THE LATE MRS.
Dorothy Parker

THE · LATE · MRS ·

Dorothy Parker

Leslie Frewin

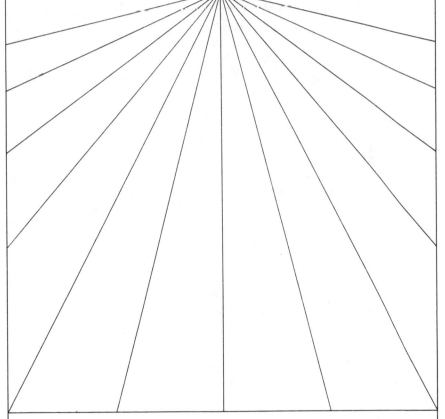

MACMILLAN PUBLISHING COMPANY · NEW YORK

Macmillan Publishing Company
866 Third Avenue, New York, N.Y. 10022
Collier Macmillan Canada, Inc.

Library of Congress Cataloging-in-Publication Data
Frewin, Leslie Ronald, 1916–
The late Mrs. Dorothy Parker.
Bibliography: p.
Includes index.
1. Parker, Dorothy, 1893–1967—Biography.   2. Authors,
American—20th century—Biography.   I. Title.
PS3531.A5855Z65   1986   818′.5209 [B]   86-5200

ISBN 0-02-541310-4

Macmillan books are available at special discounts for bulk purchases
for sales promotions, premiums, fund-raising, or educational use.
For details, contact:

Special Sales Director
Macmillan Publishing Company
866 Third Avenue
New York, N.Y. 10022

10   9   8   7   6   5   4   3   2   1

Designed by Jack Meserole

Printed in the United States of America

For Susan,
so fine in December

All her hours were yellow sands,
Blown in foolish whorls and tassels;
Slipping warmly through her hands;
Patted into little castles.

—DOROTHY PARKER,
  "Epitaph for a Darling Lady"

Now what's this?

—DOROTHY PARKER,
  "The Little Hours"

Contents

BOOK THREE   The Beginning of the End

Acknowledgments

Many people—too many to name individually—helped me in re-searching this book. There are some, however, who must be cited, the first being Professor Arthur F. Kinney, of the University of Massachu-setts, Amherst, to whom I owe a considerable debt for permission to quote from his academic monograph, *Dorothy Parker* (Twayne, Boston, 1978). I am also grateful to the following publishers, authors, agents, administrators and executors for permission to quote from books and other publications named:

Viking Penguin, Inc.: *The Portable Dorothy Parker*, copyright 1926, 1928, 1931, 1936 by Dorothy Parker. Renewed copyright 1954, © 1956, 1959, 1964 by Dorothy Parker. Copyright 1929, 1933, renewed © 1957, 1961 by Dorothy Parker. Copyright 1934 by Dorothy Parker, renewed © 1971 by Lillian Hellman. Copyright 1927, 1928, 1929, 1931, 1933 by *The New Yorker* Magazine, Inc., renewed © 1955, 1956, 1957, 1959, 1961 by *The New Yorker* Magazine, Inc. Reprinted by permission of Viking Penguin Inc.

Simon and Schuster, Inc., The Sterling Lord Literary Agency, Inc., and A. D. Peters and Co., Ltd.: *You Might As Well Live*, by John Keats.

Simon and Schuster and Eyre Methuen Ltd.: *The Last Laugh*, by S. J. Perelman, © 1981 by James H. Mathias as executor of the Estate of S. J. Perelman.

The Cole Lesley Estate, Alfred A. Knopf, Inc., and Jonathan Cape, Ltd.: *The Life of Noel Coward*, by Cole Lesley.

Little, Brown and Co.: *An Unfinished Woman, Pentimento* and *Scoundrel Time*, by Lillian Hellman.

Harcourt Brace Jovanovich: *Wit's End*, © 1977 by James R. Gaines.

Simon and Schuster: *The Diary of Our Own Samuel Pepys*, by Frank-lin Pierce Adams, © 1935 by Franklin Pierce Adams, renewed © 1963 by Anthony, Jonathan A., Timothy and Persephone Adams.

Harper & Row: *Collected Poems*, © 1922, 1950 by Edna St. Vincent Millay.

The Paddington Press, Two Continents Publishing Group: *By a Stroke of Luck!* by Donald Ogden Stewart.

Viking Penguin, Inc.: Dorothy Parker U.S. copyrights, plus *Writers At Work*, Vol. I (The Paris Interviews), Marion Capron.

Impac Literary Unit International: *Wit's End*, by Robert Brennan.

W. H. Allen and Co., Ltd.: *The Garden of Allah*, by Sheilah Graham.

Mr. Rodney C. Dennis, Curator of Manuscripts, Houghton Library, Harvard University: *The Letters of Alexander Woollcott*, edited by Beatrice Kaufman and Joe Hennessey. Quotations by permission of the Houghton Library.

Ronald A. Gregg, Assistant General Counsel, The National Association for The Advancement of Colored Peoples: literary properties of the Dorothy Parker Estate and NAACP.

Ms. Lisa Bain of *Esquire* magazine: Quotations reprinted by permission of *Esquire*, copyright material © 1986 by *Esquire* Associates.

The editor of *The New Yorker* magazine: copyright material.

The editor of American *Vogue* magazine and Condé Nast Publications, Inc., copyright material.

Atheneum Publishers, *Merry Gentlemen (and One Lady)* by J. Bryan III, copyright material.

Viking Penguin, Inc. for the poem on the jacket, "One Perfect Rose" from *The Portable Dorothy Parker*. Copyright 1925, renewed 1954 by Dorothy Parker. Reprinted by permission of Viking Penguin, Inc.

Others I must acknowledge because of their sustained help are: Ms. Elizabeth Ziman, United States Library, University of London; Dr. Howard Gottlieb and Mr. Michael Edmonds of the Mugar Memorial Museum, Boston University; Ms. Janet Sherrard, United States Embassy, London; Ms. Stephanie Kenna of the British Library; Mr. John Pinfold, British Library of Political and Economic Science (London School of Economics); Mr. Raymond Mander and Mr. Joe Mitchison of the Mander and Mitchison Theatre Collection, London; Mr. David Kepler of the Civil Archives Division, GSA, Washington, D.C.; the Director, National Archives and Records Services, Washington, D.C.; Mr. David F. Putnum of the Genealogical Society of Utah; Mr. Mark Goulden, sometime chairman of W. H. Allen and Co., Ltd., and Ms. Lucy Ellis of that company; the Director of the United States Government Printing Office, publishers of the *Cumulative Index to Publications of the Committee on Un-American Activities* (1938–1954); Ms. Kathleen Stavec of the New Jersey Historical Society and Ms. Barbara Hoskins of the Morris County Historical Society.

I wish, too, to express my thanks to the editors of *The New York Times*, the *New York Times Magazine*, the New York *Herald-Tribune*,

Chicago *Daily News*, the London *Observer*, the London *Sunday Times*, Associated Press, *Motion Picture Almanack*, *Variety*, *Daily Variety*, the *Hollywood Reporter*, *The Screenwriter*, Los Angeles *Times-Mirror* Group, the *Yale Review*, *Time*, *Newsweek*, *Reader's Digest*, *American Mercury*, the London *Daily Telegraph* Reference Library, the Research Libraries of the New York Public Library, Ms. Julia Engelhardt and Ms. Claire Harrison of Martin Secker and Warburg, Ltd., London; Mr. Stephen Roberts of the United States Information Service, London; the Chief Librarian of Cambridge University Library, Mr. Thomas Ober, Mr. H. K. Fleming, Mr. Julian Bach and Mr. Samuel Marx.

I also record my gratitude to Culver Pictures and Bettman Archives and a special word of thanks to Ms. Diana Edkins of Condé Nast Publications, Inc., and Ms. Shirley Connell of American *Vogue* for their early and considerable help and interest. For permission to quote lines from songs, I acknowledge: *We're In the Money* by Harry Warren and Al Dubin © 1933, copyright renewed by Warner Bros.; *Brother, Can You Spare A Dime?* by Jay Gorney and E. Y. Harburg, © 1932 by Harms, Inc.; *Happy Days Are Here Again* by Milton Ager and Jack Yellen, © 1929.

Finally, my thanks to Professor Peter Sainsbury, M.B., M.D., F.R.C.P., for reading the pages touching on medical matters. In relation to these, I emphasize that the words used are mine, not his.

I have tried diligently to ensure that I have not transgressed existing copyrights. If I have inadvertently done so, I crave the forgiveness of those so offended and will make every endeavor to repair any omission in subsequent editions of this book.

Prologue

How does the biographer in the 1980s, seemingly centuries away from the times and places of Mrs. Dorothy Parker, and in the face of a myriad of conflicting assessments of her persona and talents, approach the business of a life of such a lady?

Much of her adulthood and work, and too frequently a lack of work, is on record. Where it is not, especially her childhood years and early youth, one must talk with the few of her contemporaries who survive. In doing this, one must then deduce, extrapolate from hints, fragments of tired memory which—if sometimes inaccurate—are seldom without a grain or two of truth, often truth laced with venom, for Mrs. Parker was not a lady who was universally liked. One can enmesh one's desk with books, textual testimonies which sometimes provide occasional clues to the bewildering jigsaw that made up her personality, only to find oneself constantly arrested by fissures of time, place, people, sequence, event: of contradiction piled on contradiction, legend upon lie and often lie upon legend.

Does it really help, I ask myself, that one has been an intimate party to published literature concerning Mrs. Parker and her familiar Algonquin habitat in those dizzy days of the twenties, thirties, and forties; talked with an assortment of her friends and contemporaries like Noel Coward, Cathleen Nesbitt, and David Niven, among others, to skim off facets of her personality; bought Donald Ogden Stewart warm beer in Mayfair hotels while discussing at length those same fevered Algonquin days and her fashionable frolics in the South of France? Does it help, indeed, that one dined à deux on numerous occasions with Merle Oberon on the balcony of her suite at Monte Carlo's Hotel de Paris, talking into the small hours of those early days of Hollywood and of the movie star's remembrances of Mrs. Parker and that lady's halcyon habits and habitats? And, with eager ear, talked across the affected din of Belgravia parties; listened to dissections of her being, fixed in time and place, on Long Island's North Shore and other places where she was apt to run for love or cover, or both; talked to *soi-disant* contemporary luminaries like Gloria Swanson, senescently looking like a graying gargoyle of Sodom itself. Does it really help that one had once dined for four long hours seated next to Sheilah Graham in the Grosvenor Square home of a mutual friend, listening to the chanting of Parkerian particles and tales of the columnist's own paramour, F. Scott Fitzgerald, whom Mrs. Parker had swiftly loved?

Does it, I continue to ask myself, promote a deeper understanding, a fuller perception of one's subject, the mordacious Mrs. Parker, that on many occasions one has worked, slept and eaten in the assumed English ambience of New York's Algonquin Hotel, that bastion of prolific prolixity, and on at least two occasions lived in the same rooms in which the lady perversely holed herself up in the decades when the satiety of love or lust and all their attendant sadnesses had overwhelmed her? Does it, I still further ask, assist to have been a long-time member and frequenter of Jack and Charlie's "21" Club, the same "21" where Mrs. Parker had earlier walked, often unsteadily, and at whose downstairs bar some of her mordant moods, fanned by liquor, had helped to shape the listless litanies which came to her mind and then, reshaped and honed, found final force in the printed word?

Perhaps. Perhaps not.

There were, of course, other journeys, other places, other people, many other people, in the pursuit of a prescient picture of Mrs. Dorothy Parker. There were weekends at Martha's Vineyard; days and nights at Pacific Palisades, that ocean-licked inveigler of inveracity peopled as it was, and largely still is, by Hollywood escapees; there were visits to Mrs. Gertrude Benchley's plebeian fields of Blue Book respectability in Scarsdale; walks and talks in the Welsh hills, in Oxford, Wiltshire and London with David Niven; evening walks on the Côte d'Azur with Dorothy and Robert Mitchum, remembering days and times lost in a miasma of the rotting Tinsel Town of Mrs. Parker's day; a pleasant meeting with Arnold Gingrich at the offices of *Esquire*; trips to Lake Bomoseen, several trips, and visits to clinical cantons of Switzerland where Mrs. Parker had walked before me—all these, and many more, embarked on, one hoped, to help the shadowy lady re-emerge, wraith-like perhaps, within these pages.

Certainly, all the work, the travels, the people, the talk, provided years of fascinating research and endeavor culminating in this attempt to re-create the complex persona of the late Mrs. Dorothy Parker. What is certain is that my attempts to penetrate the carapace of both the legend and the lie, the drilling through of concretions of old stories and literary assessments concerning the lady and her years of work, play, frivolity, pain and despair, have been immensely rewarding. For, as in life so in death, Mrs. Parker continues to intrigue and I do not doubt that she will go on doing so. Like her or revile her, she had a mystery about her; it was, and is, a mystery she cultivated with all the irrelevant innocence which redeemed her days.

Here then, for better or worse, she is.

LESLIE FREWIN

North Devonshire, England
1985

BOOK·ONE

The Beginning

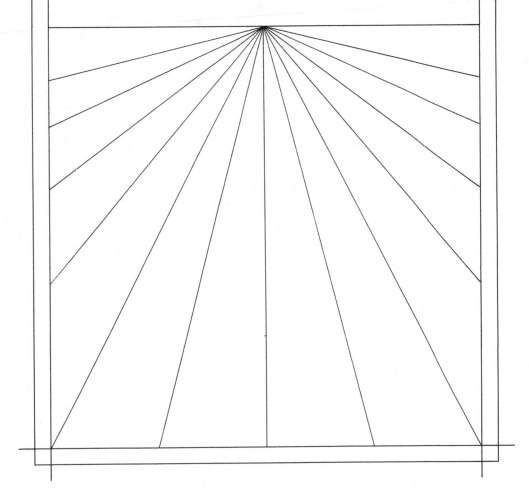

· 1 ·

A Doe-Eyed Arrival

THERE ARE two places in New Jersey called West End. The one we are concerned with is the West End of Monmouth County. Now part of the city of Long Branch, in August 1893 West End was a celebrated, snobbish resort town, where five U.S. presidents had made their summer homes during the nineteenth century. Tourism was the town's only industry. Having three high-class hotels and a profusion of well-kept homes, West End was officially described in the town's promotional literature as a cottage colony.

It was to West End, Long Branch, Monmouth County, in August 1893, that J. Henry Rothschild, "a fairly prosperous cloak and suiter" in the garment district of New York City, took his wife, their nine-year-old daughter and their two sons of six and four years, for their annual vacation. The heat of Manhattan was intense. There can be little doubt that the Rothschilds were glad to be free of the oppressive heat of the city. The cool breezes from the Atlantic Ocean offered a welcome balm to its visitors. J. Henry Rothschild was free for a few weeks from the administration of over 200 employees in his garment factory on Second Avenue and the ordered control of his large, trim brownstone at 310 West Eightieth Street, New York, with its staff of five servants.

Rothschild had a minor claim to fame. Not only was he one of the pioneers in the wholesale cloak and suit business in New York, he had also received a doctorate in Talmudic studies and thus could justifiably use the prefix Doctor to his name, which he did.

Born in Selma, Alabama, in 1851, he had moved to New York as a young man, becoming a founder of the wholesale cloak and suit firm of Meyer, Jonasson and Company. When the firm was dissolved because of disagreements with his partners, he quickly became a partner in Blumenthal Brothers, in the same line of business. In 1901, Rothschild associated himself with Oppenheim and Company, brokers, and for three years was a director of the firm. His years of hard work and growing status allowed him membership in two New York businessmen's clubs—the Progress and the Criterion.

Henry Rothschild rented one of West End's summer houses for the latter part of August and most of September. The homes were affluent

3

in appearance, totally in keeping with this man of strict propriety and formal manner. There was only one problem. His wife, Eliza, was seven months pregnant. He was hoping that the sea air, unlike the coarse winds of the Hudson River coming in across Amsterdam Avenue, would revitalize Eliza, whose health had long needed careful attention. She had always been a frail woman; now in her forties, she ran a great risk in being pregnant again. Still, there was the anticipation of trips by phaeton to Asbury Park with its elegant beach walks, drives to Point Pleasant, picnics at Toms River and the refreshing greensward of Greenwood Forest with its profusion of trees, shrubs, birds and other wildlife. These were the sights and sounds that would put fresh life into Eliza; these were the things, too, that would provide the children with memories they would recall most of their lives. Then they would return to New York where everything was already organized for the arrival of the new baby.

There is no doubt that the J. Henry Rothschilds fitted the ambience of the West End cottage colony. The three children were always immaculately turned out and Eliza customarily displayed all the trimness in dress and appearance of the schoolteacher from Perthshire, Scotland, she essentially was by nature and training: trim of bearing, ordered of coiffure and gentle of character.

True, Henry was Jewish and in a snobbish resort such as West End this could create social barriers. But money could often surmount those barriers, especially if good manners and a genuine desire to be accepted were evident. Most people in New York and its surroundings knew that Jewish garment manufacturers were almost a law unto themselves. Most of them had emigrated from Russia, and through hard work a number of them had amassed or were in process of amassing small fortunes. J. Henry Rothschild had done especially well. He had toiled long and hard for his place in society, and he and his family had acquired a certain style. He had trained his family to respect convention and to conform to the disciplines of correct social behavior. Certainly the prefix of Doctor before his name had helped their being accepted into the West End community.

There is some evidence that Rothschild had a style that was commanding, even dictatorial. But he also had good manners and an innate belief that to be both Jewish *and* prosperous was the answer to the antisemitic Blue Book socialites with their disdainful airs and graces. West End was the place where many of them came to avoid Manhattan's heat; here the Rothschilds could compete by virtue of their own quiet social graces and to some extent match the socialites' money, if need be.

On the evening of August 22, 1893, Eliza A. Rothschild, nee Marston, was suddenly precipitated into labor with her fourth child, Doctor and midwife were called, and shortly before ten o'clock Eliza gave birth to another daughter, a Virgo born on the cusp of Leo. The child was two months premature, and her arrival put an end to the planned trips and outings. We know that over the days that followed, Eliza was very ill. After three weeks, however, the doctor decided she could travel back to the brownstone on West Eightieth Street, where a nurse and servants would care for her.

The new child was christened Dorothy: just plain Dorothy, a fashionable name of the time. She was cute, with black hair and large, inquiring doe eyes. A quarter of a century later, as Dorothy Parker, she was to become a living legend of America's literati. Her early arrival in the world at West End, Monmouth County, was to be described by her as "the last time I was early for anything."

· 2 ·

A Clinical, Crucifixed
Academy

ONE THING that clearly emerges from the writings by and about Dorothy Parker is that she loathed her father. She never forgave him for her Jewish parentage and name, and regarded him as a bully, a hypocrite and an enemy. It has been said that she hated him the more because he was the parent who, by his appearance, gestures and other characteristics, marked down her own Jewishness for all to see. Certainly, even as a child, she entertained fantasies of being Catholic rather than Jewish. As biographer John Keats has said, "In the years to come she could never speak of her father without horror."

Many years later when Dorothy Parker started to collaborate with Wyatt Cooper on what she hoped would be her autobiography, she wanted to call it *Mongrel* because, said Cooper, "that term comes as near as anything to expressing how she always saw herself: as a mongrel that wanted to be a thoroughbred." She clearly believed that no thoroughbred could be Jewish, an attitude of mind that stemmed directly from her revulsion of her father.

When, six years after her birth, in 1899, her sickly mother died of a wasting malady, she was overcome with a gnawing emptiness that helped make her permanently introspective and given to depressions. At the root of this emptiness was the belief that her mother had failed her by dying when she was so young.

Her father's unrelenting pursuit of respectability, his prim and proper social fascia, insisted that he find another wife in due course. He was not long in finding the second lady of his choice, a tall and devoutly religious woman of extreme Protestant leanings who imposed tireless and tiresome fantasies of hellfire and brimstone on her stepchildren. "She was crazy with religion," Dorothy Parker later recalled. Professor Arthur Kinney of the University of Massachusetts in Amherst says that contrary to Talmudic law (by which the mother determines the Jewishness of the children), the second Mrs. Rothschild told Dorothy she was Jewish because of her father and "set a course of moral indoctrination to save her soul." If Dorothy loathed her father, she loathed her newly acquired stepmother even more. No doubt aided by his new wife's extreme religious fervor, Henry became more than ever consumed with recurrent images of a vengeful God. And he liked others to know of his God-fearing ways.

Years later, Dorothy was to remember the Sunday outings of that time. Speaking of her father, she said: "He'd take us on an outing. It was always the same kind of outing. We would go to the cemetery to visit mother's grave—all of us, including my father's second wife. Some outing. Whenever he'd hear a crunch on that gravel that meant an audience was approaching. Out would come the biggest handkerchief you ever saw and in a lachrymose voice that had remarkable carrying power, he'd start wailing: 'We're all here, Eliza; I'm here, Dottie's here and Mrs. Rothschild is here . . .' "

At home, her stepmother's religious fervor was unabating: "I'd come in from school and my stepmother would greet me with, 'Did you love Jesus today?' Now, how do you answer that?" How *did* the young Dorothy answer that? She admitted that the new Mrs. Rothschild was hurt that her sister and her brothers called their stepmother Mrs. Rothschild, but, she lamely asked, "What else? That was her name." And what did Dorothy call her new mother? "I didn't call her anything. 'Hey, you,' was about the best I could do." And clearly there was little understanding from the servants who were ruled by J. Henry Rothschild's strict domestic discipline. "In those days," Dorothy Parker was later to recall, "the well-off used to go down to Ellis Island and bring them, still bleeding, home to do the laundry." And, of course, the gentle disdain. "You know, that didn't encourage the servants to behave well. Honest, it didn't."

There was little rapport between her and her siblings. She recalled an incident when one of her brothers and his friend saw her walking down the street. "The friend pointed at me. 'That your sister?' he asked. 'No,' my brother said. That helped. There was an enormous gap there, you see. You can't bridge that, ever."

And what of her sister?

"Nine years between my sister and me. She was a real beauty, my sister. Sweet, lovely—but silly."

Even if an abiding hatred caused a rebellious reaction towards her father and stepmother, Dorothy Rothschild was compelled to conform to her parents' wishes about a school. Children were to be seen and not heard, and what this child needed, the Rothschilds decided, was a course of strict scholastic moral indoctrination, to reinforce the discipline of the Rothschild home. As a result, in 1899, Dorothy was enrolled in New York's Blessed Sacrament Convent. At that time there were few schools catering to Jewish children; moreover, the strict disciplines of Catholic education were legendary. "It was practically around the corner and you didn't have to cross any avenues, whatever that means," recalled Dorothy Parker. "Never mind, you couldn't learn anything there."

But in some way, Dorothy was pleased about going to a Catholic school; her Jewish name would not, she felt, be held against her there. The convent had been established to ensure that good manners and obedience were primary requisites to be inculcated, along with a good general education, into pupils sandwiched between a surfeit of religious instruction. Did the small girl, Dorothy, come to love Jesus? Dorothy didn't and couldn't. And by her nature, now markedly rebellious on this score, too, she made no attempt to do so. John Keats takes up the story:

. . . the school did nothing to give her the slightest reason to feel that she was welcome there. Her experience of the Catholic children made her wary of associating with any children. She hated being a child and she did not do the things that children do. She never flew a kite in Central Park; she never went to a skating rink. Each day she would walk to a school where she had no place, and each afternoon she would return to a house that had no love for her. She approached each new day apprehensively, and began to approach each person she met in a manner that suggested she wished to apologize for being alive.

"Convents," Dorothy Parker said years later:

do the same things progressive schools do, only they don't know it. They don't teach you how to read, you have to find that out for yourself. At my Convent we did have a textbook, one that devoted a page and a half to Adelaide Ann Proctor, but we couldn't read Dickens; he was vulgar, you know. But I read him and Thackeray, and I'm the one woman you'll ever know who's read every word of Charles Reade, the author of *The Cloister and The Hearth*. But as for helping me in the outside world, the Convent taught me only that if you spit on a pencil eraser, it will erase ink. I remember little else about it except the smell of the oilcloth, and the smell of nuns' garb. All those writers who talk about their childhood! Gentle God, if I ever wrote about mine, you wouldn't sit in the same room with me.

Introversion, it seems, dominated her days. She was a pretty child, large-eyed, perceptive, shy, evincing an intelligence as sharp as the knife her father used to carve the family bird on Saturdays. It seems this was the time when her satirical bent first disclosed itself. Asked by a girl at the convent, "Are you my friend, my best friend?" she is said to have replied, "A girl's best friend is her mutter." That was another way of deriding her Jewish origins, a riposte she was to repeat in print many years later. The girl, Debbie, laughed. Many years later, Debbie was to recall both the riposte and Dorothy Rothschild: "Dottie had a wonderful intelligence for a girl of her age and a dry wit that often convulsed us."

Happiness is rarely the lot of the searching, contemplative mind and clearly Dorothy Rothschild had precisely that kind of mind, the kind that had a passion for books. The nuns regarded her as quaint, a bit of a rebel, and unquestionably bright. Perhaps the brightest of all at the clinical, crucifixed academy. But she was also an irreverent child, piercingly disdainful at times, often silent, profoundly disinterested in the nuns' attempts to invade her inner being with their religious fervor for and obeisance to the Holy Mother. The flashes of astringent humor she used to repel the constant invasion of her sensibilities was her armor. A Sister of Charity asked her to explain to the class the meaning of the Immaculate Conception. "I'd say," said Dorothy, "that it was a case of spontaneous combustion."

This would never do.

She took home to her parents a respectful note paying fair tribute to her intelligence, but also the request that the Rothschilds "might do better to find a more suitable educational establishment" for their daughter. Not a precise expulsion; just a positive, pointed suggestion.

The convent did not deal in junior heretics.

· 3 ·

"I Was Just a Little Jewish Girl, Trying to Be Cute"

DOROTHY'S FATHER was predictably displeased. His social image and that of his wife were not enhanced by Dorothy's irreverent and rebellious behavior at the convent. As a form of penance, she was confined to a regimen of sober discipline in the house: early suppers and long evenings alone in her room. Occasional solace was found with her sister. Her brothers left her alone.

Clearly, something had to be done about the girl. She was nearly thirteen and needed a proper finishing education—and a respect for authority, her elders and betters, tradition and God. She had shown little respect for these disciplines at the convent. What was to be done with her? There was only one answer: A school for young ladies.

It has long been a precept of parents who have themselves known poverty or racial discrimination to seek to give to their children the means to acquire distinction and status denied them by their birth. This, in the early 1900s, applied especially to the American Jews, with their dark, sad background of immigrant history. Thus J. Henry Rothschild decided to send his youngest daughter to a well-known and socially acceptable boarding school; her brothers and sister were, it is believed, attending similar establishments in New York State.

Morristown, New Jersey, was the place nearest to New York that housed several such schools. The Rothschilds finally decided on Miss Dana's School for Young Ladies, which was known to be both an outstanding finishing and college preparatory school. Miss Dana's had an enviable reputation for being efficiently run, imaginative in curriculum and progressive in outlook. The prospectus clearly stated: "The school pays especial attention to the study of Expression and to the cultivation of the speaking voice."

The pupils, the prospectus discreetly pointed out, were cattle princesses from Colorado and the debutante daughters of successful steelmakers, brewers, physicians and bankers. The curriculum was predominantly classical: four years of Latin, English and the Bible, plus three major subjects and electives. In addition, students did a year's intensive study in the history of art, plus work in history, geometry and algebra. There were also courses in Greek, French, logic, psychology, physics, chemistry, religious instruction and music. With only fifteen girls to each class the schooling was highly personal—the girls were taught only in seminars.

After a careful investigation, the Rothschilds determined that Miss Dana's School for Young Ladies had all the qualities, atmosphere and trappings they sought for Dorothy's education. And Miss Dana herself had an impressive background.

She had been born in Blissville, Michigan, the daughter of a Congregational minister who had moved back to his native New England; Miss Dana had been educated at the Ipswich Academy, in Massachusetts. After several years of teaching Greek and Latin in high-class schools, she arrived in Morristown in 1877 to take up a teaching post in the Morris Female Institute, then conducted by Charles G. Hazeltine. This proved to be a singularly fortunate move for the young teacher.

During the 1880s, stretching through to the early 1900s, Morristown was enjoying the fruits of a golden era when many very wealthy New York families were building summer homes in the area. Indeed, one street was known as Millionaires Row.

In 1779–80 Washington's headquarters had been garrisoned over by Lafayette Avenue in the town, and Henry Ford had established an estate between the headquarters and the fashionable Ridgedale area, taking over more than a hundred acres of pastureland hard by the old D.L. & W.R. railway line which separated Ford's estate from that of the Honorable T. F. Randolph. The Roosevelt family had a summer house there, as did General Fitz John Porter. And Mrs. Whelpley-Dodge, Henry Dodge and J. S. Dodge of the emergent motorcar empire had their summer estates there.

On the other side of the railroad tracks stood the Morris Female Institute, with its imposing entrance on South Street. The institute, which had an impressive history, had been incorporated in 1860, "the original subscription amounting to $16,050 of which $15,600 was collected." The main building had been let by contract to Cyrus Pruden on behalf of himself and others who formed a syndicate. The property had originally cost, prior to an addition, $17,700 when it was leased for five years commencing May 1, 1862, to Miss Dana's employer, Charles Hazeltine. He continued to occupy it until it was leased on April 1, 1877, to Miss Elizabeth E. Dana, who, renaming the building, went on to establish Miss Dana's School for Young Ladies. It soon won high approval in academic and social circles.

Set well back off South Street, it boasted an impressive entrance drive broken by a central circular lawn, which in turn was encircled by attractive elms, oaks and silver birches. The main school building faced the drive. Victorian in concept and construction, it displayed the characteristic balconies and fussiness of design. Inside the main hall two curving stairways led to the pupils' single and double sleeping rooms, which boasted elegantly draped windows, tidy beds, closets, dressing tables, a study desk, chairs, occasional tables and in each room a school flag bearing one word: Dana.

Downstairs, through the front hall and below the curved stairways, was a lace-curtained parlor and the library. A passage led to the main classrooms and assembly hall, which, in turn, led off to a second structure, the teachers' quarters.

Behind the main building were two other covered areas; an oblong, commodious gymnasium with its floor, ceiling and walls paneled in wood, which was adjacent to a studio. At the back of the principal school buildings were the school bakery and kitchens, which adjoined tennis courts, a sports field and a woodland area through which ran a pretty stream.

The school's buildings bespoke the prosperity not only of the place but also of the people who sent their daughters there. Festooned drapes and thick Oriental rugs and carpets were set off by chandeliers with electric lighting, sofas, a plethora of potted plants, and prints and etchings on the walls.

This was to be the new world of thirteen-year-old Dorothy Rothschild. Her stepmother informed her that if accepted "Jesus will pain you to behave properly. . . .' " Mrs. Rothschild obviously didn't know that Jesus doesn't pain anybody; it is people who pain themselves and others, principally through the violence of thought that so often precedes violence of deed.

This threat did not engender the expected fear in Dorothy, who invariably kept fear at bay by closing her mind as one closes a window on a stormy night. Her parents' hypocrisy had thrown up a singular benefit to her in the shape of books, which lined several corridors as well as the library of the West Eightieth Street brownstone. They had been collected by her father, a mute symbol of perhaps some exaggerated affectation that was required to indicate to visitors the erudition of its owner. During the tortuous days of the convent, Dorothy had often taken refuge in many of the books, savoring authors like Charles Dickens, Hardy, Swift, Pope, Thomas Carlyle, Charles Reade, Thackeray, Shakespeare and Emerson. And there were the poets, too—the Brownings, John Gay,

Coleridge, Dante Gabriel Rossetti, Milton, Verlaine, Shelley, Keats and the cleric John Donne. "No man is an island entire of himself" could be applied to women, too, except that Dorothy Rothschild *was* at that time an island entire of herself.

Years later she laughingly quoted Lord Rochester's seventeenth-century witticism which she learned during this period: "Before I got married I had six theories about bringing up children; now I have six children and no theories." She also later quoted Samuel Johnson's pertinent observation in *Rasselas*, applying it cruelly to her and her stepmother: "The daughter begins to bloom before the mother can be content to fade, and neither can forbear to wish for the absence of the other." In a way, Dorothy, with her love of books, was slightly ahead of the game.

Of course, there was a formal interview to assess the girl's academic potential. Miss Dana asked questions and listened carefully to the answers. Dorothy apparently displayed a picaresque honesty in her replies which slightly dented the finely honed elegance of the principal who, to her credit, decided that here was a girl of much potential value, not only to the reputation of her establishment but, perhaps, to the community at large: the child was exceedingly well-read for her age with some evidence of a selective taste in books.

Morristown itself was a relatively small suburban area of 1,200 people but the standards established within Miss Dana's School for Young Ladies were so high as to persuade the educational authorities of New Jersey to waive set examination requirements for entrants. Those standards had to be maintained, and if she was accepted, Dorothy Rothschild would have to do her part in maintaining them.

If an expected degree of girlish innocence in the five-foot-tall Dorothy emerged at the interview, there was precious little naiveté about her. Miss Dana quickly perceived in her a social awareness in advance of her years and also noted, we are told, a provocative, well-developed figure and an attractive sexuality that belied her tender years. Dorothy's father and stepmother, who both accompanied her to the interview, were invited to enter their daughter at the start of the new term.

It has been repeatedly written that Dorothy Rothschild entered Miss Dana's in 1911, staying there for one year. This is incorrect. There is solid evidence that she joined the school in the spring of 1906 and stayed there until the autumn of 1910, when she was seventeen.

Dorothy was happy at Miss Dana's. She liked the principal and clearly approved of the curriculum. Miss Dana herself taught classes in Greek, Latin and the history of art. The seminar classes had a constructive informality. In addition, the entire school met for lively weekly discussions of current events; little that was socially important of the day was ignored. The growth of socialism, the exploitive aspects of conservatism, the problems of the slums, the plight of the underprivileged and the deprivations of the underdeveloped countries were all discussed and argued. It was a school well ahead of its time.

Much attention was paid to the written and oral exposition of the classics. Here Dorothy found her way into the magical world of the odes and satires of Horace, the verse of Virgil, the satire of Catullus, the songs of Verlaine and the philosophies of Aristotle, Socrates, Goethe, Montaigne, Martial, La Rochefoucauld, and others. She tackled her studies with zest and a perceptive willingness to learn that soon marked her down as an exceedingly bright pupil.

There were, of course, games, too, but like Oscar Wilde, whose works she devoured, she had little interest in them. As one of Dorothy's schoolmates later said of her: "She was an attractive girl, peppy and never bored. She was outstanding in schoolwork, but I can't remember her playing games." Indeed, tennis, tetherball, basketball and lacrosse had no appeal for Dorothy.

Of this period she was later to deride her own accomplishments with the self-deprecating: "I was just a little Jewish girl, trying to be cute." But she was more than that. She was a gifted scholar and markedly popular with the other girls, although she wisely kept her own counsel.

Classes were from 9 A.M. to 1 P.M., the girls being free until the 4 P.M. to 6 P.M. study period. After that, there were occasional dances to which the girls were properly chaperoned, where they would meet boys from the nearby private tennis club. A mile or so away from the school was Morristown's movie palace, showing silent films starring Edna Purviance, Pearl and Chrissie White, Buster Keaton, Ben Turpin, Chester Conklin and others, but the girls of Miss Dana's were banned from the cinema. Smoking was also banned at the school; twice during Dorothy's sojourn at Miss Dana's, girls were caught smoking cigarettes, which resulted in their immediate expulsion.

Evenings were often taken up with quiet study and religious instruction conducted by the local Reverend William E. Griffis, a worthy doctor of divinity who appealed to many of the girls not so much for his piety as for the fact that he was good-looking. For Dorothy Rothschild, it was a world away from the cloistered conformity of the Sacred Heart Convent back in New York. At Miss Dana's Dorothy flowered, happy here despite the many rules and regulations. Professor Arthur Kinney's late 1970s review of William Anthony McGuire's *A Good Bad Woman* quotes Dorothy Parker in reference to this period: "I, too, can remember those roseate days of happy girlhood when we used to skulk off to attend like dramas, thinking that we were seeing life. Ah, youth, youth . . ."

What neither Dorothy, her parents nor the other girls knew was that for all the elitist success of the school, Miss Dana was a sick woman, suffering from cancer of the stomach. Everyone was shocked when on April 26, 1908, after a short illness, the principal died in her quarters, which she shared with her sister, Mary. Also shocked were Miss Dana's colleagues of the academic establishments of New Jersey, for Morristown boasted a clutch of distinctive schools for young ladies, including the Morris Academy on South Street; the public school on Maple Avenue, which had a fine reputation under the preceptress, Mrs. R. W. Stevenson; Miss Bostwick's School for Young Ladies, also on Maple Avenue, and the kindergarten on De Hart Street. But all agreed that Miss Dana's was a unique establishment, towering over the others like the giant over Gulliver. And now, sadly, Miss Dana was gone.

The local newspaper *The Jerseyman*, of May 1, 1908, paid suitable tribute to the remarkable lady:

> In the death of Miss Dana, Morristown has lost one of the best-known and most appreciated residents. She could truly be called a rare personality . . . she kept the respect of the girls she trained by her high ideals, both religious and intellectual, and at the same time has won their attachment by the kindly sympathy and genial social nature that shone through all her bearing . . . To her friends, Miss Dana was a charming companion and an example of all that was good and strong, without any effort to do so [*sic*]. Her ideals of rectitude were distinct and influential and her varied experience of travel, her extensive reading and her love and knowledge of art filled her with stories of interest which she loved to share with her friends . . .

Miss Dana's School for Young Ladies was to survive for two more years, her work carried on by her sister, two teachers and a small band of part-time helpers and administrators. It seemed the school had never been anywhere near as affluent as its patronage had indicated; Miss Dana had simply and skillfully juggled the finances, term by term, to ensure its survival during her lifetime. It was to her lasting credit that she managed so deftly to keep the school's head above water; the costs of staff and services, care of the girls, and upkeep and maintenance of the buildings had left precious little in the kitty when all the bills were paid.

Mary bravely carried on, maintaining the school's high standards. But it was to prove too much for her. She, too, fell ill, and on August 10, 1910, there was news of her death.

After the intricate web of finances had been sorted out, the school limped along for a few months, the same standards being impeccably maintained, until the administrators had to face up to the truth. Miss Dana's was put into receivership. But Dorothy Rothschild had beaten the bell. She graduated two months before the school went into bankruptcy.

If it can be said that Dorothy Parker, nee Rothschild, was happy in the seventy-three years of her life, it is probable that her years at Miss Dana's represented a peak period of that happiness.

We know that Dorothy reveled in the wit and wisdom of classical writers; we know, too, that she became highly proficient in speaking and writing French; we know, as well, that she read and mentally romped with Fielding, fantasized with Lewis Carroll, shared *Walden*'s lovely greensward with Thoreau and delighted in the astringent wit of Wilde and others. The Restoration playwrights, too, were much enjoyed in the playground of her imagination. And it is clear that the Roman poet Martial, became a strong influence on her life. Any man who lived in the second half of the first century A.D. who could write

> Once a surgeon, Dr. Baker
> Then became an undertaker,
> Not so much his trade reversing,
> Since for him it's just re-hearsing.

or

> All of Elvira's friends have lost their life.
> I think I'll introduce her to my wife.

had to have her respect, for she had developed a marked love of the epigram, the paradox, the *trouvaille*, the wit of her betters. It was a love that was to become markedly apparent in her future years.

Despite all the efforts of Miss Dana and her devoted staff, Dorothy's rejection of established religion remained total. The scars of the convent were still there, as were the recollections of her stepmother's extreme faith. No doubt Dorothy mentally applauded Swift, whom she adored, the same Swift who had written, "Opium is not so stupefying to many persons as an afternoon sermon." All the impassioned teachings of Dr. Griffis, the school divine, had seen her remain stubbornly agnostic.

She had, too, long shunned her father's attempts to induct her into the basic tenets of the Talmud and what she regarded as the incomprehensible disciplines of the Jewish faith, always claiming an "inability to understand." But she *had* understood—understood only too well. She had never been addicted to obscurantism. She liked her words plain and simple, well-dredged to be sure, and preferably with a sting in the tail so that all could see the ironies of the human comedy. Thus she loved reading Swift, Horace and Martial. And she had discovered other, more contemporary, writers like A. E. Housman and Chesterton, whose often indiscreet anti-religious chronicles were probing the barriers which were to become forcefully challenged later in the century. And if there had been the odd girl at Miss Dana's who had snidely derided her Jewish origins, she had, in return, received a resounding clout at Christianity from her developing wit.

Many years later, in her presence at the Algonquin Round Table, Alexander Woollcott screeched at Franklin Pierce Adams: "You goddam Christ killer!" And it was George S. Kaufman who relieved the tension in a fulsome display of exaggerated indignation with: "For my part, I've had enough slurs on my race. I am now leaving this table, this dining-room, this hotel—never to return." And pausing with a penetrating glance across at Dorothy Parker, he grinned: "And I trust Mrs. Parker will walk out with me—halfway." Mrs. Parker took the point.

It is known that at this time she felt deeply about the world's inequalities. There were too many rich and far too many poor for her liking. She could not reconcile the immense fortunes of the Carnegies, Rockefellers, Fords, Mellons and the unrelated Rothschilds, with the abject poverty of the Jewish and black ghettos in virtually every major American city. Nor could she reconcile the plight of impoverished humanity elsewhere in the world with the comparative wealth of the Western nations. Such appalling inequalities could not, surely, be tolerated by a caring God: ergo, there was no God. Her deep concern about frightening social imbalances within society formed the basis of her socialist leanings later in life.

Besides arguing about the inequality of wealth and privilege in her school seminars, she began to write verses and short stories, shaping words and adapting metrical forms and rhythms.

Following her departure from Miss Dana's, she spent some months at the West Eightieth Street house. Soon she told her parents that she intended to leave home. There was, we are told, a short, sharp scene. Whatever happened, she left the brownstone with a small allowance from her father, never to return.

Her first stop was a boardinghouse at 103rd and Broadway, paying $8 a week for a room which included breakfast and dinner each day. She had already decided she wanted to become a writer. The many months in the family house had been spent in avid reading, the sketching out of stories, the writing of verse. Away from her parents and the oppressive atmosphere of the family home which stored so many unhappy memories for her, she became alive, excited.

Frank C. Brown, the American writer, had indicated her direction. Hadn't he written that "a good rooster crows in any sort of hen house"? All she needed was the hen house—and that, she knew, would come in time. Perhaps, appropriately, in women's magazines? In the meantime, she began sending cryptic verses to Franklin P. Adams's "Conning Tower" column in the New York *World,* which featured light verse and epigrams from contributors whom Adams seldom paid. He accepted some of Dorothy's items. She was later to write that Adams "raised me from a couplet." Dorothy was overjoyed. She spent her days writing and her evenings in the lounge with two other boarders, one of whom was Thorne Smith, later the celebrated author of the *Topper* stories and a contributor, like Dorothy Parker, to *The New Yorker.*

In the years to come she was to comment on that boardinghouse and its guests: "Thorne Smith was there, and another man. We used to sit around in the evening and talk. There was no money, but Jesus we had fun."

Fun she certainly had, partly because her verse had now appeared in print. And there was the fun of studying the books of verse authored by the hugely popular Edna St. Vincent Millay. Of this period she was later to say, "I thought I was Edith Sitwell."

On December 28, 1913, she received news that her father had died. His life had been of sufficient importance for *The New York Times* to run a twelve-line obituary notice. Dorothy Rothschild did not react to either his death or the notice of his death.

She did not even go to his funeral.

· 4 ·

A Nerve to Touch

THE IDYLLIC, dreamy romanticism of Edna St. Vincent Millay's verse had set its own fashion in an age when poetry was very popular. Countee Cullen, Carolyn Wells, Newman Levy, Baird Leonard were also popular, and all had been published at various times in Franklin Adams's column. But Miss Millay was the towering American poet of the day, and Dorothy Rothschild, a child of her time, quickly realized that Millay's style was the nerve to touch to reach the public. Everyone was quoting:

> My candle burns at both ends,
> It will not last the night,
> But ah, my foes, and oh, my friends
> It gives a lovely light.

Of this Dorothy Parker was later to say: "Miss Millay did a great deal of harm with her double-burning candles. She made poetry seem so easy that we could all do it but, of course, we couldn't."

Miss Millay, who had hoped to become an actress but couldn't achieve it, knew all about authorship. The young Dorothy Parker read one of her published warnings: "A person who publishes a book willfully appears before the populace with his pants down," but the poet's warning had no effect on the young woman at 103rd and Broadway.

Dorothy's sparse boardingroom became the hothouse of her youthful imagination and, meanwhile, she was keeping body and soul together playing the piano—"single notes," she was later to explain—and doing her best to teach tots dancing—"about which I knew nothing."

The "Conning Tower" column had been a start. Now she began sending her verse to magazine editors. One piece landed on the desk of Frank Crowninshield, who had replaced Donald Freeman as editor of *Vanity Fair*.

Crowninshield was a quiet, modest, cultivated man, almost quaint, and certainly out of his era. He wore starched high collars, neat suits and a "watch chain and Albert," the name given to hunter watches after their fashionable use by Queen Victoria's Prince Albert. Crowninshield's only interest outside his job was a passionate love of magic, his principal friends being Mulholland and Keating, the master magicians of the day.

19

He interrupted office routine only when the two magicians called on him. Then, together, the three would try out new tricks with coins, cards, glasses of water and opera hats, treating the staff to all sorts of sleight-of-hand tricks.

He was to play a major part in the life of the twenty-year-old Dorothy Rothschild. He summoned the young lady to his editorial offices in the new Graybar building on Forty-third Street, which housed the Condé Nast magazine empire, including *Vogue* magazine. We are told that he looked penetratingly at the pretty girl who faced him and discussed her writing ambitions and *Vogue*'s sophisticated influence in the magazine market. "I will," he said, "buy one of your poems."

As Crowninshield recalled:

I published a little poem of hers . . . a check for five dollars encouraged her, as she told me, in the belief that she was Georges Sand. A month later her father died and, having to find a job, she streaked to me for help. She had worked through the summer playing the piano, strictly by note, for a dancing class, and even given dancing lessons. She hadn't, she admitted, the faintest idea how to teach dancing . . . she wanted a literary life, and I was able to secure one for her —a job on the staff at *Vogue*, at a cool ten dollars a week . . .

Crowninshield knew precisely what he was doing. The girl had talent. He wanted to encourage its growth and control its harvest. He'd bought the talent cheaply—he had a reputation of paying his contributors the bare minimum and the five dollars was below even the bare minimum.

But for Dorothy the acceptance of her verse and the offer of an editorial job, albeit menial, was heady stuff. She returned to her boardinghouse highly elated.

The first person she ran into was Thorne Smith. That evening the two celebrated, probably on plates of cheap pasta and coffee in a café on lower Lexington Avenue, an area they frequented. There they could eat and drink cheaply while talking incessantly of their ambitions, literary images and influences. "We were both as poor as church mice, the kind that eat little but squeak a lot," she was later to remember.

Returning to her spartan room, Dorothy would read more Millay, read *Passer Mortuus Est* again and again:

> Lesbia with her sparrow
> Shares the darkness,
> Presently
> Every bed is narrow

and Millay's lines on lost love, a constant theme in much of Dorothy's later work, helped to create an indelible style in Dorothy's own sardonic

verse patterns. The Millay prose style is still recognizable when comparing Millay with Parker today:

> After all, my erstwhile dear,
> My no longer cherished.
> Need we say it was not love
> Just because it perished?

The young Dorothy perceived that Edna St. Vincent Millay was a
poet prolifically imitative, guilty of plagiarizing images and lines from
classic poets and writers as, for example, in her best-selling verses *Childhood in The Kingdom Where Nobody Dies*:

> Childhood is from birth to a certain age,
> And at a certain age
> The child is grown and puts away childish things . . .

Perhaps Dorothy identified those Millay lines borrowed from Holy Writ,
no less:

> When I was a child, I spake as a child,
> And when I grew up I put away childish things . . .

But then all art, Dorothy knew, is derivative. Great art is great only by
the imaginative use of an inborn talent which, in turn, is influenced and
guided by the example and study of past or contemporary genius.

Certainly, Thorne Smith took this view. He would often go to Dorothy's room, where she would read her verses and they would drink more
coffee and sometimes make love. They felt no guilt in not being married.
A world war had engulfed half of Europe and had produced a despairing
fatalism in the young which, externally, was shrugged off with light
abandon. Dorothy and Thorne were young and were stepping round the
light to get used to the darkness—the darkness that most intelligent
Americans of the period knew was on its way. There was a need to create
a mental cocoon of escape for the imagination.

She said at this time that "melancholy is the act of remembering."
And it was. Just as it still is. But she did not want the melancholy of
remembering her dead parents, her stepmother, the convent and the
brownstone on West Eightieth Street. Years later she simply said of the
house: "It's still standing, I believe. They sell trusses there now." Dorothy
Rothschild was concerned with the here, not the hereafter.

Although Dorothy was officially called a caption writer, Mrs. Edna
Woolman Chase, *Vogue*'s editor, plied her with many menial jobs. She
worked conscientiously at anything asked of her—captions, fillers, contents pages, slugs—all the while honing her craft with spare, telling,

pungent, terse and often mordant phraseology, always aiming for the sardonic or epigrammatic effect. According to Crowninshield:

"Her first caption at *Vogue*, which was designed to explain six photographs showing miscellaneous underwear, indicated that fashion would never become a religion with her. The caption was headed 'Brevity is the Soul of Lingerie, as the Petticoat said to the Chemise.' "

Vogue was polished, witty and urbane, glossed with the aura of the affluent luxury it catered to. It was the fount of fashion, a gilded if evanescent reflection of the American Dream, a printed preamble to the amorphous attitudes of the approaching, carefree Roaring Twenties.

Mrs. Chase consulted Crowninshield about his protégée. The girl, she said, was remarkably bright but she thought Crowninshield could make better use of her on *Vanity Fair*. She detected that Dorothy was not happy at *Vogue*. She was right. Over thirty years later, Dorothy talked of this period to Marion Capron, interviewer for *Writers at Work*. In response to Capron's question about the work Dorothy did at *Vogue*, Dorothy answered, " 'This little pink dress will win you a beau,' that sort of thing. Funny, they were plain women working at *Vogue*, not chic. They were decent, nice women—the nicest women I ever met—but they had no business on such a magazine. They wore funny little bonnets and in the pages of their magazine they virginized the models from tough babes into exquisite little loves . . .' " *Vogue* was not quite Dorothy Rothschild's cup of tea, to be sure.

That Crowninshield was the undisputed master of his market had been underscored by the wealthy Condé Nast himself in 1914, when the latter had asked him to re-launch *Vanity Fair* magazine. *Vanity Fair* had been designed to take up any slack that might have existed in *Vogue's* established market, thereby keeping other entrepreneurial magazine invasions at bay. Under "Crowny's" direction, *Vanity Fair*, whose offices were at 19 West 44th Street, had quickly become a pronounced success, embracing the hedonistic society whirl, the theater, literature, the arts. It soon boasted a stable of celebrated contributors including Gertrude Stein, T. S. Eliot, Gilbert Chesterton, Arnold Bennett, H. G. Wells, and D. H. Lawrence. Illustrations by Raoul Dufy, Léger, Henri Matisse, Marie Laurencin and Maurice Utrillo's mother, the gifted and sexually voracious Suzanne Valadon, graced the magazine.

These, then, were the distinguished company that Frank Crowninshield invited Dorothy Rothschild to join.

His offer was linked to a salary raise, predictably small but a raise nonetheless. "I'm moving you over to *Vanity Fair*," was the way he put it. "You'll have more scope and you'll occasionally review for the theater."

"I thought you would—in time." She smiled enigmatically. "You have made me very happy."

In 1920 a rising journalist named Robert Benchley wrote of *Vanity Fair:*

". . . Crowninshield . . . believes that the hope of a revival of Good Taste lies in those men and women who are college graduates, have some money, who know porcelains, and Verlaine, and Italian art, who love Grolier bindings, Spanish brocades and French literature . . . any writer who writes entertainingly may say practically anything he wants . . . as long as he says it in evening clothes."

That was exactly the measure of *Vanity Fair.*

It may have been the few times in her life that Dorothy Parker openly acknowledged happiness: She now had precisely the kind of job she had wanted.

Her business and social life, fundamentally one and the same, swung into a fiercely active period. She was encouraged at every stage by Crowninshield, who had by now gained an even more pronounced respect for her talent. Her first poem, "Any Porch," had been published in the magazine's September 1915 issue; the following month saw the publication of her first prose piece, "Why I Haven't Married." Crowninshield, who took her to first nights, soirees and press openings, also gave her the job of providing captions for the delicious drawings of an English artist appropriately named "Fish," because the artist lived in a converted sail loft in Downalong, the old fishing quarter in St. Ives Bay in Cornwall, England. He also got Dorothy to collaborate with him and George S. Chappell on a book called *High Society*, a manual of "advice as to social campaigning, with hints on the management of dowagers, dinners, debutantes, dances, and a thousand and one diversions of persons of quality." The book included drawings by the redoubtable "Fish," and again Dorothy wrote the captions.

Dorothy Rothschild was on her way. Her romantic relationship with Thorne cooled off, but the two remained good friends. With her busy life at theaters, art previews, openings and the rest, she decided it would be nice to have a regular escort. She found one in a remarkably lean, six-foot-two, well-mannered Wall Street investment broker from Hartford, Connecticut whose name was Edwin Pond Parker II.

When she met him at a summer hotel dance in Branford, Connecticut, Parker was in his early twenties and was what she later described as "a handsome Gentile." His friends called him Spook; his ancestry was upper crust. Named after his grandfather, who had been a friend of Mark Twain and pastor of the South Church of Hartford from 1860 to 1912, Eddie's background was unassailable. There was only one problem as far as the bewitching young teetotaler Dorothy Rothschild was concerned. He drank, usually a bottle or more of whiskey a day.

· 5 ·

"Even Love Goes Past..."

FOR THE FIRST TIME in her life Dorothy Rothschild was hopelessly
in love. Eddie represented the profound self-sufficiency of her ideal man.
True, his family in Hartford were pillars of the established Christian
church—even that, to her mind which still rejected any sort of religion,
didn't matter. She reveled within a cocoon of deep emotional warmth
and well-being.

On April 6, 1917, the United States formally declared war on Germany. It had been nothing more than a formality. America's European
allies, led by Britain and France, had long been aided by U.S. armaments
and food supplies. Now America and those allies were moving in for the
kill. The songs, the rabble-rousers, were ready too. "Yankee Doodle
Dandy" and "Over There" among others, were conscripted for service.

As in Europe, the young men of quality and learning were expected
to respond early to the call of war. Whatever his drinking habits, Edwin
Pond Parker II was unquestionably a young man of quality. Dorothy
Rothschild's newfound happiness was to be mortally shaken when Eddie
told her that he had enlisted as an ambulance driver in the 33rd Ambulance Company, a unit of 693, comprising mostly pacifist volunteers,
formerly of Yale, Harvard and Princeton. Among the volunteers were
Ernest Hemingway, e e cummings and John Dos Passos.

Miss Millay predictably bit the bullet in "Dirge Without Music" from
The Buck in the Snow:

> Gently they go, the beautiful, the tender, the kind;
> Quietly they go, the intelligent, the witty, the brave.
> I know. But I do not approve. And I am not resigned.

Many people in America did not approve and were not resigned,
which helped make her poetry even more popular.

It was war in its most awful sense. Hundreds of thousands of Britons,
Australians, South Africans, thousands upon thousands of young
Frenchmen, and their counterparts from the Low Countries of Europe
and from many other British-linked lands afar, had already been slaugh-
tered, maimed or gassed. As had thousands of Germans. Like it or not,
America was totally involved.

There was, at least, a brief respite for Dorothy Rothschild and Eddie Parker. He was first ordered to Butler, then Camp Merritt, New Jersey, and later to Charlotte, North Carolina, where his unit joined the Fourth Infantry Combat Division; that group moved on to Allentown, Pennsylvania, and then to Syracuse. Later still, Eddie's unit received orders to go to Vermont and later still to Saratoga Springs. There was a further lull in activity of three weeks before the 33rd moved on to Brooklyn, where the division waited.

Although the intensive training period of the division made these several moves necessary, the lovers at least managed to see each other occasionally. She spent the weekdays at *Vanity Fair* coping with all manner of editorial jobs, living only for the weekends when she could board a train that would take her to Eddie—lovely, idyllic weekends in small hotels and inns.

In June 1917, Dorothy and Eddie married and the stolen weekends continued. Sometimes, Dorothy's tiny apartment in New York, which she had acquired when she joined *Vanity Fair*, provided a further haven. When Eddie went back to camp, Dorothy again immersed herself in her work. She wrote him many letters, sometimes three a day. They were passionate letters filled with laughter and little rhymes she sent to "cheer him up" along with her hopes for their future. And when he returned to camp, she began to anticipate his next leave.

In "The Lovely Leave," a short story she wrote much later, she declared:

> There must be no waste to this leave. She thought of the preposterous shyness that had fallen upon her when he had come home before. It was the first time she had seen him in uniform. There he stood, in their little apartment, a dashing stranger in strange, dashing garments. Until he had gone into the army, they had never spent a night apart in all their marriage; and when she saw him, she dropped her eyes and twisted her handkerchief and could bring nothing but monosyllables from her throat. There must be no such squandering of minutes this time. There must be no such gangling diffidence to lop even an instant from their twenty-four hours of perfect union. Oh, Lord, only twenty-four hours . . .

Even such brief respites had now ended.

In June 1918, within a few days of the couple's first wedding anniversary, Eddie's division was ordered to France. As the huge Australian beef cargo ship, now converted into a troop carrier, moved out of the New York docks, several thousand aboard sang "Over There." They did not know they would become part of the last great Allied counteroffensive in July, from which thousands would not return.

Within a few days of landing in France, the 33rd Ambulance Company of the Medical Corps with the Fourth Combat Division established bivouac quarters to the south of Rheims. It was early July now, and the sun was high. The division was ordered into action in one of the bloodiest encounters of the war.

Back home in New York, Dorothy Parker continued to write love letters to her husband, who was dealing with the brutalities of war. Those who were with him said he was a silent soldier, full of compassion and sorrow for the wounded and the dead. Driving his ambulance from a forward dressing station, with a pitiful cargo of four badly wounded soldiers, he tried to zigzag his way out of range of enemy shellfire. A shell landed a few yards from his vehicle. The four wounded occupants were killed outright. Eddie was pulled out from his driving seat, bleeding profusely.

When the news reached Dorothy, she fancifully believed it would be but a matter of weeks before he would be given a medical discharge and would be home with her again for good.

The fierce Allied offensive had been the beginning of the end. Germany was beaten; an armistice was declared. Dorothy was filled with elation, now that Eddie would be coming home. Then came the blow. He had, he wrote to her, been medically downgraded. But he was still fit for service of a sedentary kind. He was to be posted for service with the Allied occupying forces on the Rhineland. What he did not tell her was that he was drinking again.

Dorothy waited impatiently for his return. Her frustration was clearly showing when, in January 1919, she wrote an article for *Vanity Fair* in which she said: "I'd especially like to know how those wives of American soldiers always managed to get to France—I've been trying to do it for the past year," which meant that she was ready at the drop of a pen to throw up her job with Crowninshield and *Vanity Fair* if Eddie called. But he had not.

When the emergent English poet Rupert Brooke had written:

> The years that take the best away
> Are the years that follow fast,
> And the dirtiest things we do must lie
> Forgotten at the last.
> Even love goes past,

he might have been writing of Dorothy Parker, who, faced with Eddie's long stay in the Rhineland, flung herself anew into her work. She was not, perhaps, aware that love was going past.

Things were happening at a brisk pace at *Vanity Fair*. Her verse and prose pieces were creating a following of admirers, especially her articles like "Gloom in the Spring," "Trying it on the Dog Days" and "The Star Spangled Drama." She had by this time published several of her verse *Hate Songs*. These, and her sardonic essays on people and places, were engendering warm approval among her readers and, perhaps more importantly, among the editorial hierarchy of the magazine.

Her early contributions, Crowninshield had noted, were "models of satire and wit" and offered evidence of the acidity which was to make her work renowned. "Even in those early days," he later recalled, "in the very first of her devastating *Hate Songs*, she spoke of the type of epicene and overrefined young man that was then beginning to be met within society. In alluding to such men she said:

> And then there are the Sensitive Souls
> Who do Interior Decorating for Art's sake.
> They always smell faintly of vanilla
> And put drops of sandalwood on their cigarettes.
> They are continually getting up costume balls
> So that they can go
> As something out of the "Arabian Nights."
> They give studio teas
> Where people sit around on cushions
> And wish they hadn't come
> They look at a woman languorously
> Through half-closed eyes,
> And tell her, in low, passionate tones.
> What she ought to wear.

While Eddie had been away, she had been invited several times to the home of the cultured Condé Nast, to which she had been escorted by Crowninshield. He recalled that "Though she was full of prejudices, her perceptions were so sure, her judgment so unerring, that she always seemed certain to hit the center of the mark." And what did she look like in those early days of her career?

In those days . . . her figure was slight, her eyes, with their tranquil and intensely thoughtful expression, a curious mixture of hazel and green. She wore her brownish-auburn hair in a bang and with, very often, a bun at the back. She was reticent, self-effacing, and preternaturally shy. I asked her once to suggest her own epitaph. She wrote it down:

> Here Lies
> Dorothy Parker
> Excuse My Dust!

She wore horn-rimmed glasses, which she removed quickly if anyone spoke to her suddenly. She had, too—perhaps as a result of nervousness—a habit of blinking and fluttering her eyelids. She had a fondness for the perfume *Chypre*, and for flat-heeled shoes, sometimes for black patent-leather pumps with black bows. She walked, whatever her shoes might be, with short, quick steps. Her suits, in the winter at any rate, were tailor-made. Her hats were large and turned up at the brim. Green, as a color, seemed to appeal to her greatly, whether in a dress, hat or scarf. While her disposition was to be silent, she still had the quickest tongue imaginable, and I need not say, the keenest sense of mockery. But with all her iconoclastic inclinations she was . . . capable of extraordinary kindness, generosity and loyalty.

There were now new faces on the Condé Nast scene, faces who wanted to "do things." Perhaps this period was reflected in lines she was later to write:

> People who do things exceed my endurance,
> God, for a man that solicits insurance

or, perhaps, it was an ironic aside on her life with Eddie in those immediate postwar years. Could it, alternatively, have been an ironic note for the benefit of her husband to deflect his known concern at her ascendance at *Vanity Fair*? The answer is not known. What is known is that Eddie's dogged, unromantic role of a wartime ambulance driver transporting the dead, nearly dead and badly maimed from the battlefield to the Divisional Field Hospital, and the enforced separation from his wife, had scarred his return to civilian life on Wall Street. He had learned too well Alexander Smith's observation: "Death is the ugly fact which nature has to hide."

But he had finally returned. Like many of his battlefield compatriots, he couldn't settle in comfortably. He was trapped behind a barrier of nightmares and alcohol, and things with his bride were not as they had been on those magical weekend encounters.

It had been expected that change—perhaps violent change—would start to reshape American society after the war. The expected change began to arrive and brought with it changes in the editorial structures of *Vanity Fair*. The survivors of the Lost Generation were now returning from the war, and returning to their old jobs. New faces began to appear around the offices.

Dorothy had benefited from the war years at *Vanity Fair*. And Crowninshield had kept his word to her, carefully nurturing his protégée of the lambent pen, giving her writing opportunities, sending her out on absorbing assignments. If she was having difficulties with her marriage, she was satisfied with her career. And more changes were to come.

One of the most profound changes affecting her life was to be the arrival of a journalist named Robert Benchley.

· 6 ·

A Bench for Benchley

ROBERT CHARLES BENCHLEY was appointed managing editor of *Vanity Fair* in June 1919.

His arrival at the magazine caused much interest within the Condé Nast group, and not a little concern. He had left Harvard in 1915 after editing the university magazine, *Lampoon*. It had quickly gotten around that he had not served in the forces partly because of his pacifist leanings and partly because his elder brother, Edmund, thirteen years older, had been killed in the Spanish-American war when Robert was nine. As a result, Benchley's mother had become violently antiwar, and had refused to allow her children to play with any violent toys.

Benchley had already written: ". . . if war is wrong it is wrong, and no pratings of horror can justify it." It was said that his beliefs had caused him to lose his job on the *Tribune* Sunday magazine a few months before he arrived at *Vanity Fair*. He had married a childhood sweetheart, Gertrude Darling, and her influential family had prevented him from being drafted. He had, however, been doing some freelance writing and in 1917 had taken a job doing press liaison work for the Aircraft Board in Washington.

Benchley was born in 1889 of a staunch Republican family; his grandfather had been lieutenant-governor of Massachusetts. Thus, young Benchley's pedigree was much to Crowninshield's liking, for Crowny was known to be "a bit of a snob."

Whether this had any effect on Mrs. Parker is not known, but clearly she was very attracted to Benchley. A pale, slight young fellow with the habit of biting his nails—a habit he was never to lose—"he was," Crowninshield was later to recall, "solicitous of his health to the degree of long underwear and rubbers." Mrs. Parker admired his lazy understatement, his verbal complexities which resolved themselves entertainingly into simple truths.

She approved, too, of his acute sense of satire and his irreverent approach to life, work and people in positions of esteem. Four years older than she, he was self-deprecating and droll, appearing to treat the whole of life as an irreverent joke. Some said this was a facade, for he devoted much of his spare time to working for worthwhile charities, notably settlement homes and The Big Brother organization. Highly literate, he displayed an almost alarming disregard for money and possessions. He was, too, also, in his own way, a pillar of temperance, expressing an abhorrence of both drink and drinkers.

Robert Benchley was proud of his association with Harvard, which, he reverently reminded those who didn't want to know, was "America's first college, founded in Massachusetts colony in 1636." On leaving the school, he'd taken a fleeting temporary job organizing employee clambakes for a Boston paper company about which he reminisced to Mrs. Parker: "I've never looked a clam in the face since."

Crowninshield had unstinted admiration for his new managing editor and delighted in telling the story of Benchley's Harvard days when his new executive encountered the university's final examination question. Benchley, it seemed, had been invited to:

"Discuss the arbitration of the international fisheries problem in respect to hatcheries, protocol, and dragnet and trawl procedure as it affects (a) the point of view of the United States and (b) the point of view of Great Britain."

Benchley had answered the question with a mixture of directness and tongue-in-cheek evasion:

"I know nothing about the point of view of Great Britain in the arbitration of the international fisheries problem, and nothing about the point of view of the United States. Therefore, I shall discuss the question from the point of view of the fish."

Moreover, he had proceeded to do just that—with hilarious result.

Even Crowninshield's dry wit wasn't equal to the starched, laconic humor of Benchley, who, in Dorothy Parker's estimation, rated number one in the League of Self-Mockery. The two became firm friends. Although they both led active lives, they were, in terms of ready cash, fairly impoverished. He had been appointed at a salary of $100 a week but had no real understanding of money. It has to be said, however, that he, better than anybody else, recognized his own lack of responsibility in all matters pertaining to finance.

One of the first things he did when he took the job at *Vanity Fair* was to apply for a large loan at his Fifth Avenue bank. He was surprised to be granted the full amount with no questions asked. Returning to the bank the next day he withdrew all his savings, explaining to Mrs. Parker: "I don't trust a bank that would lend money to such a poor risk."

Benchley had arrived at the same time Crowninshield hired a new drama editor: six-foot-seven-inch war veteran Robert Emmet Sherwood. Shy and given to stooping, Sherwood had dark brown hair and enormous brown eyes. Having been refused enlistment in the U.S. army because of his extreme height, Sherwood, whom his friends called "Sherry," had promptly crossed the border and enlisted in a regiment of Scottish ancestry, the kilted Canadian Black Watch. "By no stretch of the imagination can I be called an attractive fellow in kilts, but at least I can say that I'm imposing" was his comment. His erratic education, having been one of the worst students in the history of the Milton Academy, albeit one of the best liked, had proved no bar to his receiving a commission in the distinguished regiment.

His record at Milton had not been the end of his academic disgrace. He had also been thrown out of Harvard twice for poor grades and twice readmitted, his main achievement there having been his extracurricular involvement, such as the Glee Club, the Hasty Pudding theater shows, intramural football and *Lampoon*. He had left Harvard to join up in 1917 and had been badly wounded in both legs at Vimy Ridge, as well as gassed.

After the war, because of his family connections, he had briefly written speeches for the politically emerging Franklin D. Roosevelt. It was said that his wit had made a considerable mark within the White House. Once when he had accompanied Roosevelt to Philadelphia, the latter had delivered one of Sherwood's drafts. The speech had been well received and FDR took time off to compliment the author. Sherwood had deferentially bounced the compliment back, saying that Roosevelt's sense of timing had won the day. Whereupon Roosevelt smilingly asked Sherwood if he thought Alfred Lunt could have done better. To this Sherwood had cryptically commented yes. Roosevelt had much enjoyed the joke.

Sherwood joined the editorial staff of *Vanity Fair* at $25 a week. Along with Parker and Benchley, he quickly became the third member of the "laughter triumvirate." Mrs. Parker regarded him as a "pretty fast" character, wearing his straw hat at a jaunty angle.

Influenced by Benchley, Crowninshield decided that Dorothy Parker would be groomed for drama criticism—eventually. Just then Pelham Grenville Wodehouse was doing a creditable job writing theater reviews. But she was the ideal person to take over from him when he decided that he might need a change. It may be that Dorothy Parker writing occasional reviews, as his deputy, influenced Wodehouse to take a break. Certainly, he told Crowninshield that he'd always wanted to do the European grand tour and wanted to stop off in his native London. He was given an unpaid, indefinite leave of absence.

Mrs. Parker took over as drama critic on a temporary basis. She decided to use the byline "Helene Rousseau," inspired by the eighteenth-century philosopher, on her theater reviews while using her own name on her verse and prose pieces. Aware of Benchley's own attraction to drama, she asked why he did not tackle the job himself. Benchley drawled: "No. I'll stay at the desk. I do most of my work sitting down—that's where I shine."

On the basis of purely practical experience, neither Benchley nor Parker was ideally qualified for their new roles—he running the day-to-day administration of a successful magazine, she cloaking herself in what she described as "the mock mantle of Thracian drama criticism." But if there was a marked incongruity in their positions they could at least laugh together at that incongruity. And laugh they did. To her he became "Mr. Benchley—Fred" and she to him, "That there Mrs. Parker." In and out of the office, they were up to all types of larks. She remembered:

"Both Mr. Benchley and I subscribed to two undertaking magazines —*The Casket* and *Sunnyside*. Steel yourself. *Sunnyside* had a joke column called "From Grave to Gay." I cut a picture out of one of them, in color, of how and where to inject the embalming fluid, and had it hung over my desk until Mr. Crowninshield asked me if I could possibly take it down. Mr. Crowninshield was a lovely man, but puzzled."

Crowninshield's own version was this:

"I dared to suggest that it might prove a little startling to our occasional visitors and that, perhaps, something by Marie Laurencin might do as well—a hint which met with only the most palpable contempt from the emerging writer . . ."

Mrs. Parker, Benchley and Sherwood, whom Crowninshield christened "those amazing whelps," shared each other's mordant sense of humor. Benchley and Sherwood were friendly with Berthold Baer, press agent of the Frank E. Campbell funeral parlors in Manhattan and elsewhere, and would often regale Mrs. Parker with the goings-on in such establishments, much to the amusement of them all. This sick humor seemed accurately to exhibit their attitude to life, an almost casual indifference to established proprieties. They also displayed an intolerance of intelligence below their own, and clearly none of them liked the disciplines and routines of office life. But if they disliked these things, they positively reveled in each other's company.

The three lunched together daily; she came, it was said, "in order to protect" the lanky Sherwood from being "attacked by the midgets," who were then playing the nearby Hippodrome vaudeville theatre. The *Vanity Fair* offices were nearby, and when the three would stroll down the street the midgets would sneak up behind the lofty Sherwood asking how the weather was up there.

The trio would usually lunch at the Algonquin Hotel and would order either hors d'oeuvres or scrambled eggs and coffee, never straying to the relatively expensive à la carte menu encompassing such dream dishes as Lobster Newburg Cassolette, boiled Kennebec Salmon, or Minced Tenderloin of Beef à la Deutsch. As Mrs. Parker was later to say: "it cost money and we weren't just poor; Mr. Benchley, Mr. Sherwood and I were penniless," but that may have been a Parkerian exaggeration, for she was frequently given to such exaggerations, especially in later life. But it is true that while Sherwood came from a wealthy family background and had money of his own, Benchley, in particular, was hard up in those days. On $100 a week, with a wife who was used to the best and living in a house in exclusive Scarsdale, he must have been hard put to meet his home commitments, let alone those of his work, as well as his social activities. Whatever his monetary problems, he clearly enjoyed the company of his two friends and colleagues and the ambience of the Pergola Room of the Algonquin.

The editorial staff of H. L. Mencken's *Smart Set* magazine, with offices on 45th Street, also met for lunch at the Algonquin, and the place was fast becoming again a rendezvous for the New York theatrical crowd, peopled by the saturnine John Drew, the extrovert Ethel Barrymore and other stage luminaries. Certainly, when walking through the glass-and-brass revolving doors, the three invariably received a genial welcome from Frank Case, the slim, neat, bald, moustached giant who ran it.

Before long, they were joined in the Pergola Room by the erudite Franklin P. Adams—or "FPA," as he liked to be known, as well as the plump and waspish Alexander Woollcott and the gauche Harold Ross, three journalist soldiers just back from the war, who had formed the nucleus of the main editorial unit which, in Paris, had successfully run the forces' newspaper, *Stars and Stripes*.

Case invariably seated the group together at a long table between a frightful Mataniaesque mural of the Bay of Naples and a mirrored wall which effectively provided a reflection of the sextet and others who joined them.

Later, Frank Case moved the company to the Rose Room. Others in the theater and in journalism started to join the communal board. These soon included Murdock Pemberton, a Broadway press agent, who promptly christened the company "The Round Table at the Algonquin."

Thus an American legend was born.

· 7 ·

"It Had All Happened Before..."

MANY YEARS LATER, Margaret Case Harriman, daughter of the Algonquin's Frank Case, wrote: "The Round Table, or Vicious Circle as it became known, came to the Algonquin Hotel the way lightning strikes a tree."

Why she took this view is difficult to understand. The evolution of the group was, in fact, a gradual process, stretching over a twelve-year period. Long before the advent of the Round Table, the hotel had been frequented by Alfred Noyes, Mark Twain, William Makepeace Thackeray, Edgar Allan Poe, and other literary giants, several of whom ate there or stayed overnight or remained there for a time in order to write.

The twelve-storey hotel on West Forty-fourth Street, close to Fifth Avenue, had been built in 1902, and was originally to have been a temperance hotel called the Puritan. Instead it had become a haven for writers and actors. When the Round Table started to evolve, the place already boasted a list of illustrious clients such as Laurette Taylor, Booth Tarkington, Mrs. Fiske, Elsie Janis, Jane Cowl, Constance Collier, Douglas Fairbanks and Rex Beach, as well as John Drew, most of the Barrymores and itinerant luminaries of the entertainment and literary scenes.

At the time of Mrs. Parker's initial patronage along with the ubiquitous duo of Roberts, the trio christened the Pergola Room table "Luigi's Board," named after the voluble waiter who was assigned to them by Georges, the headwaiter.

The formation of the select circle was helped by a group of theatrical publicists, Pemberton with John Peter Toohey, Herman Mankiewicz, John Weaver, David Wallace and Ruth Hale. Their arrival on the scene was predicated by their jobs: They naturally followed in the wake of the journalist charter members—Mrs. Parker, Benchley, Sherwood, Ross, Adams and Woollcott—each of whom represented influential publicity outlets for the press agents and their clients.

Toohey was publicist for Broadway producer George Tyler; Pemberton, for the nearby Hippodrome; and Ruth Hale, for the Selwyn theatrical setup, while David Wallace handled public relations for William Brady Enterprises, when he was not contributing such quips as "Once there were two Jews—and *now* look!" while representing varied interests from producers to starlets like Margalo Gillmore. It was their job to stick close to the editorial honey-pot, especially since other critics and specialist journalists like Maxwell Anderson of the New York *World*, Laurence Stallings (who had lost a leg in the war) of the Atlanta *Journal*, Ben Hecht, Jane Grant, Charles MacArthur, Marc Connelly and Ring Lardner followed the trek to the Algonquin, as had the myopic Henry Miller who would sit sad-faced and silent staring at his fellow diners.

In time, the legend of the Round Table built upon itself and soon various peripheral irregulars, all closely associated with the arts, joined the party. Since luminaries like Alfred Lunt and Lynn Fontanne, Lady Gregory of the Irish theater, Ina Claire, Harpo Marx, Noel Coward, Peggy Wood, Arnold Bennett, Edna Ferber and Peggy "Peaches and Cream" Leech all turned up on occasion, the place quickly became a publicist's paradise. Frank Case predictably rubbed his hands, greeting his guests with animated warmth.

Early during this period, the table was also graced by the laconic George S. Kaufman, drama editor of *The New York Times* and an up-and-coming playwright, who usually arrived with his wife. The name of the assembly changed from "Luigi's Board" to the "Round Table," influenced no doubt by Kaufman, who disliked Luigi's habit of interrupting the flow of conversation by outbreaks of temperament delivered in fractured English. For those with an inquiring mind, it had all happened before—overseas.

In becoming established in an almost casual way, the Round Table had affixed itself to a central Manhattan hotel, thus following the pattern of similar bohemian gatherings in European capitals.

Paris had had its Belle Epoque, starting in the 1880s, centered around Fouquet's restaurant and the French intellectual magazine *Revue Blanche*, an avant-garde monthly which flourished under its founder and editor, Thadée Natanson, and his exquisite wife, Misia, endorsing the talents of such as Diaghilev, Fauré, Debussy, Dali and Picasso, most of whom frequented Fouquet's restaurant. The Algonquinites were following in the wake of this set, albeit a trifle more humbly; a close attachment to a literary magazine was soon to emerge for the Algonquinites in the shape of *The New Yorker*. The Round Table seemed, in its escalating success, sufficient unto itself, an almost enclosed society of New York's art elite.

It was the pattern to be seen in Berlin in the early twenties, where the center of artistic life was the Romanische Café, shabbily splendid and packed with artists and writers holding forth in a haze of liquor fumes, stale air and cigarette smoke, bohemians who included George Grosz, Berthold Brecht, Christopher Isherwood, Heinrich Mann, Joseph Roth, Franz Werfel, Billy Wilder, Carl Zuckmayer, Thomas Wolfe and Stefan Zwieg, as well as Albert Einstein, who was known to drink coffee and slurp boiled eggs with the best and the worst of them. Most of them buzzed around Ullstein's *Der Querschnitt* literary establishment like bees round a sunflower.

The Romanische had ricocheted off the Domino Room of the celebrated Café Royal in Regent Street, London, which, as the reprobate Frank Harris recorded, had "the best cellar on earth." This was the place where the ornate gilt mirrors reflected a formidable procession of artistic giants of the stature of Fritz Kreisler, American-born James McNeill Whistler, D. H. Lawrence, the eclectic Ronald Firbank, Oscar Wilde and Bosie Douglas, Ernest "Cynara" Dowson, Walter Sickert, Henry W. Nevison, Hugh Walpole, Eddie Marsh and T. S. Eliot, most of them contributing to the *Saturday Review*.

What the Mermaid Tavern had been to the Elizabethans, Wills' London Coffee House to the Augustans, The Cock to the mid-Victorians, the Café Royal to the late Victorians and the Edwardians, the Algonquin was fast becoming to the New York twenties literary scene.

Concurrent, too, with the Vicious Circle in Manhattan, the celebrated Bloomsbury set held sway in London—"nine characters in search of an author"—Virginia and Leonard Woolf, Lytton Strachey, John Maynard Keynes, Desmond McCarthy, Roger Fry, Clive and Vanessa Bell and Duncan Grant, leaders of a group which had another thirty or more artists, writers, poets and journalists fetching up the rear.

Between them the Bloomsburyites represented the intellectual end of the arts and crafts of British politics, fiction, biography, criticism and painting, a loftier lot, it has to be admitted, than their Algonquin contemporaries. They, too, were to center much activity on a magazine, Cyril Connolly's *Horizon*, and to a lesser extent, on Leonard Woolf's publishing house, the Hogarth Press. They took their pleasures and food in their Georgian homes and in the lesser-known restaurants of Bloomsbury, Gordon, Mecklenburgh and Russell Squares in London's Bloomsbury district, becoming known as "that elite group in which all the couples were triangles who lived in squares."

The links between the New York Algonquin and London Bloomsbury set may have been tenuous, but they were there. The affectionate, scruffy, intellectual leftist journalist Heywood Broun, who had been at

Harvard with T. S. Eliot and Walter Lippmann, and who was soon to become a familiar face at the Algonquin, certainly forged a connection between the two.

In New York in 1913, Broun met ballet dancer Lydia Lopokova, with whom he fell hopelessly in love. She returned his affection but after a year with him, she met Randolfo Barocini, Diaghilev's Italian-born secretary and manager. The two eloped to Europe and married, much to Broun's deep distress. Later the ballerina divorced Barocini, and met and married John Maynard Keynes, the sober English economist of the Bloomsbury set who was to divine and direct British fiscal policies, precursing the Thatcher era of monetarism by many years.

In manner and accomplishment, Broun and Keynes were very different. It has been said that the disheveled Broun, who loved to gamble, had a system of bookkeeping which was to put his bankroll in one pocket and his winnings in the other. When both pockets were empty, he would tell himself that he had broken even—hardly a system with which the careful Keynes would have agreed.

Yet Madame Lopokova loved the one and presumably loved, and certainly married, the other.

As Mrs. Parker, who was also briefly to love Broun, would have agreed, the tastes of women in their choice of men are often strange, stranger still than the minor parallels of history.

If the Algonquin set was something of an enclosed order, what was happening in the serious literary scene in America at large, outside the somewhat incestuous habitat of the Manhattan hotel? In artistic terms, American writing was poised for a breakthrough. Europe had unquestionably led the way; now it was time for America's new literary talents to come to the fore.

Harvard, Yale, Princeton and other universities and colleges had for some years nursed burgeoning writers who were now emerging bright, clean and possessed of an intensity of talent that was now lighting America's literary skies like a cascade of fireworks. There was Gilbert Seldes, formerly American correspondent of the *Echo de Paris* and managing director of *The Dial*, turning out a succession of incisive critical articles in that magazine. Edmund "Bunny" Wilson, a classical scholar and classmate of Donald Ogden Stewart at Yale, was the author of a series of brilliant critical essays in *The New Republic* when he wasn't engaged in helping to set a high literary tone along with the already established H. L. Mencken, or co-authoring the rampant best-seller, *The Undertaker's Garland*. And the young Princeton novelist F. Scott Fitzgerald had recently gained immediate fame with *This Side of Paradise*, following it with *The Beautiful and The Damned*, an exercise in "sentimental pessimism" that had been sold to the movies for the then considerable sum of $10,000, applauded as it had been by senior critics Mencken and George Jean Nathan.

John Farrar, also a Yale man, had made his mark not only as editor of the prestigious *The Bookman* but as author of two electrifying volumes of verse, *Forgotten Shrines* and *Songs for Parents*. John Peale Bishop, another product of Princeton and an assistant editor with Edmund Wilson on the *New Republic*, had written a slim volume of verse, *Green Fruit*, which had confirmed his talent so evident in his collaboration with Wilson in *The Undertaker's Garland*. And a Harvard graduate of "rebellious spirit," one John Dos Passos, had overtaken many of his literary contemporaries with the publication of a book entitled *Three Soldiers*, claimed by one critic of the time to be "a work of genius, because genius is an infinite capacity for giving pain."

At the same time, John V. A. Weaver was receiving plaudits for *The American*, a volume of verse written in between his duties as editor of the Brooklyn *Daily Eagle*. Stephen Vincent Benét, at the age of twenty-four, was another emerging writer of high order. He had published three books of poetry, the latest of which, *Heavens and Earth*, had won him the divided prize of the Poetry Society, while his novel, *The Beginning of Wisdom*, was a runaway success on the bookstands, a success followed by a second novel, *Young People's Pride*, which was also hitting the literary jackpot.

And there was William Faulkner making literary history with his sometimes overlong books, and the "fearsome talent" of Don Marquis with his enchanting *archy and mehitabel* books, and a man named John Steinbeck, of whom approving noises were beginning to be heard, not to mention Christopher Morley's potent "cleansing power of humor," so vivid in many of his articles and books, which Mrs. Parker summed up at the time with:

> Christopher Morley goes hipperty, hopperty,
> Hipperty, hipperty, hop.
> Whenever I ask him politely to stop it,
> He says he can't possibly stop.

Underpinning this scene of emergent talent of the new world was the growing American appreciation of the artistic achievements of Europe. They were avidly reading the works of Joyce, Proust, Cocteau and others; and lining up to view the sculptures of Brancusi and listen to the music of Stravinsky, Debussy and Fauré. Parties were being given in places like

New York's Coffee House in honor of visiting lecturers such as Margot Asquith and Clare Sheridan. Among the "cultivated clowns" of this club was Charles Hanson Towne, who specialized in giving satirical lectures on Wagner's operas when he wasn't drinking at the Coffee House with Hendrik Willem van Loon, whose *Story of Mankind* was zooming up the best-seller lists. Other writers like George Chappell, who had originated *Just the Day for a Picnic*, shared the bonhomie of the place with George Putnam, an up-and-coming young publisher, along with Charles Dana Gibson, the newly arrived owner and publisher of *Life* magazine.

America, hitherto a culturally insecure nation, was embracing the arts with latent joy; and artistically was finding its feet, helped by other emergent poets, playwrights and writers like Robert Frost, working in London; Gertrude Stein, American writer-émigré in Paris; and Ezra Pound, Sherwood Anderson, and Upton Sinclair, the last of whom had begun his literary career at the age of 15. And there was Carl Sandburg, a poet of high talent who unaccountably had a predilection for the company of goats. Wallace Stevens, too, was a poet in the ascendant. After leaving Harvard, he was earning a living as an insurance executive in Hartford to support his pen. And Sinclair Lewis had just published *Main Street*, which had been acclaimed as "a work of genius," a sensational exposé of life and conditions of the American small-town poor. Alfred Kreymborg, William Carlos Williams, Hart Crane, Mina Loy were among a clutch of poets of the time whose work displayed high literary merit. There was also the St. Louis-born T. S. Eliot, who, after Harvard, was spending much of his time in England mixing with the literati there, a pursuit unlike that of the gifted, hard-drinking playwright Eugene O'Neill, who was to win a Nobel prize but meanwhile, like Mrs. Parker, seemed set on establishing the perfect gravestone inscription:

EUGENE O'NEILL
There is something
To be said
For being dead.

· 8 ·

A Skirmish of Wit

THE FAME and notoriety which began to encompass the occupants of the Round Table attracted a variety of additional journalists, writers and artists to the Algonquin. Music critics like Bill Murray and Deems Taylor, other columnists like Broun, cartoonists like Duffy of the Brooklyn *Daily Eagle* and editors such as Crowninshield and *Harper's Bazaar's* Art Samuels joined the crowd in the Rose Room, to which the Table had now been permanently moved.

Yet another formidable talent who joined the Table at this point was Donald Ogden Stewart, who was to become Mrs. Parker's close friend and political ally in the exciting days ahead.

When he first came onto the Algonquin scene, in 1919 at the age of twenty-four, Stewart had left behind Exeter, Yale and a wartime captaincy in Chicago. He had joined millionaire Harold Talbott's aircraft business but this occupation served only to conceal a deep urge within him to write. After being fired by Talbott, Stewart promptly wrote *Aunt Polly's Story of Mankind*, a scathing satirical attack on wartime profiteers and, almost to his surprise, soon found himself published in *Vanity Fair*.

While Murdock Pemberton may have been the person who invested the Round Table with its sobriquet, it was John Peter Toohey who established the sequence of the Algonquin lunches. As one of the very early lunches was breaking up, he asked, "Why don't we do this every day?" And that was the real start of a twelve-year convocation that was to become the source of countless newspaper and magazine stories.

As the stories were repeated, refurbished, revarnished and reprinted, the reputations of those who had originally told the stories became firmly established. The Table was, as Marc Connelly, journalist and playwright, described it, "a very happy microcosm." Sometimes profane in dialogue, it was also a secular site of theatrical shop talk, bitchy gossip, epicene epigrams and rapier ripostes. It was, indeed, New York's trade center of vituperative viperisms but, most of all, as Mrs. Parker said at the time, "it was fun."

And was Mrs. Parker making her mark during those early days of the Round Table? Connelly is on record as saying, "Dorothy Parker was the most riveting presence at the table." The journalists saw to it that the best of the stories and bons mots were quoted in their columns, chiefly because many of them were so eminently quotable, and there is little doubt that several of those within the charmed circle spent waking, and often what should have been sleeping, hours dreaming up verbal strikes for the next day's assemblage in the Rose Room.

"Let's get out of these wet clothes and into a dry martini" has been variously attributed to Mrs. Parker, Woollcott and Franklin Adams. None of them said it. Robert Benchley was the author of the epigram. It was uttered by him on arriving at the Algonquin, having been caught in a rainstorm after leaving a press reception at the nearby Plaza Hotel on Central Park.

The humor continued to flow unabated and most of the Vicious Circle gave as good as they got. It was a daily skirmish of wit.

There was fun, too, away from the table. One day Mrs. Parker and Benchley were involved in a scene in an open cab near Times Square. She was seen standing up in the cab screaming to passersby as Benchley tried to gag her with his scarf. "Help! Help! This man is abducting me," she called out. But it was nothing more than just another merry jape.

And there was the occasion when Franklin Pierce Adams arrived at the Algonquin in a snowstorm. "What do you think?" he explained. "I've just seen Harold Ross on a toboggan."

"Did he look funny?" asked Kaufman.

"Well," said Adams, "you know how Ross looks when he's not tobogganing . . ."

It was Woollcott, fast becoming a dominant figure at the Table, who convulsed his friends with, "All the things I really like to do are either illegal, immoral or fattening," and who, in print, admonished the author of a slim volume of distinctly inferior verse, *And I Shall Make Music*, with "Not on my carpet, lady, you won't . . ."

And there was the time when Peggy Wood, rehearsing for the stage version of *Sweethearts*, returned to the theater after a heady Algonquin lunch. She sighed deeply, casting this pearl in the direction of the stage manager—"Ah, well, back to the mimes."

Marc Connelly, who hailed from McKeesport, Pennsylvania, had the theater in his blood, too. His father had been a stage singer and the son was now a *Morning Telegraph* reporter. Once, when Connelly was sitting next to Mrs. Parker at the Round Table, an acquaintance passed his chair and ran his hands over Connelly's bald head, remarking, "That feels as smooth and as nice as my wife's behind." Connelly responded in a flash: "So it does, so it does."

Kaufman turned up for lunch at the Algonquin after meeting producer Jed Harris in his suite at the Waldorf-Astoria. Harris, Kaufman claimed, had squatted naked on the floor throughout the meeting. When the talk ended, Kaufman, with his hand on the door handle, ready to leave, had stared at him and quipped: "Jed, your fly is open," and had promptly left.

Some might have called it banter and buffoonery but clearly there was a wide public ready to receive such laughs. The Vicious Circle's fame spread, attracting much additional business to Frank Case's hotel which he did not, as yet, own. So celebrated did the Round Table become that it brought about its own incursion into fiction. Gertrude Atherton, a well-known author, published a novel, *Black Oxen*, in which she fictionalized a Manhattan hotel and an artistic group called The Sophisticates.

According to Margaret Case Harriman, Mrs. Atherton

focused a lorgnette as powerful as Eustace Tilley's upon the Round Table describing the occupants as meeting "at the sign of the Indian Chief," where the cleverest of them are those who were so excitedly sure of their cleverness that for the moment they convinced others as well as themselves . . . There was a great deal of scintillating talk . . . on the significant books and tendencies of the day . . . it was an excellent forcing house for ideas and vocabularies . . . they appraised, debated, rejected, finally placing the seal of their august approval upon a favored few . . .

Mrs. Atherton did not wholly approve of the Circle but, it was said, that was because she wasn't invited to join it, although she did have lunch with them once or twice. If she did not approve, she shared her disapproval with others, including several influential critics and commentators, among whom was Irvin S. Cobb. He was to speak caustically of "the famous Round Table where sits in splendor Gotham's favorite wag—and his own."

But if you did not approve of the Table, you certainly couldn't ignore it; it was growing in stature from comment to comment, from story to story, from riposte to riposte. As Mrs. Harriman wrote: "The Round Table had the bloom of youth on it."

Like Mrs. Atherton, Edna Ferber, author of the Emma McChesney stories and soon to become a distinguished playwright, had only been at the Table once or twice, and while she did not wholly approve of the group she did admit:

"Far from boosting one another, they actually were merciless if they disapproved. I have never encountered a more hard-bitten crew . . . Theirs was a tonic influence, one on the other, and on the world of

American letters . . . The people they could not and would not stand were the bores, hypocrites, sentimentalists and the socially pretentious . . . Casual, incisive, they had a terrible integrity about their work and a boundless ambition." It was Miss Ferber, a spinster, who gave the visiting Noel Coward his comeuppance on her first visit to the Round Table. On spotting her seated next to Woollcott, Coward grinned and declared: "Edna, why it's you! You look almost like a man." "So," Miss Ferber replied coldly, "do you."

There were those, too, who considered the group facile, narrow and immature. But whatever the group in fact was, it was fast becoming a legend.

Robert Drennan, who in 1972 wrote a book on the Algonquin Wits, claims that the Circle came together as "any in-group must—because of their mutual interests . . . Each was possessed by the spirit of the times and each, as if touched by a common muse, found natural direction in the urge to record that spirit under the elusive mask of comedy."

Certainly, they embraced the Roaring Twenties for the fun-loving hell of it, giving the parties, setting the pace, telling and retelling the jokes, pulling the pranks, ignoring the future. Worrying was no part of their lives. As Benchley admitted at the time, "The trouble with me is I can't worry. Dammit, I try to worry and I can't . . ."

It was not uncommon for a contingent of Round Tablers to frequent the speakeasies, for Prohibition was taking its grip. Both Mrs. Parker and Benchley had now started drinking. His temperance beliefs had been lost somewhere on the way between 1919 and 1922 and although she wasn't saying much about it, Mrs. Parker was undergoing pressures at home that weren't entirely to do with her husband's drinking.

At the speakeasies, the Round Tablers would trade jokes about Mayor Walker's corrupt techniques and civic disinterest. There were those who could remember the time when the non-drinking Benchley took his first illegal drink of hooch, exclaiming. "This place ought to be closed by law!"

In accord with the times, the Algonquinites considered it a mortal sin to take themselves, or others, seriously. And several of them were radical in outlook. The left-wing Heywood Broun, for example, arrived late one evening for a dinner party at the Averell Harriman's. He apologized to his hosts, "So sorry to be late. I was down in the kitchen trying to persuade your butler to strike for higher wages." Of course, everybody laughed but, in fact, he had been doing just that.

No subject, however solemn or personal, escaped humorous comment. The comic interpretation, whether involving simple laughter, pathos or moral disapproval, seemed always to stand as their final statement on whatever issue stirred their fancy.

To discuss the names today is rather like reviewing a *Who's Who* of past American writers and entertainers, with outstanding exclusions like Faulkner, Dreiser, Hemingway and others. But in the early twenties, the names would scarcely have raised an eyebrow, they were such an integral part of the Manhattan scene. It is important to remember that the Round Tablers sought each other out before they themselves became the sought-after celebrities of Manhattan. Generally speaking, all were young, fun-loving and ambitious; all took a marked interest in literature, the theater, politics and social problems. And all were gregarious, loquacious, articulate.

This was the age of the theater of Lenore Ulric starring in *Kiki*, John Drew and Mrs. Leslie Carter in Maugham's *The Circle*, A. E. Matthews in *Bulldog Drummond* and Katharine Cornell in *A Bill of Divorcement*. It was, too, an era of songs; "Look For The Silver Lining," "April Showers," "Three O'Clock in the Morning"; and the age of Edith Wharton's *The Age of Innocence* and H. G. Wells's *Outline of History*.

It has been written of the Algonquinites that "their common bond and peculiar genius was wit, although their excellence in conversation, repartee and the delivery of bon mots may have caused them to undervalue their contributions to the community of letters." Woollcott, called by one critic of the time "the worst writer in America," underscored this when he said: "I'm potentially the best writer in America, but I never had anything to say."

FPA, after seeing Helen Hayes's performance in *Caesar and Cleopatra*, remarked that the young actress seemed to be suffering from "fallen archness," and there was the story of Benchley emerging from a midtown restaurant, asking the uniformed man standing by the doorway, "Would you get me a taxi, my good man?" "I am not your good man," was the testy reply. "I happen to be a rear admiral in the United States Navy." "In that case," drawled Benchley, "get me a battleship." Benchley's son was later to deny his father's authorship of the quip, claiming that it was the invention of a publicist; the evidence of Woollcott does not support this claim.

Underlying most of the wit and badinage was a self-deprecating strain that affected the majority of the Round Tablers, not the least Mrs. Parker, who believed that most of her writing was worthless; an attitude she was to hold throughout her life. It was an attitude shared at that time, and for most of his life, by Benchley, who, looking back years later, was to say: "It took me fifteen years to discover that I had no talent for writing but I couldn't give it up because by that time I was famous."

Their self-deprecation was, in a way, a measure of the times, a comment on their ironic, sardonic evaluation of the mad twenties whirl that they all expected, with some accuracy, to collapse at any time.

In the 1930s, Ben Hecht was to write: "Fine actors, actresses, composers and writers were among them. But their fineness was a secondary matter . . . success was the only proof of artistry, or even of intelligence. If you failed, you were a fool and a second-rater." It was, for most of them, the survival of the fittest.

As far as gender was concerned, Mrs. Parker, demure and wise, led the female contingent at the Round Table. She summed up herself in a "Hate Song" addressed to all men:

> But I despite expert advice
> Keep doing things I think are nice,
> And though to good I never come
> Inseparable my nose and thumb . . .

It was quintessentially the lady in tune with her times, and she didn't care who knew it.

By now she had become careless of displaying to others her growing contempt of her husband. Since he had returned from Europe in 1919, he had accepted Dorothy's life-style as far as he could, accompanying her to first nights and parties, and occasionally eating with her at the Round Table.

His drinking apart, by temperament he had always been a quiet man, lacking the wit of Dorothy and her newfound companions. Clearly, if there had been love once between Dorothy Parker and Edwin Pond Parker II, it had not endured. He would spend long weekends with his parents in Hartford and now became, as Margaret Case Harriman recorded, "a young Wall Street insurance man, generally liked, but seldom seen."

As for his wife, she was having fun. As she succinctly put it:

> . . . And when in search of novelty you stray,
> Oh, I can kiss you blithely as you go,
> And what goes on, my love, while you're away,
> You'll never know . . .

· 9 ·

An End to Eddie

APART FROM Crowninshield's observations and the tiny bows on her shoes and her slim, tailored suits, what did the young Mrs. Dorothy Parker look like in those early Algonquin days?

According to John Keats, what the men of the group beheld was

a tiny woman who wore her hair in a kind of pile atop her head, but then parted and combed down so as to make hers seem to be a wistful face at a parting curtain. Her voice was that of a young girl gently bred, soft and deferential. When she spoke, she had a way of putting a little hand on her listener's forearm, and of looking up at him with enormous eyes that at once pleaded for his understanding and assured him that *his* understanding was the most important thing in the world to her. She wore a feather boa that was always getting into the other people's plates or was being set afire by other people's cigarettes (someone said it was the only boa that ever moulted), and this unfortunate boa and the bows on her shoes, and the curious fact that the chic and expensive clothing she wore did not, somehow, look exactly right on her, enhanced the general impression she created. It was one of innocence, utterly feminine and utterly helpless. She was the kind of girl that any man wants to take immediately into his arms, comfort, protect, and assure that everything will be all right . . .

"She was in no more need of protection than a nest of hornets," claimed Keats.

Clearly, Edwin Pond Parker II had penetrated the shell of his wife's assumed vulnerability. Equally clearly, he had experienced—and was still experiencing—the lash of her tongue. Her friends knew that their parting was imminent because Dorothy was now inventing stories about him: She always invented stories about people she disliked.

Their tolerance of each other was marked by her enjoying the company of other escorts to the theater and the parties, which he would sometimes attend with another woman on his arm. To her friends, she would deride Eddie's proneness to accidents and they were always, according to her, *stupid* accidents. She said he would inexplicably bump into closed doors; get up from a table, trip on a carpet and crash into a passing waiter. He had once, she claimed, while following the plebeian pursuit of sharpening a pencil with a penknife while walking down a street, fallen into an open manhole and broken his arm. She was also

48

now telling friends that he had once been forcibly committed to an asylum.

As the Algonquinites knew, Eddie was a somewhat shy and markedly introspective man. His quiet nature meant little to his wife, who continued to dine out on stories of his alleged penchant to attract a series of misfortunes. She would have her friends in stitches at her unfortunate husband's propensity to do the wrong thing at the right time and the right thing at the wrong time.

Keats tells a story of the Parkers attending a funeral.

Because she was never on time for anything, Eddie told her to be ready an hour before the funeral was actually to be held. On this occasion, however, she was only half an hour late getting dressed, with the result that they arrived at the funeral home half an hour early. No one else was there, not even the funeral director. They were alone with the body, which was to be cremated. She and Eddie peered curiously at the corpse, and then, somehow or other, Eddie began to fool around with a knob beneath the casket and machinery began to hum, the casket began to move, a door opened—and casket and corpse went neatly and quietly into the hot little hell of the crematory. There was nothing she and Eddie could do but flee out a side door before the family arrived for the funeral . . .

She related the bizarre happening to the luncheon table at the Algonquin. The group all but expired with laughter.

"I don't see why we are all laughing," she said evenly. "It was really a terrible, terrible thing"—which, delivered to the nearly hysterical dining table, was said to have broken up the gathering completely.

Was it, could it all have been true? Most believed she had invented the story.

Many years later, Mrs. Parker talked briefly to her friend Wyatt Cooper about Eddie.

"He was beautiful, but not very smart. He was supposed to be in Wall Street, but that didn't mean anything. We were married for about five minutes, then he went off to war. He didn't want to kill anybody, so he drove an ambulance. Unfortunately, they had dope in the ambulance. Morphine. You know, that's not good for you. Not healthy. Well, it was one sanatorium after another. . . ."

Cooper told this story to Beatrice Ames, who was to become Mrs. Donald Ogden Stewart. She roared with laughter on hearing it.

"Little Eddie Parker a drug addict!" she exclaimed. "Impossible! He was the most harmless little man you ever saw. But that's Dottie! She's awful!"

Throughout her life, Dorothy Parker was openly to disparage the things she claimed to dislike. Some thought her sardonic hauteur was real enough; some thought it a snail-like hard shell which she assumed to protect the softness of her spirit. Many of her writings display a dismissive loathing of show business with all its traditional razzmatazz. But throughout her life she was ambivalently drawn to the glitter of the footlights of the theater and the klieg lights of the movies, the stars and the hangers-on. It was a disdain that some friends believed to be opaque. She wrote in *McCall's:* "The first-night audience is like no other assemblage of theater-goers on earth." But she could never seem to see that she herself was a component part of that assemblage. She was always an avid reader of *Variety*, the *Hollywood Reporter* and *Women's Wear Daily*.

Most people who knew her believed that her attempts to impress through her work were directed unfalteringly towards a shrewdly calculated ambition to become a celebrity. If that were true, she was now well on the way to achieving celebrity status through a writing style that exuded bored disdain and a sardonic supremacy with words, a supremacy that bordered on near contempt for the majority of the plays and many of the actors she saw. And in her opinion, most of the writers of those plays didn't count either.

As Keats said: "She was on her way to winning a public reputation as being the wittiest woman in New York before she was twenty-seven years old and before she was published anywhere outside of *Vanity Fair*." Woollcott arrived at the Algonquin one morning in something of a state. It seemed that his cat was to be put to sleep. He turned to Mrs. Parker, who knew about animals, for advice as to how to go about it. "Try curiosity," she said.

She reviewed Henrik Ibsen's *Hedda Gabler* with a clear desire to achieve her individual mark:

"Somehow, I could never seem to picture Hedda Tesman as belonging to the Susanna Cocroft type. I thought Nazimova was consistently wonderful, from the moment of her first, bored entrance to the shot that marked her spectacular final exit. Shots almost always do mark the final exit of Mr. Ibsen's heroines . . . George Tesman is one of those parts that can be overdone almost without an effort: just one 'Fancy that!' too many and you're gone . . . I never should have recognized him [George Tesman] if he hadn't used the same green and red handkerchief that he did in *The Wild Duck* . . ."

Her ever-so-gentle, sardonic underplaying reached out to the late, benighted Oscar Wilde in her review of his *An Ideal Husband*:

"Beatrice Beckley has the thankless job of playing Lady Chiltern, one of those frightfully virtuous women of Wilde's who can't utter the simplest observations without dragging in such Sabbatical expressions as 'we needs must' . . . Somehow, no matter how well done an Oscar Wilde play may be, I am always far more absorbed in the audience than in the drama . . . they have a conscious exquisiteness . . . a sort of Crolier-than-thou air. 'Look at us,' they seem to say, 'we are the *cognoscenti.* We have come because we can appreciate this thing—we are not as you, poor bonehead, who are here because you couldn't get tickets for the Winter Garden . . .' "

Even an arguably superb production of Leo Tolstoy's *Redemption* did not escape her contemptuous, derisive lash with, as always, the sting in the tail:

"I went into the Plymouth Theatre a comparatively young woman, and I staggered out of it, three hours later, twenty years older . . ." Writing of "the local Russian custom of calling each person sometimes by all of his names, sometimes by only his first three or four," she caustically added, "I do wish that as long as they are translating the thing, they would go right on ahead, while they're at it, and translate Fedor Vasilyevich Protosov and Georgei Dmitrievich Abreskov and Ivan Petrovich Alexandrov into Joe and Harry and Fred . . ."

She had shown a distinct disaffection for Edward Knoblock, the distinguished English dramatist, whose Blakeian allegory, *Tiger! Tiger!* she reviewed, evincing a particular distaste for the loquacity of the Cockney cook:

"Frances Starr never for one moment made me feel that she really was a cook . . . because a young woman says 'H'aint' and 'you was' and admits she 'don't know nothin' about art,' doesn't seem to me to be any particular reason for a man to clasp her passionately in his arms and tell her that she is a wild, sweet, fairy thing—a creature of the spring woods . . . the cooks I have known have never been in any way pathetic; they have always been the self-made, not to say aggressive, type who manage to get along very well indeed without any outside assistance, and they'll thank you to keep your sympathy to yourself . . ."

Perhaps Mrs. Parker's assessment of *Peter Pan*'s progenitor, J. M. Barrie, might conceivably avoid the lady's laceration? Overall, it seems, his *Dear Brutus* did please her mnemonic tendencies:

"The ladies' cup goes to Helen Hayes, who does an exquisite bit of acting . . . when you think of how easily she could have ruined the whole thing, her work seems little short of marvelous.

Altogether, *Dear Brutus* meant practically everything to me. It made me weep—and I can't possibly enjoy a play more than that."

In June of 1919, she could, and did, enthuse about Sem Benelli's *The Jest.* One simply had to sit up and take notice of the critic who wrote:

"The simple, homely advice of one who has never been outside of these broadly advertised United States is only this: park the children somewhere, catch the first city-bound train, and go to the Plymouth Theatre, even if you have to trade in the baby's Thrift Stamps to buy the tickets. The play will undoubtedly run from now on. You ought to be able to get nice, comfortable, standing-rooms any time after Labor Day . . ."

The following January, she took on Wilde's French translator, Pierre Louÿs, whose novel *Aphrodite* had, in turn, been dramatized by George Hamilton amid frenetic forecasts of success by the publicists:

For months beforehand, the professional publicity writers had enthused almost to the point of hysteria over the magnificence of the production; but Honest John did more for the box-office receipts in a single day than the combined efforts of the most talented and experienced press agents could have accomplished in a year. The Mayor had but to say that he had heard a rumor that there were scandalous goings-on at the Century [Theater] and if they weren't careful he would send his Committee of Welcome up to investigate, and the house sold out for eight weeks in advance.

The press agents racked their brains for such adjectives as "stupendous," "superb," "sensational" and "overwhelming"; but our own Mayor, with the simple word "indecent," did the trick . . .

. . . in dignity and impressiveness, save for those scenes played by Dorothy Dalton and McKay Morris, the production is pitifully lacking . . .

Possibly this is due, in great part, to the fact that most of the feminine members of the cast were recruited from the Century Roof, where they were trained for emotional roles in ancient Egyptian dramas by a course of dancing around between tables, singing "Smiles." Another factor is the casting of Etienne Girardot as physician to the Queen of Egypt, in which role he wears much the same makeup that he used to in *Charley's Aunt* . . .

Some time later, Mrs. Parker was to aver: "Wit has truth in it . . . wisecracking is simply calisthenics with words."

Did such reviews display real wit? Or were they simply calisthenics with words? Certainly her readers considered her writing to be devastatingly witty and on such writing she was equally certainly building her reputation.

Dorothy Parker was not much taken with the English theater and its tradition, although she seemed curiously drawn to both, touched as they were by the English intellectual literary tradition: this same tradition was evidenced, albeit with an American theme, by John Drinkwater, of whose *Abraham Lincoln* she tentatively approved in a customary Parkerian acerbic mood:

"Of the shrewd backwoodsman, there is but little trace, and of the crude humorist, the father of the unquestionably, questionable story, none whatever; this is a Lincoln that would stalk freezingly from the room if anyone said so much as 'It seems there was this traveling man . . .' "

But she was not prepared to pay full homage to Drinkwater. There had to be a bitter taste left in the mouth, a dialectic dousing for the English author, if only through the performance of Frank McGlynn, the leading actor:

"Frank McGlynn, hitherto unknown to New York, is the Lincoln of the production and, from the opening night, his unknown days were over. His is an extraordinarily real characterization; though the lasting impression is of the heroic figure, the maker of history, he has somehow managed to suggest the shrewd humor that the playwright so sedulously avoided."

Game, set and match to Mrs. Parker.

And so it went on from April 1918 through March 1920, the years of her monthly critiques in *Vanity Fair*. But she was usually prepared to praise the work of her Algonquin friends—Helen Hayes, Peggy Wood, Lynn Fontanne, Constance Collier, among others. Log rolling, they called it.

It is known that Mrs. Parker considered this work as a grind. As Professor Kinney says: "Dorothy began using her wit to distance herself from bad plays, just as it had distanced her from her stepmother and the Blessed Sacrament Convent." But if it was a grind, there were always the ebullient lunches at the Algonquin to brighten her days.

The Circle had by now attracted other occasional adherents like E. B. and Katharine White, Edmund Wilson, James Thurber, Peter Arno, Arthur Kober (who was soon to marry an unknown woman named Lillian Hellman), Nunnally Johnson, Richard Rodgers, Frank Capra, William Fadiman, Russell Crouse and Charles Addams. They, in turn, attracted others—Gus Lobrano, William Maxwell, William Shawn, Paul Robeson, Louis Bromfield, to name just a few.

However much Mrs. Parker was later to dismiss the Round Table and their talent, she showed approval of a number of its founding members. The Algonquin had become in both fact and spirit a focal point of her life. The same was true of Robert Benchley who, by this time, had become her closest friend.

In the evenings several of the group, mostly the originals, would fan out to take further pleasures in the confines of Tony Soma's speakeasy across the street, the Puncheon Club at 42 West Forty-ninth Street (which was destined to become Jack Kriendler and Charlie Berns's "21"), Polly Adler's notorious girl establishment, George Kaufman's house, Harold Ross and Jane Grant's apartment at 412 West Forty-seventh

Street, or Alexander Woollcott's place. At other times they would hive across to Bleeck's speakeasy or Neysa McMein's studio, where an admixture of distilled water, oils of coriander and lemon, glycerine and grain alcohol, was available.

Even if Dorothy Parker did find her drama criticism a grind, she was in love with life, her job and her steadily growing celebrity status.

No longer did she conceal any vestige of affection for her husband. When he turned up at the Algonquin lunch sessions he was largely ignored, mainly because of his inability to match the sardonic humor of the now-widening circle. He clearly was not of a mind to participate in word games like I-Can-Give-You-A-Sentence. Puns and double-entendres were not in his makeup or vocabulary. When, occasionally, he showed up at parties, he would usually sit alone in a corner, drinking —silent and looking bemused.

After he disappeared from the scene, his wife seldom mentioned his name. Mrs. Parker was later to dismiss him with: "I married to change my name from Rothschild to Parker—that is all there was to it."

But there were those among her intimate friends who said that Eddie had pleaded with her time and again to leave New York, promising to dry himself out, if only she would give up her job and social connections and return with him to Hartford. He claimed that his family would welcome his resettlement there with his wife; that in Hartford they would find the happiness they had once known. Dorothy used a convenient excuse that his fiercely Protestant family resented her because she was Jewish, and because of that there was no way she would go with him back to Hartford. They had walked the pitted lanes of love together and had lost their way. That was all there was to it.

Apart from the formalities, the marriage ended in 1919.

Donald Ogden Stewart perhaps best captured the essence of the girl-about-Manhattan, Dorothy Parker, when he later wrote:

I think if you had been married to Dottie, you would have found out, little by little, that she really wasn't there. She was in love with you, let's say, but it was *her* emotion: she was not worrying about *your* emotion . . . She was so full of pretense . . . that does not mean she did not hate sham on a high level, but that she could recognize pretense because that was part of her own makeup. She would get glimpses of herself doing things that would make her hate herself.

Whether she hated herself for leaving Eddie, we don't know. What we do know is that he returned to Hartford and for the rest of his life refused to make any comment on his marriage to Dorothy Parker.

· 1 0 ·

Notice to Quit

THE ALGONQUINITES, by their well-publicized antics, were now touching the hems of New York's *Blue Book* fraternity, which included the Pratts, Schiffs, Fielders, Chryslers and Morgans. To them, Dorothy Parker was the large-eyed, elegant wit of high intelligence.

She was the sardonic female jester, the dancer and the song, the wondergirl of sophisticated literary journalism, who lived for life and all that life could give her. The socializing continued unabated and Mrs. Parker was right at the center, playing the dual role of the rose and the thorn. Her caustic wit was quoted and requoted in the international gossip columns, quips that were usually picked up from Adams's "Conning Tower" column.

Now that Eddie had gone back to Hartford, it was time for Dorothy Parker to find another place to live. Taking a look around an apartment on Riverside Drive, she turned to the real estate agent and said in an even voice: "Oh, dear, this is much too big. All I need is room enough to lay a hat and a few friends."

Benchley was at her side on that visit: he was invariably at her side at this time. It was he who told her that artist Neysa McMein had secured an option for her on an apartment on West Fifty-seventh Street in the same building as Neysa's studio. "It's a lurch away from my front door" was the way Neysa had put it to Benchley. Dorothy took the apartment and moved in with an unseemly array of parcels which constituted her luggage. It is true that the place was small and unglamorous but that didn't matter. According to Herman Liebert, a friend, "it was a modest room with a kitchen stuck in one corner and a small bathroom in another. That was all." But Neysa gave a lot of parties and that in itself was good enough excuse for her taking it.

The ceaseless round of parties began to throw up rumors that Parker, Benchley and Sherwood were neglecting their jobs on *Vanity Fair*. The trio seemed not to mind such gossip; they were becoming celebrated, Mrs. Parker perhaps most of all, and people always talked, frequently lied, about those in the public eye. Dorothy's quips continued and a number of the trio's contemporaries lived in terror lest they should themselves become the subject of a Parker gibe, a Sherwood aphorism or a

55

Benchley bite—"a particular form of jest that, piercing pretense carries a reproof." But was there truth in the rumors?

It was a fact that the timekeeping of the triumvirate at *Vanity Fair* left much to be desired. That they "delivered the goods" required by the management was the timeworn, universal logic of the journalist missing from his desk, but it didn't go down well with Crowninshield when he was reminded of it by Benchley and Parker. It was true, too, that *Vanity Fair* had earlier taken to ordering members of the staff, by means of memos, not to discuss their salaries with other staff appointees. This simply resulted in Benchley and Mrs. Parker parading through the offices wearing boards that proclaimed their precise salaries.

And it was well known that the three of them took a dim view of another memorandum inspired not by Crowninshield but by an efficiency expert who had been appointed by Nast. The memo said that anyone who was late for work would have to fill out a slip explaining their lateness.

To this, Benchley had promptly completed a dog-eared slip of paper in microscopic handwriting. It told how elephants at the Hippodrome had escaped that morning. Mr. Benchley's civic duty, he claimed, was plain. He had helped round them up to prevent their boarding a Fall River steamship headed for Boston, which would have caused a marine disaster, and returned them to the Hippodrome. This noble effort had resulted in his being eleven minutes late for work that day.

After this, there were no more printed slips from the efficiency expert. The outcome, however, had been duly noted by Nast.

As far as the so-called affair between Benchley and Parker was concerned, even when Eddie had been around, one particular columnist had hardly hidden the suggestion that Parker and Benchley were involved in a torrid liaison. Before Eddie left for Hartford, they had both rushed to him to deny the story. It was, they lamely said, necessary to be seen around together; after all, they worked for the same magazine. Eddie had placidly replied that he understood, but he had not.

To most, the appearance of Robert Benchley and Mrs. Parker was of two kindred souls locked together in a life of laughter, mutual interests and a love of life. It was natural for them to be seen together; they were invited to the same parties and openings. There were those who claimed that the excuses rang a trifle hollow, but the two did not change their habits.

The people in the journalistic set of New York knew, of course, that Benchley was married, had two children back in Scarsdale and had been a teetotaler until he had met Mrs. Parker; they knew, too, that his New

England morality was still involved in worthy charitable causes which now included the YMCA and underprivileged children.

After Eddie's departure, Benchley and Dorothy became inseparable. Benchley's dry, laconic humor echoed round the party circuit and Mrs. Parker's somewhat languorous laughter followed in the wake of his quips, when she wasn't putting down people and places herself. She later recalled: "Damn it, it was the twenties; we had to be smarty. I wanted to be cute—that's the terrible thing. I should have had more sense. A smartcracker, they called me. I was the toast of two continents—Greenland and Australia!"

It was not only Benchley and Parker who were inseparable; Robert E. Sherwood spent most of his time in their company, in the office, at the Algonquin, at speakeasies and at parties.

It was Sherwood who was first called in by Crowninshield for a disciplinary discourse caused by his satirizing in the editorial columns of *Vanity Fair* the claims of one of the fashion advertisements in an earlier issue. As a result of his derisive handiwork in an article called "What the Well-dressed Man Will Wear," the magazine had to print an apology—and magazines, Crowninshield told him, didn't like printing apologies. Sherwood regarded "the lapse" as trifling and quite unimportant, and said so around the office. He was supported with comradely comment by Benchley and Parker, directed chiefly at Condé Nast.

The atmosphere in the office was becoming increasingly uneasy, while editorially Dorothy Parker's critical faculties were becoming sharper with every play she reviewed. It was clear to all that she liked to use iodine on the cuts, as when she wrote that "Avery Hopwood's plays go from bed to worse," and, in another review: "This play holds the season's record, thus far, with a run of four evening performances and one matinee. By an odd coincidence it ran just five performances too many."

She was just as dismissive of authors: "I have heard it said that it took Messrs. Shipman and Hymer just three-and-a-half days to write their drama. I should like to know what they were doing during the three days." Clearly, if she did not approve of a play, a performance or a playwright, she said so with biting acerbity, as with: "If you would get the best out of the evening, by all means leave after the first act, take a brisk walk round the Reservoir, and get back just as the curtain rises on the last act. You won't miss a thing. . . ."

Among the plays that attracted her invective was a Florenz Ziegfeld production of Somerset Maugham's *Caesar's Wife*. This starred Billie Burke, the influential producer's wife. Miss Burke was a lively blonde who was enjoying a fragment of fame as a type-cast, near imbecilic blonde. Her fame had been won principally through her appearances in motion pictures made at the Famous Players Lasky Studios on Fifty-seventh Street. Maugham's drama was "an intimate little triangle concerning the wife of the British Consul in Cairo who falls in love with her husband's young secretary within a romantic urban setting of dusky palms and sapphire sky." Miss Burke played the wife. Mrs. Parker saw the play and mercilessly likened Miss Burke to a particularly vulgar burlesque star of the period, Eva Tanguay, a vaudevillian with wild, woolly hair, well-known for her rendering of a song called "I Don't Care." Mrs. Parker set about the play and its star:

"Miss Burke is at her best in her more serious moments. In her desire to convey the gushing girlishness of the character, she plays her lighter scenes as if she were giving an impersonation of Eva Tanguay."

Ziegfeld, from his untidy aerie high above the New Amsterdam Theatre, fired a series of angry salvos across the bows of *Vanity Fair*, Crowninshield and Condé Nast. Mrs. Ziegfeld added fuel to the fire by simultaneously sending each of the miscreants her own formal letter of protest. It happened that Ziegfeld was a particular friend of Nast; he demanded the head of Mrs. Parker on a plate.

So it was that Dorothy Parker was called before the quiet, hushed figure of Frank Crowninshield during the late afternoon of Monday 24th January 1920, in the tea lounge of the Plaza Hotel. Crowninshield was precise and to the point. He told her that, regrettable as he felt it to be, Nast had ordered her to be sacked and she must leave within sixty days. She had, he said, brought it largely upon herself. There had, he added, been other complaints about her reviews. He made it plain, too, that Nast had noted her lengthy luncheon sessions with Benchley and others on the staff; also her defiant attitude to office rules and her mornings away from the office with Benchley and Sherwood for the purpose of "writing plays," when they should have been working for the magazine, had not helped.

As to the other complaints about her reviews, he was specific. She had upset David Belasco by comparing his production of *The Son-Daughter* with the tired old melodrama, *East Is West*, and had earned Charles Dillingham's ire by attacking his production of *Apple Blossoms*. Both producers, like Ziegfeld, were, Crowninshield explained, important advertisers; certainly both had made their displeasure known to Nast.

But what, he might have asked, of those on the receiving end of Mrs. Parker's lashes who were not advertisers? People like actor Wallace Eddinger, of whom she had written: "He has almost entirely lost his trick of hurrying through his speeches and ending them with a prolonged whine"; that "Lillian Lorraine has said something when she called herself a bad actress"; and that in *The Little Blue Devil,* "Harold Atteridge has badly mangled the book and lyrics and Harry Carroll has slightly rewritten most of the musical successes of the last few seasons"? It could be said that these people couldn't answer back; anyway, they were not advertisers in *Vanity Fair.*

Dorothy left the refined air of the Plaza Hotel and walked down Fifth Avenue, turning right at West Forty-fourth Street toward the revolving doors of the Algonquin. There in the paneled lounge Benchley and Sherwood awaited her. It took the two men exactly twenty minutes to write out their resignations to Crowninshield, in protest of Dorothy's dismissal. It was, in fact, a gesture not wholly unfamiliar to Benchley. In 1917 he had resigned from his short-lived job on the New York *Graphic Tribune* because his friend Ernest Gruening had been fired for allegedly pro-German sympathies. Now, here he was once again displaying his Harvard-nurtured sense of honor and fair play.

The newspapers quickly jumped on the story. The following day, *The New York Times* reported:

"Last night, over a pleasantly decorated tea-table at the Plaza, Mr. Crowninshield broke the news to Mrs. Parker that her days as drama critic of *Vanity Fair* were over. She was assured that her work in other ways would still be valued highly by the magazine. Mrs. Parker's reception of this news was complicated by the fact that she was well aware of a recent simultaneous fire of complaint on the part of offended subjects of her criticism. Both she and Mr. Benchley resigned because they were under the impression that it was these coinciding protests which had led to her removal as drama critic." The *Times* did not mention that Sherwood had resigned, too.

Mrs. Parker remained largely silent but years later, in 1938, in an interview for *Writers at Work,* she remembered: "I fixed three plays . . . and as a result I was fixed."

Interviewer: You *fixed* three plays?
Mrs. Parker: Well, panned. The plays closed and the producers, who were the big boys—Dillingham, Ziegfeld and Belasco—didn't like it, you know. *Vanity Fair* was a magazine of no opinion, but I had opinions. So I was fired. And Mr. Sherwood and Mr. Benchley resigned their jobs. . . .

Benchley, Sherwood and Mrs. Parker turned up at the office the next day wearing red chevrons upside down on their sleeves, in the manner of troops mustered out of service. They joked mightily about their departure, and at the end of the sixty days, before walking out for the last time, Benchley placed in the lobby of the *Vanity Fair* offices a money box with a sign which read: "Contributions for Miss Billie Burke."

It was a March day, cold and raining, when they took their leave of the magazine that had brought them both fame and notoriety. Sherwood had money, but Benchley's gesture of resigning, "out of moral indignation and professional ethics" had, Mrs. Parker said, "surprised her. Mr. Benchley had a family—two children," she commented. "It was the greatest act of friendship I'd known."

Here they were, three celebrated journalists, kicked out of their jobs by "commercial pressures." Where could they go from here?

· 11 ·

A Room with a View

MRS. PARKER, Robert Benchley and Sherwood needed time to take in the situation that now confronted them.

As far as the Round Table was concerned, their dismissal was not that important. Life was for living:

> Determinedly now, they [the Circle] were glorifying in their public profiles, playing happily to a city and a decade that seemed to be there for them alone. Their clothes were uniforms, emblems of style: Woollcott sported a cape and top hat to opening nights; Dorothy Parker came to be known for her splendiferous spring hats; Benchley and Stewart made an annual harvest-time ritual of buying Derbies at Brooks; Marc Connelly bought an Inverness; Neysa played hostess in pastel chalk-dust; Heywood Broun made a virtue of his *déshabille* which made Woollcott think of him as "an unmade bed." More than ever they began to honor their ambitions for each other and themselves in mutually beneficial antics outside their inner circle.

By this, writer James R. Gaines thus agreed that the tide had to rise over the mudflats, and rise it did.

Sherwood got a job as the first film critic of *Life* magazine, his column to be called "The Silent Drama." It was to help him sell a filmscript to his friend, director Rex Ingram, that Sherwood arranged a dinner party at Delmonico's for Ingram, his wife Alice Terry and some of the Round Table regulars: Connelly and Margalo Gillmore, Parker, Benchley and Mary Brandon, a young actress whom Sherwood was courting at the time.

Sherwood's co-conspirators were invited to show Ingram that Sherwood was well connected and not likely to sell his scenario cheaply, and to win the heart of Miss Brandon who, although egocentric and petulant, was nevertheless a little in awe of Sherwood's friends and quite aware of what their friendship might mean to her languishing career.

Nothing quite worked out the way Sherwood had planned: Ingram's wife, at Parker's gentle urging, became terribly drunk on pousse-cafés and kept shuttling off on Parker's arm to the ladies' room; Ingram, it turned out, had just given up movie-making and was going off to the Riviera to paint and relax; and Mary Brandon turned bellicose whenever she felt left out of the conversation. Ingram finally fell asleep at the banquet table, and Gillmore joined Terry and Parker in the ladies' room.

It was all part of the nonsense of life, the sort of nonsense that Mrs. Parker echoed in "Comment," a verse she dedicated to Benchley:

> Oh, life is a glorious cycle of song,
> A medley of extemporanea;
> And love is a thing that can never go wrong;
> And I am Marie of Roumania.

It was, too, like the Ingrams' dinner, quite crazy but such fun—the kind of fun practiced in print by Franklin Pierce Adams, who now, running a Saturday column, was even imitating the famed British diarist in his *Diary of Our Own Samuel Pepys*. His mimicking style and comment seemed to sum up the whole mad whirl of the time:

So to the baseball game with D. Stewart . . . thence to G. Kaufman's, and played cards, and lost so little that H. Ross said it was a moral victory . . . So to H. Broun's, where a great party and merry as can be, and we acted a play, J. Toohey being the most comickal of all; but I loved Mistress Dorothy Parker the best of any of them, and loathe to leave her, which I did not do until near five in the morning . . . then after to R. Sherwood's to play at cards, and an amusing game we had of it, save for the long and dreary recital of a story of H. Broun's wherein he told of the high cost of transporting provision, and ended it with *Cartage delenda est*, a feeble jape at best . . . Benchley came in to watch and did most comickal antics ever I saw in my life, what with imitating a cyclone and a headwaiter . . . so to H. Miller's again and played till two in the morning, and all very gay on the street and I threw snowballs at A. Woollcott, who chased me and washed my face in the snow, but not by strength but by weakening me with causing me to laugh at his anticks and crude remarks . . . Saw too Miss Mary Pickford . . . and in came D. Fairbanks . . . And so to dinner with R. Benchley and Mistress Dorothy . . . and so home, at nearly four in the morning. But I made a vow that I shall go to bed early forever after this. . . .

When seriousness got the better of laughter, the Round Table lashed out at bigotry, injustice, apathy and pomposity, moving hither and thither to Tony Soma's, the Puncheon Club, Polly Adler's and Bleeck's, all the while attacking tyrants, corruption and cant.

The parties continued with weekend excursions on industrialist Stanton Griffith's yacht, the guests invariably returning to the Algonquin where they formed a Saturday night gathering—The Thanatopsis Literary and Inside Straight Club—a poker-playing consortium. This was erratically rechristened The Thanatopsis Pleasure and Inside Straight Club or The Thanatopsis Chowder and Marching Society or The Young

Man's Upper West Side Literary and Inside Straight Poker Club, said to have been inspired by the Sinclair Lewis novel *Main Street*. It was also said that Mrs. Parker insisted on the inclusion of the word *Thanatopsis*, which meant "contemplation of death."

If Mrs. Parker had insisted on the word, it was Franklin Pierce Adams who had actually founded the Thanatopsis Club. He afterwards claimed he had named it after the group of card-playing journalists-turned-soldiers who had been on the *Stars and Stripes*—himself, Ross and Woollcott.

Although Mrs. Parker was out of a job, she remained a considerable asset of the Round Table fraternity. The Thanatopsis sessions were a constant delight to her. She and her cronies would play poker throughout the night and often through a weekend until sheer exhaustion would bring the play to an end. As for the men, Robert Drennan said: "Harpo Marx was popularly acknowledged as the most proficient gamester; Woollcott was unanimously voted the worst."

Mrs. Parker usually played seated at the side of Benchley. She held her cards with assured repose and acquitted herself well. It was well known that she could deal sharp verbal cards, as Mrs. Clare Boothe Brokaw, later Clare Boothe Luce, discovered when she had joined the editorial staff of *Vanity Fair*. Mrs. Brokaw had met Mrs. Parker in the revolving doors of the Algonquin:

"Age before beauty," quipped the elegant, haughty Clare.

"Pearls before swine," the bright-eyed Dorothy evenly retorted. It did not matter that Mrs. Brokaw was later to deny the encounter. It was a delicious story and that was good enough. Most knew, anyway, that a similar exchange had been used earlier by Woollcott in one of his short stories, but as far as they were concerned the origins did not matter.

It was at the Saturday evening card table of the Thanatopsis that Adams introduced a newcomer, a grain and yeast millionaire named Raoul Fleischmann. Adams sat Fleischmann next to Harold Ross, who had for some time been touting a prospectus for a new magazine he wanted to produce. It was to be called the *New Yorker*, and the prospectus promised:

Its general tenor will be of gaiety, wit and satire, but it will be more than a jester. It will not be what is commonly called radical or high brow. It will be what is commonly called sophisticated in that it will assume a reasonable degree of enlightenment on the part of its readers. It will hate bunk. . . .

Somebody said at the time that Ross evinced a scant quota of culture. Indeed, he proved a striking cultural exception among the Round Table regulars. If his old *Stars and Stripes* buddy, Aleck Woollcott, and their wartime superior officer, Captain Franklin Adams, were prototypes of the Algonquin set, Ross was the original kibitzer, accepted by the others only because (in terms of wit and repartee) he received far more than he contributed. Ross, they knew, was hard-working, "believing in a twenty-four-hour office day"; he was, too, straightforward, surprisingly non-literary and never one for verbal calisthenics. But he was "one of them" by virtue of wartime friendships.

Adams's ploy of seating Ross next to Fleischmann paid off. When, nearly a day later, Ross left the table, he had secured a promise from Fleischmann to put in a $25,000 stake to start the *New Yorker*, the title of which was John Toohey's suggestion.

Not long afterwards, at a lunchtime session with the Circle, Mrs. Parker and Benchley told the assembly that as far as work was concerned, they had decided on a course of action. They were each going freelance. To this end, they had already rented a $30 a month minuscule office on the third floor above the nearby Metropolitan Opera House, and had already adequately furnished the place with "two tables, two chairs, and a hat-rack." The room was afterwards variously described as an "oversize broom closet," "a slop room," an "Isosceles Triangle" and a "pin-room." Whatever it was, Benchley's description of it was unquestionably the most amusing of all: "One cubic foot less of space and it would have constituted adultery."

But the space sufficed. The two pinned to the wall the illustrations from the undertakers' magazines that had helped to offend Crownin-shield. The new tenants got to work. They quickly established that a contraction of their names would provide them with an apposite tele-graphic address—"Parkbench"; they also put up an office sign outside, "The Utica Drop Forge and Tool Company. Benchley and Parker, Presidents."

The poky accommodations, however, provided little in the way of congenial surroundings to help spark off their muses. There were laughs, of course, as well as frequent interruptions from Sherwood, Woollcott, Stewart and others of the Algonquin crowd, who always seemed to call when Parker and Benchley were "collaborating on a play." The naming of the characters in the play appeared to hold up the project. Dorothy suggested calling the people 1, 2, 3, 4, 5, but found that stage directions like "2 moves upstage while 3 shrinks against the backdrop" were more like bad chess instructions than good theater.

Although Mrs. Parker did try writing some fiction at this time, it took her as long as a month to smooth out a single short story. When she and

Benchley wanted a diversion, they would write on a large mirror fanciful menus of luncheons and dinners they would like, even though Mrs. Parker was a small eater. When not assisting with the menus, Benchley, who was even less productive than his office partner, perpetually wrote on dog-eared pieces of paper, "Now that wages are coming down . . ." It was a line that became a running gag for Mrs. Parker who, whatever she herself wrote at this time, would prefix every observation on the social scene with that same phrase: "Now that wages are coming down, Mrs. Vladimir Cockshy felt it in her bones . . ." and so on.

In truth, not much work was done by the pair. As a result, they were making precious little money. Benchley had his family to consider; private laughs were all well and good but they were no substitute for the necessities of life. But then, life shouldn't be taken *that* seriously; he could always get a loan. Accordingly, Benchley tried to raise enough money to buy the Crestwood Scarsdale house. Mrs. Parker gave him $200 to open an account at the Lincoln Trust Company so that he could secure a down payment. The problem, she said when she handed him the check, was that she needed the money back in half an hour for her own expenses.

Sherwood effected a temporary rescue of the situation. He enlisted the help of Edward S. Martin, who had formed the Harvard *Lampoon* with his father. Martin hired Benchley and Parker as regular contributors to *Life*. Although it paid well, the magazine was finding it increasingly difficult to survive in the now fast-changing world of periodical publishing. Benchley, however, started by writing occasional theater reviews and general pieces of a humorous nature, while Mrs. Parker was hired to produce a poem a week, one of which ironically summed up the America they knew:

> Everything's great in this good old world,
> (This is the stuff they can always use,)
> God's in his heaven, the hill's dew-pearled,
> (This will provide for the baby's shoes.)
> Hunger and war do not mean a thing;
> (Everything's rosy where'er we roam,)
> Hark, how the little birds gaily sing!
> (This is what fetches the bacon home . . .)

Despite their *Life* commissions, Parker and Benchley decided after a few months to end their freelance enterprise. Benchley took off with his family for a short holiday before taking up a full-time post on *Life*. Mrs. Parker, sad at the outcome of the enterprise, wrote to him that business had been so slow since he left she was thinking of affixing a sign to the door stating, simply, MEN. It was a kind of faltering last laugh at their foolishness in daring to hope that their joint freelance foray would work.

The Round Table on West Forty-fourth Street continued its daily pranks. Sherwood was frequently the butt of the jokes; his towering height predictably gave rise to many of them. Noting that he had been absent for a few days, Mrs. Parker wired him: "Where are you? We've turned down a vacant step-ladder for you." And it didn't matter too much if any of the members of the Circle were suffering temporary financial restrictions; they knew that Frank Case, who had now purchased the hotel, would be understanding. He customarily did not press any of them for debts. With his usual panache, and this at the height of Prohibition, he would greet all with: "How do you like it? Out of a bottle?"

One evening about this time, several of the Vicious Circle moved from the Algonquin across Fifth Avenue to the Waldorf-Astoria where, invited to a free dinner, they were seated next to a table of visiting mid-Westerners assembled for a governors' convention. The politics and speeches predictably did not go down well with Mrs. Parker. She looked in utter disdain at the assemblage and quipped: "They sound like over-written Sinclair Lewises."

But those who knew her well knew, too, that Mrs. Parker, beneath her disdainful exterior, was a vulnerable woman. Donald Ogden Stewart, who was very fond of her, was later to remember Dorothy in the early days of the twenties:

Dottie was attractive to everybody—those eyes were so wonderful, and the smile! It wasn't difficult to fall in love with her. She was always ready to do anything, to take part in any party; she was ready for fun at any time when it came up, and it came up an awful lot in those days. She was fun to dance with, and she danced very well and I just felt good when I was with her. She was both wide-open and the goddamndest fortress at the same time. Every girl has her technique, and shy, demure helplessness was part of Dottie's—the innocent, bright-eyed little girl that needs a male to help her across the street. . . .

If this was really Dorothy Parker in the twenties, then for all her helplessness she still exuded in print a pronounced cynicism about men. Robert Benchley was, of course, the exception. But men, in general, were fair game for her pen: "Men," she wrote, "don't like nobility in women. Not any man. I suppose it is because men like to have the copyrights on nobility—if there is going to be anything like that in a relationship . . ."

And what of women? How did she view the distaff side? She admitted:

"Woman's life must be wrapped up in a man, and the cleverest woman on earth is the biggest fool with a man."

She was never complimentary about professional women, particularly female writers. A friend was discussing with her the virtues of Mrs. Clare Brokaw. "Actually," said the friend, "she's awfully kind to her inferiors." "Where does she find them?" asked Mrs. Parker evenly. She was to later write: "It's a terrible thing to say, but I can't think of any good women writers." "Of course," she continued, "calling them women writers is their ruin: they begin to think of themselves that way. . . ."

The Manhattan of the time was full of the story of the lady who cornered Mrs. Parker at a party. She extolled endlessly the virtues of her mate to the bored Mrs. Parker. "He's marvelous," said the woman. "And do you know, I've kept him for eight years!" "Don't worry," replied Mrs. Parker wearily, "if you keep him long enough, he'll come back in style." Her wit had the clinical aloofness of a surgeon's scalpel, as when, reviewing a book on science, she accused: "It was written without fear and without research."

But then New York was full of stories about Mrs. Parker. Her graphic line "He gave her a look that you could have poured on a waffle" was constantly quoted.

By now, her friend Robert Sherwood had been promoted at *Life* and had decided to marry Mary Brandon. In less than a year Mary proudly announced the arrival of their first child and Mrs. Parker was quick off the mark in cabling her: "Dear Mary. We all knew you had it in you!"

This was all part of the facade. Although she had formally resigned and left, it was well known to her friends that she was still smarting under her dismissal from *Vanity Fair*. It was now that she came out with her suppressed anger. She published a Valentine poem to Ziegfeld in her *Life* corner:

> We're still groggy from the blow
> Dealt us—by the famous Flo;
> After 1924
> He announces, nevermore
> Will his shows our senses greet—
> At a cost of fiver per seat,
> Hasten, Time, your onward drive—
> Welcome, 1925!

And Benchley from his column on *Life* was still smarting for the same reason. Negatively reviewing another performance by Miss Billie Burke, this time in Booth Tarkington's *Rose Brier*, he recalled:

A few years ago a young dramatic critic lost her job for saying, among other disrespectful things, that Billie Burke had a tendency to fling herself coyly about like Eva Tanguay. Even in the face of this proof of divine vengeance, we apprehensively endorse the unfortunate young reviewer's judgment and assert that even after having her attention called to it three years ago, Miss Burke *still* flings herself coyly about like Eva Tanguay. Applications for the job of dramatic reviewer on *Life* should be sent to the Managing Editor.

Mrs. Parker and Mr. Benchley were in the ascendant again. The journalistic jungle was small and dense, but it usually gave succor to its own creatures, especially creatures like Mrs. Parker and Benchley. The latter was now hard at work, establishing an even loftier reputation for his humorous writing, and Mrs. Parker now published in *Life* her first literary criticism, a review of Kathleen Norris's *The Beloved Woman*:

"Remember, this book is by Kathleen Norris . . . everything is going to turn out for the best, and there will never be a word that could possibly give pain to any of her readers and makes sales fall off."

If Mrs. Parker was not in a permanent job, she was in fine company at *Life* magazine. Thanks to Sherwood, who had remodeled the magazine on the lines of *Punch*, the stylish and witty British weekly, *Life* now had Benchley, Kaufman, Connelly, Donald Ogden Stewart, Don Marquis, Arthur Guiterman, Christopher Morley, Carolyn Wells and a lot of other first-class writers. Dorothy rose to the occasion, positively glittering in the pages of the magazine with:

> Why should you dare to hope that you and I
> Could make love's fitful flash a lasting flame?
> Still, if you think it's only fair to try,
> Well, I'm game . . .

She had now placed a world between Miss Billie Burke and herself and her growing and widespread reputation was living proof of it. Her doldrums were at an end.

Here she was, in her mid-twenties, with an impressive readership following on from her brief years on *Vanity Fair*. She was now the author of no less than nearly 130 prose pieces and nearly seventy poems for *Life*. *Ainslee's* had now given her a monthly column, "In Broadway Playhouses," which was providing her with a regular income and the freedom to write what she liked. She had also been invited to contribute features to the *Saturday Evening Post*. As if these weren't enough, both *Ladies' Home Journal* and *Everybody's* had also called on her to contribute. Her name was becoming a household word.

As she wrote in *Life* at this time:

> I thank whatever gods look down,
> That I am living right here in town

And, amazing as it was to many, she was publicly accused by a contentious correspondent of using poor grammar. To this she declared: "Maybe it is only I, but conditions are such these days, that if you use studiously correct grammar, people suspect you of homosexual tendencies."

· 1 2 ·

The Time of Her Life

IF MRS. PARKER had had her problems, both professional and private, she was now entering a phase when she was fast becoming the darling of the social-cum-literary set of Manhattan. Her name was on everybody's lips, her put-downs persistently paraded by others at cocktail and other gatherings, her mailbox full of admiring letters. At parties, she was accosted by a succession of women who wanted to know how to emulate her. To these, Mrs. Parker would invariably deliver up some such cutting retort as "You should see your analyst: he might have a word with your ovaries," which would bring the conversation to an abrupt end. But behind the deadpan replies she was, if she could have admitted it, having the time of her life.

She was finding a much wider public now, writing for different publications, not the least being the *Saturday Evening Post* and its humor page, "Short Turns and Encores." Flippant, astringent, sardonic, self-deprecating and deflationary, her short prose pieces and verse shone from the pages like burnished baubles. Reviewing a book, *The Technique of the Love Affair*, she observed: "If only it had been written and placed in my hands years ago, maybe I could have been successful instead of just successive."

The Algonquin crowd and, in particular, Benchley, Sherwood and Woollcott, having established that she was a Jew, promptly dubbed her "Sheeny." Woollcott invariably greated her with the salutation "Hello, repulsive!" but this was just the way of the man. And there was, of course, the theater scene. Free tickets now arrived at her apartment in unspoken anticipation of any literary benediction she might endow on the senders.

More women were frequenting the Round Table now, among them Mary Kennedy, June Walker and Polly Adler, but their presence did not stop Woollcott homing in on Mrs. Parker, whom he waspishly described as "so odd a combination of Little Nell and Lady Macbeth." Woollcott, in the late days of the First World War, had met and loved a woman named Amelie Randall, who had left him to marry a successful surgeon the same year of his mother's death. This rejection was said to have haunted him; it was clear to most of the Algonquin set that he was

70

a homosexual who had gone to war "to prove himself a competent male."

There was some excitement at this time when Sherwood brought newcomers Zelda and Scott Fitzgerald to meet the Round Table crowd. Sherwood had first met the Fitzgeralds in Paris; they had since married and were now back in New York, he with his growing reputation as a novelist, she with her ambition to become a ballerina. What did Mrs. Parker initially think of the newcomers? She thought Zelda "beautiful but sulky, and both of them too ostentatious for words."

Life at the Algonquin and the Neysa McMein and Swope parties was gay, iridescent with many distractions. What the Algonquinites really needed, however, was a place to which to repair on weekends where they could write and relax. Woollcott, by now christened by his friends "The Butcher of Broadway," was predictably to find the answer—he loved to be the centerpiece of the set, which he fondly believed he was. As Helen Hayes later said:

"He was always either bedazzled or contemptuous. There was nothing in-between. He believed he was the center of the Universe and that, since he was the sun, everything and everybody revolved around him. A cosmic sport, Aleck had somehow managed to create this Universe by employing his superiors as satellites."

Woollcott knew Enos Booth, who owned the greater part of an attractive island, Neshobe, on Lake Bomoseen in Vermont. He persuaded ten of the Algonquinites to put in $1000 each (an initiation fee, he called it) to set up on Neshobe a sort of fraternity house where they could indulge in work and amusing pastimes away from their Manhattan haunts.

Woollcott quickly established his domain over the island, contriving a set of rules which his visitors were expected to obey, being urged to swim, work, play cribbage and croquet. Taking breakfast at the ungodly hour of 7 A.M. was mandatory; soon they became interminable breakfasts, with only about an hour's break before a long lunch. What had been intended as a cooperative retreat for the Algonquinites quickly became Woollcott's personal fiefdom.

In reality, little work was attempted and less was achieved; the ringmaster wanted to be surrounded by clever people at all times. Clever people came, stayed, ate and drank, had fun, talked and talked some more. The frolics seemed endless. Harpo Marx, dressed only in a boater, would regularly jump out of the bushes scaring the women; Dorothy Parker, attired in nothing but a picture hat, would gambol with Woollcott's dog, Cocaud, whom he had named after one Madame Cocaud, proprietress of a bistro near Woollcott's base hospital in Savenay, France, during the war. "Considered as a one-man dog," explained Woollcott, "she is a flop. In her fidelity to me, she's a little too much like that girl in France who was true to the 26th Infantry."

When, in the evenings, the participants weren't playing cribbage, they indulged in their favorite pastime of party games. Woollcott loved the games, particularly The Game, a bawdy version of Consequences; also played was Botticelli, Murder (with Woollcott as District Attorney) and, inevitably, I-Can-Give-You-A-Sentence. Mrs. Parker excelled herself with, "You can lead a horticulture but you can't make her think" and "I had two soft burlesques for breakfast!"

The place became nothing more than a fresh locale and the laughs came and went in familiar abundance. Woollcott regaled them with his experiences autographing copies of his new book at a Manhattan bookshop.

"What happened?" asked Mrs. Parker.

"I signed most carefully," said Woollcott. "After all, what is so rare," he asked, "as a Woollcott first edition?"

"A second edition," said Mrs. Parker, without a trace of a smile.

And what of the general run of the talk? The passions evoked by social injustices and the plight of the poor simply moved from Manhattan to the Bomoseen island house. Beatrice Kaufman, it seemed, was clearly committed to the feminist Lucy Stone League, a 1920s precursor of women's liberation. Hers was a commitment warmly endorsed by Jane Grant, who had married Harold Ross, except that she refused to be known as Mrs. Ross, preferring her maiden name, which, after she divorced Ross, she was to regain. She, in her oracular stand for the rights of women, was fully supported by Mrs. Heywood Broun, or Ruth Hale as she insisted on being known. The group discussed and verbally fought each other with opinion, fact and fancy, changing the subject whenever fatigue threatened.

Then George Kaufman would take over to explain his thoughts on the emergent Dramatists Guild. This would typically be followed, as often as not, by Woollcott, seldom out of the conversation for long, holding forth on his specialty, the literature and dark deeds of murder and murderers. At this point Cornelia Otis Skinner would usually excuse herself on the pretext of learning her lines for a forthcoming play, but everyone knew the real reason was that she became nauseated at the mere mention of anything to do with violence.

Sooner or later, the talk would return to politics, and Mrs. Parker would espouse her growing attraction to socialism. She felt deeply the plight of the poor, comparing it to the indulgences of the rich. After all, there would always be the Trotskyite who drove a Rolls, but things were, she said, "moving in the right direction." "Which direction?" she was asked. "Militant action against the system" was her usual reply. Ambivalent as she may have seemed, she would, said Woollcott describing her outbursts, "mount her fiery steed and come off on her ass."

On April 15, 1920, two Italian immigrants, Nicola Sacco and Bartolomeo Vanzetti, were arrested for robbery and murder in South Braintree, Massachusetts, and subsequently went through seven years of litigation. There was great protest, at home and abroad, of the men's ignorance of American ways. Their avowed anarchism, it was claimed, prevented a fair trial and thus condemned the two. Benchley was uncharacteristically furious when a close friend told him that Judge Webster Thayer had openly vowed at a golf club that "he would show them and get those guys hanged." Heywood Broun used his position as a commentator on the New York *World* to get the two immigrants temporarily freed. As a result, Broun had been sacked by Herbert Bayard Swope for his pains.

The Sacco and Vanzetti case had long been a hot potato in the American political arena and on August 11, 1927, Mrs. Parker joined Benchley, John Dos Passos and others in Boston, where Edna St. Vincent Millay read aloud her poem "Justice Denied in Massachusetts" to a receptive rally on Salem Street. From there, the group moved on to Governor Fuller's office to plead a stay of execution for the two Italians. Together they marched up Tremont Street to the State House grounds where they walked back and forth waiting for a meeting of the Governor's Council to finish. A big crowd gathered, which provoked the arrival of two wagons when the police grabbed "as many marchers as they could" from the forty-four actual protesters who had traveled to Boston to plead for the men's lives. Of that forty-four, thirty-nine had been arrested, Mrs. Parker, Dos Passos and Benchley among them. They were all fined five dollars and told to "behave themselves in future." Mrs. Parker afterwards protested to the newspapers that she had "been treated roughly" by the police. But the protest, like their call for clemency, had fallen on stony ground.

In tune with her political leanings, Mrs. Parker seldom exhibited external trappings of wealth. Her appearance was always neat and understated. She wore black sweaters and skirts with pearls or polka-dot dresses, occasionally sporting fancy hats. Her indulgences were confined to delicate and expensive underwear. Stewart claimed that perhaps, along with Oscar Wilde, she believed that one should take care of the luxuries and the necessities would take care of themselves. As for her anonymous Manhattan apartment, this housed little except her clothes, toilet articles, an old portable typewriter, a dog and her canary, Onan, whom she named "because," she said, "it spilled its seed on the ground." Certainly, she customarily moved around New York and its environs without money in her handbag. But she was generous in picking up the tab when it fell to her turn, and often when it did not. She seldom had enough money to pay for a taxi but then, as another of the Algonquin wags explained, "Royals seldom carry money."

Now firmly established as the Algonquinites' weekend hideout, the Neshobe Island retreat was not unanimously popular. One to whom it did not appeal was actress Peggy Wood, who in truth was never invited. Fifty years later the hurt was still there when she said:

"I wouldn't have gone anyway, I knew too much of their private lives and what went on up there, and I did not need to be involved in all that."

It is true that plenty of stories concerning these libertine weekends circulated freely among Manhattan's literati and show business sets. It was said that a double bed upstairs was known as the informative double because it creaked fiercely, causing much laughter from the listeners downstairs when it was occupied, as it frequently was, by unmarried couples.

The house on Neshobe was soon to become an annex to an even larger house that Woollcott would build alongside the original. But even this, with its comfortable appointments, did not persuade one particular member of the set to indulge in its pleasures. Robert Benchley had never been over-enamored of Woollcott and his extravagant life-style, and had always loathed house rules, especially those involving games. "A weekend guest," Benchley said, "should be allowed to wander at will, rummaging through bookshelves with permission to raid the ice-box whenever one felt hungry." To be compelled to rise for breakfast at 7 A.M. and spend much of the day playing croquet, by now a form of religion on Neshobe, just wasn't for Benchley. The record shows that he went to the island only once.

He would usually wait for Mrs. Parker to return to Manhattan and her spartan apartment, where he would put his feet up on the couch and listen to her recount the weekend's events.

Mrs. Parker was a night creature, invariably returning home late at night or in the early morning, sleeping only a few hours before getting up around eleven to meet her friends for lunch at the Algonquin. After lunch they moved on to the speakeasies and, later, to a play, a film, an art opening and more speakeasies—followed by an impromptu party at either the Ross's, at Woollcott's place, Neysa's studio, Swope's New York apartment, or somewhere else. It didn't matter where, so long as there were people and something to drink, even if it was the familiar, embellished grain alcohol stored in a cupboard in the bathroom. Woollcott, having assumed his garrulous leadership of the pack, saw to it that there was always plenty of booze in his apartment in the Campanile, a cooperative apartment house on the East River where Alice Duer Miller, Mrs. Parker and Ross also stayed during the Vicious Circle era; Mrs. Parker dubbed the building Old Manse River before she rechristened it Wit's End.

Yet for all her fun-loving activities during those years, Dorothy Parker seldom, if ever, emulated her estranged husband's drinking habits. She would be content with a gut-rot gin and orange which, friends noticed, would often last half the night. At this stage, she appeared to be able to take drink or leave it. It was akin to her attitude about money; they both seemed slightly indecent.

If this was true, she never reproached her friends when they overindulged. But she did have one hangup which everybody knew about. If Benchley or any friend dropped by her apartment, she would quickly rush to her typewriter, which usually contained some half-written paragraph, and cover it hastily with a newspaper or a towel. Her secretiveness about her work seemed to indicate that her writing was a part of her life that was totally private. It was, some said, a privacy that erected a gray stone wall around her intellectualism, a bastion to oppose the Philistine intruder. Others thought it evidence of a superiority—or perhaps inferiority—either or both begotten by her masochistic denigration of her own abilities. Some said she was afraid of her own talent.

Gilbert Seldes, a friend and fellow writer who was to win Dorothy Parker's confidence and respect, said of her at the time:

"She fascinates me. She is of the set, yet remains apart from it. She is a writer who seldom writes yet, by her presence, you know she is an artist at war with her own considerable talent. She is an enigma that none can solve, least of all her so-called friends who are in reality about as close to her as I am to Tahiti. But one thing is certain, men apart, she is constantly in love with love."

Like most young women in the twenties, Dorothy Parker had had one or two short-lived affairs, but they had added up to little. After she and Eddie separated, she had indulged in some fleeting involvements but as the Algonquin set knew, she was very choosy.

But there was one man who was gradually being allowed to penetrate the carapace. He was often at the Algonquin and sometimes over on Neshobe Island. He was handsome, with a quiet elegance of manner. It was said that he liked to play the field. His name was Charles MacArthur, a journalist who had worked on *The New York Times* and an aspiring playwright. The two dined together often, went to the theater, to parties, and to bed. Their friends soon began to predict marriage after Dorothy's divorce arrived. The affair helped her conquer her innate laziness to begin an intense period of work. But she had grown wary of men.

At this time, she prophetically wrote these lines:

> And he vows his passion is
> Infinite, undying—
> Lady, make a note of this:
> One of you is lying . . .

She was soon to discover the truth of her own words.

· 1 3 ·

The Man Who Stayed
for Breakfast

BY TEMPERAMENT, Charles MacArthur was an intellectual ally of Dorothy Parker. Born in Scranton, Pennsylvania, the son of a church minister, he had been educated at the exclusive Wilson Memorial Academy in Nyack, New York. Tall, slightly aloof, slow-speaking and something of an aesthete, he had a reputation of being generous to a fault; he would spare a dime for anyone—if he had one. But usually he hadn't, and at this time things were particularly bad for him.

During an earlier penurious period, he had roomed with Benchley at the Shelton Hotel in Manhattan when Benchley, like Thurber's Mr. Prebble, had found need to stay in the city.

MacArthur was now living hand-to-mouth as a freelance publicist. Benchley had introduced him to a Wall Street jobbing broker who had known Eddie Parker. The jobber, in turn, had introduced MacArthur to the owner of a New Jersey mausoleum who had taken him on as temporary public relations counsel.

On getting the job, MacArthur decided that the mausoleum needed a new image. He started by trying to convince his new employer to rename the establishment Fairview Abbey, "the name," he said, "connoted peace and a kind of sepulchral calm incorporating a touch of class." He went on to recommend the establishment within the Abbey of a Poet's Corner, much like that within the thousand-year-old Westminster Abbey in London. Accordingly, he decided to initiate a press campaign to transfer the bones of Henry Wadsworth Longfellow from Boston, Massachusetts to Fairview Abbey.

The owner of the mausoleum expressed some misgivings at the idea, but finally agreed to go along with it. MacArthur promptly whipped up a dispute with the Mayor of Boston, James Michael Curley, arguing with nothing if not convenient logic that since Longfellow had written in a poem:

> Life is real! Life is earnest!
> And the grave is not its goal . . .

the poet would never have approved of his burial in the conventional grave that his remains then inhabited. Nothing less, he said, than a Carrara porphyry crypt was indicated by the poet's lines. And where better to site such a crypt than within Fairview Abbey's shrine—the newly established Poet's Corner?

Unfortunately for MacArthur, Mayor Curley had done his home-work. He wrote back indignantly, claiming that the public relations counsel had not done his homework. Longfellow's bones, he said, rested not in Boston but in Cambridge, Massachusetts, and he contemptuously referred the upstart MacArthur to Cambridge's Mayor O'Flynn. Mac-Arthur lost no time in conferring with Benchley and Parker, who sent a series of much-publicized aggressive cables to the unfortunate O'Flynn:

THE COUNTRY DEMANDS THE BODY OF HENRY WADSWORTH LONGFEL-LOW. STOP. IF YOU VALUE YOUR JOB YOU WILL FORWARD IT IMMEDI-ATELY.

—further admonishing O'Flynn to:

COME CLEAN WITH 'DAT BODY! and ROLL 'DEM BONES!

These cables, among other disconcerting missives, were variously signed "The Longfellow Lovers of America," "The Longfellow Society of Union, New Jersey," "The Parochial Students League for Longfellow" and, occasionally, with the name of MacArthur himself.

Mayor O'Flynn, cut to the quick if not to the dead, applied to the police department to issue warrants for the arrest of both MacArthur and his employer. Thus ended Charles MacArthur's attempt to achieve his own special brand of well-publicized poetic justice.

The amusement of Benchley and Parker at the whole bizarre business bordered on near-hysteria, a state which abated only when MacArthur was summarily fired by the mausoleum magnate.

MacArthur embodied, as well as an evident death wish, much of the spirit of the insecure twenties, and his insecurity found its counterpart in Mrs. Parker's dry, laconic personality. In many ways the two were kindred souls, except that he regarded women simply as creatures for his pleasure. Mrs. Parker, on the other hand, was, as Seldes had said, "in love with love" and very soon she was to realize that she had fallen hopelessly in love with Charles MacArthur.

Their friends predictably had their own opinions of the affair. Anita Loos recorded: "Her crush was as fervid as it was ill-advised . . . everyone but Dorothy knew that he liked all women, and no special woman." Ben Hecht, with whom MacArthur was to write successful plays, recalled him as "a dashing, mysterious fellow who had a poet's infatuation with death . . . there was also a wildness in Charlie, but it was well-policed

. . . He had to feed the daemon in him a great deal of liquor to keep it in line. . . ."

His liaison with Mrs. Parker continued while he moved around Manhattan doing various newspaper reporting jobs, public relations having turned its back on him.

But for Mrs. Parker, this was a particularly prolific time. She continued to word hard. At this time she contributed another morsel to Franklin Pierce Adams's column, called "News Item":

> Men seldom make passes
> At girls who wear glasses . . .

The lines quickly became the most quoted couplet in America. It was gloatingly cited by girls who didn't wear glasses at girls who did, and became almost a password to conversation in the cocktail set. Its publication perhaps understandably brought forth an echoing battery of invective from the Spectacle Manufacturers Federation of America and countless opticians throughout the country as well as their colleagues in Europe. S. Omar Barker was soon to qualify Mrs. Parker's witty maxim by expressing the opinion in his book *U.S. Lady*:

"Whether men will make passes at girls who wear glasses depends quite a bit on the shape of the chassis."

For all her irreverent maxims, epigrams and bon mots, the often atrophying wit of Mrs. Parker, as most of her friends knew, ambivalently contained the seeds of a deep, personal sadness. For some years, she had worn glasses while working at home and in the office, and it had been noticed that she invariably removed them hurriedly whenever a man approached. She was never seen in glasses while Charles MacArthur was on the scene, but her sadness had little to do with that alone. Her somber mood was an in-built part of her being and it was not helped when news reached her through her friends that her lover was enjoying more than one clandestine affair on the side. She hid her hurt in a whirl of more and more late nights, refusing to acknowledge that Charles MacArthur's interest was visibly cooling, as those around her knew to be the case.

"By Christ!" said Donald Ogden Stewart at the time, "how that girl is suffering!" The perceptive Stewart was right. But then suffering, as Dorothy Parker knew, is often the main business of living for some, and she was helpless to do other than to try to come to terms with her suffering.

One of MacArthur's girlfriends was the English comedienne Beatrice Lillie. Mrs. Parker accused him of double-timing her with the actress. He admitted his deceit. She turned to Benchley for help. He said, simply, "Forget him."

But she could not. She sat down in her frugal room and wrote "Ballad of Great Weariness":

> There's little to have but the things I had,
> There's little to bear but the things I bore,
> There's nothing to carry and naught to add
> And glory to Heaven, I paid the score . . .

Dorothy Parker started to drink and smoke heavily. Her despair deepened; her defenses were down. Depression was now her roommate; darkness had overtaken her spirit again. Schiller, she knew, had said, "Weep, for the light is dead." We have it on Benchley's authority that she wept for days on end.

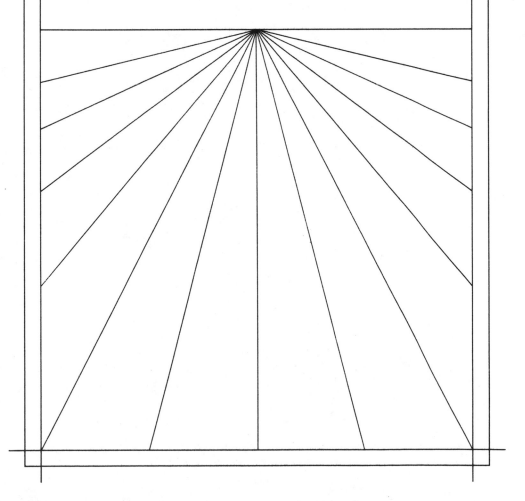

BOOK·TWO

The End of the Beginning

· 1 4 ·

"Pregnant, Bloody Pregnant..."

FROM THE UNHAPPINESS that filled the days of Dorothy Parker at this time, there was one minor compensation to distract her from the loss of her love.

The beautiful, golden-haired artist Neysa McMein wanted to paint her. Neysa, a bewitching extrovert, could take her men with her sandwiches and beer, especially if they were celebrated men. It was well known to the Algonquinites that she had had affairs with Charlie Chaplin, H. G. Wells and Feodor Chaliapin, among others. Woollcott had already described her applaudingly as "a girl with an insatiable, child-like appetite for life," which some said was putting it mildly. She was an artist with true bohemian attitudes, especially in relation to the male of the species.

Her real name was Marjorie, but nobody called her that. A numerologist, she said, had persuaded her to change it. She did just that, becoming for a brief spell a columnist specializing in numerology. But she gave that up, she said, when people started taking her advice. By 1920, she had established herself as a leading commercial artist, painting covers for *Woman's Home Companion, Saturday Evening Post* and other magazines, and creating artwork for various government agencies like Near East War Relief, U.S. Savings Bonds, and others.

Neysa, like Mrs. Parker, loved parties. She loved them even more if the guests were celebrated names, and she knew enough of them to ensure that a sprinkling were usually at her own parties. As to her personal demeanor, she invariably assumed an air of disinterestedness when the celebrity and lesser guests arrived at her atelier in the ramshackle old red building on the corner of Sixth Avenue and West Fifty-Seventh Street, opposite Carnegie Hall. She was well aware of her attributes.

Harpo Marx was one of the many who fell under her spell. "The biggest love affair in New York City," Harpo was to remember, "was between me—along with two other dozen guys—and Neysa . . . Like me, Neysa was an unliterary, semi-illiterate gate-crasher at the Algonquin . . . a lot of us agreed she was the sexiest gal in town . . . Everybody agreed she was the best portrait and cover artist of the time. . . ."

"She had the bait," Noel Coward recalled, "when guests arrived or left, with a sudden spurt of social conscience she would ram a paintbrush into her mouth and shake hands with a kind of disheveled politeness."

Woollcott was to describe her studio in his autobiography:

a bleak, high-ceilinged room, furnished by the process of haphazard accumulation. Its decoration ranges from a Briggs strip torn out of the morning's paper and pinned askew on the wall, to an original Drian, respectfully framed. The splash of vivid color on the screen is a shawl sent by David Belasco and that stretch of gray-green fabric on the wall is a tapestry which she herself bought in Paris and bore home in triumph . . .

The population is wildly variegated. Over at the piano, Jascha Heifetz and Arthur Samuels may be trying to find what four hands can do in the syncopation of a composition never thus desecrated before. Irving Berlin is encouraging them. Squatted uncomfortably round an ottoman, Franklin P. Adams, Marc Connelly and Dorothy Parker will be playing cold hands to see who will buy dinner that evening. At the bookshelf, Robert C. Benchley and Edna Ferber are amusing themselves vastly by thoughtfully autographing her set of Mark Twain for her. In the corner, some jet-bedecked dowager from a statelier *milieu* is taking it all in, immensely diverted. Chaplin or Chaliapin, Alice Duer Miller or Wild Bill Donovan, Father Duffy or Mary Pickford—any or all of them may be there . . .

While mentally rejecting Neysa McMein's desire to paint her, Dorothy Parker knew she had to make the effort to accede to the invitation. Neysa was not only a good friend; her work appeared in the best journals, and Mrs. Parker was always sufficiently astute to know the value of publicity.

The studio was quiet when Dorothy Parker arrived. There wasn't a sound of other people, noise of any kind, only the smell of stale smoke mixed with drink, odorous reminders of the night before. Mrs. Parker was characteristically laconic and seemed unable to concentrate on the static pose Neysa gave her. After sitting for two hours indulging in desultory talk while the artist worked, Dorothy Parker suddenly said she felt sick. At this, she lurched forward and burst into a fit of convulsive weeping. Neysa showed deep concern for her friend but knew that sympathy would not help. She assumed an air of aggression:

"What the hell's wrong with you?" she asked sharply.

"I'm pregnant," said her sitter coldly. "Pregnant, bloody pregnant, dammit."

Neysa is said to have stopped the sitting, given Dorothy some hooch gin, and the two discussed the remedies open to Mrs. Parker.

There was, of course, the back-street abortionist. Or one could get hold of a doctor who would get hold of another doctor who, in turn would enlist the help of another, all three to certify that if allowed to go full term, the pregnancy might result in serious psychological damage to the mother. This remedy would exact a price—a high price. The medical profession, like most other callings, had its dark corners of corruption.

Neysa helped get Dorothy into a hospital on the West Side of the city where, under the guise of a patient with stomach trouble, she had a medically controlled abortion.

The day after it was all over, Benchley went to call on his friend:

"Serves me bloody right," she told him, "for putting all my eggs in one bastard!"

Of course, the abortion had to be subject to laughs but here was the famous Dorothy Parker emerging from the same trauma as assails the poverty-stricken shopgirl; the trauma, too, of unrequited love, the same kind of unrequited love that provided the crooner and chanteuse with their bread and butter. Wit and raconteur Mrs. Parker might be, sophisticate she was, but this was still the stuff of primitive woman. Love and lust and their often inapposite results, like dying, were ever formidable levelers.

Mrs. Parker was discharged from the hospital after a week and told to rest up. Returning to her apartment, there was only her dog, which had been fed by friends in her absence, and the messy bird, Onan, to provide a welcome of sorts.

Back once more in the frenetic fold of the Algonquinites, she unaccountably began to show pointed resentment of several of those friends. Kaufman arrived at the hotel with the news that he had just come from a visit to his physician. Mrs. Parker bridled:

"What the hell did you see a quack for?" she asked.

"Oh, just a checkup," said Kaufman. "The fool told me I'm as fit as a racehorse—that I'll live to be a hundred."

Edna Ferber looked across at Parker and Kaufman with a keen gaze.

"Well, I won't live to be a hundred," added Kaufman defiantly.

"How do you know, George?" asked Ferber.

"I'll kill myself at eighty, that's why."

"How will you kill yourself, George?" asked Ferber.

"With kindness!" he grunted.

Everybody laughed loud and long. Everybody, that is, except Mrs. Parker.

Somebody, noting her glum look, asked Dorothy why she saddled herself with her pet dog, now nestled in her lap; the animal clearly needed more exercise than she had time to give it. Occasional outings to the Round Table and all-too-brief walks to wet the walls of The Little

Church Around The Corner had to be insufficient. "Isn't it a bit unfair on the dog?" asked Woollcott.

"You can't teach an old dogma new habits," she said crisply. This was the Dorothy they all knew and enjoyed.

The Algonquinites were to prove staunch friends at this time, despite Dorothy's frequent lapses into long, introspective silences. They knew, of course, of her love for MacArthur; they knew, too, of the abortion; between their verbiage and vanities they continued to give her support, albeit often of a vacuous kind. But it didn't do to take too optimistic a view of life in her presence. In a somewhat lyrical exposition of the mystery of life and its meaning, John Toohey, who in reality was trying to console her, got a flea in his ear for his pains:

"Stop looking at the world through rose-colored bifocals," she told him. He took the point. Mrs. Parker was particularly sharp-tongued at this time. Characteristically, she seldom suffered fools and there seemed to her to be too many around.

Invited to a supper party of about twenty people at the Waldorf-Astoria, she confessed that she did not know why she'd been asked. Her celebrity status had placed her next to a fussy, overattentive hostess who sat opposite a ruddy-cheeked army brigadier dressed in full military regalia. It quickly became clear to Mrs. Parker that the hostess could not keep her eyes off the officer who, truth to tell, did look rather splendid with his overabundance of gold braid and his ratchet of medals. Still ogling the soldier, the hostess nudged Dorothy:

"I can't help it," she whispered. "It's his lovely uniform. I just love soldiers."

"Yes," said Mrs. Parker evenly, "you have in every war."

It didn't help, either, that on one of his dawn forays her dog had developed the mange and had to be plied with internal and external canine potions. "He's got," explained Mrs. Parker, "a social disease." "How did he get it?" Adams asked. "From using a public lamppost," was the reply.

On assignment from *Ainslee's*, she made a quick journey to Canada and returned to report to her Vicious Circle friends the amusing aspects of her trip.

"I met a strange fellow up there," she said. "He was the tallest man I ever saw, taller even than Sherwood. He had a scar on his forehead. I asked him how he got it. He said he must have hit himself. I asked him how he could reach so high. He said he guessed he must have stood on a chair."

This was Dorothy Parker true to form. But there remained the private hell of her troubled mind and the lonely quiet of her apartment.

Few knew, as she left Tony Soma's one night, that she was in the midst of an attack of black depression. The terrible hurt of MacArthur's rejection of her and the trauma of the abortion of his child was overwhelming her. She said goodnight to the janitor and later phoned down to the nearby Alps Restaurant to send her up some supper. Half an hour later the restaurant's delivery boy, who had collected a passkey, arrived at the door of her apartment with a tray covered with a tea-cloth. She didn't answer the bell. He called out, "Mrs. Parker." Still no reply. He inserted the passkey and opened the door, still calling her name. A light glimmered beneath the bathroom door. He called out again; still no answer. He tapped on the bathroom door and slowly opened it.

She lay slumped across the bath, blood spurting from her slashed wrists. On the floor lay a razor—Eddie Parker's razor.

She screamed, "Jesus, get a doctor, get a doctor!"

The terrified youth ran out as if he'd seen a ghost, leaving the door swinging monotonously to and fro, as if manipulated by an unseen hand in the chilling aura of a room full of suicide.

· 1 5 ·

Curtain Up

THE AMBULANCE got to the shabby old red building on the corner of West Fifty-seventh Street just in time; five more minutes and Mrs. Parker would have gone to the grave, perhaps to the God she despised.

Forty-eight hours later she was propped up in bed in the Columbia Presbyterian Hospital, receiving a procession of Algonquinites that included Benchley, Broun, FPA and Woollcott. "Eddie," she told Benchley, "didn't even keep his razors sharp."

"Why do you despise yourself?" asked Benchley. "People become the thing they despise the most," she replied. It wasn't an original remark. Donne had hinted at it and Wilde had said it in his *De Profundis*, but it fitted her mood of the moment.

"Snap out of it, Dottie," said Benchley. "You might as well live." It was a remark she was never to forget. She was later to use it unforgettably in a poem, "Résumé":

> Razors pain you;
> Rivers are damp;
> Acids stain you;
> And drugs cause cramp.
> Guns aren't lawful;
> Nooses give;
> Gas smells awful;
> You might as well live.

Beatrice Ames arrived at the hospital with Marc Connelly. Dorothy Parker pressed the button marked NURSE. "This," she said, "should ensure us at least forty-five minutes' undisturbed privacy." The wit was still there, sharper by far than Eddie's razor. She had received Connelly and Beatrice wearing light blue ribbons laced into bows around her cut wrists and she showed them off like diamond bracelets. Woollcott said that when he arrived, "I found her in hospital typing away lugubriously. She had given her address as Bedpan Alley, and represented herself as writing her way out . . ."

After leaving the hospital, she started to drink heavily and chain-smoke again, both clear evidence of her inner stress.

She constantly affected her familiar state of penury yet continued to order only the best lingerie and over-garments; she was now well into her pearls-and-black-sweater phase. She ordered, too, perfumes with the scent of tuberose, the scent undertakers use for sprinkling on corpses. Another friend, George Oppenheimer, who was later to become her publisher, observed of her at this time: ". . . she is a masochist, whose passion for unhappiness knows no bounds."

If this were true, her soigné appearance and precise intonation coupled with her literary stature gave her entrée to Manhattan's best parties, to which she was now often escorted by Donald Ogden Stewart, whose Yale background helped diffuse the aura of near-notoriety of the Algonquin crowd.

Life in and around Manhattan's café society was a constant source of subject material for the newspapers, and Dorothy Parker was now frequently a guest at upper-crust gatherings, the guest of Jock Whitney and his fiancée Liz Altemus, the Averell Harrimans and the Pierre Hamiltons, among others. And Jack Kriendler and Charlie Berns soon found that their venue, the Puncheon Club—forerunner of "21"—was becoming a fashionable second home of the ritzy social crowd.

Mrs. Parker appeared to the observer the composed, placid, literary lady, understated in her personal life-style, conservative in her food and dress. As John Keats put it:

Her room was just a cheap, conveniently located place to sleep. When she dined out (she did not cook for herself), it did not seem to matter to her what she ate. She would routinely order a steak and a salad, no matter how ambitious the restaurant's menu. Food was more of a humdrum necessity for her than it was a source of pleasure or recreation, and her attitude toward food would have helped to keep its cost low for her, wholly apart from the fact that many of her evening meals would be provided by her male escorts.

She went frequently to the theater, for in those days there were as many as nine openings in a single week during the season, but this cost nothing because she attended plays together with Mr. Woollcott or Mr. Benchley, and theater critics were always assigned two free seats. The books she read were review copies given her by magazines and newspaper friends. And her greatest source of amusement cost nothing at all, consisting as it did of the company of her friends.

She was so seldom home that her private life was, in a sense, nonexistent. She would wake at mid morning and at noon meet friends for lunch. The working hours of many of the Algonquin group were elastic and nocturnal; this was particularly true of the newspaper columnists FPA and Heywood Broun and of the motion picture and theater critics Sherwood, Benchley and Woollcott. . . . after a leisurely lunch, someone might propose a thing that seemed fun to do in the afternoon, such as riding along Fifth Avenue in a carriage. Mr. Woollcott loved to do this, and Dorothy Parker was always glad to go along.

On one of these occasions, she and Mr. Woollcott found their Victoria stopped in a snarl of traffic and surrounded, like a house in a flood, by eddying pedestrians. Woollcott adopted the mood of a Bourbon monarch bored by reports that the peasants were restless. But she, amused by Mr. Woollcott's air of refined distaste, and by that quality of desperate frustration that characterizes all who use New York's streets, began to giggle. Then, playing a role of her own, she rose, blowing kisses to the commonality, and calling out: "I promise to come back and sing Carmen again for you!"

In the late afternoon of such a day, Mrs. Parker might accompany Mr. Benchley and Mr. Stewart to a brownstone on the West Side. They would somewhat furtively descend the basement steps, and Stewart would ring for admission.

It was to be another of their speakeasy afternoons.

A sliding panel in the steel door would snick back, revealing a peephole. Stewart, if not recognized to be a regular patron of the establishment, would have to mutter "Joe sent me," or otherwise give a password . . . If all went well, there would be a noise of bolts and chains, the door would slip quickly open and be as quickly shut, chained and bolted behind them. They would find themselves in a dark room, thick with cigarette smoke and loud with drunken voices, themselves now a part of an illicit camaraderie which might very well include the cop on the beat, found drinking a large whisky and a small beer at the end of the bar.

There were many styles and sizes of Prohibition speakeasies, and it was a mark of sophistication to be able to discriminate among them. There were little holes in the wall along First Avenue that had sawdust on the floor; there were bars kept by the Irish, decorated with shillelaghs; Italian establishments with marble-topped tables, bad frescoes of the Bay of Naples, and worse red wine made by the proprietors. Close to the *Tribune* newspaper's building on West Fortieth Street there was Jack Bleeck's Artists and Writers Club, catering to the newspaper crowd. On Park Avenue, across from the Racquet Club, a genial and unlettered man named Matt Winkle served a clientele that seemed to consist almost exclusively of undergraduates from Harvard and Yale. What most of these establishments had in common, apart from an atmosphere of cosy lawbreaking, was grain alcohol imaginatively flavored and even more imaginatively labeled Rye, Bourbon, Scotch and Gin. But the speakeasy the Algonquin group liked best, and which they patronized whenever they had the money, was Jack and Charlie's Puncheon Club at 42 West Forty-ninth Street. No rotgut alcohol or bathtub gin was served there, but genuine wines and spirits of first quality. And instead of steak fried thin, hard and tough, Jack and Charlie's served ambrosia prepared by a chef paid twenty thousand a year. It was not just locally known, but was internationally famous—and became wickedly expensive, for all the plebeian charm of its red and white check tablecloths.

Afterwards, Keats might have added, the guests would move down-stairs where part of the wall swung back on hinges to reveal a cavelike structure which in turn revealed a victualler's paradise.

Arriving at this establishment, Dorothy Parker and her escorts would be sure to find other of their friends there—as they would if they had gone across the street to Tony Soma's, where everyone went when funds ran low, for Tony's sold suspect liquor and rather bad Italian food, but at prices more within the reach of everyone . . .

To say that Dorothy Parker went frequently to speakeasies does not mean she drank frequently while there. Many of the Algonquin group began to drink like sewers during Prohibition, but just as their camaraderie at the Algonquin Hotel was not predicated on alcohol, so it was not predicated on alcohol at the speak-easies . . . one or two drinks would normally see Mrs. Parker through an evening . . . Dorothy and her friends might eat at Tony's, or have a drink there and move the party over to Seventh Avenue where Mr. Benchley had found "a little French restaurant completely without charm," and afterwards it might be the theater and Neysa McMein's.

Still later after a session of Consequences, Shedding Light, Cate-gories, or The Game, in what was no longer the same night but hours into the next day, the whole party might move to Polly Adler's bawdy girl shop for conversation with *les girls* and with Mrs. Adler, who would later find fame as a littérateur of sorts with her book *A House Is Not A Home,* which her house then most certainly never was.

It was such a favorite haunt of the group that one of Dorothy's friends had a charge account and kept a black Japanese kimono there.

This friend was, in fact, George Kaufman. Attired in his kimono, "he would sit down to play backgammon with Mrs. Adler for twenty dollars a game—this being the price of a girl's favor—while everyone would crowd around to see how the game came out." Although more circum-spect about his patronage, Robert Benchley also had a charge account there, of which Mrs. Parker knew and seemed not to mind.

. . . On occasion, Donald Ogden Stewart would take Dorothy to Polly's in the afternoon, and she would sit in the parlor and chat while, Mr. Stewart said, "I went upstairs to lay some lucky girl."

"The Algonquin group were by no means alone in spending so much of their time with one another," says Keats. This was the pattern of life in New York in the twenties. People tended to go out in groups, playing together, staying up all night together. The Algonquin group lived and worked in Manhattan, and could conduct all of their social and working lives, every day, within a few blocks of Manhattan's West Side between the Forties and Fifties.

The whole point of their lives seemed to be to have fun, to be clever, to know where the best bartenders were, to be knowledgeable about the city, to know all the latest catchwords and phrases, to be aware of the newest fashions and fads, to go to all the first nights and to all the Big Three football games, to go to Polly's and be satirical and blasé, and to do as little work as possible. Certainly no one saw any evidence that Dorothy did any work. There was no littered desk in her small apartment, no wastebasket filled with manuscript drafts . . .

"It was one of the things you didn't do," Donald Stewart explained.

She and Bobbie [Benchley] and I never actually talked about our work, much as we saw of each other. I wouldn't call it an amateur spirit, but it was a little like that. I mean, we weren't professional literary people in that sense of discussing each other's work. The only discussions there would be . . . I had a deadline to meet, and Bobbie would have to get out one of his theater reviews, and there were various jokes over the telephone about the poor editors, such as "Hasn't that piece got there yet?" when you hadn't even started to write it.

All this was very much in keeping with Ernest Hemingway's remark in *The Sun Also Rises* that it was then an important part of the ethics of journalism to pretend *not* to be working . . . some people felt that Dorothy Parker was not just pretending. She was always available to do anything else instead, or so it seemed, and some of her friends thought that she was lazy. She chose to admit the charge, rather than refute it. Asked what inspired her to write, she replied, "Need of money, dear," as if to say that when she had money, writing was the last thing she wanted to do. . . . The Algonquin group was somewhat in the position of Puck saying "What fools these mortals be," although they were not so far above the battle as Puck. They felt themselves to be an elite, and they had considerable reason to believe they were right. From there, they went on to set another standard for the nation, to create a different intellectual climate. But they did this *en passant*.

Harold Ross's *New Yorker* was rapidly becoming the smart magazine for the in crowd; its understated humor was becoming the fashionable read for the witty and wealthy, later in part sustained by talented cartoonists and illustrators like Charles Addams, with cartoons in which a nurse outside a maternity ward was shown handing a baby to a Frankenstein-looking father, saying, "Will you take it with you, or will you eat it here?" The Algonquinites continued to lead the field in the frenetic social whirl of mid-Manhattan. They ate, drank, worked, talked, played and loved; most of all they laughed, laughed as if there were no tomorrow. And quipped. "That woman," said Dorothy Parker of one café society habituée, "is so highly educated that she speaks eighteen different languages. And she can't say no in any of them." Benchley told her a story about an actress who had broken her leg. "How unfortunate," said Mrs. Parker, "she must have done it sliding down a barrister." When Franklin Pierce Adams told her that Harold Ross had been expecting her to call on him, she said, "Tell him I've been too fucking busy, or vice versa."

Mrs. Parker was frequently on the move during this period; she was edgy, unsettled. Even when she had a semipermanent address, she would frequently move into a hotel for a few weeks simply for a change of scene. During one such spell she moved into Manhattan's Marmont Hotel, which had been recommended to her by George Oppenheimer. She was put into rooms immediately below his suite. Mrs. Parker liked Oppenheimer. He was, after all, expressly a writer and a writer's editor, as well as something of an entrepreneur and in many ways great fun, albeit a little too extroverted at times. She and several other Algonquinites often teased him unmercifully about his name-dropping habits, at which, it must be said, he was a master.

He had invited a number of literary and show business people for cocktails in his rooms, and Mrs. Parker, also invited, had said she would join the party later, using the excuse of a meeting with Benchley and Sherwood. The party upstairs was in full swing when she, Benchley and Sherwood suddenly reacted to a resounding crash which shook the ceiling above them. The noise stopped all conversation. Turning to Benchley with just a slight glance upward, Mrs. Parker quietly observed: "Dear, dear. There goes George dropping another name."

All such stories and quips were relayed to the Manhattan set who chuckled with glee. "Did you hear what Dorothy Parker said today?" became the question that opened many conversations in Manhattan at this time.

Speaking of a well-known stage director whom she despised, Mrs. Parker dismissed him with the assessment, "He's a cad. A card-carrying cad." She suggested again that her epitaph read, "Excuse my dust," which she later amended to "This one is on me," and went on further to discuss women. "Most good women," she said, "are hidden treasures who are only safe because nobody looks for them," and she totally ignored the fact that she had become a featured character, hidden in a fictional name, in Donald Ogden Stewart's best-selling novel, *The Crazy Fool.*

And what of Mrs. Parker's close friend Robert Benchley? He, too, was becoming the rage. He had left *Life* after asking for too many advances in lieu of his salary and had now become a star contributor and simple line-illustrator for *The New Yorker*. He had finished up his *Vanity*

Fair stint with a screamingly funny piece, "The Social Life of The Newt," about a raunchy newt that had been disconcerted by the proximity of an office eraser. As a result, Benchley had become something of a cult figure, albeit a still fairly penurious one, and his star was again in the ascendant.

Corey Ford was later to dub this period "The Years of Laughter." It was certainly no less than that in Dorothy Parker's life. For her, the Algonquin was the clique and the claque of her days and nights, the apotheosis of exciting living. Her abortion and suicide attempts had by now receded into the past. She had collaborated with Adams in a book of light, frothy verse called *Women I'm Not Married To: Men I'm Not Married To*, a spinoff from a piece that originally appeared in the June 17, 1922, issue of the *Saturday Evening Post*. The book's cover showed an upside-down photograph of the two authors and had done well in sales.

Now she was contributing to *The New Yorker* alongside Benchley and other of their literary friends, and she was writing well. Her *Diary of a New York Lady* was considered wise, contemporary, acerbic and mordantly funny. And she had earlier extended her freelance activities with occasional contributions to H. L. Mencken's magazine, *Smart Set*, which had earlier published her first short story, "Such a Pretty Little Picture."

Now, too, she took over occasionally from Benchley in reviewing plays for *The New Yorker*. The theater was clearly one of her major interests. And as early as 1920, in *Vanity Fair*, she had expressed her admiration of a man who had changed his name from Elmer L. Ritzenstein to Elmer Rice, whose mystery play she had reviewed, observing that the author "follows the regular formula so faithfully that there is not a chance of any slip-up." Mr. Rice was now the toast of Broadway, an idol, too, of her close friend Robert Sherwood. Even the ubiquitous *Variety* had kissed Mr. Rice in print with the description: "Masterful."

Dorothy Parker told her friends of the Round Table that she was all set to write a play with that same Mr. Rice, to be called *Soft Music*.

· 1 6 ·

The Perils of Parker

THE ROUND TABLE was agog at the news of Mrs. Parker's fresh literary enterprise. It had been Mr. Benchley who had persuaded her to "do something different"; here she was doing just that.

Soft Music was soon changed to *Close Harmony or The Lady Next Door* and was to be of three-acts "in tune with the jazz age, about two frustrated people who start up an adulterous affair."

It appeared to be the right time for this collaborative effort. Broadway had been getting up steam since the beginning of the decade. The annual rate of new productions had leaped from about 120 during the immediate pre-war years to about 256 in December 1924. Of course, there had been the long runs like *Abie's Irish Rose*, which had chalked up 2,397 performances; Leon Gordon's *White Cargo*, with 864 performances; Frank Davis's *The Ladder*, with 789 money-spinning nights and days; Austin Strong's *Seventh Heaven*, with 704 performances; Colton and Randolph's classic adaptation of Somerset Maugham's *Rain*, with 648; and David Belasco's presentation of *Kid*, with 600 performances to its credit.

Success was there on and around Times Square, and there seemed no good reason why the combination of Elmer Rice and Dorothy Parker could not create a play that would compete with the best.

Close Harmony, its final title, opened in a pre-Broadway tryout in Wilmington, Delaware, on November 22, 1924, moving to Broadway on December 1. That same evening, five other plays also opened on Broadway. Inevitably, this crowded concentration of new theatrical fare diffused the critical reception of all six. Mrs. Parker, at the hub of the journalistic scene and having many friends within it, predictably attracted many of the reviews, despite the simultaneous opening of Fred and Adele Astaire in *Lady Be Good*.

The day after *Close Harmony*'s Times Square debut, the management learned the truth. Despite some good reviews they knew they would have to fight to survive. Battle was joined with a barrage of paid advertising and editorial publicity, both to no avail. The play closed after twenty-four performances. As if anticipating the Round Tablers' inevitable derisive reaction, Mrs. Parker got in first. On the afternoon of the last day of the run, a telegram from her was delivered to the Vicious Circle:

CLOSE HARMONY DID A COOL NINETY DOLLARS AT THE MATINEE TODAY. STOP. ASK THE BOYS IN THE BACK ROOM WHAT THEY WILL HAVE.

The whole enterprise had been little short of a disaster for all concerned, but disaster was becoming a frequent companion to Mrs. Parker.

To her credit, she continued to work hard, capitalizing on her recent experience of abortion with a story called "Mr. Durant," which was published in *American Mercury*, as well as a piece of fiction entitled "Bobbed Hair," which was a chapter from a novel—a gangster story—she had tackled earlier but had not published. This appeared in *Collier's* in January 1925.

The course that much of her future life would take began at this time. George Kaufman invited her to collaborate in the writing of a movie short, *Business is Business* for Paramount Pictures. The two got to work and delivered the script within six weeks. Like so many film projects, it was made but soon disappeared without trace.

Public life for Mrs. Parker, like her intensely private inner life, now became a series of highs and lows.

How had she really reacted to the failure of *Close Harmony*? She herself was devastatingly frank. "It was dull," she told her friends. "You have my apologies." Just that, and no more. Nonetheless, the business of collaboration still appealed to her. In her earlier collaboration with Franklin Pierce Adams on *Women I'm Not Married To: Men I'm Not Married To*, she had extended her boundaries, and it had certainly done her no harm to be associated with one such as Adams, whose books like *The Book of Diversion, Half A Loaf* and *The Diary Of Our Own Samuel Pepys* had met with both critical acclaim and healthy sales figures. It had been the same Adams who, when applying for an Algonquin charge account, had written in the space marked "Professional Position" a single word—"Horizontal!"; this was the kind of humor Mrs. Parker greatly approved of.

Adams, then, had been the first collaborator; Elmer Rice the second; and George Kaufman was the newest. That the film hadn't taken off didn't much matter; life seemed full and rich for Mrs. Parker. But was it?

Well, at least she was occupied with work, and as for play the wits were still hard at work and New York was immersed in a nightly whirl of the Charleston, the Georgella Blues, the Rag-Time Rag, the Mayfair Quickstep, the Bermuda Foxtrot, and tangos by the score. And, too, there were the afternoon and evening pleasures within the metal-grilled speakeasies, not to mention the ceaseless round of parties like those given by the Swopes at Great Neck, Long Island, where, as Edna Ferber remembered: "People just came in and out, carefree . . . at an unbelievably luxurious clubhouse . . . tea at six or seven, dinner at ten or eleven, supper at three or four . . ."

There was much activity, too, within the brownstone at 412 West Forty-seventh Street, where Harold Ross, the son of an agnostic failed silver prospector, and his wife Jane Grant were building a force of contributors to his *New Yorker* magazine. Raoul Fleischmann had kept his promise and invested in the magazine to help it off the ground, but now more money was needed.

Several of the leading Round Tablers had been named by Ross as advisory editors, which surprised them since none had knowledge of the fact until they saw their names listed in the magazine. These included George S. Kaufman, Alexander Woollcott, Dorothy Parker, Marc Connelly, Alice Duer Miller, Edna Ferber, Laurence Stallings, artist Rea Irwin and an editor and artist named Ralph Barton. "Fine and dandy," Benchley had commented, "if only we'd known about it."

It obviously hadn't mattered too much because they all turned up at the Ross home for the launching party of *The New Yorker*. Charlie MacArthur stood on the pavement outside handing out invitations to passers-by to join in the festivities upstairs: "Do come in, your ghost is in there waiting for you."

When *The New Yorker*'s finances were again at a perilously low ebb, Fleischmann was prevailed upon to inject yet more capital into the enterprise. Heir to a vast baking and yeast fortune, he was heavily caught up in the pranks of the Vicious Circle, just as he now was well and truly involved in the financial fortunes of the magazine.

The Roaring Twenties were in a full and unabashed spate; Flaming Youth, as they called it, was mocking middle age. Manhattan was a magically alive place. From Harlem echoed the sounds of jazz; Greenwich Village was growing a noticeable bohemian bulge, and the North Shore society of Bright Young Things, which included Alexander and Pierpont Hamilton, Robert and Adele Lovett, and Charles and Joan Payson, accepted reciprocal party invitations from the Algonquinites. During the season, the Whitneys had taken a suite of rooms for some of the Round Tablers at the Saratoga races, and Manhattan and Long Island, like the rest of America, echoed to the ribald rhythms of "Everybody's Doing It, Doing It, Doing It. Everybody's Doing It, Doing It Now!" But the song was a bit of a misnomer.

In reality, precious few were doing it, and those who were—largely the monied, cultured, discriminating haut monde—were now cavorting with the demi-classe of the literary set who shared their hedonistic natures, if not their dash or cash. Life was a lovely lark for all who were fortunate enough to participate in the effervescent whirl of Manhattan. If you were in the social set, in or on the periphery of the arts, as were Mrs. Parker and her immediate friends, most likely you were enjoying the exuberant life of the city to the full.

To the observer it was, as writer and society girl Ethel Mannin put it, "an exciting time in which to be young; it was a decade of uninhibited living—relatively. In another sense it was an Age of Innocence in which foreign travel was a real adventure and falling in love, no matter how ephemerally, was endowed with romantic passion!"

Even the flaunted promiscuity, it seems, was both romanticized and sentimentalized.

Miss Mannin, who darted back and forth across the Atlantic, enjoyed the best of both continents. "The 1920s," she later averred, "was a decade of paradoxes, of surface gaiety and hidden misery, of a generation dedicated to the pursuit of happiness in terms of sexual freedom, and to good times in terms of cocktail parties, dancing, night life, but all of it a gaudy superstructure imposed on the black, rotting foundations of the coming economic depression."

Everybody, it seemed, was out on the town at parties, dancing to the persuasive rhythms of the Charleston and the tango, or smooching to the dreamy music and lyrics of current hit songs like "Poor Butterfly." Clubs, restaurants and theaters were packed nightly, the more formal-minded sticking to the popular matinee performances. By 1924, Broadway had seemingly totally recovered from America's participation in the Great War: show business and its adjuncts flourished. *Artists and Models* was "packing them in" at the Schubert Theatre; France's Alice Delysia was a palpable hit at the Winter Garden in *Topics*. The youthful writing team of George Kaufman and Marc Connelly were enjoying a hit with *Beggar on Horseback* at the Broadhurst, while Fay Bainter performed nightly to ecstatic plaudits on stage at the Morosco in *The Other Rose*. The Guild Theatre Players were enjoying a successful run in the Garrick Theater's production of Shaw's *Saint Joan*, while Laura Hope Crews and Grace George were winning applause with their performances in Laurence Eyre's comedy *The Merry Wives of Gotham* at the Henry Miller Theater on West Forty-third Street. In characteristic Barrymore fashion, Lionel Barrymore, with Irene Fenwick as his leading lady, was stunning audiences in *Laugh, Clown, Laugh* at the Belasco.

Almost inevitably, the new winter edition of Flo Ziegfeld's *Follies*—

"the greatest of the series"—was playing to full houses at the New Amsterdam, while Times Square and its environs were enjoying box-office hits like Lillian Gish in *The White Sister* at the Lyric and Douglas McLean in *The Yankee Consul* at the Central. *Jesse James* was enjoying a great vogue at the Little Theater, featuring a Paul Whiteman Band, one of fifty such bands then being presented by the overweight musician-impresario throughout the country.

The movies, too, were taking in big money in New York and other major cities. At the Cosmopolitan Cinema on Columbus Circle, *The Great White Way* was breaking records, with publicity proclaiming Harold Bell Wright's "amazing photo drama." *When a Man's a Man* was being shown at the Cameo, just off Broadway, to audiences who had often waited in line for hours.

And while the bobbed Mae Murray was electrifying the audience at Loew's State in *Fashion Row*, Virginia Valli was enchanting audiences in *A Lady of Quality* at Loew's New Lexington cinema on Lexington Avenue. The Broadway, the Tivoli, the Rialto, the Plaza, the Olympic and most other movie palaces in Manhattan were enjoying good seasons with such varied fare as *Don't Call it Love* and *A Woman of Paris*. Even the Moscow Art Theatre was breaking records at the Al Jolson Theater. And no less than the kilted Sir Harry Lauder, with his lilting rendition of "I Love A Lassie, a Bonnie, Bonnie Lassie," was successfully transporting the heather of the Scottish highlands to the stage of Manhattan's Opera House.

Manhattan was seemingly full of jazz bands in the dance salons, restaurants and clubs. Itinerant jazzmen like Duke Ellington, Benny Carter, Fletcher Henderson, Jimmy Lunceford, Pee Wee Russell, Mezz Mezzrow, Bix Beiderbecke, Bunny Berigan, Eddie Condon and the crippled little drummer Chick Webb, along with Wingy Manone, Red Redman, Frank Teschemacher, Louis Armstrong and others beat out their brash convulsive rhythms in clubs on Harlem's Lenox or Seventh Avenue and elsewhere where any one of Paul Whiteman's touring bands attempted more polished renditions of the jazz of Harlem, New Orleans, Louisiana, Chicago and the middle Mississippi valley in dance halls, restaurants and theatres. Classical artists included Fritz Kreisler, Sergei Rachmaninoff, Josef Stransky, Walter Damrosch, Jascha Heifetz, Moriz Rosenthal, Leopold Stokowski, John McCormack, Amelita Galli-Curci, Mary Garden, Alma Gluck, among others, while critics like William Henderson, Leonard Liebling, Henry Osborne Osgood, and P. R. Sandborn judged the performances in the newspapers and magazines.

It was a similar scene in London, which often followed American patterns. The theaters of Shaftesbury Avenue and the Haymarket within the square mile of the capital's entertainment center echoed to a collection of musicals, straight plays, comedies, vaudeville shows and revues. Nightclubs like the Kit-Kat were packed with people who wanted to enjoy themselves. At the Florida, one danced on a glass floor lit from beneath. If discreet and rich enough, one might see the Prince of Wales dancing with one of his several mistresses at Ciro's Club. As in Manhattan, life for those at the center of things seemed to be a succession of wild parties full of flappers and other Bright Young Things who included gallant-looking young officers of the Brigade of Guards, many of them scions of wealthy families, living it up with carefree abandon, sating their thirsts with champagne, White Ladies and Manhattan cocktails, or the new and fashionable dry martinis, the heavy consumption of which was a challenge to be met only with laughter and clinking glasses, starched evening shirts and tails.

No matter that within the confines of Hester Street and its environs on the Lower East Side of Manhattan the area was swarming with hand-outs and poverty, full of Jews who did not manage to get a square meal in weeks. It was the same in London's East End and other impoverished areas of the British Isles.

The war to end wars had been fought and won, the world had surely been made safe for democracy. Little notice was taken now of the politicians who talked glibly of "reconstruction"; the young bloods in New York and London were largely unconcerned with such platitudes. "Ain't We Got Fun" was the title of a popular song of the time, evincing the mood of the days—and nights. It was sardonic, of course, but as Ethel Mannin recalled: "We liked it, we sang it on Broadway and in Piccadilly, we danced to it kicking up our heels. We laughed a lot, danced a lot, told each other risqué stories—we called them 'saucy' stories. We used to ask each other at parties—'Heard any good stories lately?' Most of them were fairly funny; sometimes they were crude. But we liked them and wondered who invented them, or originated them."

Like the one about Tallulah Bankhead. During a visit to England, the actress had had a torrid affair with a very blue-blooded gentleman of the shires. His family disapproved of the actress and succeeded in breaking up the relationship by persuading him to become engaged to a girl of his own background and aspirations—he would, in time, inherit a dukedom. The two families were dining at the Savoy Grill, when Tallulah swept in. Walking straight up to their table, the actress greeted her former lover effusively. He, embarrassed, turned his head away, ignoring her.

"What's the matter, dahling?" cried Tallulah, sufficiently loud for both families at the table to hear. "Don't you recognize me with my clothes on?"

Despite the risqué stories, the period was in its way an Age of Romanticism. The crooners through their megaphones sang: "If you could care for me, as I could care for you-ooo . . ." "It was," as Ethel Mannin remembered, "as simple as that." We were a very believing generation. Unashamedly we could declare love to be at first sight, a reaction underlined by the dreamy words and music of another popular song of the time:

> I took one look at you
> That's all I meant to do—
> And then my heart stood still . . .

The Bright Young Things of New York and London further declared: "You felt that if you turned up to lunch in a loincloth, nobody would take much notice."

On the literary front, publisher George Doran of Manhattan was enjoying great acclaim for his international parties embracing the social scene of each city. His guest lists boasted the upper echelons of New York and London society, with such guests as Arnold Bennett, Hugh Walpole, Somerset Maugham and up-and-coming young writers like Beverley Nichols. The parties continued throughout much of the twenties until Doran amalgamated with Doubleday. Even that did not matter —there were others to take his place within the confines of transatlantic society.

If the girls and boys sang and danced to "I want to be happy, but I won't be happy, 'til I make you happy too," they meant it. It was the fashion of the times.

There was, too, George Glaenzer, an executive at Cartier, the jewelers. His fashionable East Side home echoed to the merry din of parties throughout the twenties. Mr. Glaenzer believed in mixing business with pleasure; many of the celebrities and socialites he entertained bought their valuables and jewelry from him, including Jack Dempsey, George Gershwin, Charles Chaplin, Lord Louis and Lady Edwina Mountbatten, Douglas Fairbanks, Noel Coward, Fanny Brice, Jascha Heifetz, Gertrude Lawrence, Fred and Adele Astaire, and Maurice Chevalier. Gershwin was there because of his newfound fame—in 1919 he had written a joyful, unpretentious song, "Swanee," which, in Al Jolson's rendition of it, had swept the world; nobody mentioned that it had first been performed by his brother, Morris Gershwin, on a comb wrapped in lavatory paper.

The long cigarette holders in Manhattan and London, which affectedly held Virginian or Turkish cigarettes, were not a sign of "putting on the Ritz" as much as a defiant accouterment to the largely discarded standards of convention and "proper" behavior; standards that were conveniently tossed out the window by flappers and their escorts. On the stage, it was the height of daring for an actress to appear in cami-knickers which is precisely what a number of actresses on both sides of the Atlantic did; to them they were garments that were comfortable, pretty, free and loose, replacing as they did the constricting corsets of the earlier age. Garters too, frilly, ribboned with rosebuds and lace, provided a provocative and often hopeful invitation when knees were crossed, especially if they sported a touch of feather or marabou. Such "naughty" additions to the female dress, along with headbands and cloche hats and pure silk stockings, enhanced many a lovely female. It was all part of the soigné look; you simply had to have "It."

The mysterious and elusive quality of "It" was totally necessary to the girl who sought completeness in the sexually liberated mores of the day. "It" had been devised, or invented, by the romantic fiction writer Elinor Glyn. "It" was something that every young girl *ought* to have—"It" meant, quite simply, *sex appeal*. Miss Glyn liberally filled her books with torrid doses of "It," so much so that a rhyme was current in New York and London at that time:

> Would you like to sin
> On a tiger-skin
> With Elinor Glyn
> Or would you prefer
> To err
> On another fur?

Mrs. Parker was to deal with the likes of Miss Glyn in due course but not before the vocation of a freelance writer had been perfectly and humorously defined by Robert Benchley. It had already been defined as "One who gets paid per word, per piece." Benchley's version was the classic: "One who gets paid per word, per piece or perhaps."

Mrs. Dorothy Parker loved the laughter of the age, especially Mr. Benchley's kind of laughter. But unlike others she also secretly loathed the noisy festivities, the billowing party laughter. She told Benchley that she disliked the domed dance floors and the ghostly, night-veiled swimming pools alive with giggling, thirsty human bodies. But behind these protestations, did she really abhor the cascading hooch, the starched wing-collars of the men and the tight-lipped, tight-legged immaturity of the head-banded girls? She herself after all was, in a sense, one of them.

Yet, perversely, she was not. Back in 1920 she had written in *Life* what amounted to a plea for socialism, deploring the gilded affectations of the self-absorbed female snob. On going to a Yale prom with Donald Ogden Stewart she had astringently observed of the society girls there: "If all these sweet young things were laid end to end, I wouldn't be at all surprised."

In this age of the New Thing—the Cocktail Cult—she made no bones about her loathing of that, too. Asked if she had enjoyed a party, she quipped: "Enjoyed it? One more drink and I'd have been under the host!"

The laconic lunacy apart, she was, as George Oppenheimer had said, "a masochist whose passion for unhappiness knows no bounds." This evaluation fairly summed up Dorothy Parker, who seemed to grip life like a steel vise, certain that it would be torn away from her if she let go. Yet, paradoxically, she was obsessed with death. There were those who said that her extroverted hedonism was an outflow of her inner fear. She had, indeed, written in a verse: "I'll not be left in sorrow," but sorrow seemed resolutely slow to leave her. That she was still suffering hurt in the aftermath of love was revealed in "The Burned Child," which she wrote at this time:

> Love has had his way with me.
> This my heart is torn and maimed
> Since he took his play with me.
> Cruel well the bow-boy aimed,
> Shot, and saw the feathered shaft
> Dripping bright and bitter red.
> He that shrugged his wing and laughed
> Better had he left me dead. . . .

The sophistication was gone. It disappeared as it always disappeared when she was alone in the vacuum of her apartment, when the japish jazz was silenced and the laughter had spirited itself away like smoke in a drafty room. There was no love in her life now, and she, Dorothy Parker, could not live without love.

After a party, Benchley walked Dorothy Parker to the elevator at the Algonquin, where she was temporarily staying. The dawn outside was hidden by swift stalking clouds as the two said goodnight. She entered her room, brushed her teeth, changed into a nightdress and got into bed. We know that she was in a highly emotional state. She took a large vial of barbiturates and swallowed them. Before she passed out, she hurled her drinking glass through a window. It fell into the well of the hotel yard below; the noise wasn't noticed, perhaps a dishwasher had smashed a glass, that sort of thing happened often.

When she did not appear for lunch next day, Benchley, with the help of a porter and a passkey, entered her room. Dorothy Parker lay on the bed inert and pale, hardly breathing.

She had, if any had cared to perceive it, already warned her friends of the likelihood of another suicide attempt in her recently published poem, "I Shall Come Back":

> I shall come back without fanfaronade
> Of wailing wind and graveyard panoply;
> But, trembling, slip from cool Eternity—
> A mild and most bewildered little shade.
> I shall not make sepulchral midnight raid,
> But softly come where I had longed to be
> In April twilight's unsung melody,
> And I, not you, shall be the one afraid. . . .

The would-be ghost did not quite make it to the shades.

· 1 7 ·

Enter Ernest...

THE FIRST TIME Dorothy Parker had attempted suicide her friends rallied around, some displaying unexpected compassion. The second time was rather different. When Benchley visited her in the hospital, he looked at her dolefully and said: "Dottie, if you don't stop this sort of thing, you'll make yourself sick."

He planned to use hard-hitting tactics this time, to try to frighten her. Her friends, he claimed, did not want to know. Her repeat performance was not simply a nuisance, it was more than that. It was "a bloody great bore." "If you could have seen how utterly repulsive you looked when we found you," he scolded, "you would never have done it. You looked a drooling mess." And then, to soften the hurt, he said, "If you had any consideration at all for your friends, you'd shoot yourself cleanly and not be so revoltingly messy!"

Benchley was the one who knew and understood her better than any of the Algonquin crowd. He knew that her familiar gaiety was nothing more than external drapery for her unhappiness. He knew, too, that she was always at war with her demons; that they seldom left her. And he was deeply concerned for her. She had been put in an oxygen tent for a day or two during her last suicide attempt when she had said to him, "Can I have a little flag for my tent?" "I'll get you the Medal of Freedom, if you want, Dottie," he answered, "but go easy on this suicide stuff. First thing you know, you'll ruin your health."

Heywood Broun was a constant visitor to her hospital room. His visits were well remembered by psychiatrist Dr. Alvan Baruch, who had treated Dorothy since her first suicide attempt:

She was already a pathological drinker, and a great deal of our time together was directed at eliminating that symptom. Of course, when I had her in the hospital that time I could keep her sober, at least at first I could. Then, after a couple of days, on my four o'clock visit she would be fine but at six she would be tight. I couldn't figure out what was going on, how she was getting any liquor, until I found out that at five every day she had a visit from Heywood Broun who was another of my patients . . . despite the fact that he knew she should get over it, despite his ideas, he fed her his gin from five to six. Such an interesting part of Heywood's character—so idealistic and yet so willing to play the little boy and try to outwit me. I think, in a way, he was testing my affection the way a child would: love me no matter how bad I am . . .

Baruch may not have been the world's most perceptive psychiatrist, but he understood the Algonquinites, most of whom he knew professionally and socially:

They were all living lives of extreme casualness. . . . They always had to be witty, playful, entertaining. They never spoke about anything for more than a minute, and never in depth, and so they were being forced to sell short on the other side of their nature: the purposeful, striving side. They wrote to make money or to be witty and, knowing instinctively that something was missing, they needed the security the group gave them. The exclusiveness of the group, the amount of time they spent together—I saw and still do, as an index of how insecure they all were. One of the results was a terrible malice. Nearly all of them had a terribly malicious streak.

Although suicide was then a felony according to the law, Mrs. Parker's attempt to end her life once again was largely hushed up by the group at Benchley's behest. She soon rejoined Benchley and the others, happy that at long last she had met, through Donald Ogden Stewart, Ernest Hemingway.

The aura of Sylvia Beach's bookshop in Paris—of Gertrude Stein, Alice B. Toklas and other American émigrés—surrounded the bearded writer. Mrs. Parker felt an instant rapport with him. Hemingway, for his part, displayed nothing more than a passing interest in her. A hedonist with a growing reputation for high-living and near-dying, he exemplified to her all the anarchistic traits of the bohemian littérateur. Above all, he was a fine, spare, taut writer of high talent, the total embodiment of a real artist.

On first meeting Benchley and Parker, Hemingway told John Dos Passos that he found them "obviously attractive people," an opinion that, in relation to Mrs. Parker, was not to endure. She, for her part, wrote of him:

"Hemingway has an unerring sense of selection. He discards detail with a magnificent lavishness, he keeps his words to their short path. His is, as any reader knows, a dangerous influence. The simple thing he does looks so easy to do . . . he is clean . . . exciting. . . ." For once in her literary life she had found someone to look up to.

The trauma of her attempted suicide was now receding—or so it appeared. She rode the swell of more parties. One evening she was approached by a good-looking young man who, awed by her celebrity stature, nervously discoursed at length about people and their behavior at parties. "I simply can't bear fools," he exclaimed. "How odd," replied Mrs. Parker. "Your mother could."

A woman named Muriel King, who ran a dress shop at 49 East Fifty-first Street, knew her well at this time, since Mrs. Parker often bought clothes from her. "She was charming, darling—and loathsome," King later recalled. "No, not really loathsome, disappointing. When you thought you were friends, you didn't expect her to slap you down. She'd come in and ask, 'What did you do yesterday?' You'd tell her. Then she would say in a flat, bored voice, 'That is a very interesting story.' One felt totally deflated." But that, as her friends knew, was the way she was.

If confirmation were needed, Kitty Hart, wife of Moss Hart, a stage actress of the time who was to become a movie personality in the 1930s as Kitty Carlisle, confirmed to the venom of the lady. She told Joseph Bryan III of this incident:

> When Dottie realized she wasn't going to get a rise out of Moss, after persistently baiting him that Moss was not his real name, she came over and sat by me, sweet as sugarcane, and begged me to tell her about my debut on the stage. I should have known she was half-loaded, but I didn't, and I—little Miss Innocence—plunged ahead. It was in *Rio Rita*, I said, the title role, and the theater was the famous old Capitol, in New York. I was all wound up, describing the thrill of walking in the footsteps of the great stars who had played there, when she put her hand on my arm and breathed, "They made you do *that*? Oh, you poor *child*! That *huge* place, and all those people out front *staring* at you, waiting to *devour* you! Just to *think* of it makes my heart *ache*!"
>
> I said, "It wasn't that way at all! They were a marvelous audience, and I enjoyed every minute of it." Dottie said: "You don't have to pretend with *me*, dear. How *brave* you are! What a *brave* girl! Oh, I *admire* you so!" I can't swear there weren't tears in her eyes. I kept protesting that there'd been nothing for me to be brave about—that I'd absolutely loved it—but Dottie kept oozing sympathy and calling me, "You dear, brave *baby*!"—and then, suddenly, I woke up. She was putting me on, trying to see how much of her molasses I'd swallow. I felt like a *fool*!

She tried a similar technique on Bryan on the evening they first met. Mrs. Parker "dropped her lighter, which bounced under the sofa." Bryan recalls: "I had to kneel to reach it, and when I knelt, my knee joints popped and crackled. Dottie rubbed her hands together and spread them toward me. 'Ah', she beamed, 'there's nothing like an open fire!' "

One evening, at a particularly boisterous party, she was accosted by a woman who asked her: "Where on earth do all these people come from? And where do they go when they leave here?" Mrs. Parker looked vacantly across the assembly. "When it's all over," she said, "they crawl back into the woodwork."

Most of the time, she affected an air of ineffable boredom, particularly when admirers cornered her. At one party, someone observed that their hostess of the evening was "outspoken." "Outspoken," asked Mrs. Parker, "by whom?"

Neshobe Island continued to have an irresistible appeal for her. Her weekends quite often became extended by weeks, and when she tired of her hosts she would move on to other friends, usually displaying her familiar attitude of merciless boredom. At one such party on the Pennsylvania estate of George H. Lorimer, editor of the *Saturday Evening Post*, she asked him if she could send a wire to Robert Benchley. He agreed, and she wired:

PLEASE SEND ME A LOAF OF BREAD AND DON'T FORGET TO INCLUDE A SAW AND A FILE.

The text was repeated to Lorimer. She was never invited to his home again.

The swift, laconic swipe, delivered in a soft, clear sardonic voice accentuated by delicate, precise diction, was never far from the surface, as was evident at a Halloween party given by the Swopes on Long Island. Several of the Round Tablers were there helping to devise new versions of established party games. On Mrs. Parker's arrival, Swope told her they had invented a new version of the Halloween game "Ducking for Apples." She looked straight at him and said: "There, but for a typographical error, is the story of my life."

Despite her apparent boredom, her zest for parties and fun seemed insatiable. At this time, she was mixing a good deal with the Manhattan homosexual set who were usually evident at the town's theatrical parties. One night, all but over the top with rotgut gin, she climbed on to a balcony festooned with drapes and balloons, gaily brandishing a bottle of champagne. "Come and get me, boys," she called out. "I'm a man!"

Sometimes, in search of escape from her frenetic life, she would call on the frail, beautiful, yet volatile Elinor Wylie at her home on West Ninth Street off Fifth Avenue. Wylie's biography of Shelley had deeply impressed her; her poetry had impressed her even more. Wylie would encourage her to sit and work in a back room, amid a library full of books. It was a place which Mrs. Wylie allowed few to penetrate, still less to work. Benchley heard of her visits and encouraged her to go there more often.

This apart, she sardonically summed up the literary scene of the time with: "The two most beautiful words in the English language are 'check enclosed.' " But she knew better than most the private rigors of authorship and all the effort perfection entails: "If you are going to write," she said, "don't pretend to write it down. It's got to be the best you can do, and it's the fact that it is the best you can do that kills you."

This was the most prolific time of her life. She wrote ninety-one pieces for *Life*, sixty-three poems and twenty-eight squibs.

The longer prose continued to have a sardonic, clinical aloofness, her irony the point of a rapier, her wit the stinging lash of a whip. Contemptuous of married bliss, she sneered: "A man defending husbands versus wives, or men versus women, has got about as much chance as a traffic policeman trying to stop a mad dog by blowing two whistles."

She sank the matrimonial knife even deeper with: "Wives are people who get invited out somewhere and the husband asks if he ought to shave and they say 'No, you look all right.' And when they get to wherever they are going they ask everybody to 'Please forgive Luke as he didn't have time to shave.'" Wives, moreover, were the people "who think that when the telephone rings it is against the law to answer it."

Her distaste for the role of housewife may, of course, have had its origins in her own lack of success as a wife and domesticated woman. She admitted that she couldn't even boil water, much less cook a three-minute egg. Nonetheless, she continued to deride the ladies: "Wives are people whose watch is always a quarter-of-an-hour off . . . but they would have no idea what time it is, anyway, as daylight saving gets them all balled up." She appeared not to have much in common with her own sex.

Yet she could be charmingly feminine when she chose, particularly when surrounded by the predominantly masculine Round Table assembly. Once, rising tentatively from her chair at lunch, she sought their indulgence: "Excuse me," she said, "I have to go to the bathroom." This remark was followed by a short pause before she added, "I really have to telephone but I'm too embarrassed to say so."

She was seldom kind to women writers, particularly novelists, whom she described to James Thurber: "As artists, they're rot, but as providers they're oil wells—they gush . . ."

With MacArthur out of her life but not out of sight, for he still remained on the Algonquin scene, she began to hate even more the loneliness of her apartment. It was clear to her friends that she desperately needed a deep, emotional involvement, if only as a sacrifice to her familiar state of being in love with love.

When teased by the Round Tablers, she would reply with characteristic irony: "I require only three things of a man. He must be handsome,

ruthless and stupid." Was that an underlying truth or was she wearing
her customary mask?

Whatever the truth, she was now to test her tenets once again. She
was invited to call on Seward Collins, who was considered to be a catch
for any woman, literate or otherwise. He was a patron of the arts, whose
Virginian family had made millions from the sale of tobacco through a
large chain of retail shops. More important to Mrs. Parker was the fact
that he was the new owner of *The Bookman*, the distinguished publication which boasted the work of many of the best literary names. At lunch
with him, he commissioned her to write several articles for his magazine.
She liked the commission and she liked the man, and told Benchley of
her interest. "Go to it, Dottie," he said, "smoke him out!"

Mrs. Parker decided to go to it in her poem "The Whistling Girl," in
which she wrote some appropriate lines:

> Better be left by twenty dears
> Than lie in a loveless bed,
> Better a loaf that's wet with tears
> Than cold, unsalted bread.

By no stretch of the imagination was Mrs. Parker prepared to continue to lie on a loveless bed but she was, clearly, as bewildered as ever
about her inability to sustain a loving relationship, as she recorded in
another poem, "Conjecture":

> Into love and out again—
> So I went, and thus I go.
> Spare your voice and hold your pen—
> Well and bitterly I know
> All the songs were ever sung,
> All the words were ever said;
> Can it be, when I was young,
> Someone dropped me on my head?

· 1 8 ·

Smoke with Fire

WHEN not at Neshobe Island, the Algonquinites converged on the Swope mansion at Great Neck, by the Manhasset shoreline, frequently a replay of midweek festivities at Swope's glittering twenty-eight-room apartment on West Fifty-eighth Street in Manhattan. The much-traveled Herbert Bayard Swope, red-haired, long-legged and loud-voiced, at one time New York City's Racing Commissioner, evinced perfect joy at any prospect of a gamble, especially if it involved horses, croquet or pretty women.

Life at Great Neck was what Swope's wife, Margaret, described as "an almost continuous house party" and "an absolutely seething bordello of interesting people." Mrs. Swope was a woman acerbic in both manner and speech. Before a single guest drove up the dirt road, no less than sixteen servants had been housed to service the festivities. Indoor meals were taken in an ambience of spinach-green walls (painted by Elsie de Wolfe), Waterford crystal and George III silver candlesticks.

Before her marriage, Beatrice Ames had spent a weekend with the Swopes and had gratuitously given Margaret Swope's address as "Sourpuss, Great Neck, Long Island," which, to some, accurately summed up the hostess. Mrs. Swope had been particularly cold when a male guest had brought along a lady she considered to be of easy virtue. She told the young man, "Everybody who comes here must have a visible means of support." Of another female of questionable morals, whom Beatrice Ames thought to be "a charming woman but somewhat free with her body," Margaret Swope's tart comment was, "That's the only way she can dispose of it." Herbert Swope was executive editor of the New York World and a somewhat lordly but lasting and beneficent patron of the Round Table group, whom he thoroughly enjoyed entertaining at his mansion.

Close by lived Ralph Pulitzer, owner of the World. Also in the area were the Talbotts, with a huge estate, and Ring Lardner, one of the quieter members of the Vicious Circle, who had moved to Great Neck in 1921. Others who had impressive houses nearby were Fanny Brice, George M. Cohan, Laurette Taylor, Jane Cowl, Eddie Cantor and Ed Wynn, as well as Neysa McMein, who had just married Jack (Joe) Bar-

111

agwanath, a successful mining engineer. The marriage was as much a surprise to her many lovers as it was to the Algonquinites. Scott and Zelda Fitzgerald were also at Great Neck in a rented house. The Swope mansion was seldom silent when the owners were in residence. Swope boasted, "No one in my house goes to bed before 3:00 A.M." The Algonquinites often played croquet by hand-held flashlights on the lawn. "Jesus Christ," remarked Mrs. Parker on seeing this, "the heirs to the ages!"

A small army of servants provided a nonstop buffet of hot and cold food and an endless supply of drinks, "sometimes serving breakfast, lunch and dinner to various guests simultaneously." The plentiful supply of food and good liquor helped, as one put it, "to cement important connections with publishers and editors." Harold Guinzburg, founder of the Viking Press, was predominant among these. Faces frequently seen at the Swopes' included Charlie Chaplin, Alice Longworth, Raoul Fleischmann, Franklin Pierce Adams, Robert Sherwood, Edna Ferber, old Mrs. Cornelius Vanderbilt, Ruth Hale, Al Barach, Sonny and Marie Whitney, Nelson and Patty Doubleday, Birdie Vanderbilt, Peggy and Harold Talbott, Irving and Ellin Berlin, the Irish St. John Irvine, Harrison Williams (with or without Mona), Alicia Patterson, William Bolitho and Bernard Baruch.

Other frequent guests were Ethel Barrymore, Fanny Brice, Heywood Broun, Peggy Leech, Charlie Schwartz, Frank Case, Benchley, George and Beatrice Kaufman, Harpo Marx, Woollcott and, of course, Mrs. Parker. "At Swopes' you belonged," said Ruth Gordon. "If you didn't, you didn't get asked twice." Games predominated, and if the games were about words, so much the better. Predictably, Mrs. Parker was at the forefront of the word games. As Scott Meredith has recorded:

. . . the group derived considerable pleasure from trying to top one another with various kinds of play on words, and the more terrible the pun or joke the better. "I'd like to give you a sentence with the word 'punctilious,' " Kaufman told Frank Case. "I know a farmer who has two daughters, Lizzie and Tilly. Lizzie is all right, but you have no idea how punctilious." "If you are so smart," Frank Case countered, "give me a sentence with the word 'paraphernalia' in it." Kaufman thought for a while. "Well," he said, "I know a man who ate the wax cover off a jar of jelly. Can you guess what people asked him?"
"No?"
"They asked him, does that paraphernalia?" Case, in another rejoinder, told Kaufman that he, too, knew two sisters, two poor girls who were in a terrible quandary. "Their names are Bettina and Anna," Case said. "And I'm afraid they're Bettina devil Anna deep blue sea."

The gags grew more and more awful, with Adams adding to the horrors by wishing people a meretricious and a happy New Year.

It was Kaufman who came up with the perfect title for a play about Swope and his friends: *The Upper Depths*. Kaufman also posed an unexpected question when Charlie Chaplin remarked one day that his blood pressure was down to 108. "Common," Kaufman asked, "or preferred?"

It was, on the face of it, simple-minded stuff, but it honed the word-sense of Kaufman and his friends to a fine cutting edge and often gave magazines like *The New Yorker* more value for money than the contributors were receiving.

The camaraderie of Mrs. Parker, Benchley and Robert Sherwood was underscored when Benchley told them he had received an offer to work in Hollywood. Studio mogul Jesse L. Lasky had invited him to write additional dialogue and subtitles for a Paramount movie. Benchley discussed the offer with Parker and Sherwood. Their warm encouragement persuaded him to accept. But it wasn't a hard decision to make. He needed the money.

Donald Ogden Stewart had already left New York for Hollywood, where he was working for $250 a week on *Brown of Harvard*, a sort of *A Yank at Oxford* in reverse. Stewart planned to marry the young and beautiful Beatrice Ames and had sent a message to Benchley that he wanted him to be best man at the wedding. To help matters along, another of Benchley's chums, Laurence Stallings, was in Hollywood, too, writing a picture called *Old Ironsides*, and others like Herman Mankiewicz, John Weaver and Charlie Chaplin were also on assignments there, providing support to their visiting Algonquin friends.

Having been given a merry sendoff by Mrs. Parker, Sherwood and others of the group, Benchley traveled by train to Los Angeles. He'd hardly been there a day when he broke a leg negotiating a darkened porch, but he gamely played the role of best man to Stewart helped by splints and crutches.

It wasn't long before he was back in his familiar Fifth Avenue environs. The Avenue and its well-ordered blocks had long been the territory of the pacesetters of America. Not many years before it had been the mecca of the business tycoons, as well as artists and writers, who had contributed so much to the legend of Manhattan. The robber barons, with arcane stealth, had built their town palaces on and around the Avenue, sometimes with a tastelessness matched only by the outward swagger of their extrovert life-styles, which frequently displayed a wealth staggering in its enormity. Fifth Avenue was the thoroughfare where

Diamond Jim Brady had pedaled its length on a gold-plated bicycle encrusted with precious stones; where Edward VII of England, then Prince of Wales, had taken a trip on the world's first vertical railway, now identified as the common elevator; where, too, until the turn of the century, Jews and Catholics had been automatically banned from the Ward McAllister world of high society.

It was all markedly different now. But the Fifth Avenue environs to which Benchley now returned were still in many ways redolent of their wildly affluent origins. Many of the town palaces remained, converted now into stores and apartments, including the mansion of the traction king Charles T. Yerkes, who had kept both his respectable wife and his young and beautiful mistress, Emelie Grigsby, enclosed in the same sumptuously decorated building. Yerkes had manipulated stocks and shares to finance London's first underground travel system, at the same time enjoying and adding to his $4 million art collection, before his debt-ridden death.

Unlike Yerkes, Benchley, to whom Hollywood had tentatively beckoned, was devoted exclusively to the arts, and to writing in particular. But writing for Hollywood, he said, was another ballgame. He had done his job there with sober application but had found the ambience unconducive to his creativity. That wasn't precisely the way he put it, but his description amounted to the same thing: "Hollywood is seventy-two suburbs in search of a city."

Benchley booked into the Algonquin, planning to return to the family house at Scarsdale after he had finished writing some additional subtitles. With the proximity of Mrs. Parker and his fellow Round Tablers, however, he found life somewhat distracting there. One evening he sat down in his room to work, the typewriter in front of him. It contained a blank piece of paper. He typed the word "The", got writer's block, rose from his chair and paced round the room. He then rode the lift to the lobby. Sitting around in the lounge with assorted Round Tablers, he spent a couple of hours talking and drinking before returning to his room. Seated at the typewriter again, he stared at the solitary word for a long time. Other words would not come. In a fit of inspiration, he dashed off three more words to join the definite article: "The," it finally read, "hell with it!" He then descended once again to rejoin Mrs. Parker and her cohorts for an impromptu party that went on well into the small hours.

He told Mrs. Parker and Frank Case that he simply could not work at the hotel. Case became worried. Anxious to keep his celebrated guest happy, the hotel proprietor promised that he would arrange things so as to ensure that nobody was allowed in or near the Benchley rooms during working hours. "You might keep them from coming up, but you can't keep me from coming down," quipped Benchley.

In a further effort to impose some discipline into his working life, Benchley took a suite at the Royalton, a small hotel then almost opposite the Algonquin. While he and Mrs. Parker attempted to write a play there, Ernest Hemingway arrived, unheralded. Mrs. Parker's idol, it seemed, was en route for Spain. While Benchley and Parker were finishing off a scene, Hemingway browsed through the books on the coffee table until he came upon Mrs. Parker's copy of his own book, *Our Time.*

The copy was a heavily censored edition, evidencing the excision of some Anglo-Saxon expletives and other such words. These were indicated by gaps in the printed lines. Hemingway turned every page of the book, filling in the missing expletives and four-letter words. Before handing the book to Mrs. Parker, he wrote on the flyleaf: "Corrected edition with filled-in blanks. Very valuable copy—sell quick!" It became one of the few, very few, things Mrs. Parker was to treasure for the rest of her life.

On the eighth day of his sojourn at the Royalton, Benchley received an urgent call to return to Hollywood. Mrs. Parker agreed to take over the room for her own work. She would, she said, "hold the fort so long as I can drink with the Indians." It was, after all, just across the street from the Algonquin and it was in this room that she applied herself to writing her first pieces for *The Bookman.* It was from this room, too, that she applied her warpaint for a succession of intimate dinners with the publisher.

Work was all very well but Mrs. Parker was clearly becoming restless. Many of her friends were talking of the gay life in Paris and on the French Côte d'Azur. She needed a holiday, but there were the commitments of her work.

George Oppenheimer, who had by this time joined Boni and Liveright, had earlier commissioned her to prepare a slim volume of her verse for publication. It was now due to appear, and she decided to dedicate it to Elinor Wylie, "with love, gratitude and everything." The volume, *Enough Rope,* duly appeared, its title derived from Rabelais—"You shall never want rope enough . . ." The book, priced at $2, had, at her suggestion, a dangling noose on the front cover.

Within two weeks it was a bestseller. Unable to keep up with public demand, Boni and Liveright pumped out edition after edition. Henry Louis Mencken, enjoying his reputation as a literary journalist as well as co-editor of *Smart Set,* applauded *Enough Rope* in print, as did several of her Algonquin journalist pals. Edmund Wilson, a student of Catullus, described her verse as: "Extraordinarily vivid . . ." The literati fell over themselves to quote some of her best lines:

> Scratch a lover and find a foe.

> Women and elephants never forget.

> Inertia rides and riddles me
> The which is called philosophy.

> Woman wants monogamy,
> Man delights in novelty.

In "Epitaph for a Darling Lady," she revealed, some said, something of herself:

> All her hairs were yellow sands
> Blown in foolish whorls and tassels;
> Slipping warmly through her hands;
> Patted into little castles.

Her indifference showed in "Indian Summer":

> Now I know the things I know
> And do the things I do,
> And if you do not like me so
> To hell, my love, with you!

In "The Satin Dress" she sardonically inquired:

> Where's the man could ease a heart
> Like a satin gown?

And she became pensive in "Recurrence" with:

> Where unwilling, dies the rose
> Buds the new, another year.

And, of course, she remained insouciantly casual in "Faute de Mieux," almost to the point of ennui:

> Travel, trouble, music, art
> A kiss, a frock, a rhyme.
> I never said they feed my heart
> But still, they pass the time.

The New York Times waxed lyrical:

"In these verses, perfected with simplicity of words and fine craftsmanship, there is more than facility—there is an outspoken manner that explodes pretense sharply and turns its sorrow into mordant wit . . ."

Enough Rope was reprinted thirteen times and if Mrs. Parker could have been described as well-known before its publication, she was now more, much more, the literary celebrity. Some actually called her "The Mistress of Manhattan," which seemed to sum up her status in the literary scene.

The book illustrated the elliptical Dorothy Parker at her best: The droll, almost bored, prismatic author, immersed in a desire for beauty, in love with the lacerating stillness of death in life, and always sardonic in her cerebral exercises. She was the large-eyed lady who seemed to ignore love and affection while defying the world, her world, which appeared to be balanced on the edge of the ramparts of doom.

How did Mrs. Parker herself react to her renewed acclaim? "Glad of the money" was the way she put it. Certainly the money was now flowing in.

If her verse displayed traces of masochism, she knew that the masochism of mortals was as old as time. It was a habit more than just familiar to all, including the lady herself, who had studied classical literature. From Lycophron to Hippolytus; from Proust and Kafka on, masochism was usually there in plenty. Self-imposed flagellation of the mind, body and spirit was punishment habitually practiced by writers upon themselves.

George Oppenheimer had earlier described her as a masochist. Another who could be so termed had been introduced to the Algonquin set by Franklin Adams in 1922. His name was Ring Lardner, and he had a face that looked like a tidy grave.

Like Mrs. Parker and other Round Tablers, Lardner had early contributed to Adams's "Conning Tower" column. Mrs. Parker knew and had long respected Lardner's growing reputation. He had been thirty-seven when they had first met; she had been instantly intrigued by his tall, thin, cadaverous appearance. A man infinitely sad of spirit, he was also beset with self-loathing and deep, depressive tendencies—seemingly a soulmate to Mrs. Parker.

He had begun his career as a sports writer and had quickly made a name for himself with his dry, informed humor in his Chicago *Tribune* column, "Letters of a Bush-League Ball Player." His reputation had been cemented with the publication in book form of his short stories, starting with *You Know Me, Al*. Both Mencken and Edmund Wilson had acclaimed his work. He had become a master of the short story, proving himself skillfully adept at handling midwestern rural dialect in the Mark Twain tradition of folk humor—gentle, unassuming humor tinged with a strain of bitterness, irony and, frequently, despair. His literary reputation had grown out of the pressures involved in writing seven columns a

week for the *Tribune*. These he filled with monologues full of excruciat-
ing grammar in the dialogue of uneducated country types.

Ever since Adams had first brought him to lunch in 1922, Lardner
had become known to the Algonquinites as "The Quiet One." His sense
of humor was always acute. It was perfectly displayed when Heywood
Broun invited him to a Thanatopsis poker game, to which Lardner had
replied: "I can't make it tonight, Heywood. It's my little son's night out
and I've got to stay at home with the nurse." Seldom saying much, he
would occasionally give vent to such dry quips as: "Last night President
Harding and I attended *The Merry Widow*—but not together."

At the all-male Friar's Club dinner of show business personalities, a
fellow member asked Lardner to read aloud a confection in verse form,
which had been written by the man's brother who had died twenty years
earlier. Lardner complied, and when finished, he turned casually to the
man and asked, "Did your brother write it before or after he died?" On
another occasion Lardner had returned to the Algonquin after a meeting
with President Calvin Coolidge. He had, he said, told the President a
humorous story. "How did he respond?" asked Franklin Adams. "He
laughed until you could hear a pin drop," replied Lardner.

Mrs. Parker was fascinated by the man. His dark, impassive eyes
looked out from a face that was remarkably reminiscent of Buster Keaton, his high cheekbones accentuating a look of infinite sadness. Lardner
and Mrs. Parker shared quiet dinners together. Their favorite place was
Delmonico's, well known to the Algonquin group. Predictably, it wasn't
long before everybody knew of the affair. On the face of it, Lardner was
happily married to an attractive brunette, seemingly enjoying life with
her and their four sons in a spacious house in Great Neck, where Mrs.
Parker often spent her weekends, some of which stretched into weeks.

Being a lady of few words, Mrs. Parker had met her match. Lardner's
spare writing and laconic way of speaking were best illustrated in his
celebrated cryptic paragraph, "Shut up, he explained." Writer Corey
Ford described his first meeting with Lardner as "a brief, wordless encounter." Ford, like others, found him "solemn and unsmiling, yet curiously appealing." Certainly, Mrs. Parker found him just that. She was
honored when he asked her to approve a telegram he was sending to a
friend, which read: "When are you coming back and why?" and she
adored his story of an ex-coroner in St. Paul whose ode to his mother
included the line: "If perchance the inevitable should come . . ."

Few knew why, but one of the primary reasons Mrs. Parker spent so
much time at the Swope mansion on Long Island was that Lardner's
front lawn faced its entrance. Whether Mrs. Lardner knew of her hus-

band's affair with Dorothy Parker is not recorded, but since Mrs. Lardner was herself very much in the swing of the Algonquin group it is likely that she did. In any case, she did not mention it.

The affair lasted just short of six months.

Mrs. Parker's respect for Lardner, both as a writer and man, was considerable and perhaps it was predictable that she withdrew with grace from a somewhat graceless situation. It is known that Lardner was devoted to his family. It is therefore likely that Mrs. Parker's withdrawal was engendered by the sheer hoplessness of the situation in which she found herself.

We know that he told her that he was still in love with his wife and that nothing would persuade him to leave her and his family. But she and Lardner were to remain close friends right up to his death in 1933 at the age of 48, caused by heart failure brought on by excessive alcoholism, an end "when he had," said his friends, "closed his eyes for the last time with a half-smile of infinite relief."

Scott Fitzgerald, Lardner's close friend, said of him: "He is a proud, shy, solemn, shrewd, polite, brave, calm, kind, merciful, honorable man who has made no enemies . . ."

Mrs. Parker found respite from the aftermath of her love affair by the continuing success of *Enough Rope*. On the crest of that success, Harold Ross invited her to become literary critic of *The New Yorker* under the pseudonym of "Constant Reader." Love had come and gone again, but at least there was work to be done; she accepted Ross's invitation.

The New Yorker, now settled in after its near-catastrophic early months, had enlisted an enviable array of top journalists, editors and illustrators. These included E. B. White, James Thurber, Peter Arno, Wolcott Gibbs, Corey Ford, Ralph Ingersoll, James M. Cain, Russell Maloney, Benchley, Frank Sullivan, Sally Benson, Ogden Nash, Clarence Day, Katherine Angell, Sidney Perelman, John O'Hara, and Thorne Smith.

The lady was now keeping the best of company.

· 1 9 ·

"Constant Reader"

MRS. PARKER'S "Constant Reader" was to run in *The New Yorker* virtually every week from October 1927 through May 1928, and occasionally after that until 1933. It was a feature which, because of its power of wit, irony and often devastating dismissal, helped make some reputations, including her own, and frequently shattered others. In all, she was to contribute forty-six such pieces, in which she trenchantly dealt with books such as Katherine Mansfield's *Journals*, edited by J. Middleton Murry, the English critic who Mrs. Parker knew had been accused of exploiting his subject and her work. "It was the saddest book I have ever read," she observed. She went on to dissect *The Best Short Stories of 1927*, edited by Edward O'Brien—"Sedulous agony has become as monotonous as sedulous sunshine. Save for those occasions when you come upon [in its pages] a Hemingway or an Anderson or a Lardner in your reading, the other stories that meet your eye might all have come from the same pen. . . . "

She tackled direct and often full assessment of many well-known and not-so-well-known writers. In dealing with Miss or "Madame," as she called her, Elinor Glyn of the "It" syndrome, she said:

And this, ladies and gentlemen, is the finest day that has yet broken over the bloody and bowed head of your girl-friend. On this day there first fell into these trembling hands The Book, the Ultimate Book. There is grave doubt that I shall ever be able to talk of anything else. Certainly, I have read my last word. Print can hold for me now nothing but anticlimaxes. *It*, the chef d'oeuvre of Madame Elinor Glyn, has come into my life. And Sherman's coming into Atlanta is but a sneaking, tip-toe performance in comparison. I didn't know. Truly, I didn't know . . . I have read but little of Madame Glyn. I did not know that things like it were going on. I have misspent my days . . . Where, I ask you, have I been that no true word of Madame Glyn's literary feats has come to me?

Emily Post's *Etiquette* provided her with

the sweetly restful moment of chancing on a law which I need not bother to memorize, let come no matter what. It is in that section called "The Retort Courteous to One You Have Forgotten," although it took a deal of dragging to get it in under that head. "If," it runs, "after being introduced to you, Mr. Jones" (of course, it would be Mr. Jones that would do it) "calls you by a wrong name, you let it pass, at first, but if he persists you may say: 'If you please, my name is Stimson.'"

No, Mrs. Post; persistent though Mr. Jones may be, I may not say, "if you please, my name is Stimson." The most a lady may do is to give him the wrong telephone number.

Of actor Lou Tellegen's *Women Have Been Kind:* "Mr. Lou Tellegen has recently seen fit to write his memoirs . . . it is at least debatable that it would have been more public-spirited of him to have sent the results to the zoo. . . . "

Tackling her review of Aimee Semple McPherson's autobiography, *In the Service of The King,* headed "Our Lady of the Loudspeaker," Mrs. Parker showed her teeth again: "Her [writing] manner takes on the thick bloom of rich red plush . . . With the publication of this, her book, Aimee Semple McPherson has replaced Elsie Dinsmore [the put-upon heroine of twenty-six books for girls by Martha Finley] as my favorite character in fiction."

She headed her review of Dashiell Hammett's *The Glass Key* with "Oh, Look—a Good Book!" and prefaced her assessment of *The Ideal System for Acquiring a Practical Knowledge of French,* by a Mlle. Valentine Debacq Gaudel, with the heading "The Grandmother of the Aunt of the Gardener," going in for the kill with "How am I not to be bitter, who have stumbled solo about Europe, equipped only with 'Non, non et non!' and 'Où est le lavabo des dames?' "

Dealing with Anne Parrish's new novel *All Kneeling,* Mrs. Parker ended her review with: "It is true that the book is occasionally overwritten, that certain points are hammered too heavily. But, as I was saying to the landlord only this morning, you can't have everything. . . . "

Reviewing Tiffany Thayer, who attained wide notoriety and record sales for his sex novels, including his "very own" version of *The Three Musketeers,* Mrs. Parker wasn't impressed with his *An American Girl:* "I am at a loss to comprehend," she wrote, "why this was the selected title, since the book displays any number of American girls, all alike in seeming to be, as Henry James said of Georges Sand, highly accessible . . . he might care to change his present rather pastel title to the possibly more provocative *I Am a Fugitive from a Daisy Chain Gang.*"

As for Mabel Dodge Luhan's *Background,* the first book in a planned series to comprise the author's *Intimate Memories,* "It may be in her forthcoming volumes, when she gets into her stride of marrying people, things will liven up a bit. But *Background* is to me as dull, and with that same stuffy, oppressive, plush-thick dullness, as an album of old snap-shots of somebody else's family group. . . . "

Mrs. Parker had her favorites of course: Hemingway, Lardner, George Jean Nathan and Fitzgerald among them. They were, in-terestingly, either friends of hers or friends of friends, which is not to say that she was unduly influenced by such although, like most of the journalists of the Round Table, she could not escape the accusation of log-rolling. People read her column, however, because they expected—and usually got—trim, well-honed syntax and frequently amusing word constructions that made them either think, laugh or admire her gift of literary satire exercised at the expense of book, author or both.

Her readers knew, of course, that A. A. Milne, Sinclair Lewis and others would inevitably be burned at the stake by her dismissive sarcasm, the very content of their books crying out for roasting. And an author like Nan Britton, who dared to write a book with the title *The President's Daughter*, subtitled *Revealing the Love-Secret of President Harding*. Miss Britton, according to Mrs. Parker, was "one who kisses, among other things, and tells." It seems the author wrote her book "solely as a plea for more civilized laws affecting the standing of the children of unmar-ried mothers," which was rather asking for Mrs. Parker's whiplash. "Maybe she did," suggested Mrs. Parker. "And maybe the writer of *Only a Boy* set down that tale just for the purpose of arousing interest in bigger and better crèches . . . "

No matter, let "Constant Reader" get into her stride with the Presi-dent and his mistress. "Throughout her book, Miss Britton protests, perhaps a shade too much, that she and President Harding bore each other a love which she insists, in a phrase that I am fairly sure I have seen before some place, could not have been greater had they been joined together by fifty ministers; yet they seem to have been, at best, a road-company Paolo and Francesca. Theirs is the tale of as buckeye a romance as you will find. It is, and a hundred percent, an American comedy."

Miss Britton went on to tell of the President tucking thirty dollars in her brand new silk stockings. She told, too, "about that afternoon when the house detective put them firmly though gently out of an hotel room, despite the President's plea that they weren't disturbing any of the other guests." "Gee, Nan," recorded Mrs. Parker in a repetition of the Presi-dent's dialogue, "I thought I wouldn't get out of that under a thousand dollars."

"One can but feel," Mrs. Parker wrote, "after several of these anecdotes, that Miss Britton was doing admirably to get that thirty dollars tucked into her stocking."

The Counterfeiters, a novel by André Gide, the French intellectual who won a Nobel Prize for Literature, was so heavily publicized that Mrs. Parker did not need to mention the author's name in her review, but uncharacteristically declared: "To say of it 'Here is a magnificent novel' is rather like gazing into the Grand Canyon and remarking, 'Well, well, well; quite a slice.' Doubtless you have heard that this book is not pleasant. Neither, for that matter, is the Atlantic Ocean."

Fannie Hurst, an established writer since the success of her two earlier novels, *Humoresque* and *Lummox*, had written another novel called *A President Is Born*. "No," protested Mrs. Parker, "it is not a companion piece to the Nan Britton book. I have a deep admiration for Miss Hurst's work. Possibly in your company I must admit this with a coo of deprecating laughter as one confesses a fondness for comic-strips and . . . chocolate almond bars . . . This, they say, is her Big Novel . . . I can find in it no character nor any thought to touch or excite me."

She intensely disliked Ford Madox Ford's *The Last Post*, ending her review with: "And now this review is over, do you mind if I talk business for a moment? If you yourself haven't any spare jobs for a retired book-reviewer, maybe some friend of yours might have something. Maybe you wouldn't mind asking around. Salary is no object. I want only enough to keep body and soul apart. The one thing I ask is that I have an occasional bit of time to myself. I want to read the papers."

She had again used her quip about keeping body and soul apart to good effect, having first used it when discussing salary on joining *Vanity Fair*. And, too, the retired book-reviewer plea contains much of the essence of Benchley's appeal when, years after it happened, he revived Mrs. Parker's sacking by Crowninshield in print.

Mrs. Parker was now to take on a doctor, Thew Right, A.B., M.D., F.A.C.S., who had written a book called *Appendicitis*, a popular treatise that the author hoped would bring an understanding of the malady to the laity. Commented "Constant Reader": "For who that has stood bareheaded and beheld the peritonium by moonlight can gaze unmoved by its likeness? It is really terribly hard to keep from remarking, after studying 'the fascinatingly anatomical illustrations,' . . . 'That was no laity; that's my wife.' It is hard, but I'll do it if it kills me," she wrote. "Only once did I dash sleep from lids. That was at the section having to do with the love-life of poisonous bacteria. That, says the author, is very simple and consists merely of the bacterium dividing into two equal parts. Think of it," pleaded Mrs. Parker, "no quarrels, no lies, no importunate telegrams, no unanswered letters. Just peace and sunshine and quiet evenings around the lamp. Probably bacteria sleep like logs. Why shouldn't they? What is Spring to them?"

The flippancy and waspishness of Mrs. Parker's reviews appeared to know no bounds. The perceptive reader knew, of course, that reading her was an exercise in obliquitous burlesque with words; it was satire saturated with sass, and that was what the customers seemed to want, and if that is what they wanted she surely was going to give it to them. The sensibility of conventional literary assessment was not part of the game as such. The game was played, in fact, using an easy dexterity of her chosen words combined with an irritation, if not an exasperation, with anybody who chose to write books. To Parker, acerbity was the pivot and the point of her work.

As she had written of Hemingway, "The simple thing . . . looks so easy to do. But look at the boys who try to do it." She might also have included the girls.

· 2 0 ·

Sounds of the Sea

ALTHOUGH HER WRITING implied she was well traveled and urbane, Mrs. Parker, while certainly the latter, was remarkably untraveled for a woman of her distinction. The only frontier she had ever crossed was the line between America and Canada. But now her travels were about to begin.

The Stewart-Ames wedding in Hollywood had been a glamorous affair, with newsreels covering the arrival of celebrities outside the chapel at Montecito. A couple of weeks after the champagne reception, the Stewarts boarded the *Twentieth-Century Limited* to Chicago, traveling on to New York, where they were to meet up with Seward Collins, Mr. Benchley and Mrs. Parker, before boarding the S.S. *Roma* en route for the south of France. Stewart had arranged for Collins, Benchley and Parker to be the guests of his longtime friends Gerald and Sara Murphy, at their elegant Villa America at Cap d'Antibes. It was to become in the memory of most of them "the golden summer of 1926."

Besides being a much-needed holiday, the trip held an added excitement for Mrs. Parker. Ernest Hemingway had also been invited to stay with the Murphys, as had Scott and Zelda Fitzgerald, the Gilbert Seldes, and Ada and Archibald MacLeish. Murphy had known Stewart and Hemingway in Paris back in 1924. Like them, he was good-looking and his wife, Sara, was benignly beautiful. The couple was wealthy: she was heiress to a considerable fortune, while Gerald had inherited the well-known leather goods firm, Mark Cross, which had made Gerald a millionaire several times over.

Murphy had studied architecture at Yale, where he had been a close friend of Cole Porter. Afterwards, he established himself in Paris with the idea of becoming a painter, and began studying with Léger, largely abandoning his business life. His wealth had provided him with an apartment on the Quai des Grands-Augustins that displayed a considerable tribute to his good taste: Aubusson carpets, Sèvres china, exquisite silver and a valuable collection of post-Impressionist paintings by Léger, Bonnard, Vuillard, Braque and Picasso, several bought through his friendship with those artists.

In the early 1920s, Gerald had written a ballet, *Within the Quota*, with Cole Porter. With the libretto, costumes and scenery by himself, and the music by Porter, the ballet had been presented in 1923 by the Ballet Suédois at the Théâtre des Champs-Elysées to poor reviews.

Donald Ogden Stewart described the Murphys and their life-style:

Gerald Murphy . . . was intelligent, perceptive, gracious, and one of the most attractive men I have ever known. His wife Sara was the perfect complement to these virtues. If this sounds like a child's fable beginning "Once upon a time" . . . that's exactly how a description of the Murphys should begin.

They were both rich; he was handsome, she was beautiful; they had three golden children. They loved each other, they enjoyed their own company, and they had the gift of making life enchantingly pleasurable for those who were fortunate enough to be their friends . . . They had an apartment overlooking the Seine near the Place St. Michel.

When they entertained at home their guests might include Picasso or Léger, Cole Porter or Douglas Fairbanks, or some struggling young artists they happened to like . . . They gave a party for the entire corps of the Diaghilev ballet, and rented a Seine river steamer one evening for another of their galas.

With Sara and Gerald I came closest to enjoying what might be termed "gracious living." It was a closed circle, it was privileged, but within those narrow limits it was immensely stimulating. . . .

As Fitzgerald observed at the time, "Gerald Murphy was not rich, he was *very* rich," and apart from playing host to American writers and artists in Paris and on the Côte d'Azur, his importation of American culture also extended to bringing Harlem jazz as well as Negro spiritual music to Antibes.

The Murphys were enchanted by Dorothy Parker. When she arrived at Antibes, she was given a cottage, La Bastide (small country house), in which to work. But life that sultry summer was to include precious little work for Parker.

There were lazy, sun-drenched days on the beach at the Hôtel du Cap; a never-ending succession of dinner parties at quayside restaurants at Villefranche and soirees on the terrace of the Carlton Hotel, in Cannes; outings to Frank Harris's flat on Cimiez Hill; gourmet excursions to Grasse, Mougins and Menton; and repeated repasts at an enchanting restaurant not far from the railway arch at La Napoule, where Oscar Wilde had supped secretly with Lord Alfred Douglas.

The south of France that summer was full of celebrities. Woollcott had taken the Villa Ganelon nearby and was lavishly entertaining Somerset Maugham, Harpo Marx and Cornelia Otis Skinner, while in other villas and hotels Grace Moore, Edmund Wilson, Charlie Chaplin, Paulette Goddard, Lady Mendl, the Moisewitzes, Mary Hopkins Joyce,

Joan Bennett and the Fredric Marches entertained and were entertained from dusk to daylight. Cole Porter, in his stately ivy-covered villa at La Garoupe, high above the beach looking across Angel's Bay, gave elegant parties where good taste united with high living. When Bernard and Mrs. Shaw arrived, the only person Shaw asked to meet was Dorothy Parker. After their introduction, he turned to Woollcott and said, "I'd always thought of her as an old maid."

The expansive Elsa Maxwell, diamonds flashing like harbor lights, was entertaining a galaxy of names on the same stretch of coast, including Irene Castle, Sidney Lejon, Gertie Sanford, actress-writer Ruth Gordon, and Daisy Fellowes, of the Singer sewing machine fortune. The latter, who boasted two yachts, a string of lovers and no humor, told Woollcott: "You people are all so talented. You write or dance or sing or act. But I do *nossing*." Woollcott, sipping his fruit cup, quietly observed, "My dear, I have heard different."

The Murphys held festive boards at the exclusive La Réserve in Beaulieu, and with their guests played the tables at the Monte Carlo Casino when not being entertained on yachts owned by other friends. There were trips up the coast to Amalfi, Naples and across to Capri, and lunches on the Iles de Lérin. There were visits to Maugham's Villa Mauresque, with the Arabic symbol of the Evil Eye glowering down over the front entrance.

It was all quite glittering and glamorous. Mrs. Parker, however, was having a disturbing time trying to equate the gilded, golden-coast life-style with her Socialist conscience and convictions. And, as her friends knew, she was not winning. Frequently in her cups, she became greatly intrigued by Woollcott's relationship with Harpo Marx, who was the very antithesis of him in both stature and bearing. Everybody knew Harpo to be shrewd but illiterate. The journalist and the comic made an unlikely pair but it was plain for all to see that Woollcott cherished Harpo. Mrs. Parker mischievously related to Edmund Wilson that Woollcott had been told by a Jungian psychiatrist that he was in love with Harpo. It was, he said, a downright lie but Mrs. Parker was convinced that it was true.

The sybaritic life on the Côte d'Azur that summer was not all it seemed. Scott and Zelda Fitzgerald spent many nights fighting it out in their rooms, she accusing him of ogling the women. And Hemingway didn't help when at a Villefranche party he told Zelda that he thought she was mad. James Thurber, who had taken a temporary post on a Riviera newspaper to help subsidize his stay, observed inconsequentially that only Gertrude Stein and Alice B. Toklas were missing, and wasn't that good?

Certainly Thurber's observation summarized the hedonism of that summer. It seemed that the New York social scene, augmented by America's show business elite, had moved itself en masse to the stretch of the Mediterranean coast from St. Raphael to Menton. Americans mingled agreeably with Europeans in the villas, hotels, yachts, casinos, restaurants and bars in Monte Carlo, Cannes, Nice, St. Jean-Cap Ferrat, Mougins, Grasse, St. Tropez, Beaulieu, Juan-les-Pins. Early in the season, ships and trains brought in Rudolph Valentino, Mistinguett, John Dos Passos, Alice Terry, Maud Kahn, playwright Philip Barry, screenwriter and author Charles Brackett and his wife Margerite Namara, thriller writer E. Phillips Oppenheim, the violinist David Mannes, Floyd Dell, Max and Chrystal Eastman, Etienne de Baumont, actress Isadora Duncan, journalist Charles MacArthur, socialite Chato Elizaga, and scores of others. The place was alive with gossip and stories; it was a newspaper columnist's paradise.

The best story of the season, it was claimed, occurred at a farewell party given for Woollcott and Elizaga. After a number of meaningless toasts, Zelda Fitzgerald got up unsteadily and cried: "I have been so touched by all these kind words. But what are words? Nobody has offered our departing heroes any gifts to take with them. I'll start off." She then pulled up her dress and stepped trimly out of her black lace panties, throwing them at the feet of Woollcott and Elizaga. It was a gesture calculated to inflame the simmering anger of her husband, a defiant insult to Scott and his warring alcoholism, another gesture of her enveloping schizophrenia.

Zelda had earlier insulted Isadora Duncan when it became clear that the actress had selected Scott as a bed companion. After the fracas, Zelda had thrown herself down a long flight of stairs and, at the bottom, had laid prone in the road in front of a car, daring the driver to run over her.

For his part, Scott Fitzgerald was at his worst that summer, primarily because of Zelda's irritating presence. As a group of them emerged woozily from a dimmed restaurant in Antibes late one sunny afternoon, Fitzgerald knocked over a street vendor's elaborate display of nuts. He did this deliberately and for some reason found it immensely funny. No one else did. "Look, wasn't that funny?" he kept repeating to blank reactions. Finally he gave the vendor a 500-franc note as if to make up for his foolishness. "There," he said to the others. "I've given him 500 francs. Wasn't that funny?" The others, embarrassed, turned away while Fitzgerald kept repeating and repeating, "Wasn't that funny, old sport, wasn't that . . . "

If Fitzgerald was unsure of himself in the company of his friends, no such uncertainty was apparent in his admiration of Dorothy Parker or her work. He wrote to Max Perkins, his editor at Scribner's, urging him to sign her to a contract. "She is," he wrote, " . . . at a high point as a producer and as to reputation. I wouldn't lose any time about this if it interests you. . . . " Perkins did not pursue the suggestion.

The two-storey Villa America, with its elegant sun-roof and checkered marble terrace, was not only to become the setting for a Hemingway recollection and Fitzgerald's *Tender Is the Night*; it was also to be used as the background for Philip Barry's play *Hotel Universe*, in which the playwright drew the character of Lily Malone, a girl who was "able to impart to her small, impudent face a certain prettiness." The character was based on Mrs. Parker.

One evening, when Mrs. Parker had not been present at a party at the MacLeishes, Hemingway had acidly toasted her in absentia with: "Here's to Dorothy Parker. Life will never become her so much as her almost leaving it," a cutting reference to her suicide attempts.

As for Mrs. Parker and her current paramour, Seward Collins, whom Benchley thought in many ways resembled Eddie Parker, she was becoming increasingly tetchy in his company. Her irritation at what she considered to be Collins's somewhat gauche behavior was at first confined to small things—when he meekly remonstrated with a waiter or when he moved his chair to be close to her. Collins, the embodiment of the traditional wealthy, upright young scion of an upper-class American family, appeared to be uneasy in her company, yet it was plain for all to see that he adored her. Stewart thought the cause of her testiness was sexual frustration. Whatever it was, she grew more and more spiky towards him and the Murphys were perceptive enough to arrange place settings so that the two were usually not seated together.

Worse for Dorothy, Benchley received a cable from Hollywood requesting his return there, interrupting his vacation much to his—and her—annoyance.

Mrs. Parker's prickly relationship with Collins finally drove her to seek refuge in her work. She asked the Murphys to lock her in her rooms so that she could write undisturbed. They did so, but each time she got drunk and fell asleep.

Towards the end of the summer many of the guests were finding that the "unadulterated gaiety" was slowly turning into a living nightmare. Like Father Schwartz, the mad priest in Scott's story "Absolution" who, as Professor Mizener was later to put it, "had found the distant prospect of the world's fair so enchanting," several of them had discovered that if you had ventured too close to the scene, "you felt only the heat and the sweat of life," and it wasn't pleasant. But, as Fitzgerald himself was later to put it: "It was the summer of a thousand parties," a summer of song. Indeed, the hand-cranked gramophones ceaselessly echoed to the current French and German hit tunes and to America's "Pardon Me, Pretty Baby (Is it Yes, Is it No, Is it Maybe?)," "In a Little Spanish Town," "What Can I Say, Dear, After I Say I'm Sorry?" "Always," "Remember," and "All Alone."

Hemingway, who had by now left for Spain, wired some of the Murphy guests to join him there. Mrs. Parker, having been told of his toast to her, at first chose to ignore the invitation. Then she changed her mind. Hemingway, after all, was her god, and gods had to be forgiven all things. Seward Collins, too, was eager to go. Indeed, he offered to underwrite the entire trip if Gilbert Seldes, then writing his *Seven Lively Arts*, and his pregnant wife would go along with them.

The four arrived in Spain. Hemingway had arranged for them to participate in the Fiesta of San Fermín and the running of the bulls in the streets of Pamplona; he had also bought them tickets for a bullfight. As far as the hysterical dash with the almost demented bulls through the Pamplona streets was concerned, this was not Mrs. Parker's idea of fun. And when the bullfight became too gory, as it did, she ran from the enclosure and was later found crying outside the stadium.

A few days later, Gerald Murphy called the party and invited them to his apartment in Paris. By the time they got there, Mrs. Parker and Collins were openly quarreling. She had become sullen and moody and was drinking heavily. Seldes had a theory that it was her contempt for the rich that was upsetting her, and she was taking it out on Collins. Others said it was her attitude of mind—"I loved them until they loved me."

After yet another party at the Murphy's apartment, Mrs. Parker and Seward Collins returned to their quarters at five o'clock in the morning. A blazing row ensued. Collins did not bother to go to bed in the suite he was sharing with her; he packed his bags in total silence and left. A few hours later, Dorothy packed her bags and left to rejoin the honeymooning Stewarts on the Riviera, by which time Seward Collins was en route back to America—alone.

Rudolph Valentino had left the Riviera to return to New York, feeling quite ill. Now, towards the end of that same season, the Côte d'Azur hardly reacted to the news that Valentino had died in the Polyclinic Hospital back in Manhattan, thus plunging millions of people all over the world into deep mourning.

After all, there were still lots of parties to come. The Americans were betting furiously on the outcome of the imminent Jack Dempsey–Gene Tunney fight at Madison Square Garden. It was no time for tears, anyone's tears. Not even Mrs. Parker's.

· 2 1 ·

"Oh, God, These People
Bore Me..."

DOROTHY PARKER'S FRIENDS were not altogether surprised at her split with Seward Collins. There was one who, mimicking Brecht, whispered, "What happens to the hole when the cheese is gone?" It was a good question and no one except Mrs. Parker knew the answer.

Collins's adoration for her had been more than evident in New York, on the Riviera and, to some extent, in Paris. What, then, had really gone wrong?

It was known that after displays of her temper, he had needlessly apologized to her in order to keep the peace. She, in turn, had declared her disgust at his meek apologies. Perhaps *that* was what had been wrong? Her friends agreed that she needed a dominant man in her life. Collins, to put it simply, had not been a dominant type; he had been merely an adoring and often a compliant lover.

According to Donald Ogden Stewart, on top of his remark about Mrs. Parker's suicidal tendencies, Hemingway had also related "a viciously unfair and unfunny poem"—a rhyming dirty joke—at her expense which, too, had reached her ears, but still the bearded writer could do no wrong in her eyes. He even accused her of not returning the portable typewriter he had lent her, which, in fact, she had.

The trip then had not been altogether a happy one for Mrs. Parker. But for one or two of her friends something positive had come out of it. Scott Fitzgerald was to enshrine the Murphys as Dick Diver and his wife, a rather pitiful couple, in *Tender Is the Night*, and was himself to receive a slighting reference as "that man Scott" in the pages of *The Snows of Kilimanjaro*. Hemingway was to accord his Riviera hosts a grudging kind of immortality in the pages of *A Moveable Feast*.

Dorothy Parker was not among those whom Hemingway would deal with in print, although he had written the ugly poem about her that was to end his close friendship with the Stewarts. Had he portrayed Mrs. Parker unsympathetically as a character in one of his books, she would not have minded or, if she had, she would certainly not have shown her resentment to others. She worshiped his talent which, in her view, provided the best excuse for his sometimes insufferable behavior. She knew, Stewart said, the truth of Jung's dictum: "Great talents are the most lovely and often the most dangerous fruits on the tree of humanity. They hang upon the most slender twigs that are easily snapped off." But there were those who swore that Hemingway resented Dorothy Parker's celebrity status, which, he said more than once, was based on "puerile journalism."

Sherwood swore that Dorothy Parker was in love with Hemingway. If this were so, Hemingway himself was indifferent towards her. He was married, anyway, and was transparently in love with his work if not his wife.

If there had been bad feeling between herself and Seward Collins, or suppressed annoyance at Hemingway, in time the vacation in France produced its benefits for her, too. It had broadened her horizons and she had met and become close friends with the civilized Murphys, who were to visit her and Benchley in New York the next year.

Meanwhile, plaudits for her verse flowed in. She was described in *Poetry* magazine as part of a celebrity class with "the Theatre Guild, Gramercy Park, H. L. Mencken and the Prince of Wales." This was heady stuff, but she was already abreast of the tide. In "Philosophy," part of *Enough Rope*, she explained her attitude towards fame:

> If I should labor through daylight and dark,
> Consecrate, valorous, serious, true,
> Then on the world I may blazon my mark;
> And what if I don't, and what if I do?

And predictably, she rose above those who criticized her behavior towards the clean, adoring figure of Seward Collins. For had she not already written, in "Prophetic Soul":

> Because your eyes are slant and slow,
> Because your hair is sweet to touch,
> My heart is high again; but oh,
> I doubt if this will get me much . . .

Little, indeed, it had gotten her.

In New York, Neysa McMein's finished portrait of her was being exhibited. It turned out to be an image of fine sensibility. Now, on her return to Manhattan, here was the celebrated G. T Hartmann, a painter of considerable renown, asking her to sit for him as he produced a full-page illustration of her in *Arts and Decoration*. This accomplished, the portrait proved immensely disappointing to her. In it she was represented as the archetypal sullen, bitter, city woman with a selfish and cynical look. Hartmann had captured the dark side of the lady, and Mrs. Parker did not approve of this kind of truth.

Yet, she probed for the truth in others. On meeting people, she invariably would take them, drink in hand, to a corner and question them on the most intimate details of their lives. With the force of her riveting gaze, she would convince the victim of her undivided attention. After the person had exposed his or her innermost secrets, Parker would join other friends, the person then becoming the object of a Parkerian catechism of insult. She would finally evict the entire assembly with a remark like, "Oh, God, these people bore me. How they bore me. . . . "

And more often than not, people *did* bore her, especially those who seemed to be her intellectual inferiors. Yet, inexplicably, she could produce almost a torrent of tears when told of some wretched injustice affecting those of a social order lower than her own. She was a walking, talking, thinking, dreaming succession of paradoxes.

Early one day in 1928, the telephone rang in her apartment. Answering it, she learned that her application for divorce from Edwin Pond Parker II had been listed for March 31. She went to Hartford alone that day, testifying before the court to Eddie's cruelty. She won her divorce. That night, she went out with Benchley, drinking into the early morning.

In her work for *The New Yorker*, Mrs. Parker had found a niche for her talents as literary reviewer. America pretended it did not know for certain that the pseudonym of "Constant Reader" hid the one-time Dorothy Rothschild, now elegantly grown up as Dorothy Parker. People argued about her. But of course America *did* know. Everybody knew and everybody talked about her. Benchley was now getting more work in Hollywood and Mrs. Parker was asked to stand in for him as theater critic during his absences. She began by assessing the work of playwrights like J. M. Barrie, Rudolf Besier, he of *The Barretts of Wimpole Street*, William Doyle and Bernard Shaw. Predictably, many of the authors did not emerge too well from their Parkerian pawing.

New Yorker editor Ross admired Parker, but was suspicious of her. Years later, James Thurber recalled that Ross had said at the time:

"You've got to watch Woollcott . . . and Parker . . . they keep trying to get double meanings into their stuff to embarrass me." As a result he begged Thurber: "Question everything they write. We damn near printed a story about a girl falling off a roof. That's feminine hygiene; somebody told me just in time. You probably never heard the expression in Ohio," whence Thurber had come. Thurber replied: "In Ohio, we say the mirror cracked from side to side. . . . " "I don't want to hear about it," said Ross, prudishly.

Meanwhile, Dorothy Parker did little to soothe Ross's threatened ulcers with metaphors such as "like shot through a goose."

While the magazine was constantly improving with its distinguished team of writers and illustrators, which now also included Elmer Davies and Gluyas Williams, financially it was still not quite out of the woods. And Mrs. Parker clearly knew this. Thurber also remembered:

"One evening during that summer of Harold Ross's greatest discontent, the harried editor ran into Dorothy Parker somewhere. 'I thought you were coming into the office to write a piece last week,' he said. 'What happened?' Mrs. Parker turned upon him the eloquent magic of her dark and lovely eyes. 'Somebody was using the pencil,' she explained sorrowfully."

Now, in one of her stand-in reviews, she displayed sardonic agitation for her old and dear friend Robert Benchley, to which she added a postscript: "Personal. Robert Benchley please come home. Nothing is forgiven." And there was the matter of A. A. Milne's play *Success*, whose title had been changed to *Give Me Yesterday*. After a devastating review, she explained:

"Now I have gone into this opus at such dreary length not only out of masochism, but from bewilderment . . . Ladies and gentlemen, I have told you the tale of the play they saw. My case rests. If *Give Me Yesterday* is a fine play, I am Richard Brinsley Sheridan," to which she added yet another postscript appeal: "Personal. Robert Benchley *please* come home. Whimso [meaning Milne] is back again."

She continued to write articles and essays for a number of magazines, including *Vanity Fair*, on subjects as varied as Films; Life in Summer Resorts; Deadly Suitors; Is Your Little Girl Safe?; Dogs; The Arrival of Spring in New York; and biographical pieces on some of her friends, including "A Valentine for Mr. Woollcott!" whom she did not particularly care for but found amusing and thus tolerable.

She was also exacting in her demands of the professional writer. In a review of a book by Theodore Dreiser, she advised: "It is the first job of the writer who demands rating among the good, to write well."

Regarding herself, she did not think she wrote well at all. Was the reason for her disenchantment with her own writing to be found in her deep admiration of Katherine Mansfield, at that time incarcerated in a tower-abode next door to D.H. Lawrence and Frieda at Zennor in Cornwall? She may, as Kinney has hinted, have thought of herself in terms she applied to Mansfield:

"She was not of the little breed of the discontented; she was of the high few fated to be ever unsatisfied. Writing was the precious thing in life to her, but she was never truly pleased with anything she had written. With a sort of fierce austerity, she strove for the crystal clearness, the hard, bright purity from which, she considered, streams perfect truth. She never felt that she had attained them."

That, to her friends, sounded like the precise persona of Mrs. Dorothy Parker: the lady was showing her slip again.

· 2 2 ·

A Trinity of Men

MRS. PARKER'S FASTIDIOUSNESS for the purity and purpose of the written word was shared not only by Hemingway, who saw little of her now, but more particularly by Scott Fitzgerald, who grew increasingly close to her.

Zelda was becoming obsessed by the fantasy of her future as a ballerina, while her husband was playing fast and loose with other women. He had recently ended an affair with an English actress, an elfin-like beauty named Rosalinde Fuller, who had played Ophelia to John Barrymore's Hamlet in the New York production of 1922. A friend of Charles Chaplin, Edmund Wilson and Aleck Woollcott, she had met Fitzgerald at a party at the Plaza and had been whisked off by him in a fiacre stationed outside. The couple had disappeared for a couple of days. Now, Fitzgerald turned his attention to Mrs. Parker, the literary purist who shared his devotion to language and addiction to love.

His affair with Mrs. Parker was also surprisingly short—a week or two —but, according to him, "ecstatically sweet." Fitzgerald could not bask in another's glory, and living in the mental turmoil of his private Styx did not help matters. The two emerged from the frenzy of their affair without regrets, and Mrs. Parker was to remain his friend until the end of his life.

Dorothy returned to her pen with gusto. Reviewing Katharine Hepburn in a wispish play called *The Lake*, she treated the star to dismissive contempt: "Miss Hepburn," she wrote, "ran the whole gamut of emotions from A to B," an assessment that was to echo round the party circuit.

Years later, in 1970, Garson Kanin was to write of this critical roasting of his friend in a piece of what seems to be inaccurate reporting in his book *Tracy and Hepburn*. He remembered:

It was in the lobby of the Martin Beck Theater, during the first intermission of a performance of *The Lake*, that Dorothy Parker made one of her most celebrated remarks . . . Somebody said to Mrs. Parker, "Kate's wonderful, isn't she?" "Oh, yes," agreed Mrs. Parker. "She runs the gamut of emotion all the way from A to B."

The crack is remembered better than the play.

It should be noted that by this time Mrs. Parker had married Alan Campbell, who had been one of Kate's many beaux.

Some years later, I was working on a film with Dorothy Parker [presumably, Kanin's own story, *The Good Soup*]. In the course of a casting discussion, she began to sell Katharine Hepburn. I was astonished.

"I thought you didn't like her," I said.

Those great brown eyes became greater and browner.

"Me?" said Dottie. "I don't think there's a finer actress anywhere."

"But what about all the way from A to B?" I reminded her. "Or didn't you say it? Or do you think she's improved?"

Dottie sighed. "Oh, I said it all right. You know how it is. A joke." She looked distressed. She shrugged and swallowed. "When people expect you to say things, you say things. Isn't that the way it is?"

If we are to believe the story, memory was playing tricks with both Kanin and Dorothy Parker because, first, she did not say it, but wrote it in her review of *The Lake* (as recorded in her *Collected Works*), and, second, she had not yet met Alan Campbell. In retrospect, Miss Hepburn herself agreed with Mrs. Parker's critical assessment of her performance. She said: "I'm sure I gave a *foul* performance in *The Lake* —chaotic."

Mrs. Parker continued in her social rounds. She attended the celebration dinner in honor of W.E.B. Du Bois's ninety-second birthday. Seated next to him, she enjoyed an African spear dance which involved lots of chanting and flashing of spears. One or two of them had come within inches of Du Bois's head. Mrs. Parker turned sweetly to him and quipped: "Watch it, mate, or you'll never see ninety-three."

And here she was again with another volume of verse on the presses. *Enough Rope* had been reprinted with monotonous regularity. Her publishers had pressed forward with almighty speed to follow it with a second volume, *Sunset Gun*.

Her articles and verses continued to appear to considerable acclaim. She was now working a little, playing hard and drinking heavily. But what did it matter? Alcoholic or not, could one ignore a critic who, paraphrasing Dowson, could write of Ford Madox Ford's *The Last Post*: "I have been faithful to my duty in my fashion"?

Now, as always, she was a didactic personality, the darling of those who wanted to know and usually didn't. To them she remained largely oracular, always mercurial, unexpected and frequently ambivalent. She had always been the big question mark of the Algonquin set, a driven woman and writer, who seemed at times to be the embodiment of the helpless female. "Dark she was and limpid eyed," she was to those who really knew her, and few did, a woman who was unstable, neurotic and obsessively private yet on the exterior "a fun girl."

She was to lash out at the subject of sex in the novel. "It's not just Lady Chatterley's husband," she wrote, "it's that after this week's course of reading, I'm good and through with the whole matter of sex. I say it's spinach, and I say to hell with it. . . . " She was sending up sex because that made her more readable.

Through her life-style, she appeared to reject the staid and dull, yet she frequently displayed a perverse and quaint penchant for dull and staid businessmen, which was evident when she met John Garrett, the grandson of the founder of the Pacific and Orient shipping line, at Tony Soma's. Marc Connelly introduced them; he had spent a month cruising with Garrett on the Mediterranean.

Garrett was strikingly like Eddie Parker in appearance. According to Mrs. Parker's friends, he soon became enamored of her. Benchley saw the warning signs: "It was sufficient that he loved her and exhibited his love at the drop of a fork. We knew it couldn't last; he wasn't her type, yet perversely he was. He was a nice man, batteringly dull . . . He was her beau, so she had to be protected. We all knew she was heading for the furnace but with Dottie you didn't interfere. . . ."

Dorothy soon tired of Garrett, who disappeared so quickly from the scene that her friends were quite taken aback. From the day of his disappearance, she never mentioned him again.

Following Garrett, there was another love affair, of a different kind. To this day, no one has discovered the man's name, possibly because he was known to be "highly respectable" and married with three children. Successful in business, he owned an elegant townhouse in the West Seventies as well as a snug pied-à-terre in the East Fifties. Like most of her men to date, this one, too, was tall, extremely good-looking, polished, urbane. All that was known of him was that his family were wealthy Pennsylvania farmers and horse-breeders.

The liaison lasted only a few months. Word got out that he was treating her poorly, but this did not seem to change her feelings for him. She confided to Benchley that he had struck her so hard she had fallen across the room; her right hip and lower back were badly bruised for weeks. Benchley told her: "Drop him, Dottie, he's a killer." She did not take Benchley's advice.

One evening Gerald Murphy called to take her to dinner. She opened the door looking as if she'd been in a prize fight, displaying a black eye, cuts and bruises on her face and arms and congealed blood at the side of her mouth. Apparently, her lover had just left the apartment. Horrified at her appearance, Murphy said: "How can you bear that man, Dottie? He's a very dirty cad." Mrs. Parker stared straight at Murphy and gently admonished him: "Stop it, Gerald. I can't let you talk about him that way." Mrs. Parker kept this affair very secret; even today, the man remains nameless. Even her friend Lillian Hellman could not identify him, either then or years later when she wrote her portrait of Mrs. Parker.

That same lover, in a fit of nervous frenzy at Martha's Vineyard airport some time later, was to fire a gun into his own mouth, blowing half his head off. Mrs. Parker wasn't there to see it happen but when she heard about the suicide she commented blandly: "There goes my whipping boy; I hope he left his whips behind."

Now her second book of verse appeared on the bookstalls. *Sunset Gun* had originally been called *Songs for the Nearest Harmonica*, a plaintive enough title that was changed, close to publication, to the somewhat funereal *Sunset Gun*, which referred to a gun in the grounds of West Point Military Academy traditionally fired at sunset; it was the gun that had frightened the life out of Mr. Benchley, who had once been present when it was fired. The book was dedicated simply "To John," perhaps John Farrar, another admirer at the time, but most thought the dedication referred to John Garrett.

The volume included a poem dedicated "To RCB," her friend Robert C. Benchley. It was applaudingly reviewed by *The New York Times* and other publications. There were those who correctly identified in it the influences of A. E. Housman and Martial. And it embodied aspects of her private philosophy, especially in the direction of love, as in her poem, "To Newcastle:"

> Oh, Dallying's a sad mistake
> 'Tis craven to survey the morrow!
> Go give your heart, and if it break—
> A wise companion is sorrow.

There were those who faulted the scansion, but few argued with the characteristic Parkerian outlook: the wise companion, inevitably, was, indeed, *her* own familiar soulmate, sorrow. The irony was faultless, as in "The Parable for a Certain Virgin":

> How amply armored, he, to fend
> The fear of chase that haunts him!
> How well prepared our little friend
> And who the devil wants him?

Robert Sherwood with his chorus in the revue "No, Siree!"—"an anonymous entertainment by the Vicious Circle of the Algonquin Hotel" performed at the 49th Street Theater on Sunday, April 3, 1922. Dorothy Parker wrote this number, "Everlastin' Blues." The ladies of the chorus are (*left to right*) Constance Binney, Helen Hayes, June Walker, Lenore Ulrich, and Margalo Gillmore. (*Photo by James Abbe, courtesy of Washburn Gallery*)

Harpo Marx kissing Dorothy Parker after her first radio appearance in 1933. (*Culver Pictures*)

Frank Crowninshield gave Dorothy Parker her first job at *Vanity Fair*. (*Culver Pictures*)

Harold Ross, "a born outsider and a chronic loser at cards." (*Culver Pictures*)

Robert Sherwood in 1944. (*Culver Pictures*)

Robert Benchley, Dorothy Parker's close friend and confidante.

Alexander Woollcott, known as "der Führer of Neshobe Island." (*Culver Pictures*)

Dorothy Parker in 1933 at the time of the publication of her second book of short stories, *After Such Pleasures*. (*Culver Pictures*)

Dorothy Parker, chairman of the Women's Division of the North American Committee to Aid Spanish Democracy, with a symbolic Christmas stocking which she presented to the Spanish Ambassador to the United States in 1937. (*UPI/Bettman*)

(*Left to right*) Norma Shearer, Frank Case (owner of the Algonquin Hotel), Charles MacArthur, and Helen Hayes (*UPI/Bettman*)

Dorothy Parker with Alan Campbell in the mid-forties. (*Culver Pictures*)

Dorothy Parker (right) with Lillian Hellman at a dinner to launch the Spanish Refugee Appeal Campaign on March 27, 1945. (*Culver Pictures*)

Who indeed? Certainly not Dorothy Parker. Her poem "Interior" was recognized to be very personal Parker, if one omitted a feminine frill here and there:

> Her mind lives in a quiet room,
> A narrow room and tall,
> With pretty lamps to quench the gloom
> And mottoes on the wall.

With disciplined derision, *Sunset Gun* quickly and sardonically disposed of several literary giants, among them Byron, Shelley and Keats, as well as Thomas Carlyle, Walter Savage Landor, Alexandre Dumas *et fils*, Alfred Lord Tennyson, Dickens and Dante Gabriel Rossetti. And even Harriet Beecher Stowe was chucked in "The Ash Bin":

> The pure and worthy Mrs. Stowe
> Is the one we are all proud to know
> As mother, wife and authoress—
> Thank God I am content with less!

If many of her poems exuded the familiar, dismissive last lines, she romped home with her applause of Oscar Wilde:

> If, with the literate, I am
> Impelled to try an epigram,
> I never seek to take the credit
> We all assume that Oscar said it!

Here she might have been at odds with Massachusetts-born James MacNeill Whistler, who had long accused Wilde of stealing his best lines. But no matter, it was amusing verse, dealing admiringly with one of her heroes. She was to be equally amusing in assessing aspects of Georges Sand:

> What time the gifted lady took
> Away from paper, pen and book
> She spent in amorous dalliance
> (They do these things so well in France!)

Happily for Mrs. Parker, *Sunset Gun* followed in the wake of the success of her earlier volume of poems, the sales of both becoming mightily enhanced when it was reported that, on being told that President Calvin Coolidge was dead, she crisply remarked: "How can you tell?"

Successful versifier that she was, she did not neglect her literary criticism, taking on such authors as Theodore Dreiser, who had achieved stature with *The Financier, The Titan* and *The Stoic.* His eminence did not frighten her. She concerned herself with his new novel, *Dawn,* which provided for her but little light on the horizon: "The reading of *Dawn* is a strain upon many parts, but the worst wear and tear falls upon the forearms."

This was the stuff for the sophisticated set, as was her reply to an effusive woman she encountered at a party. The female gushingly inquired: "Are you *really* Dorothy Parker?" Mrs. Parker replied, "Yes, do you mind?"

If, at this point in her life, Dorothy Parker was particularly disenchanted, she gave little evidence of it in her autobiographical verse. Her poem "Bohemia," for example, was full of life and "wise-cracking bravado"; specifically, it treated her Algonquin compatriots to some distinctive disdain:

> Authors and actors and artists and such
> Never know nothing, and never know much.
> Sculptors and singers and those of their kidney
> Tell their affairs from Seattle to Sydney.
> Playwrights and poets and such horses' necks
> Start off from anywhere, end up at sex.
> Diarists, critics and similar roe
> Never say nothing, and never say no.
> People Who Do Things exceed my endurance,
> God, for a man that solicits insurance!

She was clearly tiring of the Algonquinites and, more important, she was emerging as a serious poet, capturing the sonnet form vividly and expertly in "A Dream Lies Dead":

> A dream lies dead here. May you softly go
> Before this place, and turn away your eyes,
> Nor seek to know the look of that which dies
> Importuning life for life. Walk not in woe,
> But, for a little, let your step be slow,
> And, of your mercy, be not sweetly wise
> With words of hope and Spring and tenderer skies.
> A dream lies dead; and this all mourners know.

Mrs. Parker had long reached out for happiness, but it had been denied her. Life was a business of constant pain; to survive one had to learn to live with that pain. She had not yet discovered that the destruction of dreams is the foundation of hope.

· 2 3 ·

Prize for a Lady

WHEN Harold Ross had appointed Mrs. Parker to become "Constant Reader," he had sent her to see Fillmore Hyde, his literary editor, to discuss money. "Money," she had told Hyde, "is no object; I only want to keep body and soul apart." But whether she cared about money or not, she was now making quite a lot of it.

Enough Rope was still selling buoyantly; *Sunset Gun* was being reprinted yet again; and her many and varied freelance outlets were greedily using almost everything she wrote. But the pressures of notoriety were taking their toll. She was drinking far too much, which greatly concerned Benchley, who finally persuaded her to consult with Alcoholics Anonymous.

Afterwards, she met with Benchley, Sherwood, the Stewarts and Aleck Woollcott at Tony's. All were eager to learn about her consultation. She was unusually quiet. Benchley broke the ice:

"What do you think about AA, Dottie?" he asked.

"I think it's an admirable outfit," she replied.

"Are you going to join?"

"Certainly not," Mrs. Parker retorted. "They want me to stop—now!"

If this was lighthearted banter it did not hide her suffering from her friends. As Freud had said, "The sadist is a masochist at heart." Although highly successful as a literary journalist and poet, she was quickly getting another reputation that was less than complimentary. Of late, she had become careless of deadlines and markedly irresponsible about her commitments and promises to various editors. She hated herself for her neglect. Stewart's wife, Beatrice, who was close to her, said: "She respected her talent, she had an absolute solid gratitude for it. She said to me, 'I'm betraying it; I'm drinking. I'm not working. I have the most horrendous guilt':" guilt she indisputably had.

Vincent Sheean, who knew her well, said of her: "If the doorbell rang in her apartment, she would react and say, 'What fresh hell can this be?' —and it wasn't funny, she meant it. I think she drank because of her perception. She wanted to dull her perceptions. Her vision of life was almost more than she could bear."

If that were true, she struggled to hide her unhappiness. As far as her book reviews were concerned, her bite was growing even worse than her bark. Reviewing William Lyon Phelps's *Happiness*, she growled: "It is second only to a rubber duck as the ideal bathtub companion," and her reaction to another dose of A. A. Milne's whimsey with the publication of *Winnie the Pooh* was, "Tonstant weader fwowed up." She failed to perceive that Milne's book would become a lasting classic.

Neysa McMein feared the worst when she got a call from Mrs. Parker close to midnight saying that she was in acute pain. Neysa rushed across to the apartment, called an ambulance and Mrs. Parker once again was rushed into Columbia Presbyterian Hospital. Within two hours she was operated on for the removal of her appendix. Predictably, there were those who said it was another abortion. She dismissed the whole episode as "a mere scratch."

At the end of two weeks, she was well enough to return home, resuming her familiar habit of attending parties at Aleck Woollcott's apartment on the East River. And there were still the weekend sojourns to Neshobe Island.

Although during that summer of 1929 Neshobe was frequented by many of the old gang, as well as the celebrated Otis Skinners, Alfred Lunt and Lynn Fontanne, Noel Coward, Ethel Barrymore and others, and although the Algonquin lunches seemed as gay as ever, the more perceptive among the group realized that the Round Table was gradually sliding into decline. Mrs. Parker, who that year wrote a column on the New York scene for *McCall's* and contributed her work to *Ladies' Home Journal* and *Everybody's*, realized it perhaps more than the rest. She had long been acutely tuned in to the movements and moods of the Vicious Circle.

Her literary journalism in *The New Yorker*, like her reviews and verse, continued to find their mark, and at this time she burst forth with more praise for Ernest Hemingway. In her profile entitled "The Artist's Reward," she called him "the first American artist," which some thought was putting it a bit high. She applauded him for "avoiding life in New York . . . he has the most valuable asset an artist can possess—the fear of what he knows is bad for him." At this time a female journalist quizzed her with "Where is the best place to write?" "In your head," quipped Mrs. Parker.

With her two books enjoying excellent sales, her friend George Oppenheimer, who had moved from Boni and Liveright to Viking, now wanted her to collect her published short stories in a book. But she put aside the idea for a couple of months while she helped Marc Connelly type out the final manuscript of his moving play *Green Pastures*, which was to win a Pulitzer prize.

She was amused to read in *Women's Wear Daily* that actress-writer Ruth Gordon, a frequenter of the Algonquin, had written a new play entitled *Over 21*. That in itself was no major revelation except that the play "concerned the life and good times of an un-named Manhattan lady scribe," whom everybody would recognize as Dorothy Parker. Following quickly on this, Oppenheimer, now turned part-time playwright, portrayed Mrs. Parker as the character of Mary Hilliard in his play *Here Today*. At precisely this time, too, another publisher approached her to write her autobiography, offering her a substantial amount of money. Would she tackle it? "No chance," she said. "Ruth Gordon and George Oppenheimer would sue me for plagiarism!"

If she was much fancied by publishers and editors, she was also greatly feared by playwrights and writers—and not without reason. Anyone who could write as she did in her short story "The Little Hours": "And I'll say of Verlaine too, he was always chasing Rimbauds!" could not be ignored.

Apart from the bright quips and epigrams, there was almost always the now-familiar acid in the lady's pen. Another writer whom she considered to be indecently overpraised, learned this on reading *The New Yorker*: "He's a writer for the ages. For the ages of four to eight." In the same journal, she also observed: "Looking at a list of our authors who have made themselves most beloved and therefore most comfortable financially shows that it is our national joy to mistake for the first rate, the fecund rate. . . . "

There was, too, the incident of the young playwright who was introduced to the Algonquin set by Helen Hayes. In a quickly whispered aside, Aleck Woollcott told Dorothy that the young man had lifted original Parker lines and had incorporated them into his latest play. On being introduced, Mrs. Parker asked him, with her usual direct stare of intimate concern, to describe his new unproduced play. "Well," he stammered, "it's rather hard to describe, except that it's a play against all 'isms.' "

"Except plagiarism?" she sweetly inquired.

In 1929 her book of thirteen sketches and short stories, *Laments for the Living*, was in proof form. Mrs. Parker dedicated the book to Adele Quartley Lovett, the wife of banker Robert Lovett, both of whom were friends and had been with her in France in the summer of 1926. Several of the stories were rather moving, most were acutely perceptive; but by the time the proofs arrived for correction, she was bored by them all. Oppenheimer, anxious to publish the book quickly, could not persuade her to concentrate. He finally had to lock her in a room in the house of a mutual friend with a bottle of whiskey at her side to get the corrected proofs out of her.

It was at this time that her short story "Big Blonde" won first place in the eleventh annual O. Henry Memorial Prize for the best American short story. The prize money was $500, then a tidy sum. To her friends, it was perhaps small wonder she had won the prize—there were more than 2,000 entries; for the story of Hazel Morse—the "Big Blonde"—was the story of Dorothy Parker—a Dorothy Parker compressed into a beautifully turned portrait of a woman who lives with her depressions and attempted suicides brought on by loneliness and ill-fated love affairs. It was the monologue of a party girl revealing herself to herself while taking an excessive number of Veronal tablets in front of a mirror.

"It has," Kinney has since declared, "the beauty of bones stripped bare of artifice and detail, clean with truth."

If her attitude was defensive to most, all her defenses came crashing down the night she met John McClain in Tony's. A former college football star, he was extremely well-built and "almost unbearably good-looking." One of her group described him as an arrivist on the prowl. When she was pointed out to him in Tony's, he said, "You mean that's Dorothy Parker, the famous writer?" He was assured that it was. "Boy," he said, "give me air." Without further ado, he sauntered across and introduced himself. Like others before him, he revealed that he was "on Wall Street." He was, in fact, a clerk in a firm of jobbing brokers, doing spare-time reporting of ship news for the *Sun*, in a column called "On the Deck." It was afterwards to be revealed that he made a habit of latching onto others to enjoy the free party circuit of New York; it was also revealed that he was given to discussing the details of his conquests, who were usually society women or young actresses. David Niven described him as "a Teddy Bear"; Joe Bryan as "the male equivalent of a Rubens nude."

Mrs. Parker was over ten years older than McClain, but she was clearly attracted to him. They left the party together, moving across to the Algonquin. After a brief talk with Frank Case, the two were given the key to a room upstairs.

In the glow of his own conceit, McClain subsequently used that night to regale Dorothy Parker's friends with detailed descriptions of her sexual mores. "There wasn't much," he claimed, "that Mrs. Parker couldn't teach her mattress worthies." Her friends became genuinely concerned at the dangers inherent in the relationship; they saw disaster looming ahead again. They were not wrong.

Mrs. Parker grew boringly possessive of her new lover. She checked with his friends and his office when he made excuses for not being around to attend to what he described as her "voracious sexual appetite." She frequently demanded to know where and with whom he had been. Thus cornered, he usually lied. Time and again she exposed his lies. There were repeated quarrels between them, culminating in a particularly ugly scene in the Algonquin lobby that was witnessed by Benchley and Franklin Adams. "This pathetic woman," McClain said angrily, "wants me to go upstairs and spend the night with her again." Mrs. Parker quietly remonstrated with him, at which he lost his temper. "I don't want to spend another night with you," he spat. "You're a bloody lousy lay."

Mrs. Parker never afterwards denied the story. It was repeated to her by Neysa McMein who asked if it was true.

"Yes," she said simply, "his body went to his head."

There were a succession of subsequent midnight calls to the Algonquin desk with dramatic messages to be conveyed to her lover; threats of suicide among a succession of hysterical outbursts over the telephone. What was crystal clear was that the beefy lounge-lizard had taken his pleasures of Mrs. Parker and was now moving on to other women. It was a sordid affair. She knew that. But she did not care what her friends called it. She was being dominated again, and was taking her punishment with no trace of reproach for her man. She learned that on leaving her he had moved in with a wealthy woman. She told Benchley, who was upset at her hurt, "Don't worry. He'll come back to me when he's finished licking all the gilt off her bottom."

Without a word to her friends she moved out of the hotel and temporarily out of their lives. She did, however, leave a message for them with the bell-captain. It was short and to the point—"I've gone away."

But she had not gone far. Like the lion of Babel, she had simply retired out of sight to lick her wounds.

· 2 4 ·

An Alligator in
the Bath

DOROTHY PARKER did not leave Manhattan. After packing her bag and leaving her bill unpaid at the Algonquin, she checked in at the Plaza; a few days later she moved into the Lowell Hotel on East Sixty-third Street, then a service-apartment establishment which housed fairly well-to-do provincial visitors to New York.

Alarmed at her disappearance, Benchley, Woollcott and Frank Sullivan tracked her down to the Lowell, sympathetically asking for an explanation. She said: "There is no explanation. I just had to rid myself of all those lousy people; I had to get me some peace." They knew, of course, that she had been crying her heart out for McClain. They told her to snap out of it. Plainly the man was a louse and she had more going for her in life than the accommodation of louses.

That night, after her visitors left and she was alone in her darkened room, she tried to kill herself again. She swallowed over half a phial of Veronal tablets and was found barely alive in the morning when they rang to ask what she wanted for breakfast and received no reply. She was shuttled into the hospital. Once again she had beaten the bell.

Her Algonquin friends rallied round her once again; flowers, messages and callers arrived. She quickly regained herself; within two days she was as droll as ever. When the patient was ready to leave the hospital, the bill was sent up. Beatrice Ames Stewart, Neysa McMein and Edna Ferber were with her when it arrived. She looked agonizingly at it. "God," she said, "I can't pay this. I haven't any money." She had often told her friends that she was "poorer than poverty itself." The three women put their heads together. Mrs. Stewart found the answer: they would borrow the money for her.

Even though she had made a good deal of money in recent times, she appeared to her friends to be fluctuating between near-penury and passable affluence. She had long regarded money as something that ought not to be discussed; indeed, it should be totally disregarded unless absolutely necessary to her continuance as a human being. No one seemed to know quite how she spent the large sums she earned, least of all herself.

Mrs. Parker agreed to her friends' suggestion but warned them that they were to be careful from whom they obtained the loan; she was not in the habit of taking money from those of whom she did not approve. She made them swear they would not approach any of her wealthy Manhattan friends. Beatrice Ames Stewart explained to the hospital office that they would have the money in a few days.

In fact, the women had no idea how the money could be raised; Mrs. Stewart had simply suggested borrowing the cash. Later she got an idea. While in Hollywood, she and her husband had become friends with the wealthy screen idol John Gilbert, who had several times told them of his admiration for Mrs. Parker and her work. When Beatrice Stewart approached him for the loan, he readily agreed.

After three weeks of "convalescence," taking in the theater with Benchley and Woollcott, and spurts of diligent reading, she was soon back to her old self. And she was back at her chopping block: "French nouns ending in 'aison' are 'feminine' "; in reviewing Channing Pollock's play *House Beautiful*, she declared in print: "*House Beautiful* is the play lousy." She dismissed another so-called "sensational" novel with: "This is not a novel to be tossed aside lightly. It should be thrown with great force. . . . "

Although there was no male love in her life, there was at least a Scottish terrier she adored, whom she christened Alexander Woollcott Parker because Woollcott swore that the creature had earlier, in turn, christened him no less than three times during a single automobile ride.

She had long had what she described as "this thing" about animals. Some years before, her dachshund Robinson, named after the Swiss Family, died after a fight with a huge Dalmatian on Forty-third Street. Mrs. Parker had sworn fiercely at the Dalmatian's owner, who claimed that Robinson had started the fight. "And I have no doubt," spat Mrs. Parker, "that my dog was also carrying a revolver." According to Woollcott, Robinson had been succeeded by a blue Bedlington named John who, in turn, had been followed by another canine called Woodrow Wilson, "because," as Mrs. Parker explained, "he was full of shit." And, too, there had been Amy, a Scottish terrier, whom Woollcott remembered as:

. . . an enchanting, woolly, four-legged coquette whose potential charm only Dorothy Parker would have recognized at first meeting. For at that first meeting, Amy was covered with dirt and a hulking truckman was kicking her out of his way. This swinish bi-ped was somewhat taken aback to have a small and infuri-ated poetess rush at him from the sidewalk and kick him smartly in the shins—so taken aback that he could only stare open-mouthed while she caught the frightened dog up in her arms, hailed a taxi and took her up to Neysa McMein's studio to wash her in the bathtub. There Amy regained her trust in the human race, achieving a fearful air of harlotry by eating all the rose-madder paint, of which a good deal lingered to incarnadine her face, and eventually won her way to a loving home. . . .

Dogs to Mrs. Parker were an essential part of life. She had already written a poem about one, "Verse For A Certain Dog," which Edmund Wilson claimed she had based on Thomas Hood's "A Parental Ode to My Son, Aged Three Years and Five Months." The mood of Hood's poem, evincing great love for his child, was certainly the structural form of her poem, the central character being transposed from child to dog:

> Such glorious faith as fills your limpid eyes,
> Dear little friend of mine, I never knew.
> All-innocent you are, and yet all-wise.
> (For Heaven's sake, stop worrying that shoe!)
> You look about, and all you see is fair;
> This mighty globe was made for you alone,
> Of all the thunderous ages, you're the heir.
> (Get off that pillow with that dirty bone!)

There had once been a baby alligator, too. Mrs. Parker claimed that she found it in a taxi. The story went that with the help of the janitor, she had gotten it to her bathroom, where the two lodged it in the tub. She then left to keep an appointment. On returning a few hours later, she was confronted by a note written in lipstick which had been left by the occasional maid. This, according to Woollcott, had read: "I will not be back. I cannot work in a place where there are alligators. I would have told you this before, but I didn't suppose the question would have come up." When the alligator was ejected by the apartment-block owners, there was left only Onan, the seed-spreading canary, and the Scottie dog.

There is little doubt she had a rapport with animals. Dray horses would nose her affectionately; cats, as if directed by unseen forces, ma-neuvered themselves to her, although she was not particularly attracted to them. Dogs had long been her joy, a joy she had had ever since her days on *Vogue*. Yet, as her friends noted, she would often keep her animals locked up, without food, in apartment or hotel rooms for hours on end.

The dachshund named Robinson might not have, if it could have spoken, subscribed to his mistress's oft-professed love of animals. As Frank Sullivan later perceptively observed: "That poor Robinson! That poor little dog spent more time in Tony Soma's speakeasy, in that smoky atmosphere, under the table, at two in the morning. I thought that for all her vaunted affection for animals, she could have been a little more considerate." This, too, was the view of Beatrice Ames Stewart, who also adored dogs: "Stories about Dorothy, the friend and champion of dogs would fill libraries," she said. "Actually, she disliked some of the many dogs she had during her life; she was so bored by one of them that she fed it only a single slice of tongue a day, as if hoping it would die, but not wishing to be charged with having starved it to death."

On and off, Mrs. Parker had been racked by guilt over her lack of religious faith and purpose. Her agnosticism had always been shaky, so it was no surprise to her friends when, after her abortion and three suicide attempts, she appeared to be flirting with Catholicism. She said little about her newfound faith at this time but it was there, to be seen and felt in her poems "The Gentlest Lady" and "The Maidservant at the Inn":

> I never saw a sweeter child,
> The Little One, the darling one!
> I mind I told her, when he smiled
> You'd know he was his mother's son.

That was not her best, but it was improved on in "Prayer for a New Mother":

> Let her have laughter with her little one;
> Teach her the endless, tuneless songs to sing,
> Grant her right to whisper to her son
> The foolish names one dare not call a king.

Learning of Dorothy's newfound faith, Benchley observed: "Work for the Lord. The pay is terrible but the fringe benefits are out of this world!"

· 2 5 ·

Train to Tinsel Town

IT WAS NOW 1929 and if "the public manifestation of the twenties—the speakeasy and high-life cultures, the theatrical boom, the age of the flapper, the fads of entertainment that came and went" had been in any sense real, it was coming to an end.

Since 1926, unemployment had been increasing but, except for Mrs. Parker, Benchley, Broun, Stewart and the few others of radical mind, the Algonquinites had hardly noticed.

The year had been heralded by the most "extravagant bash" at the Swopes' new estate at Sands Point, a mansion and grounds far more commodious than their place in Great Neck. Mrs. Parker was now working on the short stories for her next book as well as penning her *New Yorker* contributions; Sherwood was writing successful plays and was now in Vienna for the opening of one of them; Benchley was commuting to the film studios in New Jersey and Hollywood, making short films of seemingly inconsequential ideas that were very popular. He had decided to take another break on the Riviera, this time with his family, staying with the Murphys. Kaufman, Woollcott, Lardner, Broun, Alice Duer Miller, Neysa McMein, Ruth Gordon and the rest were busy working on projects.

For the ordinary citizen, there was little to presage the disaster that had been hovering over America since 1927.

In October 1929, the stock market trembled violently for a nightmare of days and then crashed with a reverberancy that echoed round the world. On October 29—Black Tuesday—prices plummeted. The stocks and shares of the major companies hit rock bottom—Adams Express dropping $96 a share, Commercial Solvents, $70, Otis Elevators, $40, Westinghouse, $35, and General Electric, $20. By 3 P.M. the second largest figure of daily trading had been traded at a disastrous loss, the worst losses in the history of the American stock exchange.

Covering the scene for the London *Daily Telegraph*, Winston Churchill stood on the balcony of the trading floor of the New York Exchange and saw it all happening. Most of the other major shares began to tumble: International Telephones, General Motors and the rest—few escaped. Alfred Noyes, financial editor of *The New York Times*, assessed the situation: "The crisis," or "decline," as he called it, "had come about because of lack of support and exhaustion of margins, the selling by many frightened persons who had owned stocks outright, and a recreation of a wave of fright which swept the speculative markets last week." But it was more than that.

In mid-year, the New York stock market had been spiraling dizzily in the most exhilarating bull market America had ever known. Caught up in a frenzy of get-rich-quick visions, hundreds of thousands of small investors had poured their cash, often their life savings, into Wall Street with reckless abandon while "the great bulls, the shadowy figures of the financial giants," were investing millions, manipulating stocks ever higher for their personal profit. The bears, standing on the sidelines, would then attack the market when a break in prices seemed imminent.

Now the market had all but collapsed, and not even the liquor in their hip flasks, during this eighth year of Prohibition, could offer the high-flying investors, bankers and brokers any degree of effective sustenance.

It had not been uncommon for the "big boys" to buy shares with only 10 percent cash to call on, the remaining 90 percent being "borrowed" from the brokers, who, in turn, borrowed it from the "call money market." If the value of the stocks fell, the investor would be required by the broker to put up more "margin," which in simplistic terms meant more cash. And if the investor could not do so, the shares would be sold by the broker so that the broker himself would have the cash to pay back the money *he* had borrowed. And if he couldn't pay, the system simply did not work and dire crisis fell upon the speculators, as now it had.

Many suicides were reported. Innumerable speculators had lost everything; over one weekend, more than three million Americans had been wiped out financially, and there were countless others whose finances had plummeted to rock-bottom. The approaching aftereffects were too awful to be faced with any sort of equanimity.

Bernard Baruch, Winston Churchill's associate and a patron of sorts of the Round Table, had long been a friend to Herbert Swope. He had given him, as well as Churchill, investment tips. Now, not even these were worth anything. At the beginning of October, Swope had had $14 million on paper. By the first of November, he was $2 million in the red.

Joe Baragwanath, who had been playing gin rummy with the Prince of Wales and Harold Talbott at Fort Belvedere, in Sunningdale, England, the night before the crash, hurried back to New York with Talbott, only to watch the ship's ticker tape spell their joint stock market doom. Kaufman had been relatively lucky: the one stock in which he had invested had gone down to the tune of $10,000, but he could survive that since his collaborative playwriting was earning him high rewards. Mrs. Parker "had never," she confessed, "the sophistication to play the market," which had been just as well.

Now, as James Gaines observed, "the champagne of the twenties had gone flat" and with it the Algonquin Round Table was approaching its end, like so many of the pleasures of the decade. Mrs. Parker gave no hint of any regret she might have felt. "Money," as she was later to say, "is only congealed snow."

A year or two earlier Dorothy began to date a man she had met at the apartment of Vincent and Diana Sheean. At the time, Joseph Bryan was a young recruit to *The New Yorker*. His piece for the magazine on the celebrated London madame Rosa Lewis of the Cavendish Hotel on Jermyn Street, had caused something of a stir; it had displayed considerable wit and had proven the author to be a remarkably talented journalist.

To her friends, Dorothy excused her interest in Bryan by declaring it to be "more out of admiration for his writing gifts than for his sex appeal." The two had, as she called it, "a swing round the lampposts." Then, quite inexplicably and with the passivity of a guru, she stood him up one night on the pretext of not remembering the date or "who the man was."

Woollcott, Bill Crawford and Jack Leonard teasingly reproached her for her casual treatment of Bryan; it was, they knew, the mind of Mrs. Parker performing arabesques around the image of a man she had clearly fancied and who had not, it seemed, responded to her as she wished. When that happened she customarily told herself that the man simply did not exist. She appeared to be a social diptych, two images uncomfortably posed side-by-side, each contemplating the other in distaste. To the more rational of her friends, her summary of the man seemed crassly rude, if not downright ungrateful, but gratitude for love—or sex—was not, it seemed, in her makeup. There had been other occasions of a like nature, as Edmund Wilson was to remember:

"When I told Dorothy Parker once—what she didn't know—that a former lover of hers had died, a young, good-looking and well-to-do fellow who had suffered from tuberculosis, she said crisply: 'I don't see what else he could have done.' On an earlier occasion . . . we ran into Condé Nast in the lobby of the Algonquin. He said that he was going on a cruise: 'And, Dorothy, I wish you would come with me.' 'Oh, I wish I could!' immediately followed, as soon as Nast had gone on, by 'Oh, God, make that ship sink!' " Mrs. Parker clearly had her own distinctive taste in men and the words to dismiss them if they did not measure up to her requirements. Interestingly, Joe Bryan, the accomplished ex-Princeton journalist, both before and after his marriage to another lady, Joan, was to become a good, if not close, friend of Mrs. Parker.

Meeting Scott Fitzgerald and Zelda at the Algonquin, Wilson sat with Mrs. Parker "at one of those tables too narrow to have anyone across from you, so that one sat on a bench with one's back to the wall." Mrs. Parker greeted the Fitzgeralds with: "This looks like a road company of the Last Supper."

It has been said that the hotel at 59 West Forty-fourth Street, was "a kind of Camelot." If that were so, it must surely have been a tossup between Adams, Benchley and Woollcott for King Arthur; certainly, and unmistakably, Mrs. Parker was Guinevere. Her literary reputation was now widespread and Hollywood wanted to use her skills. Her interest in writing for Hollywood might well have been at the insistence of several of her friends who had already written for the screen; Donald Ogden Stewart, George Kaufmann, Herman Mankiewicz, Charles MacArthur, among them.

The mighty Metro-Goldwyn-Mayer, symbolized by a roaring lion and the ungrammatical legend *Ars Gratia Artis*, began to woo her; her winning of an O. Henry prize had impressed more than one Hollywood producer. She said at the time, "I need the money." Besides, the West Coast would certainly provide a change of scene for her, a change she badly needed, and she might just as well take part in the glittering gold rush, even if it was adjudged to be the market place where materialism ruled. She decided to accept the MGM offer.

Her contract was for three months. It was generous in terms and restrictive in conditions, similar, she discovered, to the contracts signed by several of her friends. The trip to L.A. was four days and four nights by train, with two changes. On her arrival, she was given a cube-like office, her tasks being to rewrite the work of others, to read books for possible films, and to write screen treatments.

Predictably, she was invited to a round of parties; Dorothy Parker was the newcomer to Hollywood, a fresh image; and images, she had always declared, responded to images. But that wasn't exactly true, certainly not of her screenwriting work, which she soon came to loathe. She was, however, prepared to sit it out. It was as if she knew that there would come another time when she would be able to write for the screen on her own terms, her current foray with MGM providing a sort of apprenticeship.

At the end of the three months, MGM said they were delighted with her work and bade her goodbye. The atmosphere had been anathema to her creativity: she longed to be in New York again. Her stint in Hollywood had been made palatable only by the presence of various members of the Algonquin crowd. Harry Kurnitz, a bright newcomer to Hollywood, said at the time, "Movie writing is a horrible ordeal in which sadistic producers torture you almost beyond endurance by holding your jaws open while they drop a monotonously maddening succession of gold dollars into your helpless mouth!" Well, she, like others, had done her chores, opened her mouth, and now the train was pulling her back into her familiar and beloved New York.

She immediately took up again with the homosexual theatrical set, and her friends believed she did so because there was no special man in her life. Several of the men took her out on dates, occasions which were interpreted by some of the Algonquinites to mean that she found the "inaccessibility of the queers attractive." By others it was read that she wanted to avoid any further pain of rejection, especially after what had happened with McClain. Characteristically, she even made fun of this situation. In "Diary of a New York Lady," subtitled "Days of Horror, Despair and World Change," which ran in *The New Yorker*, she reported:

"Called up and found I could get two tickets for the opening of *Run Like a Rabbit* tonight for forty-eight dollars. Told them they had the nerve of the world, but what can you do? Think Joe said he was dining out, so telephoned some *divine* numbers to get someone to go to the theater with me, but they were all tied up. Finally got Ollie Martin. He *couldn't* have more poise, and what do I care if he is *one?*"

She did not seem to care, but clearly she had put on her mask again.

Mrs. Parker's era of the twenties had all but passed.

She had been at the center of a literary scene in America that had reacted enthusiastically to the publication of a rising swell of books by the new and established literary lions from Europe: Axel Munthe, Virginia Woolf, Robert Graves, R. H. Mottram, Arnold Zweig, Osbert and Edith Sitwell, E. M. Forster, Herbert Read, Siegfried Sassoon, Maugham, Aldous Huxley, Galsworthy, Shaw, Norman Douglas, Ronald Firbank—all quintessentially of the age, as was Richard Aldington, T. E. Lawrence, D. H. Lawrence, Arnold Bennett and the satirical Evelyn Waugh, a disciple of Firbank who had electrified the literary establishment with his irreverent *Vile Bodies* and *Decline and Fall*. Towards the end of the decade that same establishment had risen up and banned Radclyffe Hall's *The Well of Loneliness* and D. H. Lawrence's *Lady Chatterley's Lover*, which had featured a character named Michaelis, an Irish writer who was her ladyship's lover before the gamekeeper Mellors arrived on the scene. Everybody in the literary set knew that Lawrence had based Michaelis on the Armenian novelist Michael Arlen. Mrs. Parker is known to have been fascinated by the gossip but her real interest lay predominantly in Ernest Hemingway, whose new book, *A Farewell to Arms*, was hitting the literary jackpot in late 1929. Her continuing praise of the novel was noticed by Sherwood, who teased her about it. "He really is your hero, isn't he?" Sherwood asked.

"What of it?" she replied. "We all need heroes, don't we?"

· 2 6 ·

Death in Switzerland

AT THIS TIME, as during so many other times in her life, Mrs. Parker was consumed with guilt, with which she tried to come to terms. She felt that she was achieving nothing save an ephemeral, empty fame; and her love life was nonexistent. That there was a mystical answer to her guilt she was convinced, but the answer eluded her. Her friends, she knew, provided her with an escape from the tortures of that guilt; but this escape was only fleeting. For solace, however, there remained the beckoning promise of the bottle; for her there was no other way out.

She fell into another spell of black despair and, to his credit, George Oppenheimer recognized the symptoms. He told her that she needed a change of scene: new sights, new sensations, new sounds.

Oppenheimer got in touch with Gerald and Sara Murphy, who cabled Dorothy and invited her to stay with them in their Chalet LaBruyere at Montana-Vermala in the Swiss Alps. They even extended the invitation to any friends she might want to bring along, Mr. Stewart, for example. She accepted, but before she left she partied vigorously with her homosexual friends. She told the Round Tablers that she "needed good fairies to take care of her."

George Oppenheimer had promised to see her off. When it came close to her hour of departure, neither the Stewarts nor her publisher could find her. Eventually, Oppenheimer laid siege at Jack and Charlie's, where he discovered the lady intoxicated and maudlin. As he recalled, "I poured her into a cab and she met up with the Stewarts." On the ship at Brooklyn docks she waved goodbye to Oppenheimer, calling out:

"Guess who's on the boat—Marlene Dietrich! And guess who's not on the boat—my trunk!" Oppenheimer had already shipped the trunk to the liner and Dietrich was endlessly showing her legs to the photographers, or trotting out boring cooking recipes to any who cared to listen.

Mrs. Parker spent nearly a month at Antibes, where Woollcott and others had gone ahead for their now customary summer revels. She met up once more with Somerset Maugham, looking like an embalmed

Doge, at the Villa Mauresque, and Bernard and Mrs. Shaw were again there, as was Harpo Marx. But it was all becoming rather jaded, as if everyone was trying a little too hard. Mrs. Parker left the Côte d'Azur to move on to the Murphys in Switzerland, clutching a volume of verse by Ernest Dowson, many of whose poems she had learned by heart.

The Murphys were at the station to meet her. Stewart and his wife joined the Murphys and Mrs. Parker. He recalled that:

We made a quick visit to Gerald and Sara Murphy upon whom tragedy had suddenly and overwhelmingly descended. Their son Baeoth had been stricken with tuberculosis and had died. And now, as if fate had not been cruel enough to this glorious family, the youngest boy Patrick [aged 9] was fighting for his life in one of the magic mountain resorts high in the Swiss Alps. The moment that Patrick's doctor had told them that this was the one hope for saving the child's life, Gerald and Sara had abandoned everything, and were living in this last-resort community of dying men and women to be close to their son.

. . . when Bea and I arrived, it was infinitely more grim than we had imagined, even though Patrick was "improving." Gerald and Sara were as gaily charming as ever, and Dottie Parker . . . tried her best to cover the horror with tenderness and laughter.

Gerald warned us that the first night of sleep was usually difficult for the newly-arrived and he was right. Not because one couldn't sleep, but because of the horrible dreams which emerged in the topmost Alpine atmosphere. But even before bedtime, the haunting shudders closed down with the early setting of the sun behind the mountain peaks. For four years, Bea and I had spent our evenings in an atmosphere of excitement, either in the theater, in a speakeasy, or at a party or, if at home, with guests who, even if dull, could usually be transformed by mutual application of alcohol into what seemed to be fascinatingly intelligent companions. We had resolutely and successfully shut out sorrow and pain—and were even beginning to be able to avoid inconvenience. And here, trapped on this desolate snow-covered silent mountain, with death seeming to be waiting mockingly in the cold clear air outside, were the two people who had been our models for The Happy Life.

They themselves gave no sign of any change. Gerald remembered the special cocktails Bea and I had loved on our honeymoon, and Sara had outdone herself with amazing variations of Swiss cookery. Dottie was at her best. After dinner, Gerald played new records he had discovered in Germany, including one by Marlene Dietrich called "Der Blaue Engel." Sara and he told us of the macabre life-in-death with which they were surrounded, and to which they were attempting to bring some of their own brave gaiety. When one of the patients was given his death warrant by his physician, it was now the custom for him to appear at the club with a small replica of his coffin; those who were also about to die, saluted him with champagne. Sara had found some musicians and had actually persuaded them to open a night club, which had been extremely successful. At the end of the evening, Gerald went on the piano and Sara, in her lovely alto, sang with him. At the end of the evening, Bea and I found ourselves in our bedroom crying our eyes out. Something of reality had tapped on the windows of our dream house and we hastened to close the shutters.

Next day we fled, taking Dottie with us. The descent from Hell to Earth was almost as nerve-shaking an atmosphere change as had been the sudden elevation to the mountain. On the train to Paris, I exploded into my one and only row with Dottie and attacked her bitterly for a profile of Ernest Hemingway she had written for *The New Yorker*, in the course of which she had praised Ernest as one writer who would never, never, never be a slave to the society inhabiting the north shore of Long Island. *Touché*—and it hurt like hell especially, ironically enough, coming from Dottie for whose sake years before I had had a quarrel with Ernest which had helped terminate our friendship. Dottie, of course, disclaimed that she had been referring specifically to me, and by the time we got to Paris all was love and cognac. And by a curious coincidence, Ernest, with his new wife Pauline, were on the boat which Bea, Dottie and I took for New York.

The Murphys' tragedy was to become infinitely greater than appeared at this time. Of their three children—they also had a daughter Honaria —the two boys eventually died within two years of each other, Baeoth in 1935 of spinal meningitis and Patrick in 1937. What Stewart did not say was that Mrs. Parker had drunkenly accused him during their time together in Switzerland of "trading in his pen for an alpenstock."

Apart from three or four book reviews mailed back to *The New Yorker* office, the long months Dorothy Parker spent in Switzerland was a fallow period, full of great sadness for her friends the Murphys. Perhaps her poem "Little Words," fueled by that same sadness, echoed her feelings at this time:

> When you are gone, there is no bloom nor leaf
> Nor singing sea at night, nor silver birds;
> And I can only stare, and shape my grief
> In little words.

Dorothy Parker returned to New York early in 1931, after nearly a year with the Murphys. At a party given by the Howard Dietzes, she was introduced to an actor who was part of the homosexual set and upon whom she subsequently called to escort her to openings, parties and receptions. He was a close friend of Katharine Hepburn and a solid admirer of Dorothy Parker, the writer. Some years before, he had graduated from the Virginia Military Academy and had later decided on an acting career. With the build of a latter-day Adonis and the overt breeding of an Edwin Pond Parker "without the lad's habits or inhibitions," he was, Mrs. Parker soon discovered, utterly star-struck. And Mrs. Parker, as she quickly perceived, was the principal star in his personal constellation.

His name was Alan Campbell.

· 2 7 ·

Laments for the Living

ALAN CAMPBELL was the embodiment of the attitude of mind and body which in a future generation was to become known as "camp." Extroverted, witty, intelligent, he was a bright, theatrical conversationalist with unusual and decidedly flamboyant tastes in decor, food and friends. He had, too, a pronounced liking for high living, good clothes, wine and parties. Mrs. Parker quickly learned that those around him declared him to be bisexual, but that was not of singular importance to her: he was, as she described him at the time, "fun, a bundle of fun."

Noel Coward invited the two of them to a party, along with others of his friends and the English members of the cast of *Set to Music*. The play starred Beatrice Lillie, an actress whose stage cavortings hid a woman of title, Lady Peel, a lady, indeed, whom Mrs. Parker did not particularly like. She had been involved in Mrs. Parker's sad love affair with Charles MacArthur and, although she kept her own counsel, Mrs. Parker found it difficult to forgive those who had caused, or helped to cause, her unhappiness. Cole Lesley—or, to give him his correct name, Leslie Cole—Coward's alter ego, was later to remember the party:

Helen Hayes and Ruth Gordon, who were there, I thought much gayer and funnier than Dorothy Parker, who looked miserable, verging on the disagreeable, emitting not one Parkerism for us to treasure. However, she made up for this with one at about that time, which remained Noel's favorite. She produced a personable young man, of which she seemed to have a supply, to fill in a last-minute cancellation at a literary dinner party. Faced with such distinguished guests, through nerves he knocked back too many martinis and was drunk by the time he got to the table, from which he soon got up, loudly announced "I wanna piss," and staggered from the room. "He's very shy," said Mrs. Parker, "actually he only wants to telephone."

It was a variation, timely and apposite, of one of her own exits from the Algonquin table some years back, but that did not matter. It was still funny, the more so delivered as it was by Mrs. Parker in her poker-faced fashion. The nervous escort of Dorothy Parker that night was, in fact, Alan Campbell.

Helen Hayes was now being courted by MacArthur and had lately been present at a number of Algonquin parties. There was one, at Woollcott's "Wit's End," that she had painful cause to remember. Mrs. Parker, George Kaufman, and Joe Hennessy, Woollcott's secretary-amanuensis, had watched while Woollcott concocted a particularly ferocious cocktail brew, which he had christened "The Alexander," an addition, he claimed, to current fads of the Manhattan cocktail, whiskey sour and sidecar.

Miss Hayes was invited by Woollcott to sample his concoction and she was later to recall her initiation into the efficacy of the brew:

The first time I ever got tight in my life was with Aleck Woollcott . . . I was given an awful cocktail made with cream and creme de cacao and something else . . . "The Alexander" it was called . . . lethal mixture . . . it tasted like ice cream . . . I drank one down and took another and drank it down, and I was blind. I sat there and can remember so vividly my distress, my agony, because I thought they're all going to know I'm tight if I can't say something to prove I'm not. So I was thinking, working up to saying something. I had a piano and was moving to another apartment which was smaller. I didn't want that piano any more, and this began to come into my drink-sodden mind. I waited until there was a pause in the conversation and then I said with a great intake of breath, "Anyone who wants my piano, is willing to it," and this terrible silence followed and Kaufman said, "That's very seldom of you, Helen . . . "

Mrs. Parker's cryptic comment to MacArthur was, "That's what comes of lying in the Hayes. . . . "

At this time, Dorothy Parker was interviewed about her experiences in Hollywood. The work, she said, had been agony: "I just sat in a cell-like office and did nothing. I would imagine the Klondike would be like that—a place where people rush for gold." She might have added that they were still rushing. Benchley, it seemed, had all but taken up permanent residence there, as had Sherwood, Connelly and others of the Algonquin set, and there were many others who were now following in their wake.

Nevertheless, there were compensations for her now. It was still 1930 and her first book of short stories, *Laments for the Living*, was on the bookstalls and selling fast. Professor Kinney's summary of the book, her first prose collection in hardcover, later provided a piercing analysis of human frailties:

The book "contains some of Dorothy Parker's more popular but lesser stories, as well as some of her best. Some remind us of her early, experimental fiction," he was to write.

"Dialogue at Three in the Morning," between "the woman in the petunia colored hat" and the "man with the ice-blue hair" is the angry, trivial monologue of a woman who feels she is being jilted and a man who wishes to apologize but gets no opportunity: its chief technique is repetition; its end, our boredom, paralleling the boredom of the characters . . . "The Mantle of Whistler" is representative flapper dialogue between a couple who have just met at a party. "You Were Perfectly Fine" unravels the night before as a woman helps her companion recall some of the stunts he performed when drunk . . . "Just a Little One" is another study in jealousy: as the couple converse in a speakeasy dark as Mammoth Cave, the woman gets more and more drunk: on the way home she asks for a little horse as she had spent the evening asking for little drinks. "New York to Detroit," in which an estranged couple discuss their separation, uses a bad telephone connection to insinuate their own faltering relationship. And, "Arrangement in Black and White" . . . daring for its time, follows the familiar Parker outlines, the woman anxious to display her tolerance by talking to a colored man and finally overcome by her ability to shock her husband in reporting what she has done . . .

"Mr. Durant" parallels a man's cruelty to his secretary, Rose, whose affair with him ends in an abortion he will only partly pay for, and to his children, whose dog he intends to be rid of as soon as they are in bed. Yet his coldness is not the subject so much as the cause of his coldness; his need for order and discipline . . . Dorothy Parker shows no shred of sympathy in this story—she achieves the distancing Hemingway asked for but she has a fine sensitivity in "The Sexes" and "The Last Tea." In the former, a young man is puzzled and spiritually defeated by the unreasonable jealousy of his date: in the course of his manly attempt at reconciliation, he finds himself falling to her standards. "The Last Tea," narrating the breakup of a romance at which both parties interrupt each other to express the demands on them by other dates . . . what each fights to maintain is not so much reputation as self-respect.

Three stories in *Laments for the Living* are full and, in distinct ways, moving. "The Wonderful Old Gentleman" shows the parasitic nature of humanity; two daughters and a son-in-law show differing responses to an old man's imminent death . . . The story . . . studies the variations of funereal sorrow, the irony inherent in the slow revelation of a couple's exploitation, succeeded, in the final lines, by the blatant unconcern of another character.

We can see Dorothy Parker's use of social detail—reminiscent of Fitzgerald —in the opening of *Little Curtis*, but what seems at first too elaborate, with its shaggy-dog ending, is only the story's premise, for Mrs. Matson continues to apply the same polished surface to her treatment of people, her staff and her friends . . . as to her adopted son, Little Curtis . . .

All of these stories gain strength through their concentration. Yet Dorothy Parker's best story, "Big Blonde," is astonishingly panoramic. In its portrait of the birth and growth of alcoholism and suicidal despair and its clinical analysis, painfully detailed and piercingly accurate, we have an unrelenting study of the possible brutality of life. Despite the breadth of time, the sharp focus on Hazel Morse is close and steady.

From the start, Hazel Morse finds no advantage in living. She never knew the pleasure of family; her later popularity is artificial. But she has no distorted sense of herself; she is willing to settle for Herbie Morse to gain some security and stability. Herbie leads Hazel to alcohol which, in turn, produces tenderness, self-pity, "misty melancholies." Herbie finally leaves her, despising himself, despising him in her, and she becomes a party girl.

Hazel Morse is mirrored in her husband, the speakeasies, her lovers, and, finally, the maid, yet all these painful doublings are not nearly so pathetic as the comparison Dorothy Parker makes between Hazel and a wretched horse, nor as tragic as Hazel Morse looking at herself in a mirror when taking Veronal . . . Here, at the moment of suicide, the best she can manage is a bad joke: "Gee, I'm nearly dead . . . that's a hot one!"

But that is not the end of Hazel Morse. As she survived desertion by her husband and subsequent lovers, so she survives the deadly poison; her punishment is to remain alive amidst the squalor of the poor and unfortunate yearning to breathe free. Yet what survives is at best what we see when Hazel Morse, drugged, is at greater peace with herself:

Mrs. Morse lay on her back, one flabby, white arm flung up, the wrist against her forehead. Her stiff hair hung untenderly along her face. The bed covers were pushed down, exposing a deep square of soft neck and a pink nightgown, its fabric worn uneven by many launderings; her great breasts, freed from their tight confiner, sagged beneath her armpits. Now and then, she made knotted, snorting sounds, and from the corner of her opened mouth to the blurred turn of her jaw ran a lane of crusted spittle.

This, by the best of standards, was good writing. It richly deserved the accolade it had won as the Best Short Story of the year, and here it was again included in Mrs. Parker's first volume of collected prose writings. T. S. Matthews, writing in *New Masses* for September 17, 1930, cogently observed:

"Dorothy Parker is an able prosecutor, and one who knows the limitations of her case. No one could write with such unhappy wit, manage such a savage humor, who did not feel herself a blood sister to her victims, who did not also regard them as a pernicious race of odious little vermin." Writing in the late 1970s, Professor Kinney regarded Dorothy Parker as "very much of our day; the thrust of her wit is apt to tickle as it wounds, her most sympathetic gesture always has some horror in it."

This was largely true. She was, indeed, a blood sister to Hazel Morse, the pathetic, drained woman who felt the need to expire and watch herself expiring, if only for the hell of it; a similar mental hell to which Mrs. Parker seemed more and more attracted as the years went by. Her deep introspection, the overwhelming sadness that so often encompassed her life, the repeated suicide attempts, the disharmony of her private life, her morbid obsession with death, the seeming hopelessness of her private world, were all disturbing behavioral traits. What then, one might ask, was really ailing her? What did her doctors and psychiatrists diagnose? Was there a clear and reasoned medical explanation for her acute depressive state, her sense of ever-increasing despair about her life and the world she lived in; why such a lasting and obsessive preoccupation with dying and death?

To look behind the exterior of her persona, we know that she did not suffer any organic disease of the body: it was not her body that troubled her, it was her mind. The psychiatrists of the twenties who treated her knew that her attempts to leave her mortal life were the desperate responses to a psychotic condition which they could have admitted they did not then fully understand.

They had earlier called it dementia praecox, a label given to a wide grouping of mental disorders. It was labeled thus by Jung and used by him as a title to one of his books, although it had earlier been delineated under that heading by Kraepelin and earlier still by Morel. The condition had been deeply researched by Jung and his findings had been endorsed by Freud, who declared the condition as having its origins in human sexuality. What Kraepelin, Morel and Jung called dementia praecox, Bleuler later described as schizophrenia, the term which survives. Mrs. Parker's symptoms were familiar enough to psychiatrists of the time—then invariably called psychologists, sometimes alienists. Today, those symptoms would indicate that she was assuredly what we know as a manic depressive, suffering from the first depressive syndrome in the psychiatric book—endogenous depression, endogenous indicating that the trouble is generated from within and not as a result of external misfortune.

Although in the 1980s it is claimed by the medical profession to be a treatable condition, it must be remembered that up until World War II, little was known of its cause and effects. Of the various known categories of depression, the endogenous type often affects the patient for no apparent reason, it being one facet of the wider rubric manic depression or psychosis. Its now familiar symptoms are, first, a deep decline of interest in normal affairs underlined by an accompanying decline in initiative and emotional response. At the onset of the illness, matters of normal

importance cease to attract the sufferer's attention; work or everyday
commitments cease to have any real significance: an attitude of marked
indifference takes over—all pronounced aspects of Mrs. Parker's personality.

Victims of the condition are usually agreeable people, often highly
talented. They are mostly people who have formerly been reasonably
well organized and conscientious. For this reason the sufferer struggles
inside in an effort to fight back against the illness, but marked indecision
usually takes over. The personality, now at war with lethargy and indecision, develops the misfortune of a self-recriminatory attitude. Psychiatrists today refer to this sequence of change as psychomotor retardation:
it also manifests itself in a slowing up of both thought and movement,
even of such physiological functions as digestion and excretion. Sufferers
normally evince other characteristics previously unknown to themselves;
these include depressive stupor, depressive facial expression and the
waning of concentration. They will attempt to read a book and the words
simply do not register. At this stage the mind has reached a plateau of
bewilderment which in turn adds to the state of intense depression. So
the patient comes to believe that life is pointless and attempts at suicide
may well take over; purpose and ambition having become virtually nonexistent.

Another marked and principal feature of the illness is self-reproach.
Victims irrationally blame themselves for all sorts of imagined "cata-
strophic" happenings for which there is no basis in fact. When these
delusions come to the fore they are usually identified as such by
family and friends, seldom by the sufferer. The application of logic by
others has little or no effect because the sum total of the illness at this
stage is a state of almost total delusion of futility. There may even be
displayed delusions of hypochondriasis—the belief that the sufferer is
being taken over by bodily disease when, in truth, no disease exists.
When agitation is a prominent feature this state is sometimes called
involutional melancholia; it often appears in women at the change
of life.

An interesting characteristic of the condition frequently occurs in the
senile period when delusions of poverty are displayed. These were
strongly apparent in Mrs. Parker's later life when she was in the habit
of telling her friends, Lillian Hellman in particular, that she was penniless when, in fact, she was quite well off. Another aspect of the
condition is a loss of sexual enjoyment with the result that the patient
becomes even more addicted to self-reproach and goes "over the top"
in sexual endeavor because he or she feels that they are likely to

disappoint their partner. Loss of appetite is another symptom. From the early days of her involvement in literary journalism Mrs. Parker ate little, evincing scant interest in food. Insomnia, too, is another marked characteristic of the complaint; it is known that Dorothy Parker seldom slept well. The result of the condition's persistent insomnia often persuades the sufferer to swallow tablets to induce escape into sleep. Mrs. Parker was a frequent pill-taker for this same reason. Such is the travail of mind that frequently—too frequently—the sufferer takes too many pills, sometimes mixing the taking of them with too much alcohol.

In summary, then, it seems clear that Mrs. Parker, with her classic swings of mood was, indeed, a manic depressive, a sufferer of recurrent psychosis in which periods of depression of the endogenous type were punctuated by periods of well-being and achievement, with bursts of overactivity, sometimes loquacity or euphoria (irritability, in some) amounting to mania, the swings moving from being overtly depressed to periods when she performed at an above-average level of originality and productiveness.

It could be argued that her pronounced ups and downs amounted to hypomania because this cyclical pattern, too, is frequently evident in successful writers, politicians and others in the arts and public life, accounting for exceptional creativity and achievement. But hypomania as we know it, with its overactive, garrulous moods, doesn't fit the overall recurrent trends and changes in her personality. Her exuberant wit and loquacity are clearly evident in "Just a Little One" and "The Lady with the Lamp," in particular—but perhaps she labored long and hard at these outpourings. We do not know. But what we do know is that she had good and clear remissions from her depressive illness as on the occasions when her wit shone brilliantly through in both her work and play.

Psychiatry, then as now, is a profession of highly complex signals, with many areas still ill-defined. As to Mrs. Parker, "The Little Hours" is recognized by experts as "text book hypomanic talk." But, one asks, did it all just spill out in her first draft, then to become organized by her to read in the irresistible way it does? We shall never know. Poets and writers like Donne and Cowper and, in this century, Sylvia Plath, describe depression—of whatever type—so much more effectively than the textbooks of modern psychiatry. Donne's habit of rehearsing his death by habitually lying in a coffin is surely more eloquent than reams of medical dissertations.

Suffice that Mrs. Parker was clearly manic depressive; she herself called her mind "a little den of demons." It was no less an agony, however she or others tried to describe it.

Alan Campbell was well aware of her deeply depressive nature. Supreme optimist that he was, he believed that he could do much to alleviate the effects of the malady that plagued her days and nights.

· 2 8 ·

An Empathy of Genes

THE SUM AND SUBSTANCE of Alan Campbell within the life of Dorothy Parker, his apotelesm, was soon evident in the year of 1932 in his ability to become the core, the very oxygen of her existence.

Soon after the marriage of Neysa and Joe Baraganwath, Mrs. Parker had moved out of her apartment adjacent to Neysa's studio and was now living in rooms on the extreme edge of East Forty-ninth Street. Alan, who had stayed at the apartment with her, moved in with her at the new one and took over as "household administrator, cook, launderer, bartender, schedule arranger and," even he admitted it, "meal ticket." He set about his many tasks catering to her whims, tending her dog and canary, laughing at her jokes, making her appointments, tidying the rooms, doing the household accounts and sating her physical desires. He also escorted her to the theater and parties. He even helped her with taxes, staving off the Internal Revenue Service. He kept her books and when they occasionally entertained, he cooked as a passable parody of Escoffier.

Campbell strove to become everything to her and it wasn't long before Dorothy Parker was echoing in the fashion of the times, "Where have you been all my life?"

After military college, he had fluttered around the theatrical parties, on the periphery of the Algonquin set, getting a stage bit-part here, a modeling job there. He had become friendly with Katharine Hepburn when he was given a few lines in Jed Harris's production of A Warrior's Husband, in which the actress had starred. Known in Hollywood as "Katharine of Arrogance," Hepburn had taken to him and he had stooged for her when Selznick tested her for the lead in the movie Holiday. Now he was Mrs. Parker's amanuensis, and both were loving every moment of the liaison.

She continued to do reviews and write magazine features. She had dealt with the ladies of the English social scene when reviewing the aristocratic Countess of Oxford and Asquith's The Autobiography of Margot Asquith, and the English society queen had not come out of it well. She had also gotten to the peeress's second tome, Lay Sermons, a tempting enough title for Mrs. Parker's pickings:

Through the pages of *Lay Sermons* walk the great. I don't say that Margot Asquith permits us to rub elbows with them ourselves, but she willingly shows us her own elbow, which has been, so to say, honed on the mighty—"I remember President Wilson saying to me," "John Addington Symonds once said to me," "The Master of Balliol told me": thus does she introduce her anecdotes. And you know those anecdotes that begin that way; me, I find them more efficacious than sheep-counting, rain on a tin roof or Alanol tablets. Just begin a story with such a phrase as "I remember Disraeli—poor old Dizzy!—once saying to me, in answer to my poke in the eye . . ." and you will find me and Morpheus off in a corner, necking. . . . *Lay Sermons* is a naive and an annoying and unimportant book. The author says "I am not sure that my ultimate choice for the name of this modest work is altogether happy." Happier I think it would have been, wrote Mrs. Parker, if, instead of the word "Sermons," she had selected the word "Off."

It was as dismissive as the manner in which she had dealt with Margot Asquith's earlier autobiography. At that time, Mrs. Parker predicted: "The affair between Margot Asquith and Margot Asquith will live as one of the prettiest love stories in all literature."

There had, however, been more alluring aspects to her job. She had turned her attention to the latest Hemingway book, *Men Without Women*. Hemingway, immersed in his perpetual themes of war, love, courage and death, had held out hope for her: "It was a warm gratification to find the new Hemingway book, *Men Without Women*, a truly magnificent work. It is composed of thirteen short, sad and terrible stories . . . I do not know where a greater collection can be found." Ernest, she knew, would love that.

In reviewing *My Life*, the posthumous autobiography of Isadora Duncan, Mrs. Parker had written:

"Here was a great woman; a magnificent, generous, gallant, reckless, fated fool of a woman. There was never a place for her in the ranks of the terrible, slow army of the cautious. She ran ahead, where there were no paths. . . . "

There were those who likened Mrs. Parker herself to that description of Isadora: certainly she was given to running ahead where there were no paths. But there was a path she was now to take which was clearly defined. She made it known to her friends that she wanted to marry Alan Campbell.

It had been slightly ironic that Joseph Bryan III had first introduced her to Alan at the Dietzes' dinner party. Then and there she convinced herself that there simply had to be an empathy of genes between them despite the fact that he was a Southerner, a breed she had up to then disliked. Like her, Alan was half-Jewish and his father had been of Scottish descent, a direct member of the Duke of Argyll's premier clan of Scotland—the Campbells. Mrs. Parker was half-Jewish and with a Scots mother. And, too, the basis of their separate upbringing was not that dissimilar.

Like her, he had been something of a family reject, the product of a shrewish woman, Hortense, second daughter of a Jewish butcher from Richmond married to a husband who was "something in tobacco" from Virginia. When, following the death of his father, Alan had got bit-parts on Broadway, his mother had followed him to New York. It mattered not to her that her son was bisexual. He was an extremely well-built young man, six-foot-two, and strikingly handsome with a presence and wit that would see him through to success. Like Alan, Hortense had long believed that if her son did not make it as an actor, he'd make it as a writer—he had always been gifted that way even as a boy when he had won essay prizes at school. She knew too, that despite his versatile sexual proclivities, he'd as likely as not settle for a woman in the end, provided the woman was attuned to his ambitions.

Now, here was her son Alan, shacked up with New York's Dorothy Parker, celebrated literary journalist, poet and wit. If Hortense Campbell was happy at the news of her son's new liaison, Mrs. Parker was not perceivably inspired at the prospect of acquiring Hortense Campbell as a future mother-in-law. She dismissed her by saying:

"Hortense is the only woman I know who pronounces the word 'egg' with three syllables."

Still a victim of spasmodic black, introspective moods, Mrs. Parker was becoming much happier now. Love—the real thing—it seemed, had come at last and with it a harvest of caring affection and an abundance of help.

· 2 9 ·

A Light on the Horizon

IN THE EARLY THIRTIES, following the Wall Street crash, America was lurching in a sea of contradictions and extremes.

Since the mid-1800s, it had absorbed thousands of immigrants attracted to the ideal of the American Dream. Now, "God's own country," as the immigrants had called it, was entering the dust-bowl years of the Great Depression. Murder and violence were rampant across the country. Food and the necessities of life were in pitifully short supply, nailing Herbert Hoover's lie of 1928 when he had declared, "We in America today are nearer to the final triumph over poverty than ever before in the history of any land. The poor-house is vanishing from among us."

In thoroughfares such as Manhattan's Twenty-Fifth Street, the women's section of the Socialist party distributed bread, soup and coffee to lines of bedraggled human beings who had little hope for the future. Even those usually found in such places were conspicuously absent now, their places having been taken over by tired and hungry clerks, engineers, civil servants, office workers, factory hands, housewives, professional men. Petty racketeering was rife. Many could not pay their rent and were evicted, some riding the trains from Times Square to Coney Island, swinging round the loop and returning just to get some sleep in the warm railroad cars. Bodies were nightly stretched out on all available park benches; hundreds of thousands of feet were swollen with blisters from tramping the sidewalks for days and nights in search of odd jobs and food, anything to avoid the breadline to which they were inevitably destined to return.

It was life in the raw and it was, too, a raw winter of cold reality, the reality that America had lost its way; that the bubble of the American Dream had burst.

Even when the spring of May 1930 had arrived, it had not helped when Hoover sought further to assure the people of America:

"We have been passing through one of those great economic storms which periodically bring hardship and suffering upon our people. While the crash only took place six months ago, I am convinced that we have now passed the worst and with continued unity of effort we shall rapidly recover. There is one certainty in the future of a people of the resources, intelligence, and character of the people of the United States—that is, Prosperity."

While the rest of the country suffered, the Chicago gangsters prospered. Ironically, the notorious Al Capone, with a Colt revolver strapped beneath his jacket, was actually funding a breadline operation in Chicago, while respectable housewives in many areas of the country were turning to blatant prostitution in order to feed their families, their favors often being turned down with such remarks as, "Christ, kid, if I had any dough I'd rather eat." Children were fainting at school due to lack of nourishment. There were a few, however, who had the crisis in perspective, one such being Will Rogers:

There is not an unemployed man in the country that hasn't contributed to the wealth of every millionaire in America. The working classes didn't bring this on, it was the big boys who thought the financial drunk was going to last forever and over-bought, over-merged and over-capitalized . . . We've got more wheat, more corn, more food, more cotton, more money in the banks, more of everything in the world than any nation that ever lived ever had, yet we are starving to death. We are the first nation in the history of the world to go to the poorhouse in an automobile.

An anonymous lyricist had written a sardonic song, "The Happy American," which, sung at Democratic meetings, closely approached Mrs. Parker's sense of irony:

> How happy to be an American
> One of the chosen breed,
> Who lived in a land of abundance
> Where no-one is ever in need.
> As long as a man is willing to work
> He is bound to get on well,
> And there are two chickens in every pot,
> There are, like hell!

There was irony too, when a while later Gorney and Harburg penned another song which swept America and the rest of the world, touching the nerve of mass disenchantment:

> They used to tell me I was building a dream,
> And so I followed the mob—
> When there was earth to plow or guns to bear
> I was always there—right on the job . . .
> Once in khaki suits,
> Gee, we looked swell,

Full of that Yankee-Doodle-de-Dum,
Half a million boots, went sloggin' through Hell.
And I was the kid with the drum.
Say, don't you remember, they called me Al—
It was Al all the time,
Say, don't you remember, I'm your pal,
Brother, can you spare a dime?

If the Depression was all but draining the life out of the nation, it had little effect on Mrs. Parker and her friends. The media, give or take a few bankrupted journals, remained largely intact and she had not been asked to take cuts in her fees. She had, however, identified herself with the plight of the masses, doing what she could to help by donating money to soup kitchens and charities.

There was, as far as she and Alan Campbell were concerned, a light on the horizon. While the economic crisis had had a fiercely detrimental effect throughout commerce and industry, one of the few industries that had survived intact and was, indeed, booming, was the film business, centered in Los Angeles.

For many people the cinema was now the escape route from the harsh reality of the grim, real world; it was a fantasy world of sumptuous riches and fine homes, where the men and women who lived in the affluence of the flickering movies seemed deliciously unreal and totally, infinitely glamorous. And the place where it was all happening was Hollywood, the place where Benchley, Sherwood, Stewart, Connelly, Stallings and others were making salaries ranging from $500 to $2,500 and more a week.

Alan Campbell believed that Hollywood would again beckon to Dorothy Parker; that the moguls would cable her and make it possible for her to return in style, with full acknowledgment of her formidable status as a writer. And he, Alan Campbell, would be there at her side to become, in full professional terms, a screenwriter himself.

Campbell's friends knew he was star-struck; that he adored the gossip of show-business; that he thrived on stories laminated with a sheen of bitchy venom. They knew, too, that Alan loved the lunches, the dinners, the intimate suppers, the parties, the celebrity-studded ambience of the Algonquinites and the foolishness they exuded. A number of the Algonquin crowd were now established playwrights, authors, actors, featured syndicated columnists, composers, lyricists, and several of them had already won top writing awards and other accolades, including the newly initiated prestigious Pulitzer prizes.

Alan Campbell now was close friends with most of the Algonquinites.

It mattered little that many of them who worked in Hollywood despised the place, hurling dismissive epithets on the town and its moguls. This attitude was the old problem of the artist prostituting his art for a mess of potage.

No such grandiose thoughts consumed Alan Campbell, even though Dorothy declared the place to be "a shit heap." The studio moguls and story department heads had the perfect answer to this accusation: "Yeah," they said, "it's true, but all these pontificating intellectuals give in and come here in the end. They all come out here shouting 'shit' and stay to eat it!"

That, to Campbell, was the reality of the place and he was nothing if not a realist. To him, there was much about the place that was infinitely appealing and he desperately wanted to make his mark. He, as a would-be screenwriter, exuded no craving for culture: if he was expected to execute a dance for deification, he'd do it for dollars, and only for dollars. In his view, Hollywood added up to Money and Fame and that to him was an acceptable enough panacea for any loss of writer's integrity.

Meanwhile, if the masses on the breadlines were having a hard time, life in New York for Mrs. Parker was buoyant.

Oppenheimer, her publisher at Viking, had staged his play, *Here Today*, starring an eccentric lady writer who was clearly the mirror-image of Dorothy Parker. It mattered little that the show had closed within five weeks to become destined for a kind of jerky immortality in summer stock. And, too, writer-director Charles Brackett had been inspired to feature Mrs. Parker as a puffy-eyed, self-pitying writing celebrity in his astringent play *Entirely Surrounded*. Dorothy Parker had, indeed, become a cult figure, and cult figures laid themselves open to be ridiculed on stage which is exactly what her friends, Kaufman and Hart, did when featuring her as Julia Glenn and the Algonquin crowd as themselves in the Coq d'Or restaurant scenes in *Merrily We Roll Along*, which proved at this time to be a decisive hit on the Broadway stage. The authors featured Julia Glenn as "a woman close to forty. She is not unpretty but on her face are the marks of years and years of quiet and steady drinking —eight, ten hours a day."

It was all heady stuff, exhilarating and exciting. The exhilaration and excitement were such that one evening Alan and Dorothy went to a party that ended up in a tattoo parlor in Greenwich Village. Under the influence of too much alcohol, Dorothy Parker wanted to be tattooed on the arm. Alan was against the idea but when Dorothy made up her mind, there was no arguing about it. The tattoo was to stay on her arm for the rest of her life. As far as Alan was concerned, there was one symbolic aspect of her impulsive act: She had chosen to be tattooed with a star.

Alan Campbell was his wife's adoring acolyte, responding to her every whim, laughing at her jokes. "He took her and probably kept her living," Donald Ogden Stewart was later to recall. "He was important insofar as taking care of her was concerned, and to him she was well worth taking care of. Alan was an actor and he may have been playing a part which, little by little, took over, but he wasn't a villain. He kept her living and working." The fact that she was, indeed, living and working was underlined by Woollcott who, at this time, took Stella (Mrs. Patrick) Campbell to the theater to see *The Cherry Orchard*. He later remembered:

> I could not help hearing Stella try to drown out Nazimova. I thought this was naughty of her, and as the curtain fell on the first intermission, I tried to scowl a reproof in her direction. Unabashed, she held me in the aisle with inquiries about Dorothy Parker, whom she admires enormously, but whom she usually refers to, for some mysterious reason of her own, as Dorothy Warren. Mrs. Campbell told me she had been having great success in her lectures by reciting one of Mrs. Parker's lovelorn poems which ends with the lines:
>
> > There is no edgèd thing in all this night,
> > Save in my breast.
>
> By this time the whole audience was watching us, and I felt a thousand pair of eyes critically surveying my contours as she cried out with considerable archness, "There's no use denying it. I am sure *you* are the edgèd thing in her breast!"

· 3 0 ·

A Meeting with Hammett
and Hellman

IN THE *Bookman*, Dorothy Parker had been described by her friend John Farrar as "the giantess of American letters," a description which showed a lack of acrimony on the part of her former lover, Seward Collins, who owned the magazine. And now 1931 had seen her new book of poems, *Death and Taxes*, appear on the bookstands. As a result, she was the recipient of further critical accolades. A poet could hardly hope for a more glowing assessment than that given to her by Henry Canby in the *Saturday Review*: " . . . verse of a Horatian lightness . . . exquisite certainty of technique . . . like the lustre on a Persian bowl. . . . "

There seemed, at last, to be full and unequivocal justification for her stance as a wit and poet: Raymond Kresensky perceptively noted when reviewing her book in *Christian Century* that "it is a well-known fact that often the court jester is a serious philosopher beneath his cap and bells." And her old friend Franklin Pierce Adams appeared to be indulging in some log-rolling when writing in *Books*: "In this new collection the painful hunger for beauty and the heartbreak of its impermanence, the uncompromising idealism, are even acuter than in her previous volumes. It is her saddest and her best book." To others, too, it was precisely that, her epigrammic mastery being well to the fore in "Sanctuary," in which she admitted:

> My land is bare of chattering folk,
> The clouds are low along the ridges,
> And sweet's the air with curly smoke
> From all my burning bridges . . .

Her sardonic humor also hit the target in "Salome's Dancing Lesson".

> She whose body's young and cool,
> Has no need of a dancing school . . .

It was, predictably, a book of moods, as varied as the colors of a Vermont autumn, ranging as it did from her cycle of epigrams, "Tomb-

178

stones in the Starlight" to "The Little Old Lady in Lavender Silk." In structure her verses formed their own identity from vers libre to sonnet, joking like Catullus in "From a Letter to Lesbia," to French verse form in "Ballad of a Talked-Off Ear." The lady was unquestionably versatile. And, as if in quiet gratitude, she had dedicated the volume simply: "To Mr. Benchley."

Mrs. Parker now occupied herself with writing for *Harper's Bazaar, The New Yorker* and *Cosmopolitan,* plus about four other publications, and she was delighted when her friend James Thurber invited her to write an introduction to his book of drawings *The Seal in the Bedroom and Other Predicaments.*

Thurber, who had joined the staff of *The New Yorker* in 1927, was an artist, illustrator and storyteller of exceptional and unusual talent, a man "who did not make up jokes in his mouth like so many clowns, but somewhere between the optic nerve and the unconscious, an area where the slightest tilt can lead to torment and madness." Thurber, as well she knew, "was at his best when he wasn't saying anything about anything" as, for example, "I said the hounds of Spring are on winter's traces, but let it pass, let it pass." As somebody else said at the time: "That's art and that's Thurber."

It was a similar sort of humor to that of her friend Robert Benchley, vaguely reminiscent of the time when a man at Tony's showed Benchley and Mrs. Parker a so-called indestructible watch. Thurber recalled the incident:

"They whammed the watch against a tabletop, then put it on the floor and stamped on it. The dismayed owner picked it up and put it to his ear. 'It has stopped,' he said incredulously. 'Maybe you wound it too tight,' said Benchley and Mrs. Parker together."

In both a literary and personal context, Benchley, Thurber and Sid Perelman were her special kind of funsters. There was another, Ogden Nash, who now dedicated his new book, *Hard Lines,* to her.

The success of her *Death and Taxes* volume demanded a celebration. George Oppenheimer decided to throw a cocktail party in her honor. He chose the Algonquin. The Vicious Circle, as it now scarcely remained, was an ectoplasmic image of what it had once been, now no longer a force, a full-bloodied entity, its members being half in Hollywood and half on Broadway, with one or two, like Sherwood, in England and elsewhere. Those who were still around the New York literary scene and Times Square, turned up at the Algonquin, fully expecting a drinking bash. One such was Tallulah Bankhead, dressed for the kill and characteristically in the mood to hog the limelight. She was not at the party for more than an hour, all the while dispensing an effusion of *"dahlings!"* when somebody noticed she had slipped indecorously to the floor in a drunken stupor. With a total lack of ceremony, the actress was bodily transported to an adjoining room to sleep it off. Seeing this, Mrs. Parker put her head round the door of the room and casually inquired, "Has Whistler's mother passed out?"

Tallulah, with her customary contempt for conformity, and with no perceivable lack of aplomb, turned up for lunch at the hotel next day. Mrs. Parker was there at the Round Table, her doe eyes giving nothing away. Taking her seat, Tallulah produced a mirror and gazed ruefully into it. "Dahlings," she proclaimed languorously, "the less I behave like Whistler's mother the night before, the more I look like her the morning after." Touché to Miss Bankhead.

The dispersal of the Algonquinites from the hotel on Forty-fourth Street had now all but been effected. The early rose blush of the place had faded and the members of the Round Table and the peripheral hangers-on were now frequenting other hotels, dining in other restaurants, drinking in other bars. The parties, too, were less in evidence; life was becoming rather more staid.

The Hotel Sutton on East Fifty-sixth Street was attracting the interest of Mrs. Parker and her escort, Alan Campbell. Let their friend Sid Perelman describe the place:

If, in the latter half of 1932, you were a mid-Western music student at Juilliard, a fledgling copywriter with a marginal salary, or a divorcée rubbing along on a small alimony, the chances are that you lived at one time or another at the Hotel Sutton . . . The Sutton was a fairly characteristic example of the residential, or *soi-disant* "club" hotel designed for respectable young folk pursuing a career in New York. There was nothing in the least club-like about it, and it was residential only in the sense that it was an abode, a roof over one's head. Otherwise, it was an impersonal sixteen-storey barracks with a myriad of rooms so tiny that their walls impinged on each other, a honeycomb full of workers and drones in the minimum cubic footage required to avert strangulation.

The decor of all the rooms was identical—fireproof early-American, impervious to the whim of guests who might succumb to euphoria, despair or drunkenness. The furniture was rock maple, the rugs rock wool. In addition to a bureau, a stiff wing chair, a lamp with a false pewter base, and an end table, each chamber contained a bed narrow enough to discourage any thoughts of venery. As a further sop to respectability, the sexes had been segregated on alternate floors, but the liftmen did not regard themselves as house-mothers, and for the frisky a rear stairway offered ready access or flight.

The waitresses in the coffee shop on the ground floor wore peach-colored uniforms and served a thrifty club breakfast costing sixty-five cents. You had a choice of juice—orange or tomato—but not of the glass it came in, which was a heavy green goblet. The coffee, it goes without saying, was unspeakable. . . .

The manager of the Sutton was Mr. Nathanael West, who happened to be Perelman's brother-in-law. West was destined to achieve future eminence as a novelist. The place, as well as being a haven for the young, was also a sort of sanctuary for unknown writers, to whom West gave considerable succor, especially when they were hard up. "But," Perelman later remembered, "the one writer of celebrity in the establishment was something of a recluse. This was Dashiell Hammett, who, in the pages of magazines like *Black Mask*, and four novels, had revolutionized the whole concept of police fiction."

Tall, gray-haired and emaciated, with a face that looked like a deflated football, Hammett was holed-up at the Sutton with a lady named Lillian Hellman, who, born in New Orleans, had spent her childhood between there and New York, had attended New York University and Columbia, worked as a story assistant in Hollywood and as a reader for publisher Horace Liveright, and had married Algonquin frequenter Arthur Kober. Separated from him, she was now living with Hammett, at the same time seeking her own identity as a playwright, struggling at the Sutton with her first play, *The Children's Hour.*

It was to the Sutton that Mrs. Parker and Alan Campbell came one night, before going on to a party at William Rose Benét's apartment, to which Hammett and Hellman were also invited. If Mrs. Parker knew little or nothing about Miss Hellman, she was more than familiar with Mr. Hammett and his works. According to Miss Hellman:

I first met Dorothy Parker . . . shortly after I moved back to New York with Hammett. She caused a wacky-tipsy fight between us. She had read *The Maltese Falcon* and *Red Harvest*, perhaps a year or two before, and she had written about them, but she had not met Hammett until a cocktail party given by William Rose Benét. I was already uncomfortable at this party of people much older than myself, when a small, worn, prettyish woman was introduced to Hammett and immediately fell to her knees before him and kissed his hand. It was meant to be both funny and serious, but it was neither, and Hammett was embarrassed into a kind of simper.

I had a habit in those days—there are still often hang-overs of it on other levels—of making small matters into large symbols and, after enough cocktails, I saw the gesture as what New York life was going to be like for an unknown young woman among the famous. That night I accused Dash of liking ladies who kissed his hand. He said I was crazy, I said I wasn't going to live with a man who allowed women to kneel in admiration, he said he had "allowed" no such thing, didn't like it, but if I wanted to leave right away, he would not detain me. I said I'd go as soon as I finished my steak, but I guess by that time we were fighting about something else, because a few months later he said if ever I reminded him of the incident again, I would never live to finish another steak!

Strangely, at the sequel to that meeting, Dorothy Parker won in Lillian Hellman a friend for life. And by that single ostentatious gesture, made of Dashiell Hammett an enemy who in later days would move out rather than tolerate Mrs. Parker as a houseguest of Lillian Hellman in the home he shared with her.

· 3 1 ·

A Juvenile's Bride

LIGHT-YEARS away from the cosseted confines of the literary set of
New York, the abject poverty of most of the citizens of New York and
the seemingly unending vista of utter hopelessness remained until
Franklin Delano Roosevelt entered the main American political arena.

In his Democratic nomination acceptance speech of 1932, Roosevelt
made a clarion call to the people:

"I pledge you—I pledge myself—to a New Deal for the American
people. Let us all here assembled constitute ourselves prophets of a New
Order of competence and of courage. This is more than a political campaign; it is a call to arms. Give me your help, not to win votes alone but
to win in this crusade to restore America to its own people."

It was not long, the next year, in fact, before Roosevelt, swept up in
the euphoria of his own election promises, fell a victim to hate. On February 16, 1933, a man named Giuseppe Zangara shot at him, missed,
killed Chicago Mayor Anton Cermak and wounded four others in Miami.

On November 8, 1932, 22,815,535 Americans voted for Roosevelt to
Hoover's 15,759,930 votes.

But if there had been hatred abroad, there was now song, Franklin
Roosevelt's election song:

> Happy days are here again,
> The skies above are clear again!
> Let's all sing a song of cheer again—
> Happy days are here again!

And even if happy days had not returned, two songsters, Warren and
Dubin, in sunny Hollywood, were helping to create a false image of
American affluence during this, the end of Prohibition:

> We're in the money, we're in the money,
> We've got a lot of what it takes to get along,
> We're in the money, the skies are sunny,
> Old man Depression you are through, you done us wrong!

At this time, Alan Campbell received an invitation to do a summer
stock season at the Ellitch Gardens Theatre in Denver, Colorado. Ever

the optimist, Campbell was buoyant at Roosevelt's pledge and full of hope for the future. He considered that the job offer indicated that the fallow years were indeed past and that this was an indication to prove it. He and Dorothy made several decisions. First, they decided he would accept the job and they would move to Denver. Second, they would get married there, the fairly easy morality of the city being what it was. The gap in their ages did not seem to bother either of them; Dorothy Parker was forty; Alan was twenty-nine.

They bought a 1929 banger, packed in two Bedlington terriers and were soon unpacking their bags in Denver. Although Alan had previously done the cooking and attended to most of the household chores, Mrs. Parker tried ineffectively to take over the domestic reins, appearing destined—albeit briefly—for a life of contented domesticity.

Keeping in touch with some of the old Algonquin crowd, who had by this time tried unsuccessfully to set up a replacement venue at Jim Moriarty's establishment in Marlborough House at 15 East Sixty-first Street, she wrote to Alexander Woollcott. Denver, it seemed, was much to her liking. Or was it?

"We have met three or four nice people, which is big for a continent," she wrote. "I thought I was going to hate it, and I love it. I love being a juvenile's bride and living in a bungalow and pinching dead leaves off the rose bushes. I will be God damned."

To this day, nobody quite knows when they married or precisely where. The International News Service reported the marriage took place in October 1933 at her sister's home on Long Island, while the divorce papers she filed in 1947 claimed it was in 1934 in Raton, New Mexico. INS also reported a prank, whereby Denver's socially prominent people were invited to a party at the Campbells', which neither bride nor groom knew anything about. The *Los Angeles Times'* first reference to the union was emblazoned beneath a headline which read: "Dorothy Parker's Secret Marriage to Actor Bared." Bared it might have been in journalistic terms, but neither Alan nor Dorothy was telling.

It seems likely that the marriage did, in fact, take place in New Mexico in 1934 because by that time, at the end of Alan's summer stock job, the two moved on to Hollywood. New Mexico was not that far away and once in Hollywood they were soon to throw a memorable party that underlined their status as newlyweds.

As far as their Algonquin friends were concerned, most of the group in Hollywood were now well established and those in New York and elsewhere were not doing too badly, either. Marc Connelly's *The Green Pastures* was a hit on the Broadway stage and George Kaufman, now temporarily in Hollywood had, with Moss Hart, achieved a big success on the New York stage with *Once in a Lifetime:* Kaufman also had yet another hit running with *The Bandwagon.* Robert Sherwood had turned out the memorable *Waterloo Bridge* and *Reunion in Vienna* shortly after the Wall Street crash, and Woollcott had written a best-selling book, *While Rome Burns,* and had made a great success when Mutual Broadcasting network station WOR had established him as a major star as "The Town Crier" on radio. Edna Ferber had published *Cimarron* and *American Beauty* to high acclaim, and Heywood Broun's revue *Shoot the Works,* to which Mrs. Parker, as we shall continue to call her, had contributed a sketch and a lyric, had run eighty-seven performances on Broadway. Harpo Marx, together with Peggy Wood, Helen Hayes, the Lunts and other actors and actresses of the Algonquin set, had severally become firmly established names in the theater.

Before leaving New York, Mrs. Parker had desultorily started to collect and edit her three published books of poetry. She vaguely planned in the future to publish an omnibus edition of the best of all three under the title *After Such Pleasures,* deriving the title from Mercutio's sardonic death-speech in *Romeo and Juliet.*

It was 1933 and money-wise, there was yet more gainful expectancy on the horizon. With Denver behind them and bliss their companion, the two duly arrived in Hollywood, plus dogs, where George Oppenheimer's house was available to them to provide temporary shelter and considerable comfort.

Before leaving, the two had been in touch with the influential film and theatrical agent Leland Hayward, who was handling the representation of writers at the New York end of the Myron Selznick–Frank Joyce agency, a talent organization in time destined to become the Music Corporation of America. Hayward had been delighted to accept both Dorothy and Alan as clients, more particularly as a writing team, and had sent enthusiastic signals to his associates in the West Coast branch.

Soon Hayward had negotiated a six-picture deal for them as collaborative scenarists for Paramount Pictures at $5,200 a week.

Dorothy Parker phoned the news of their arrival and the Paramount deal to Robert Benchley, who was still at the Garden of Allah. "Great," he said, "come on over and meet the Almighty and his Disciples." He meant, of course, the aging Paramount mogul Adolph Zukor and his minions.

As Alan had predicted, Mrs. Parker had arrived back in Hollywood in style. And Alan himself had arrived at his Shangri-la. The couple, feeling good at the turn of events, called a cab and instructed the driver to take them to the Garden of Allah.

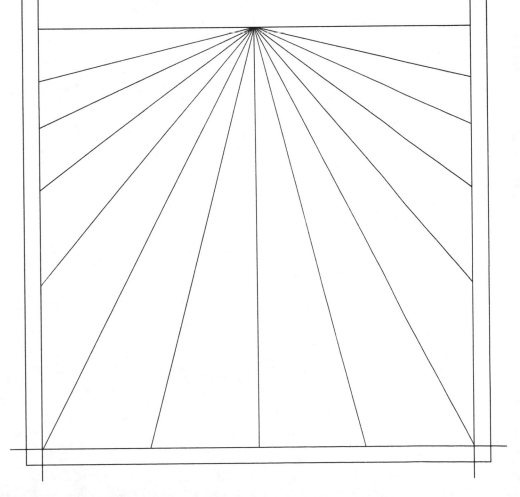

BOOK · THREE

The Beginning of the End

· 3 2 ·

The Garden of Allah

THE LEGEND of the Los Angeles suburb which was becoming the world famous Hollywood had begun in 1905. That year, a languorous Russian actress, Alla Nazimova, arrived in America with a company of players known as the Orlenoff Troupe. The lady quickly discarded them and embarked upon a career as a silent movie star.

In 1918, shortly after the end of the First World War, that same dark-haired screen siren paid over $55,000 for a ninety-nine-year lease on a huge Spanish-type structure at 8150 Sunset Boulevard in West Hollywood, a garish, green-roofed, sprawling edifice with ancillary buildings and four acres of exotic palms, banana, bamboo, cedar, grapefruit and orange trees. The collection of rare, squawking Oriental birds inhabiting the trees seemed to some to be the epitome of bad taste; to its Crimean-born owner it was a world of delight.

She soon reorganized her assets and converted the place into a hotel. With a touch of Eastern promise, she named it the Garden of Allah, which some said might have been an allegorical allusion to the lady facing Mecca with a bankbook in one hand and a prayer rug in the other. The hotel boasted—and never was a word more fitting—a main building and bar, a redesigned swimming pool—"the biggest in Hollywood"—and some thirty or more self-contained cottages or apartments, variously described as bungalows, apartments or villas. They were little more than ocher hutches, either square or elongated in shape and all undistinguished in their architecture, each creating a monotonous anonymity in their pseudo-Spanish similarity.

The Garden of Allah opened for business on January 9, 1921, and was given an "official launching" with an indescribably vulgar party which lasted a full and raucous twenty-four hours. Four hundred and fifty guests had attended, at least three hundred of whom turned out to be frenetic freeloaders.

As time passed, the central hotel building and its stuccoed satellites became known as either "the Beverly Hills Bathhouse," "Ali Baba's Alley" or "The Whores' Hang-Out." It became a custom to organize parties for residents who had died, "rave-ups" as somebody put it, "to send the departing spirits on their way." With the inevitability of night, the place quickly became its own legend, largely created by the bizarre opulence of the complex and the extrovert antics of its habitués.

If the Algonquin had had its pranks in the twenties, they were nothing compared to what went on in the Garden. John Barrymore was given to taking drunken midnight dives, fully dressed, in the pool, and Tallulah Bankhead's cavortings at five o'clock in the morning, stark naked, were monotonously heard of around the same azure waters. John Carradine, of Villa Number 15, frequently orated Shakespearean passages grandiloquently at dawn, directed towards the Hollywood hills above, customarily cheered on loudly by his wife, Sonya. There was also Charles Laughton's nightly gambolings around the pool while sporting a huge and horrific hump on his back, a penalty of his role in *The Hunchback of Notre Dame*; it took too long to remove the hump and reapply it, so Laughton took it home with him.

The Garden was the place where mid-European expatriate moguls, agents, producers, directors, and other show-business entrepreneurs scattered their alms for Allah, and most of the lower orders who stayed there grabbed hungrily for those same alms. Frequent patrons of the hotel included Sergei Rachmaninoff, (who liked to practice on the piano at dawn); Clara Bow, the "It" girl; Rex Ingram; Greta Garbo; Roland Young; Ramon Novarro; Vilma Banky; Rod La Roque; Ronald Colman; Buster Keaton; and Edmund Lowe. Ever since its ostentatious opening the place had accommodated a continuous flow of movie people: Lilyan Tashman, Gloria Swanson, Conrad Veidt, Mrs. Patrick Campbell, William Powell, Ernst Lubitsch, Francis X. Bushman, Maurice Chevalier, Carole Lombard, Charles Chaplin, among them. Like the legends of the place itself, the list of its patrons seemed endless.

Robert Benchley was in Villa Number 16 when Dorothy Parker and Alan Campbell arrived in Hollywood. Benchley, with his frequent trips to the West Coast, his short films, books and now his roles in feature films, had early established his claim as "the patron saint of the Garden." Moss Hart, Kaufman and Alice Duer Miller were there, too, at the time; as were Donald Ogden Stewart, Ben Hecht, Charles MacArthur, Noel Coward and the stately Dame May Whitty, a long way from her flat in Covent Garden, London, rehearsing as the nurse to Vivien Leigh's Juliet and Laurence Olivier's Romeo. Dame May's daughter, Margaret Webster, the renowned theater director, was another temporary resident.

Benchley quickly initiated Dorothy and Alan into the frolics of the place and, as he called it, "the local cold chicken and coleslaw circuit." The stories about Hollywood were already vast in number and Benchley delighted the newcomers with a droll collection of the latest. There was the Lubitsch one he liked; the director had explained his directing technique, adding, "I let the audience use their imaginations. Can I help it if they misconstrue my suggestions?" There was also the one about John Barrymore, who after throwing a fish at a coughing theater audience, had called out: "Busy yourself with that, you damned walruses, while the rest of us proceed with the play."

Within a few days of the arrival of Mrs. Parker and Alan Campbell, Alexander Woollcott checked in at the Garden. He did not like Hollywood but was addicted to his friends, and a lot of those friends were there. Laurence Stallings told him that he could earn at least $1,000 a week writing for films, to which he replied: "When I take up streetwalking, the streets will be Broadway, not Hollywood Boulevard." It echoed the sentiment of many of the writers there; disenchantment had set in early, but, as they put it, they had a living to make.

Other friends of George Oppenheimer were due to arrive at his Hollywood house, so the Campbells moved out and checked into the Garden of Allah. In 1933, the place was said to be "a world within the world of Hollywood" and that is precisely what it had become. The Campbells swiftly learned the social customs of the hotel. It was the order of the day that someone gave a party each afternoon in one of the villas, and each of the old Algonquin set in his or her turn staged a raucous après-lunch get-together. These parties were augmented by further ones given by people like writers John McClain, Eddie Mayer, Muriel King, John O'Hara, Frances and Albert Hackett. Charles Butterworth, a well-known screen comedian of the time, a small dyspeptic-looking man with a penchant for endless whiskey sours, was a familiar guest at virtually every party—he was to become a firm friend of Mrs. Parker and Alan.

Orson Welles, a bright young man of the theater, was holed up in a villa at the Garden working with two writers in an attempt to "update" the Lord's Prayer, which he planned to orate in a movie. "You can't do that," said one of his writers. "It's God's word." "Don't tell me about God's word," shouted Welles. "I am God!" The place was, as somebody called it, "the uterus of Flickerland."

Dorothy and Alan got to work on their assignments. They had signed with Paramount to produce an original story for Carole Lombard and Lee Tracy. When they finished it, they moved on to write dialogue for two further films, *Here is My Heart* and *One Hour Late*. Leland Hayward had made it a condition of their employment that they should be allowed to work at home if they wished, attending the studio only for script conferences and the like. Hayward had fixed this useful arrangement but sometimes, as with other of his clients with a similar facility, the arrange-

ment hadn't always worked, and he had not always been told when this
was the case. As he himself was to recall:

> One day I got a call from Metro. They were completely confused over there
> and they wanted to know where in hell was my client, William Faulkner. They
> were pretty sore, nobody was supposed to walk out of Metro without letting the
> front office know where he'd gone. I didn't know where Bill was. He hadn't told
> me he was going anywhere. I got the office to start making calls all over the
> damned place, and finally we thought of trying him at his home in Mississippi,
> and sure enough, there he was. "What the hell are you doing down there?" I
> yelled on the phone, and he said, "Well, ah asked my producer if ah could work
> at home, and he said fine, so heah ah am. . . ."

And there, indeed at home, like Mrs. Parker and Alan, he was. Results were what mattered; films were being made in every available corner
of Hollywood, in the studios, on the backlots, on location, and there
wasn't time to bother too much about writers and their "integrity" or
where, in special cases, the scripts were actually written. Time was
money, and Leland Hayward had the pulse of time, especially when his
big-name clients were providing him with a steady and handsome succession of 10 percents. Moreover, he could prove it, as he later explained:

> Ben [Hecht] and Charlie [MacArthur] did the script for *Wuthering Heights* in
> two weeks flat," he recalled. "They didn't bother too much with the Brontë book
> —they did it from an outline. Walter Wanger sold it to Sam Goldwyn and Sam
> made it into a big hit. Ben was always good at pressure jobs. He worked on *Gone
> With the Wind* for David Selznick—never read that either. Claimed reading the
> book would only confuse him and, you know, maybe he was right.

Maybe, too, Will Rogers was right. He said at the time: "There is only
one thing that can kill the movies—and that is education." Or it could
have been, as Darryl Zanuck opined: "Public taste is an ascending spi-
ral." The trouble was that Zanuck failed to say to what it was ascending.
As far as the producer was concerned, there were always wits around to
denigrate the people who made movies, wits like Oscar Levant, another
Algonquinite, who described Mr. Zanuck's own ascent as "From Poland
to polo in one generation."

Working at home, however, had its distractions. Mrs. Parker and
Alan had taken up golf, and each week when they played they sent the
chauffeur the company had provided to collect their salary check from
the studio treasurer. Their pay was particularly generous because of Mrs.
Parker's literary eminence, but husband and wife both knew how to
spend the money. Mrs. Parker thought nothing of paying $86 for a hat

and it is known that she settled one bill for $628 in respect of a couple of sets of handmade lingerie. She also repaid John Gilbert the $2,500 he had loaned her for her stay in hospital.

At this time she became close friends with Helen Hayes, who was on the coast making a film; other friends whose company she and Alan enjoyed were Bing Crosby and James Cagney. Mrs. Parker was settling into Hollywood but was developing an even more pronounced abhorrence for screenwriting as prescribed by the moguls. She wrote her sister in New York State: "Aside from the work, which I hate like holy water, I love it here." And she did love the place, not least because other writers of her intellectual parity were arriving in the film city. These included her "darling" friend F. Scott Fitzgerald, as well as Thomas Wolfe, who was working on the screenplay for his book, *Look Homeward, Angel.* Wolfe, when told about the Garden of Allah, had refused to believe that any such place existed: "I'll be damned if I believe anyone lives in a place of that name."

But the place did exist. Moreover, it now housed Dorothy Parker and Alan Campbell who, after afternoon sojourns to the celebrity villas, would join the crowd to move on to other parties in the houses up in the hills, often finishing up early the following morning in Schwab's Drugstore on the corner of Sunset Boulevard and North Crescent Heights.

Mrs. Parker and Alan were soon very much a part of the film city's social scene and the lady herself underlined this by joining Benchley, John O'Hara and Jock Whitney in investing in the Mike Romanoff's new restaurant on the north side of Wilshire Boulevard on North Rodeo Drive.

As a hotel, the Garden of Allah had, as everybody knew, a reputation for "devastating decadence," and there were few who would deny it that reputation. It was the hotel where countless affairs, one-night stands and, occasionally, marriages had begun, ripened, endured or ended, often as a result of the calumny of two ego-drunk columnists, the Misses Hedda Hopper and Louella Parsons, the former who wore outrageous hats and lisle stockings and the latter who boasted an indecent power complex, a drunken doctor husband and a holy crucifix in her hall.

One such affair concerned F. Scott Fitzgerald, who, with Zelda away in a sanitorium, turned his attentions to the blonde, beautiful Sheilah Graham, a former Cochran chorus girl. Cochran's chorus had also included Winston Churchill's daughter, Sarah. Miss Graham had been glamorously transformed by time and fortuitous meetings with several rich men, including an English viscount, from an impoverished, illiterate, orphan into a syndicated Hollywood columnist. She lived at the

Garden next door to Errol Flynn. According to Miss Graham, formerly Lily Sheil:

Dorothy Parker was the most unpredictable woman I ever met in the Garden of Allah, or anywhere else. I had met her in New York before I came to Hollywood. She had been tattooed in the Bowery and the New York *Mirror*, which I was working for . . . sent me to get an interview with her. She was staying at the Lowell Hotel, and when she could not pay her bill there she ordered an ambulance and was carried out on a stretcher . . . Alan Campbell, John O'Hara and John McClain were with her when I arrived. They were hanging on her every word . . . Dorothy was apologetic. The tattoo, she said with shy embarrassment, was only on her arm. The newspaper had expected it to be somewhere more exciting. She gave me tea, and offered me her undying friendship.

Dorothy Parker made Miss Graham promise to call her, which she frequently did, but Mrs. Parker was always "out" or "not available."

"It was," recalled Miss Graham, "rather embarrassing for me to meet her again in Robert Benchley's bungalow at the Garden. But she was friendly, and she said she was delighted to see me again. I was to see a lot of Dorothy, mostly with Bob [Benchley] . . . He was the only person I did not hear her malign as soon as he left the room." With great percipience, Miss Graham added, "I can well imagine what she said about me after I had left."

"Dorothy," she continued,

wore her rather sparse black hair in sticky-looking bangs on her forehead above her over-round smudges of black, doleful eyes. . . . I thought she looked like a tired Renoir. She wore the weirdest clothes. Once I saw her going to dinner at the Sheekmans wearing tennis shoes and black stockings with a blouse and skirt . . . Whenever she saw me she would take my hand and hold it tensely, and sometimes tears rolled down her white cheeks, and she would say how glad she was to see me, behaving just as she had done at the hotel in New York. . . . But now I knew her, and I said as little as possible when we met at the various bungalows at the Garden and at dinners in the homes at Beverly Hills.

If Mrs. Parker had ever affected real friendship towards Graham, it was scarcely evident when, years later, she reviewed *Beloved Infidel*, Miss Graham's intimate memoir of her life with Fitzgerald. "She was murderous," recalled Miss Graham. What *had* Mrs. Parker said about the book? "They—the authoress and her collaborator, Gerold Frank—not only dug up his bones but they gnawed on them."

The feud between Miss Graham and Mrs. Parker—and to the on-looker it was never a feud but a friendship, full of charm, sweetness and light—was to continue in another of Miss Graham's books. Again, Dorothy Parker came in for the Graham whiplash:

"Dorothy Parker was just as bitchy when the party was her own. She telephoned songwriter Harry Ruby and said, 'Harry, this is Dorothy Parker. I'm giving a party on Wednesday. Can you come? Everyone will be there—Hammerstein, Benchley, Butterworth.' Harry arrived at the party to be greeted by his hostess who gushed, 'It's so nice of you to come. Isn't this a lot of shit?' "

Miss Graham was not finished with Mrs. Parker:

"Dorothy's was the lashback usually given after the person she was lashing had left the room. People were afraid to leave the room for fear of inspiring one of her vicious remarks."

Patently, it wasn't only Mrs. Parker who could roll the splenetic dice. Hear more from Miss Graham:

"I attended one of Dorothy Parker's parties with Scott Fitzgerald. It was Friday the thirteenth. Three of the people at the party were dead by Sunday morning: Scott, Nat West and his wife Eileen who were killed on Ventura Boulevard in a car crash. Everyone then remembered it had been Friday the thirteenth at Dottie's." The date, of course, had been merely coincidental.

Often the Hollywood parties were rudely interrupted by studio producers demanding that a writer or artist "get your ass over here," a frequent and peremptory cry made usually either late at night or in the early hours of the morning. They had tried it on Scott Fitzgerald when the story of that alluring lady of the French Revolution, *Marie Antoinette*, was due to go into production. Hunt Stromberg, the producer, rang Fitzgerald at a Parker party, where Scott had been drinking steadily all evening. Stromberg demanded Fitzgerald's presence at his home immediately. Fitzgerald put the phone down, turned to Dorothy Parker and told her that he had no intention of responding to the demand. Instead, he sat down and wrote a note which he sent over by messenger to the producer. It read:

> Stromberg sent for Poppa
> Tho' Poppa hadn't et,
> To do what Jesus couldn't—
> Save Marie Antoinette . . .

The pace of life at the Garden of Allah, with its unceasing round of parties, was hardly conducive to work. The fun and the gaiety were fine in their place but Paramount started to become more demanding of the talents of Mrs. Parker and her husband. Of those talents Miss Graham said:

"While Dottie and Alan worked together during their marriage, he never received personal credit for his contribution. Everyone believed Dorothy was carrying him. But he was quite a good writer and an industrious one, which," Miss Graham concluded, "his wife was not."

One afternoon, Dorothy and her husband welcomed their old friend Donald Ogden Stewart to their villa. He arrived looking remarkably elegant, attired in a new spring suit. Kyle Crichton, another Garden writer, was there. He recalled: "To the roar of welcome and congratulations, Don replied by patting the lapel of his new jacket humbly and saying, in an apologetic voice, 'This spot belongs to another suit.'" Such witty remarks were fun enough, but there was work to be done. Work, however, did not stop the flow of stories about the place. When the talented scenarist Frances Marion was asked by Lillian Gish what she thought of Hollywood, she declared: "It's a bloody lie!" Even Aleck Woollcott, who could climb on anyone's bandwagon or invite himself to anyone's estate, was even more derogatory: "It's the sort of place you expect to find down a rabbit hole." It might well have been both a lie and an unsalubrious warren, but it provided a diverting shelter and comfortable income for Dorothy Parker and Alan Campbell. She had continued to correspond with Woollcott, who was now back on the East Coast. Her letters were laced with both irony and humor:

Alan and I are working on a little opera which was originally named *Twenty-Four Hours by Air*, but it has been kicking around the studio for a long time, during which aerial transportation had made such progress that it is now called *Eleven Hours by Air*. By the time we are done, the title is to be, I believe, *Stay Where You Are*. Before this, we were summoned to labor on a story of which we were told only, "Now, we don't know yet whether the male lead will be played by Tullio Carminati or Bing Crosby. So just sort of write it with both of them in mind." Before that, we were assigned the task of taking the sex out of *Sailor Beware* [sic]. They read our script and went back to the original version. The catch for the movies, it seemed, was that hinge of the plot where the sailor bets he will make the girl. They said that was dirty. But would they accept our change, that triumph of ingenuity where the sailor just bets he will make another sailor? Oh, no! Sometimes I think they don't know *what* they want.

For his part, Woollcott considered his friends in Hollywood to be "slaves, indentured servants or dupes." He not only mentally proscribed most of them, pitied them, but took time off to tell them so to their faces, or at least through the mails.

Despite the lushness of their lives, or because of it, Mrs. Parker and

Alan were drinking steadily—and too much. They began to quarrel in front of their friends and the language she used towards him became more and more vulgar and profane. They were playing too hard and working too hard; both needed a rest.

They decided that they had had enough of "Sodom-in-the-sun" or "Poughkeepsie with Palms," the place where they both knew that if you didn't dirty your napkin too much, the moguls would now and then "throw you a tablet down from Mount Sinai."

It was time to leave, to escape from those interminable script conferences where Dorothy Parker would pull out her knitting from an unprepossessing woolen bag and monotonously click away with her needles, dog at her feet and a look of monumental boredom on her face while Alan brightly spouted the platitudes the producers wanted to hear. Somebody said the producers were "Caligulas all" and Mrs. Parker was prepared to say "Amen" to that.

If it was true that, in her own opinion, she had achieved in Hollywood little that had been worthwhile, she had, by working in her spare time and attending informal meetings in the homes of some of her friends, at least succeeded in another area; she had helped form the first trade union for Hollywood's screenwriters—the American Screenwriters Guild. Not only that, the little lady who appeared to many of those same friends to be incapable of timing an egg, had suddenly emerged as a skilled organizer and fundraiser for the emerging Anti-Nazi League. She had worked energetically alongside Donald Ogden Stewart, the league's first president; Fredric March; March's wife, Florence Eldridge; Norma Shearer; Oscar Hammerstein; and others to make Hollywood aware of the dangers that were being signaled from Europe. Of this time, Stewart was later to remember: "It was the time when Dottie and I arrived at the politically conscious stage of our lives. Hitler had arrived in our view. And we didn't like what we saw."

· 3 3 ·

A Place of One's Own

MRS. PARKER'S and Alan's "escape from the cultural boneyard"—
her description of their departure from Hollywood—was not to be their
final escape. It is true that they had not received many screen credits for
their various assignments, but they had received credit as dialogue writers for *Here Is My Heart*. Film credit did not seem important to Dorothy,
but Alan believed that after money, credits were the top priority of the
craft. During her visit to Hollywood in late 1929, Dorothy had worked
with Cecil B. DeMille on the screenplay of *Dynamite* and had lately,
and somewhat surprisingly, contributed the lyric to a song, "How Was I
to Know?" which eventually turned out to be a modest hit in the Bing
Crosby film *The Big Broadcast of 1936*, made in early 1935. The pair had
also contributed dialogue to *One Hour Late*, but the business of credits
in Hollywood was the business of jungle law, as Donald Ogden Stewart
was later to recall:

> The competition was very great—you couldn't make mistakes because there
> were other writers waiting to step in and fix your script up the way you were
> fixing somebody else's. . . . In those days, the first thing you had to learn as a
> writer if you wanted to get screen credit was to hold off until you knew they were
> going to have to start shooting. Then your agent would suggest that you might
> be able to help. The producers had the theory that the more writers they had to
> work on the scripts, the better they would be. It was the third or fourth writer
> who always got the screen credit. If you could possibly screw up another writer's
> script, it wasn't beyond you to do that so that your script would come through at
> the end . . . it became a game to be the last one before they started shooting so
> that you would not be eased out of the screen credit.

Years later, Mrs. Parker was to give her version of life in the Hollywood writing jungle:

"I tell you, nobody can do anything alone. You are given a script that
eight people have written from a novel four people have written. You,
then, they say, write dialogue. What a curious word! Well, you know,
you can't write dialogue without changing scenes. While you are doing
it, eight people back of you are writing beyond you. Nobody is allowed
to do anything alone."

Charles Brackett, who was in Hollywood at the time, later swore that Mrs. Parker received equal credit on work largely done by Alan. If that was true, it had to be admitted that she had been engaged by Paramount not only for her work but for her "name." She certainly added bright dialogue to Selznick's movie *Nothing Sacred*, with Carole Lombard. The script was by Ben Hecht and "provided a fine cynical view of small-town narrow-mindedness and big-city exploitation." Also she and Alan did considerable work on a Garson Kanin screen project, *Passport for Life*, but the film was never made.

Towards the end of 1936, the screen credits of Mrs. Parker and Alan were tallied up and, by Hollywood standards, were found to be not insubstantial. They had done the screenplay of *Three Married Men* for Paramount and had written and were credited with additional dialogue for *The Moon's Our Home*, adapted by Isabel Dawn and Bruce DeGaw from a novel by Faith Baldwin. It was a Walter Wanger film for Paramount, which starred Margaret Sullavan, Henry Fonda and Mrs. Parker's friend Charles Butterworth. Alan and Dorothy were also given joint credit, along with Horace Jackson and Lenore Coffee, for *Suzy*, an MGM film, for which they had been loaned out to Dorothy Parker's principal Hollywood employers. This was based on a novel of the same name by Herbert Gorman, and starred Jean Harlow, Franchot Tone and Cary Grant. *Suzy* had proved to be difficult to make. The supervisors, as MGM's executive producers were then called, struggled with the script, and it wound up as rather confused. It was not unpopular, but hardly the hit one might have expected considering the box-office strength of its stars. The principal producer, Bud Lighton, a ponderously slow man, had all but driven Dorothy Parker and Alan to distraction with his lengthy and confused script conferences, and things were made worse by the presence of two other senior administrative executives: Maurice Reynes, who by common consent "knew almost nothing about moviemaking," and Eddie Mannix, who as well as being a top studio executive was also manager of the entire MGM plant, hardly a creative position.

Another film, about which she had written so amusingly to Woollcott, was *Sailor Beware*. For this, Alan and his wife were credited, along with Harry Ruskin, with the screen adaptation of the play by Kenyon Nicholson and Charles Robinson; the final title was *Lady, Be Careful*. This, too, was a Paramount movie, one which starred Lew Ayres. It was not a major success but it did well enough at the box office to please Paramount's moguls.

It is doubtful, therefore, that Adela Rogers St. Johns was right when she later wrote:

"Like a lot of famous writers . . . Dorothy and Alan had been brought to Hollywood for more money than they had ever before seen, and then discovered they couldn't write a shooting script. . . . So some poor underpaid fellow would have to sweat it out to get a script. This would cause Dorothy and many like her to weep and wring their hands and say how much they hated Hollywood." Miss St. Johns, as may be deduced, was another Hollywood newspaper columnist.

As Mrs. Parker's friends knew, she disliked her work because of Hollywood's attitude towards writers and serious creative writing. What she seemed unable to appreciate was that, in reality, Hollywood was a factory, turning out an assembly-line product for which there was a constant and ever-increasing demand. She was simply not an assembly-line writer, although Alan, for his part, reveled in the whole system and loved working on *any* script, at which he was very good.

On leaving Hollywood, the two told Leland Hayward they would be available to continue script work in New York. They were making good money and their joint bank balance had been rising steadily. They could choose their work place and largely their own terms, but not before Mrs. Parker had written a poem about their Hollywood foray:

> Oh, come my love, and join with me
> The oldest infant industry.
> Come, seek the bourne of palm and pearl
> The lovely land of boy-meets-girl.
> Come, grace the lotus-laden shore,
> The Isle of Do-What's-Done-Before,
> Come, curb the new and match the old win
> Out where the streets are paved with Goldwyn . . .

They were both tired on returning to New York. Many of their friends had homes in the country, at which they often spent time. They decided the time had come for them to look for property in the country.

In Bucks County, Pennsylvania, many of their friends rented or owned farms or houses, including Oscar and Dorothy Hammerstein, Moss Hart, Theron Bamberger, Kelcey Alley, Arthur Bachrach, Louise Closser Hall, Gus and Ruth Goetz, Sidney and Laura Perelman, Budd Schulberg, Joe Shrank, John Hess, St. John Terrell, Artie Shaw, Tom Ewell, Louis Calhern, Jerry and Rhea Chodorov. Also there were Beatrice and George Kaufman, who on purchasing the fifty-seven-acre Barley Sheaf Farm for $145,000 had promptly rechristened it Cherchez La Farm.

Mrs. Parker and Alan checked in at the Water Wheel Inn, near Doylestown, Pennsylvania. From there they surveyed the scene, looking for a property to their liking. The lush green pastures, the serene plains and soft, secretive hills seemed to provide the ideal setting for their desired life-style. They consulted Sidney and Laura Perelman, who had often regaled them with seductive stories about the rural life in Bucks County. Mrs. Parker liked the Perelmans and had first met Sidney at a party a few years earlier. Perelman remembered that meeting:

The occasion was a cocktail party given by Poultney Kerr, the bibulous producer of *Sherry Flip*, the revue I had written some sketches for and which was about to begin rehearsal. The show at that point lacked a title and Kerr, seizing on any pretext for a bash, invited 40 or 50 social and theatrical acquaintances to drinks in his office in the hope that someone would come up with a frisky and forceful name for the enterprise. Halfway through the proceedings Mrs. Parker arrived, visibly gassed but dressed to kill in a black confection by Lanvin, a feathered toque, and opera-length gloves. Thirty-nine years old and a very toothsome dish, she immediately made every other woman in the assemblage feel dowdy, and for a moment the sound of their teeth gnashing drowned out the buzz of chit-chat.

When Kerr introduced us, she straightaway fired off a barrage of compliments likening me to Congreve, Oscar Wilde and Noel Coward. Inasmuch as my total Broadway output was confined to one sketch in *The Third Little Show*, I thought the praise a mite excessive, but I blushingly accepted the tribute. Having fortified the company with several rounds of malt, Kerr called for silence, explained the purpose of the gathering, and bade everyone don his thinking cap. Needless to say, all heads turned towards Mrs. Parker, who accepted the challenge.

"Let me see," she pondered. "What about 'Sing High, Sing Low'? No, that's defeatist! It needs something frothy, sparkling—wait, I know! 'Pousse-Café!' "

There was an imperceptible ripple, and several willowy young men murmured, "Splendid . . . Yes, definitely . . . Oh, I love it." In the hush that followed, I suddenly became aware of Mrs. Parker's eyes fixed on me with cat-like intentness. "What do *you* think of 'Pousse-Café,' Mr. Perelman?"

"Great!" I said, striving to put conviction into my tone. "It's gay and—sparkling, you're right. But it lacks—how shall I say?—*punch*. I mean, *pousse*-café—it's too soft, somehow."

"Oh, really?" she asked, with a slow and deadly inflection. "Well, then, here's something punchier. How about 'Aces Up'?"

" 'Aces Up,' " I mused. "That's marvelous, very good, I just wonder, though, if we can't find something a *tiny* bit sharper, less static . . . "

"Well, goodness me." Mrs. Parker's words dripped sweet poison. "Whatever shall we do? Our wrist has just been slapped by the house genius there, who feels that we're a bit dull-witted. Of course, he's in a position to know, isn't he, leaning down from Parnassus?"

"Look, folks," Kerr broke in nervously. "Have another drink—don't go, it's still early."

"How privileged we are to have the benefit of Mr. P's wide experience!" she overrode him. "How gracious of him to analyze our shortcomings! I wonder, though, if Mr. P. realizes that he's a great big etcetera, because he is, you know. In fact, of all the etceteras I've ever known . . . "

Well, fortunately for me, the bystanders who had witnessed the carnage recovered their tongues at this juncture, and the rest of Mrs. Parker's diatribe was lost in the babble. I made my escape, and when Kerr phoned me the next day to apologize for her conduct, I swore that if I ever met the woman again, I'd skewer her with one of her own hatpins. That evening I received a dozen magnificent roses from her accompanied by a note steeped in remorse.

It was a gesture that was to establish a long and lasting friendship between Dorothy Parker and the Perelmans—a friendship that was to become slightly worn at the edges only when she and Alan Campbell sought their support in their search for peace and quiet.

"When my wife and I saw her again on the coast," continued Perelman:

she was married to Alan Campbell and from all outward appearances was prosperous . . . Laura and I, who shared her detestation of Hollywood, spoke often of our place in Bucks County; we tended to become lyrical about the countryside, the farmhouses and the relative simplicity of life there, and evidently our encomium had an effect. In time we began to notice the recurrence in Dottie's speech of the word "roots." "We haven't any roots, Alan," she would admonish him after the fourth Martini. "You can't put down any roots in Beverly Hills. But look at Laura and Sid—they've got *roots*, a place to come home to. *Roots, roots.*"

It was practically foreordained, hence, that a month or two after we settled down at our place, the Campbells suddenly materialized on the doorstep with shining faces. They were surfeited with the artificiality and tinsel of Hollywood, they declared; they wanted a farm near ours and they wanted us to help them find it. Property was still cheap in our area, though farther down the Delaware around New Hope, George S. Kaufman, Moss Hart, and several other playwrights had acquired houses and Bucks County was becoming known as a haunt of writers and artists.

Dottie and Alan, however, were imbued with what might be called the creative spirit. Not for them a manor house equipped with creature comforts like bathrooms, stainless steel kitchens, and laundries. They wanted a place that "had possibilities, something they would have fun remodeling . . . "

Perelman decided that Alan and Dorothy Parker's dreamhouse, thus described, "was clearly an assignment with Jack Boyle . . . a stage Irishman who was by way of being a real-estate agent" and one "who spent a good deal of his time seated on the steps of the local post office telling yarns."

"A couple of days thereafter," Perelman went on,

Laura and I accompanied the Campbells on an inspection tour of several farms that Boyle listed. The second one we saw was such a plum that, had our friends hesitated, we ourselves would have snapped it up. The dwelling and its outbuildings, reached by a long lane that guaranteed privacy, lay on a gently rolling southern slope of one hundred and twenty acres, and the asking price was $4,500. As Boyle quoted the figure and all our jaws dropped in unison, he raised his hand:

"A word of advice before you grab it, friends," he told the Campbells. "I think you ought to see the inside first. It needs—well, it needs a little attention." Even with his warning, none of us was prepared for the actuality. The interior of the house was in an appalling state; floors had rotted out in places, revealing the cellar below, fragments of plaster hung from the ceilings, woodwork gave way at the touch. A disused incubator for baby chicks was balanced crazily in the largest room, and a thick film of poultry feathers and cobwebs shrouded everything. It seemed incredible that the ruin was inhabited, yet, said Boyle, an old Ukrainian couple had been living there for several years.

"There is," continued Perelman,

a specially insidious form of self-deception affecting house-hunters wherein they confuse themselves with Hercules, equal to any Augean stable they encounter, and the Campbells promptly succumbed to it. They ran around envisioning the rooms a clever architect could fabricate out of the shell, the baths and bedchambers, and butler's pantries, necessary for country living, and in all conscience we did nothing to disillusion them, for the prospect of having Dottie as a neighbor was a stimulating one. It did not occur to us that we had taken on the role of mid-wives, that the Campbells had expected us to accouche the birth of their dreamhouse, and that we would be called upon to provide sympathy and counsel —to say nothing of anodynes like Martinis—for the manifold problems plaguing them.

As Perelman went on to say, "The next few months were a caution." The pair installed themselves back in the Water Wheel Inn and from here

they groaned through all the legal complexities of acquiring their place, choosing an architect, and approving his plans. Infatuated with him at first, they fell out of love with him in short order; he was stodgy, unimaginative and old-fashioned. The Ukrainians, who had been given notice to vacate, turned obstinate; they refused to adapt themselves to the new owners' time-table and hung on, maddening Alan beyond measure. He turned in desperation to Jack Boyle who pointed out, reasonably enough, that the old people had chickens they were preparing to market, standing crops not yet ready for harvest.

"That's their problem," Alan retorted passionately. "Don't they realize it's costing Dottie and me a small fortune to stay away from Hollywood?"

The Ukrainian couple had long been tenants of the colonial field-stone farmhouse, Fox House Farm, which was owned by Franklin G. Fox of Easton; it had been in his family since 1775. The main farmhouse had fourteen rooms and three fireplaces and, as Dorothy Parker discovered, had earlier been used as a station on the Underground Railroad. It overlooked the Delaware River with the Netcong Mountains of New Jersey in the distance and it would, she believed, be the ideal retreat for Alan and herself. The peace of their surroundings would certainly be conducive to better work and would be ideal for the dogs, now numbering nine.

In an atmosphere of urgency, accusations, recriminations and apologies between architects, owners and builders, Fox House Farm, near Pipersville Village, was in time gutted and remodeled. The main living room was painted in nine shades of red, large ornate mirrors were affixed to the dining room walls to bring more of the landscape into the house, rooms were lined with bookshelves and a new butler's pantry and servants' quarters were erected. Electricity was led up to the house at a cost of $3,000 and a swimming pool, costing $2,600, was started. In less than eight months the house which had cost $4,500 to buy had had close to $100,000 spent on it. On the first floor the remodeled house boasted a kitchen, dining room, a book-lined living room, a study, a bathroom and a butler's pantry. Upstairs were three bedrooms, each with its own bathroom suite. In addition, a five-room apartment for servants had been built out of the stone barn adjoining the house; also built were other offices and terraced gardens.

Even though much of their 120 acres was waterlogged, Dorothy Parker and Alan had created their dream home. And, most important, they were away from the Hollywood of which Leo Rosten had said: "Nothing is certain there but death, taxes and agents," an epigram that had given Mrs. Parker the title for her successful book *Death and Taxes*, published in 1931. And now, late in 1936, her fourth book, *Not So Deep as a Well*, was on sale all over America, representing her collected poems with the addition of five new ones, "Sight," "The Lady's Reward," "Prisoner," "Temps Perdu" and "Autumn Valentine." The sad lyricism that had characterized so much of her earlier verse was again beguilingly evident in her new poems. "The wittiest woman of our time has suddenly taken on new stature," said William Rose Benét; her poem "Sight" was surely the aperture through which one could still see glimpses of her own mordant sadness:

> Unseemly are the open eyes
> That watch the midnight sheep,

That look upon the secret skies,
Nor close, abashed, in sleep;
That see the dawn drag in, unbidden,
To birth another day—
Oh, better far their gaze were hidden
Below the decent clay.

Not So Deep as a Well was a huge popular success, if not a marked critical success since much of the book had been published before. It went into five printings, from which she earned $32,000, a princely sum for poetry. From the proceeds, she bought a "pitifully inexpensive" black and white sketch of Scott Fitzgerald drawn by Zelda. She was always a lady who quietly remembered her lovers.

In the late fall, she and Alan seemed to have papered over the cracks of their marital difficulties, and the signs augured well for a happy life in their new home. Together they spent much time planning the final decorative touches and drawing up a list of guests for weekend visits.

They had not been living in Fox House Farm more than three months when the *Hollywood Reporter* carried an item that swept through the literary and theatrical communities of America like a hurricane.

Dorothy Parker—wit, literary journalist, poet, screenwriter and the most unlikely mother in the world—was pregnant, expecting a child in June of next year. Louella Parsons screamed:

"A baby? How positively ludicrous. Can you imagine Dorothy Parker changing a diaper?"

In truth, none of her friends could.

· 3 4 ·

A Night of Pain

MRS. DOROTHY PARKER was embarking rather late on the adventure of motherhood. She was now forty-three years old, a dangerous age for a woman to start producing and raising a family. And, her friends declared, the excesses of the previous years—the untold packs of Chesterfields; the small rivers of gin, whiskey, martinis and, during the years of Prohibition, the hooch alcohol; the continuous late nights; her work commitments; and irregular eating habits—were not exactly conducive to a healthy pregnancy.

Nonetheless, Mrs. Parker plunged happily into the business of preparing the layette for her expected child. She converted a room at the farm to serve as a pretty nursery. She tended the gardens with love because flowers, as she often said, meant a great deal in her life. She busily directed the final labors of the workmen. She arranged pictures and ornaments, ordered rugs and accessories and designed the lighting of the rooms as if they were settings for an avant-garde play. Several of the designs could hardly have been described as appropriate to an old colonial Pennsylvania farmhouse, but as with most things, Dorothy had little regard for the opinions of others. Writing an article for *House and Garden*, she wasn't in the least contrite:

"We caused hard feelings in the country. There are no folks so jealous of countryside tradition as those who never before have lived below the twelfth floor of a New York building . . . they found us vandals . . . "

As with her writing, if her color schemes and furnishings offended, that was of little concern to her. And if her theatrical and literary friends were disparaging about her design ideas, she did not lack for houseguests nor for invitations to the homes of nearby friends. Alan busied himself about the house and cooked with flair, if with little regard for the urbane palates of several of their guests. As he was the first to admit, what skill he lacked in the culinary arts, he made up for in theatrical brio, especially when serving, a task he insisted should be done by none but himself.

Alan and his wife had facing desks and typewriters in their study and got down to work. In the evenings she would sit contentedly by the fire, and talk, drink and knit baby clothes. Her contentment was full and as complete as it was ever likely to be. It was marred only by the fussy presence of Hortense, Alan's mother, who took it upon herself to direct much of the household management because, she said, she did not want her pregnant daughter-in-law to exert herself. "We must all take care of the little one," she would coo.

Dorothy Parker hated having Hortense around but, at Alan's insistence she was taking it easy, avoiding lifting, fetching and carrying. "Hortense," he said "would cope." And when Alan wasn't creating scenes of almost violent discord with his mother, his mother was creating them with her son. If there was a dull patch in the lively environment of hostility, Dorothy, because of Hortense's interfering presence, would verbally set about Alan. It was, as one wit called it, "a triumvirate of tension," a tension that was to become increasingly apparent to their houseguests.

In the winter of the previous year, Dorothy Parker had again met Lillian Hellman in Hollywood. Miss Hellman, by now a dramatist of growing reputation, was to recall the meetings in her memoirs:

I was not to meet Dottie again until the winter of 1935 in Hollywood and then, having glared at her for most of the evening in memory of that silly first meeting, we talked. I liked her and we saw each other the next day and for many, many other good days. . . . It was strange that we liked each other and that never through the years did two such difficult women ever have a quarrel, or even a mild, unpleasant word. Much, certainly, was against our friendship: we were not the same generation, we were not the same kind of writer, we had led and were to continue to lead very different lives, often we didn't like the same people or even the same books, but more important, we never liked the same men. When I met her [again] in 1935 she was married to Alan Campbell, who was a hard man for me to take. He was also difficult for her and she would talk about him in a funny, half-bitter way not only to me but, given enough liquor, to a whole dinner party. But she had great affection for Alan and certainly . . . great dependence upon him. If I didn't like Alan, she didn't like Hammett, although she was always too polite to say so. More important, Hammett, who seldom felt strongly about anybody, didn't like Dottie, and in the later years would move away from the house when she came to visit us. He was not conscious that his face would twist, almost as if he had half-recovered from a minor stroke, as she embraced or flattered a man or woman, only to turn, when they had left the room, to say in the soft, pleasant, clear voice, "Did you ever meet such a shit?" I think the game of embrace-denounce must have started when she found it amused or shocked people, because in time, when she found it didn't amuse me, she seldom played it. But Hammett found it downright distasteful and I gave up all efforts to convince him that it was the kind of protection sometimes needed by those who are frightened.

Lillian Hellman continued:

I am no longer certain that I was right: fear now seems too simple. The game more probably came from a desire to charm, to be loved, to be admired, and such desires brought self-contempt that could only be consoled by behind-the-back denunciations of almost comic violence.

If she denounced everybody else, I had a right to think that I was included, but now I think I was wrong about that, too: So many people have told me that she never did talk about me, never complained, never would allow gossip about me, that I have come to believe it. But even when I didn't, it didn't matter. I enjoyed her more than I have enjoyed any other woman. She was modest, this wasn't all virtue, she liked to think that she was not worth much—her view of people was original and sharp, her elaborate, overdelicate manners made her a pleasure to live with, she liked books and was generous about writers, and the wit, of course, was so wonderful that neither age nor illness ever dried up the spring from which it came fresh each day. . . .

Perhaps Miss Hellman, with her comment about Mrs. Parker being generous about writers, was being particularly generous about her friend.

"The joke," continues Lillian Hellman,

has been changed and variously attributed to Mischa Elman and Heifetz, but it is hers, because I was there when it happened. We were knitting before the living room fireplace in the country house that she and Alan . . . owned in Pennsylvania. Upstairs Alan was having an argument with his visiting mother. The afternoon grew dark, it began to snow, we made the fire very large and sat in silence. Occasionally, the upstairs voices would grow angry and loud and then Dottie would sigh. When the voices finally ceased, Alan appeared in the living room.

He said, immediately, angrily, "It's as hot as hell in here."

"Not for orphans," Dottie said, and I laughed for so long that Alan went for a walk and Dottie patted my hand occasionally and said, "There, there, dear, you'll choke if you're not careful. . . . "

The visits of houseguests like Lillian Hellman were interchanged with calls on friends who had bought property in Bucks County. Mrs. Parker had reviewed a book by George Kaufman and Moss Hart in *The New Yorker* and she was not kind to either the book or her two friends. She had waded into Kaufman and Hart with unexpected severity: " . . . so much kudos for so little talent . . . " she had written. The weekend the review was due to appear in the book section of the Sunday *Times*, she and Alan, along with Lillian Hellman, were guests at Cherchez La Farm.

To avert any embarrassment, Mrs. Parker and Miss Hellman hid the book section of the paper. At the same time, they decided that it would be prudent for them to take a long, long walk in the countryside, hoping that if the paper was found by the time they returned, Mrs. Parker's comment might be forgotten in the general welter of chitchat. They had clearly not counted on the fact that Moss Hart, living in Bucks County himself, would have his own copy of the paper.

It was getting late as the two ladies sneaked back into the Kaufman house. They went to their rooms, collected their bags and moved downstairs for formal goodbyes before leaving. George Kaufman was seated at a table in the living room, playing solitare. All appeared to be well. The women thanked Beatrice Kaufman for an enchanting time and were about to leave when George lowered his cards, looked over his glasses and asked: "Dottie, did you take the real estate section of the Sunday *Times?*"

Kaufman, as many claimed, had a wit as dry as a tinderbox. It was well known in Bucks County and elsewhere that Kaufman was never enamored of Mrs. Parker, nor she of him. But away from her sophisticated friend and enemies, she seemed now to be a woman in the throes of change—change for the better. It was three months since she had conceived, and those same people knew that the quiet expectancy she felt for the child was amounting to what Dorothy Parker considered nearly perfect fulfillment. Yet this happy state was not to last. One night, after Hortense had left Fox House Farm for New York and the couple had taken hot drinks to bed, Dorothy Parker was racked by internal stomach pains—she had miscarried her child.

The next morning, with placid resignation, she gave cool instructions to Mr. and Mrs. Hiram Beer, the local couple engaged as cook-housekeeper and general handyman, to get rid of everything associated with the expected child, starting with the nursery. The room was speedily stripped and the same day decorators moved in to change the decor completely. The expensive layette and pregnancy wardrobe were both flung unceremoniously into the trash.

Dorothy Parker never spoke a word to anyone about this disastrous event.

· 3 5 ·

A Cry from the Heart

AFTER THE MISCARRIAGE, Alan persuaded Dorothy to spend a few days on her own in New York; he would occupy himself on a screen treatment which needed to be finished. She agreed and checked in at the Leonori Hotel where she spent a few days looking up old friends. In response to columnist Leonard Lyons's inquiry about her farm, she asked, "Want it?"

Legend has it, which even Lillian Hellman refers to it in her memoirs, that Dorothy Parker, alone in her room for nearly two hours, recorded a heart-rending record of the misfortunes of her birth, her love affairs, her great and continuing unhappiness and what she felt to be the total purposelessness of her life. To this day the recordings have not been discovered or, if they have, the full detail of the agonizing content has never been revealed.

The outpouring of her abject sadness may well have effected a kind of self-therapy because she returned to Bucks County and Alan and threw herself into her work. She had not been back at the farm more than a week when the phone rang. Leland Hayward was calling from Los Angeles and said that Paramount had agreed to loan out the services of Alan and herself to MGM and Selznick for several assignments. Would they please return to Hollywood as soon as possible?

Thus, early in 1937, they went back there, but not to the Garden of Allah. They rented an imposing white colonnaded house at 520 North Canyon Drive in Beverly Hills, complete with four servants. If one believes Miss Sheilah Graham, "Dorothy had rugs on each side of the bed with raised chenille letters that spelled out the inviting word 'Welcome.' " If the story was true, Mrs. Parker had clearly not lost her sense of humor.

She and Alan started to tackle the work awaiting them. Hayward had first loaned out their services to Selznick, who after seeing the 1932 film *What Price Hollywood*, starring Constance Bennett and Lowell Sherman, had given Hayward an idea for a drama based on Hollywood itself. He originally had gone to William Wellman and Robert Carson, who had jointly developed it on paper; now Selznick wanted Dorothy Parker and Alan to do a complete rewrite of the project.

The film was called *A Star Is Born*. Unknown to the Campbells, Selznick had also taken the script to Roland Brown, Budd Schulberg and Ring Lardner, Jr., the eldest son of Mrs. Parker's late lover, for secret rewritings. Wellman heard about it and, as a result, much of the original script was restored in the final film, which starred Fredric March and Janet Gaynor. It won several Academy Awards, including one for best original story, the award going to Wellman and Carson. Alan and Dorothy's final screenplay was nominated but it did not win. However, they were probably happy with the review of the film in *The New York Times*, which said it was "the most accurate mirror ever held before the glittering, tinseled, trivial, generous, cruel and ecstatic world that is Hollywood."

Asked by the Los Angeles *Times* how she liked being back at work in Hollywood, Mrs. Parker placatingly replied: "It's all right. You make a little money and get caught up on your debts. We're up to 1912 now."

She and Alan were now loaned out to United Artists to work on a film for Sam Goldwyn, who had once proclaimed that he sought only to make entertaining films, that "messages were for Western Union." For Goldwyn, Dorothy Parker and Alan adapted a farce, *Woman Chases Man*. The film starred Miriam Hopkins and Joel McCrea. Mrs. Parker defined Miss Hopkins's screen character as "a flab, a young snip who climbs ladders upside down blindfolded."

But Mrs. Parker was once again deriving scant consolation for what she considered her demeaning work:

"I was coming down a street in Beverly Hills, and I saw a Cadillac about a block long, and out of the side window was a wonderfully slinky mink, and an arm, and at the end of the arm a hand in a white suede glove, wrinkled round the wrist, and in the hand was a bagel with a bite out of it," she told an interviewer.

Despite her continuing disenchantment with the work, she was nonetheless enjoying a round of parties that somewhat competed with those of the Algonquin days. To make the place happier, Robert Benchley was there, now a featured player in several movies with Deanna Durbin and other top stars. Benchley had become more and more the bland, bowtied, hair-parted-near-the-center, poker-faced movie humorist, celebrated for such roles as a lovable, inane drunk.

By this time, many of Mrs. Parker's and Benchley's friends had established themselves in the higher echelons of American drama and literature. At one of the parties at her North Canyon Drive house, Benchley was there with F. Scott Fitzgerald and Robert Sherwood, who was by now a leading playwright with two of the three Pulitzer prizes he would gain. Late, after drinking too much, Benchley, lurching slightly, was heard to say: "Those eyes—I can't stand those eyes looking at me!" At this, everybody turned to witness Benchley backing away from his old friend, Bob Sherwood, waiting for the big joke they expected to come. Benchley, it turned out, had never been more serious. Pointing directly at Sherwood he said: "He's looking at me and thinking how he knew me when I was going to be a great writer . . . and he's thinking, now look what I am!"

It was a sad little episode, an incisive commentary on the vagaries of fate in a town that had been equated with "a world's fair that had been up a year too long."

Its luxury, its sheer madness, its potent atmosphere of unreality was summed up by Beatrice Kaufman, who by this time had been appointed Sam Goldwyn's Eastern story editor. She wrote to her mother in Rochester:

It's like old home week; the Swopes arrived yesterday and Oscar [Levant] is coming on Wednesday. I really could close my eyes and think that I was back in New York with my buddies around me, which is both pleasant and unpleasant, according to how you look at it.

The party at the Donald Ogden Stewarts was great fun the other night, and my evening was made for me when Mr. Chaplin sat down beside me and stayed for hours. He is very amusing and intelligent and I enjoyed talking to him a great deal. Pauline Goddert [sic] was there too—very beautiful; everyone says they are married. Joan Bennett, Clark Gable, the Fredric Marches, Dottie Parker, Mankiewiczes, etc. A delicious buffet dinner, with talk and bridge afterwards. Their house is lovely, Saturday night's party which Kay Francis gave was swell, too. She took over the entire Vendome restaurant and had it made over like a ship— a swell job. I seemed to know almost everyone there—there were over one hundred people. A sprinkling of movie stars, James Cagney, the Marches again, June Walker, etc. I arrived home at a quarter to five—completely exhausted, having danced and drunk a good deal.

Before it, we went to Pasadena to have dinner at the Alvin Kingsbachers, you remember them. Mrs. K. asked particularly to be remembered to you, Mother. Said she thought you were so beautiful. They had an assortment of people to meet us—not much fun, really. And last night we went to dinner at Zeppo's [Marx] and later to a small party at the Goldwyns where I played bridge. The Goldwyns are off to England in a few days. And today I am lunching with Ruth Gordon and Maggie [Swope], having my hair done afterwards, dining with Mr. K. and going to the opening of *Merrily We Roll Along* [the play that ridicules Dottie Parker]. And so it goes. I am dated up all week, but I am thinking of going to the desert instead. There is difficulty in getting a room, however. It's a little too much like New York for me here and rather exhausting. One could have luncheon dates, tea dates and dinner dates every night here indefinitely, I suppose. . . .

Mrs. Kaufman's supposition was correct. Filling their days with work and play is precisely what Dorothy Parker and Alan Campbell were doing, except that following the wave of New Radicalism in 1935, Mrs. Parker was now taking a very active interest in the California political scene, reading and talking with Hollywood's radicals, of whom there were a surprising number.

She was often seen attending private and public meetings espousing the cause of Socialism or, as her enemies claimed, "preaching the pink gospel of Marxism." Clearly, she did not wish to recall the words of the sage who had said that "politics are the greatest depravity of man." Politics, she believed, was the future of mankind, and she enthusiastically carried the message to many of her friends. The Kaufmans listened and smiled. He, perversely and doubtless with an eye to box-office trends, wrote at the time an astringent musical about Franklin D. Roosevelt called *I'd Rather Be Right*, which turned out to be a big hit. "How could he do this?" asked Alan Campbell of his wife. "There's nothing funny about a dead elephant," she replied tartly.

In Hollywood, the movement towards radical politics was gaining ground. A new resident in town was Herb Kline, a young magazine editor who was politically to the extreme left. He had moved after launching his Broadway magazine *New Theater* and was, it appeared, living on $10 a week; the same amount, it was noted, that the Communist party paid their functionaries. Kline, according to Donald Ogden Stewart, was "a devoted and selfless fighter in the struggle for Socialism." It was not long before Kline was tutoring Mrs. Parker and the Fredric Marches in the finer points of that struggle.

Clifford Odets, a talented young playwright, suddenly arrived from New York to make an "inspirational" speech at a fund-raising meeting for Kline's magazine. "Then," according to Stewart, "came the announcement that there was to be another meeting of those interested in the anti-Nazi struggle." This was to be held at the Hollywood Women's Club. A play called *Bury the Dead*, by an unknown writer named Irwin Shaw, was to be read by the Marches.

Stewart recalled the occasion: "The sleeping Hollywood Dragon-in-Wonderland stirred for a moment uneasily in his comfortable cork-lined castle; then, concluding it was only something he had eaten at Romanoff's, went back in search of the slumbering contentment of his habitual happy dream." This was part of Stewart's retrospective view in the late 1970s; in reality, the movement towards socialism was well under way and Mrs. Parker, aided by Stewart and others, was taking a leading part in its progression.

While showing some tolerance for his wife's radical leanings, Alan preferred to steer a middle course; he begged his wife to compromise. His insistence started to generate more resentment in their progressively difficult relationship.

Taking a few weeks off from their Hollywood base, they returned to their Fox House farm, where they gave yet another house party, at which Mrs. Parker got into one of her anti-Alan moods, excusing herself to work on a movie script. "Do forgive me," she said, "but I have to go to that fucking thing upstairs," adding pointedly, "and I don't mean Alan Campbell!"

For all the irritation she frequently felt for her husband, Dorothy Parker nevertheless continued to collaborate with him professionally. Apart from a few stories ("But the One on the Right" was published in *The New Yorker*, and "Clothe the Naked" by *Scribner's*), she had all but given up writing other than for Hollywood. In one or two of the few pieces she did publish at this time, she revealed her radical political stance.

Back at *The New Yorker*, Harold Ross despaired of seeing any real supply of new material from her. When a piece did arrive he was grateful beyond words. He knew, as all their friends did, that she and Alan were making a great deal of money in Hollywood; they had little need for income from magazines.

As far as her short story work was concerned, she found a ready excuse. She was, she said, now writing her stories by hand before retyping them, two fingers at a time. "It takes me six months to do a story," she said. "I think it out and then write it sentence by sentence."

The two had recently completed a sugary script called *Sweethearts*, a musical for MGM starring Jeanette MacDonald and Nelson Eddy, and were now at work on a screenplay of *Trade Winds*, from Tay Garnett's story which would be produced by Walter Wanger and star Fredric March and Joan Bennett. The couple had also written the screenplay of *Mr. Skeffington* for Warner Brothers.

Whatever Mrs. Parker's critics may have felt about her neglect of the short story and verse forms, she was keeping majestic literary company in Hollywood. Her office was close to those of William Faulkner, John O'Hara, Sinclair Lewis, Thornton Wilder and Willie Somerset Maugham, hardly the company indicated by the caustic wit Fred Allen, who observed at the time: "Hollywood's a great place to live—if you're an orange!" And that writer's list was by no means comprehensive; others were Zoë Akins, Maxwell Anderson, Dikran Koujoumian (or Michael Arlen, he of *The Green Hat* fame), Vicki Baum, Stephen Vincent Benét, Samuel Hoffenstein, Sidney Howard, Aldous Huxley and Christopher Isherwood, not to mention old Algonquin friend Ben Hecht, who later recalled his first day in the film city.

I was given an office at Paramount. A bit of cardboard with my name inked on it was tacked on the door. A soiree started at once in my office and lasted for several days. Men of letters, bearing gin bottles, arrived. Bob Benchley, hallooing with laughter, as if he had come from the land of Punch and Judy, was there, and the owlish-eyed satirist Donald Ogden Stewart, beaming as at a convention of March Hares. One night at a flossy party Don appeared on the dance floor in a long overcoat. "That's silly and showing-off to dance in an overcoat," said the great lady of the films in his arms. "Please take it off." Don did. He had nothing on underneath.

Clearly, for some, their first day in Hollywood marked out their territory. The first day Robert Benchley had arrived at MGM, he had ignored the office allocated to him. Another larger and more luxurious suite was assigned to him. This, too, he ignored. Finally, he was persuaded to look it over. Benchley expressed his delight. That afternoon he returned to the room almost submerged in a welter of maps, graphs and blueprints. These he carefully affixed to the walls, stuck into them a succession of colored pins and shut the door after him. He never set foot in the place again.

If by her attitude Mrs. Parker was exposing her radical stance in her political activities, she was still possessed of her familiar astringent and mordant humor, as was markedly evident when she wrote to her friend Woollcott, back on the east coast:

> Selznick International Pictures, Inc.
> 9336 Washington Boulevard,
> Culver City, Cal.

Dear Gerald, [she frequently joked with pseudonyms]
So last week the board of directors of Selznick Pictures, Inc. had a conference. The four members of the board sat around a costly table in an enormously furnished room, and each was supplied with a pad of scratch paper and a pencil. After the conference was over, a healthily curious young employe [*sic*] of the company went in to look at those scratch pads. He found:
Mr. David Selznick had drawn a seven-pointed star; below that, a six-pointed star, and below that again, a row of short vertical lines, like a little picket fence.

Mr. John Whitney's pad had nothing whatever on it.

Dr. A. H. Giannini, the noted Californian banker, had written over and over, in a long, neat column, the word "tokas," which is Yiddish for "arse."

And Mr. Meryan [sic] Cooper, the American authority on Technicolor, had printed on the middle of his page, "RIN-TIN-TIN."

The result of the conference was the announcement that hereafter the company would produce twelve pictures a year, instead of six.

I don't know, I just thought that you might like to be assured that Hollywood does not change.

If Hollywood did not change, the same could hardly be said of Mrs. Parker, who was now vigorously espousing the plight of the poor and similar subjects. She held forth with impassioned zeal at parties and meetings on the disgraceful treatment and segregation of blacks in America; on the appalling unemployment of vast numbers of people; and most important, the ghastly situation in Franco's Imperial Spain, which half the world, excepting America, was metaphorically up in arms about. The United States and Spain were, to the people of America, two entirely separate worlds. Mrs. Parker, however, considered that the destinies of these countries were intertwined, that the liberty of the free world was in mortal peril. Hers was a cry from the heart:

"These are not the days for little, selfish, timid things," she claimed, but few seemed to be listening.

· 3 6 ·
Left Turn

IF ALAN CAMPBELL was not a committed political ally of his wife, Donald Ogden Stewart most certainly was. The two were now seeing a great deal of each other, attending rallies and fund-raising affairs, while Alan waited in the wings.

Stewart was by now a highly successful screenwriter in Hollywood. The time had long since passed when, in the *Vanity Fair* era, he—a young, ambitious graduate of Yale—was "the cultivated Don Quixote with Beauty on his shield, looking for giants." He had killed a good many giants since then. Now, buoyant with material success, he totally embraced the truth of Marxism and espoused it, especially to Dorothy Parker, with whom he had much earlier "fallen in love" in that tiny triangular cubbyhole above New York's 'Met' in those far-off Algonquin days.

By this time, Stewart could boast not only a succession of acclaimed screenplays made into films, but a clutch of published satirical books and novels as well. His achievements had provided the leisurely breeding ground for a greater political awareness than he had had in the twenties in Paris when he had hobnobbed with Hemingway, Gertrude Stein and other "lefties." And he had proven a loyal friend to Mrs. Parker when, in Archibald MacLeish's apartment, Hemingway had read to the assembly his vicious and cruel poem about her. Stewart had vigorously defended her, attacking Hemingway for his calumny. That attack had brought his friendship with the bearded writer to an abrupt end. Being the person he was, Stewart had not taken kindly to Mrs. Parker when she had turned on him by "sucking up," as he put it, to Hemingway in print. But Dottie Parker, as he always maintained, was a "one-off," and he confessed to being honored when she agreed to become the godparent of his son, Ames.

Now he and Mrs. Parker were together again, united in a political cause, organizing meetings and parties to help provide funds for the Spanish Loyalists, arranging benefits to assist blacks, as well as other charitable enterprises in aid of suffering humanity. If Mrs. Parker and Stewart felt deeply for the war-stricken oppressed and underprivileged, their feelings did not stop them from attending, with Alan, parties of the

Hollywood social set. Mrs. Parker's ambivalence was all too familiar to her friends.

At a party given by Stewart for Beatrice Kaufman, now recovered from a short illness—which Mrs. Parker and the host christened The Nervous Breakdown soiree—the guests arrived at noon in full evening dress, headed by Elsa Maxwell in the clinical attire of a psychiatrist. She was followed by Mrs. Parker and Alan, the Stewarts, Benchley, Clark and Rhea Gable, Richard and Jessica Barthelmess, Kay Francis, Lewis Milestone, David Niven, British actress Elizabeth Allen, New York society playboy Whitney de Rham, Fred and Phyllis Astaire, Sam and Frances Goldwyn and Grace Moore with her current beau. "The Nervous Breakdown party? How sick can you get?" one guest was heard to ask.

It did not matter if some did not approve. If one happened to be radically inclined, he or she could always retire to the swimming pool and read up on Malraux's *Man's Fate*; or turn the pages of *The Coming Struggle for Power*, *The Nature of The Capitalist* or *Crisis*; or browse through one of the plentiful radical magazines, such as the *Nation*, *The New Republic* or *The New Masses*, which were strewn around; such literature was frequently in evidence in Hollywood homes.

One could usually find literature that was even more radical, such as pamphlets by Kyle Crichton, who was using the pseudonym Robert Forsythe on his feature writing for *Collier's*. Or one could at some point attend lectures by Herb Kline, the dedicated Marxist, and others.

Many in Hollywood now were, or seemed to be, activists, which in simplistic terms meant pro-Communist because, they predicted, the Soviet Union would inevitably become the victim of the Nazis even though Russian planes were, along with German aircraft, bombing defenseless Spanish towns and villages, like Guernica.

To many it did not quite add up but Mrs. Parker and Donald Ogden Stewart made it perfectly clear where their sympathies lay. Franco, they claimed, was the mortal enemy of democratic civilization.

Predictably, Mrs. Parker and Stewart—who later said of his friend, "she went left before I did"—sought to enlist the benign Robert Benchley to the Spanish cause. He claimed he was "non-committally understanding." Stewart, persistent in cornering his prey, persuaded Benchley to turn a few pages of Sidney and Beatrice Webb's *Soviet Russia—A New Civilization*. Benchley studied the book and appeared unconvinced. Donald Stewart was later to remember the occasion:

I don't think Bobby got much further into the book, but after a few more pages, he suggested that I have a physical checkup by a wonderful new doctor whom Lewis Milestone had discovered. I suspected that Bobby might be hoping that the doctor would cure me of my unfortunate attack of political activity, but I agreed that I would let the doctor work on me if Bobby would take the same treatment. The physician's name was Cecil Smith, and after a preliminary examination he sent both of us to a hospital for a week of "further checking up."

It was a marvelous week. Bobby and I were in adjoining rooms; the meals were excellent and we were allowed wine with some of them. Cecil recommended that Bobby take a certain pill for one or two nights, "just to see if we're on the right track." On the third day, Cecil came to Bobby's Garden of Allah bungalow and asked him if the pills had had the desired affect. Bobby replied: "Well, I'm not quite sure," and when he pulled off his shirt, we saw that a frighteningly realistic growth of silver-fox fur extended from Bobby's neck down to his rectum. "Is this what you meant?" he asked poor Cecil.

Mrs. Parker and Donald Stewart were fiercely intent on marshaling the intellectual force and money of the Hollywood left into a cohesive whole, having been prime movers in the formation of the Hollywood Anti-Nazi League in the autumn of 1936. The league had an impressive membership, which included Eddie Cantor, Marc Connelly, Dudley Nichols, Marion Spitzer, Herbert Biberman, among others. Initially, a few producers nervously loaned the league some facilities, feeling impelled to acknowledge the important names who headed it. Later, several of them sought to be excused when additional requests for help were received. Stewart continued:

"Gradually the producers had been made suspicious that the league might be a Red organization. It was not long before many of our 'name' supporters had also yielded to the fear of being associated with communism . . . Our League continued to grow, however, even without the big producers and the 'names,' and we gradually achieved a membership of some five or six thousand. . . . " While his figures might be questioned, his enthusiasm could not. Dorothy Parker later recalled:

"It is to my pride that I can say that Donald Stewart and I and five others were the organizers of the Hollywood Anti-Nazi League. From those seven, it grew in two years to a membership of four thousand—the last figures I heard—and it has done fine and brave work."

The league had come to the forefront of her activities, underlining what those in Hollywood believed about Mrs. Parker's political leanings —that she was, in fact, a Communist.

Mrs. Parker, along with Lillian Hellman and Dashiell Hammett, had become a chief organizer of the newly constituted Screen Writers' Guild, which she had helped to found. The guild had become so strong and

effective that by April 1936 it had called on the House Patents Committee
for legislation to strengthen authors' rights in deciding how their work
was to be used. She later wrote:

"With Donald Stewart, I served on the board of the Screen Writers'
Guild. Some claimed that every writer for the screen received for his
trash $2,500 a week. Well, you see, the average wage for a screenwriter
is $40 a week, and that for an average of fourteen weeks in a year, and
that subject to being fired with no notice. . . . "

With the guild leading the way, writers in Hollywood were now organizing groups for economic and political action designed, they said, to
oppose local and even international fascism. Mrs. Parker and her friends
were clearly prepared to stand up and be counted.

With Stewart and others, she believed that films could be "a powerful
weapon in the defense of our democratic heritage." While not everyone
in Hollywood was prepared to share her view, she persisted in an article
in *New Masses*, revealing:

I cannot tell you on what day what did what to me [but] there I was, then,
wild with the knowledge of injustice and brutality and misrepresentation . . . At
that time I saw many rich people and, in this I am not unique—they did much
in my life to send me back to the masses, to make me proud of being a worker,
too. One must say for the rich that they are our best propagandists. One sees
them, clumsy and without gaiety and bumbling and dependent . . . I saw these
silly, dull, stuffy people, and they sent me shunting. It is not noble that hatred
sends you from one side to the other; but I say again, it is not unique.

As if her forays in print were not enough, Dorothy Parker, now the
untiring political activist, started to organize the Western branch of The
League of American Writers, "an organization," she defined, "to get
writers out of their ivory towers and into the active struggle against
Nazism and Fascism." She also became acting chairman for the Spanish
Refugee Appeal and national chairman for the Joint Anti-Fascist Refugee Committee and other politically oriented organizations.

Ella Winter, widow of the left-wing extremist Lincoln Steffens and
later the wife of Donald Stewart, claimed at a rally in Hollywood: "Dorothy Parker and Donald Ogden Stewart can help us more than a thousand jargon-filled pamphlets."

When this was delivered, Alan Campbell, seated in the audience and
looking smooth in a new tuxedo, visibly winced. A distinctly uncomfortable rope around his neck was dragging him reluctantly behind a cart
pulled by a sophisticated and pronouncedly more affluent version of
Mother Courage in the person of his wife, Dorothy Parker. It was a

sensation that was to continue to give him a prolongation of considerable unease. But his wife continued to say: "Oh, the years I have wasted, being a party girl and smart arse, when I could have been helping all the unfortunate people in the world."

· 3 7 ·

Ernest Makes a Scene

DOROTHY PARKER had always been prepared to stand up and be counted when she believed wholeheartedly in a cause. If the opinion of others disagreed with hers, she was contemptuous of that opinion and was prepared even to reject old and valued friends like Benchley, if they did not agree with her consuming radical tilt. Early in 1931, Kaufman, Benchley and Mrs. Parker, together with others of the Algonquin crowd, had actually donned waiters' uniforms when the restaurant staff had gone on strike at the hotel, but Benchley, it was said, had participated more for a laugh.

The group had, they claimed, "moved in to help Frank Case out," but many had seen this gesture of friendship in a different light. Heywood Broun, ever an impassioned Socialist, heard about the incident and had taken Benchley to task for "trying to break the strike." Broun, who was away covering a story in Philadelphia, had berated Benchley, Parker and other of his friends in his column, but there clearly had been some doubt about their true intentions. It was said, in their defense, that they had been "fooling around." Benchley, in turn, had accused Broun of printing "second-hand accounts—the way you want them for your column" and had added, "you know damn well that they aren't true, and I'll thank you not to make a column out of a story which you know had no foundation in fact."

That incident had signaled the beginning of the end of the era of the Round Table. Even Frank Case's attempt in 1933 to reinvigorate it by starting an Algonquin Supper Club—with an expensive inaugural dinner attended by celebrities like Betty Starbuck, Richard Halliday, Tallulah Bankhead and Joseph Bryan III—had fallen by the wayside, as had Case's attempt to revive the Thanatopsis, which had finally moved to the Colony Restaurant, where Herbert Swope and FPA had long been well known. As Ogden Nash observed at the time: "After all those years of intimate and secluded sipping, I find that to order and drink in a hotel gives me the naked feeling of a scallop torn from its shell." That was one way of putting it, and Nash, as all knew, certainly had a way with words.

There had been others who had doubted the sincerity of Mrs. Parker, Benchley and Woollcott when they had supported the waiters' strike at the Algonquin. The group had lobbied the diners to walk out in sympathy with the strikers and had been harried by house detectives for their pains. To the "house dicks" they had "kept up a running fire of extemporaneous bon mots and wisecracks." Woollcott summed up the evening in a single phrase as he swept out with Mrs. Parker and Benchley on each arm: "It was," he said, "just a swirl of ugly passion."

A year or two afterwards, Mrs. Parker and Alan gave a benefit buffet in their North Canyon Drive mansion to aid the Scottsboro Boys, an event which had raised several thousand dollars.

The current activities of Mrs. Parker, Stewart and their Hollywood political allies were not, however, all plain sailing. Their efforts were vigorously opposed by staunch right-wingers like Adolphe Menjou, Robert Taylor and Gary Cooper, and those who belonged to the strong pro-Fascist groups like Victor McLaglen's Light Horse Cavalry (a branch of Pelley's Silver Shirts) and Guy Empey's Hollywood Hussars, both evoking an equine imagery which some said denoted an intention to ride roughshod over all opposition. Mrs. Parker and her friends were indifferently disdainful of their opponents.

On trips back to New York, and what were called "rest" periods at Fox House Farm, Dorothy and Alan joined a committee of authors working for Roosevelt's reelection. They also traveled to Biltmore and other towns to attend dinners to provide funds for the Anti-Nazi League.

Mrs. Parker's round of activities on the political front did not prevent her from spending a succession of spirited social weekends with her show business friends. She, like others of the Hollywood fraternity, was a frequent guest at William Randolph Hearst's ostentatious castle, La Cuesta Encantada (the Enchanted Hill), formerly known as Camp Hill. The baroque complex looked down across the tiny village of San Simeon and the Pacific Coast highway, standing aloof like a fantasy in space, spilling random images down the hill in a mesmeric confusion of marble and tile borrowed from Spanish, Italian and Moorish traditions. Its pure fantasy had been summed up by a previous visitor, George Bernard Shaw, who said of it, "This is probably the way God would have done it if He'd had the money."

The castle was presided over by Hearst's mistress, movie star Marion Davies, who had succeeded another actress, Miriam Hopkins, in Hearst's life and bed. The publishing multimillionaire had given Davies an excess of diamonds and other gifts, and had even bought her a movie studio to help make her a star, an effort which had largely succeeded. Originally a comedienne, she wanted to make people laugh, but Hearst saw her as a haloed, virginal heroine and exercised a strange fetish by having her

parade before the guests at San Simeon in what was then fairly revolu-
tionary attire—men's trousers. Each weekend Miss Davies would assem-
ble a large cross-section of guests at the castle, mostly from the Blue
Book colony and Hollywood:

"The society people always wanted to meet the movie people, so I got
them together," was her later comment.

There was one fairly strict rule at San Simeon. Hearst disliked alcohol
and thus limited his guests to one cocktail as they assembled for dinner.
Marion Davies, however, usually managed to subvert the rule, boasting
to her close friends that she had once got Calvin Coolidge tipsy on Tokay
by persuading him that her applied beverage was non-alcoholic. "Best
darned non-alcoholic drink I ever drank in my life," the former president
had exclaimed as he passed out.

Mrs. Parker was at San Simeon one weekend with Herman Mankiewicz, who was far from being an abstainer. The two of them allegedly
got rather high, much to Hearst's chagrin. The press baron issued orders
to his mistress that while he was prepared to tolerate Mrs. Parker—he
confessed to "liking her style"—Mankiewicz was henceforth to be
crossed off the invitation list. Mrs. Parker took quiet issue with both
Hearst and Davies. It seemed that the Elysian playground was peppered
with statues of the Blessed Madonna. One, at the entrance to Miss Davies's dressing room, was pointed out to Mrs. Parker by Miss Davies as
having come from King Ludwig II's castle in Bavaria. Mrs. Parker was
later to remember the statue, Miss Davies and Mr. Hearst—in verse:

> Upon my honor
> I saw a Madonna
> Standing in a niche
> Above the door
> Of a prominent whore
> Of a prominent son of a bitch.

And Mankiewicz was to get even in his own way by reporting on the
bizarre place and its activities to Orson Welles, thereby starting the web
of fantasy and fact that became the memorable *Citizen Kane*.

It was at this time that Mrs. Parker attended a party where the British
actor Herbert Marshall was holding forth, continually referring, in
upper-class English, to his "schedule." After a while, Mrs. Parker could
stand it no longer. She interrupted him in full flow with, "If you don't
mind my saying so, I think you are full of skit."

If her mordant humor did not, in the view of some, quite fit the mood
of these serious times, it well fitted Mrs. Parker's life-style. Her busy life

at this time appeared to be echoed in her own lines in "The Flaw of Paganism":

> Drink and dance and laugh and lie,
> Love, the reeling midnight through
> For tomorrow we shall die
> (But, alas, we never do)

She was still turning out screenplays and film treatments with Alan by day and many of her nights were taken up with attending millionaires' soirees. At the same time she was vigorously seeking to create in Hollywood the crystallization of the New Socialist Dream. She spent much of her time meeting with anti-Fascists who turned up regularly in Hollywood and New York to appeal for more money and support for Spanish Loyalists. The visitors included Eduard Beneš from Czechoslovakia, Louis Aragon from Spain and France, Beatrice Webb and Sylvia Townsend Warner from England, Professor Harold Laski from his base at the London School of Economics. When invited to take part in a Hollywood show with Stepin Fetchit, she refused, saying that "Black people have suffered too much ever to be funny to me." The flow of visitors was supported by a parade of radical American writers and artists like Vincent Sheean, Louis Bromfield, Norman Corwin, Alan Lomax, Langston Hughes, Joseph Freeman, H. V. Kaltenborn, Max Wylie and others.

France's André Malraux, who had flown a plane for the Loyalists in Spain, arrived in Hollywood to conduct an impassioned appeal for support of the freedom fighters. Mrs. Parker, along with Hammett, Stewart and others, met him at Lillian Hellman's home, where he delivered a moving address. As one result, Dorothy Parker and Lillian Hellman each contributed $1,000 to the cause, enough to buy two ambulances.

Ernest Hemingway was in Hollywood, too, in his now customary flight of rhetoric. He had been in Spain making a pro-Loyalist documentary film, *The Spanish Earth*. In Morales, just outside Madrid, he and the cameramen had been close to a Republican attack and were shot at.

Hemingway was now at the height of his success, made stronger by the acclaim of *The Snows of Kilimanjaro*. With Scott Fitzgerald, Mrs. Parker, Alan, Lillian Hellman, Dashiell Hammett and others present, he screened the final cut of *The Spanish Earth* in the home of Fredric and Florence March. Lillian Hellman remembered what happened after that screening:

When we left the Marches, Dorothy Parker asked a few of us to her house for a nightcap. . . . I had met Scott Fitzgerald years before in Paris, but I had not seen him again until that night and I was shocked by the change in his face and manner. He hadn't seemed to recognize me and so I was surprised and pleased when he asked if I would ride with him to Dottie's. My admiration for Fitzgerald's work was very great, and I looked forward to talking to him alone. But we didn't talk: he was occupied with driving at ten or twelve miles an hour down Sunset Boulevard, a dangerous speed in most places, certainly in Beverly Hills. Fitzgerald crouched over the wheel when cars honked at us, we jerked to the right and then to the left, and passing drivers leaned out to shout at us. I could not bring myself to speak, or even to look at Fitzgerald, but when I saw that his hands were trembling on the wheel, all my rides from Metro came rushing back, and I put my hand over his hand. He brought the car to the side of the road, and I told him about my old job at Metro, the awful rides home, my fears of California drivers, until he patted my arm several times and then I knew he hadn't been listening and had different troubles.

He said, "You see, I'm on the wagon. I'll take you to Dottie's but I don't want to go in."

When we finally got to Dottie's, he came around to open the door for me. He said softly, "It's a long story, Ernest and me . . . "

I said, "But Dottie wants to see you. Everybody in that room wants to meet you."

He shook his head and smiled, "No, I'm riding low now."

"Not for writers, nor will you ever. *The Great Gatsby* is the best . . . "

He smiled and touched my shoulders. "I'm afraid of Ernest, I guess, scared of being sober when . . . "

Miss Hellman was sympathetically attentive.

I said, "Don't be. He could never like a good writer, certainly not a better one. Come. You'll have a nice time."

I put out my hand and, after a second, he smiled and took it. We went into the hall and turned left into the living room. Nobody saw us come in because the four or five people in the room were all turned toward Ernest, who stood with his back to the door, facing the fireplace. I don't know why he did it, or what had gone on before, but as we started into the room, Hemingway threw his highball glass against the stone fireplace. Fitzgerald and I stopped dead at the sound of the smashing glass: he stepped back into the hall and turned to leave, but I held his arm and he followed me through a swinging door as if he didn't know or care where he was going. Dottie and Hammett were in the kitchen . . .

I said, "Ernest just threw a glass."

Dottie said, "Certainly," as she kissed Fitzgerald.

Clearly, Lillian Hellman was not aware until that moment of the friction between Hemingway and Fitzgerald. But Dorothy Parker knew what had caused the scene. In *The Snows of Kilimanjaro*, a dying novelist had recalled to an old friend:

"The rich were dull and drank too much, or they played too much backgammon. They were dull and they were repetitious. He remembered Scott Fitzgerald and his romantic awe of them and how he had started a story once that began, 'The rich are different from you and me.' And how someone had said to Scott, 'Yes, they have more money.' But that was not humorous to Scott. He thought they were a special glamorous race and when he found they weren't it wrecked him just as much as any other thing that wrecked him."

Lillian Hellman had not known that when Fitzgerald had read the book, he had written to Hemingway in stinging terms to protest. As a result, in later printings "Scott Fitzgerald" had become Julian.

When Dorothy Parker, on being told of the glass incident, coolly remarked, "Certainly," her comment was in tacit approval of the gesture made by her idol. In spite of her long friendship with Fitzgerald, Ernest Hemingway could do no wrong in her eyes—a fact of which Miss Hellman was obviously not aware; or if she was, she chose to ignore it.

Why had Fitzgerald displayed such reluctance to meet again with Hemingway, and why the bravura gesture by Hemingway as Fitzgerald walked into the room with Hellman? Clearly, each resented the presence of the other.

The two men had known each other for many years, since the early twenties, when they used to dine together at James Joyce's favorite restaurant, the Trianon, and at the Closerie des Lilas, the Dome, the Café des Deux Magots and other Parisian venues. It is true that Zelda Fitzgerald had at one time accused Scott of having a sexual relationship with Hemingway. Scott had written indignantly to her that, "The nearest I ever came to leaving you was when you told me that I was a fairy in the Rue Palatine . . . "

That rumor had been started by Robert McAlmon, Fitzgerald's first publisher in France, but Scott had been on to him. Scott wrote to Max Perkins, his American editor, that "McAlmon is a bitter rat and I'm not surprised at anything he says or does . . . He's a failed writer . . . Part of his quarrel with Ernest some years ago was because he assured Ernest I was a fairy—God knows he shows more creative imagination than in his work. Next he told Callaghan [a mutual friend] that Ernest was a fairy. He's a pretty good person to avoid!"

As far as is known there had not been an affair between Hemingway and Fitzgerald. However, there was always a curious reluctance on Hemingway's part to acknowledge the literary accomplishments of Fitzgerald. On the other hand, Scott had constantly been fulsome in his praise of Hemingway's work; to a large extent he shared Mrs. Parker's hero worship. But there were those who believed that Fitzgerald was intimidated by his own idolatry of Hemingway.

· 3 8 ·

Frolics on the Farm

MRS. PARKER'S, and to an extent Alan's, political activities in Hollywood and New York now impinged into their lives at Fox House Farm. Their friends perceived they were growing apart, united only by their collaborative screenwriting activities. Alan frequently invited friends to stay at the farm, several of them ostentatiously "camp." Mrs. Parker invited a succession of her political allies, mostly writers and some of her old Algonquin friends, several of whom exhibited a refined intellectual mockery that contrasted with the waspish gaiety of Alan's coterie. But whoever happened to be in the guest rooms, one thing was certain: they usually went to bed at dawn and would rise shortly before noon and take a swim in the pool, a present from Dorothy to Alan. Enjoying pre-luncheon cocktails, the guests would be treated to Parkerian witticisms often delivered at the expense of her husband:

"Did you ever see Alan on stage? It was like something Vassar girls would do—only *nicer*" or, "Scratch an actor—and you'll usually find an actress!" She would tease him with appellations like "My friend, the wickedest woman in Paris," and if he referred to one of their homosexual friends she would comment, "How d'you like that for competition?"

Alan customarily shrugged off the insults. He would simply concentrate on other things, like creating some gastronomic delight, aided by the stolid Mrs. Beer, who was more than a little intimidated by his antics. Fed up with the late-night and early-morning parties at the farm, Hiram and Mrs. Beer had quit three times, each time being assured by Dorothy that Alan and the guests would behave better; also Dorothy had given them raises to persuade them to stay.

To Mrs. Parker nothing seemed sacred. Even her descriptions of country life were derisory:

"Every year, back Spring comes," she wrote, "with nasty little birds yapping their fool heads off and the ground all mucked up with arbutus."

Life, despite its many problems, was still to be approached with humor, if not total scorn. At this time, she heard from two friends who had decided to get married after living together for many years. She sent them a wire: WHAT'S NEW?

To many of her friends, Fox House Farm was becoming known as

Animal Farm, for Mrs. Parker had collected no less than nine dogs, four cats, two cockatoos and a clutch of chickens. Often, when she, Alan and their guests dropped in on friends in neighboring homes, they would return to the farm to find the rooms dotted with randomly dropped animal ordure, the result of their locking up the animals with no concern for their natural functions. Confronted with the resultant mess, shrieks of laughter would ring through the house as the occupants and guests excitedly called out, "There's a lot over here." "And, look! A lot over here, too." "Some more here, as well."

And it seemed not to matter to anyone other than the housekeeper that in the normal course of events, when Alan was busy with his guests, Mrs. Beer was asked to serve dinner at eight. The martinis, of course, had to come first—and last—and if Mrs. Beer's repast became burned up by one A.M., the kitchen crisis seemed only to add to the hilarity. As one of the guests would later remark: "It was all too, too much. Too much self-indulgence!"

While at the farm, Mrs. Parker and Alan would sometimes suddenly embark on frenetic spells of writing to catch up on their scriptwriting, becoming oblivious to their guests. Although she had made no secret of hating screenwriting, she tried to fulfill her commitments. But it was Alan who pressed her to work. His doggedly persistent star-struck attitude was in no way constricted by his wife's disapproval of Hollywood that "it looks, it all feels as if it had been invented by a Sixth Avenue peep-show man." The only time she had ever agreed with the hated Hedda Hopper had been when the columnist had written: "Our town worships success, the bitch-goddess whose smile hides a taste for blood." For Dorothy Parker, Hollywood remained a place bereft of ethics or art.

This was the face she showed to the world. But she was still deeply troubled. Her morbid preoccupation with death rarely left her. But now, additionally, it was the death of thousands of loyal Spanish freedom fighters; the deaths, too, of hundreds of European and American radicals who had gone to Spain to join the anti-Franco International Brigades, the 15th, the Lincoln.

At this time, she met with an old friend, Leland Stowe, who convinced her that she should go to Spain and write about the oppression and the horror of fascism there. She must write about it, he said, and "tell the world." She went straight to the editor of *New Masses* seeking to persuade him to give her accreditation to cover the Civil War for his magazine. He agreed to send her.

Mrs. Parker's social conscience had been clearly troubling her. She had been living among Hollywood's gilded images of affluence and success, while outside that privileged, enclosed community, in Spain, poverty, death and destruction were the rule. In Spain, there was a harsher world than she had ever dreamed of.

Had she, on the eve of her trip, perhaps glimpsed the struggle which she had earlier described in "Prisoner":

> Long I fought the driving lists,
> Plume astream and armor clanging,
> Link on link between my wrists
> Now my heavy freedom's hanging.

For, in a way, it was.

· 3 9 ·

Whistling in the Graveyards

IN 1938, Dorothy Parker left for Europe on the S.S. *Normandie* with Alan, Lillian Hellman and Dashiell Hammett. In Paris they met with the Murphys and dined with James Thurber. Thurber thought she was over-reacting in her impassioned reasoning about the civil war and later wrote E. B. White: "It is the easiest thing in the world nowadays to become so socially conscious, so Spanish war-stricken that all sense of balance and values goes out of a person." It was true of many and there were those who held it to be true of Mrs. Parker.

She left her husband and friends in Paris and moved on to Spain, where Miss Hellman had preceded her. She had promised the readers of *New Masses* she would concern herself exclusively with objective war reporting. She was to keep that promise, even if her reportage was to be colored with a deep, emotional response.

In Spain, King Alfonso XIII, the puppet king, had already cleared out the coffers and left the country in 1931. The ruling Falangist party constituted the upper classes, who were allied with the established mili-tary forces and the Spanish Catholic church; the regime, dominated by Fascists, was being supplied by Fascist Italy and Nazi Germany with troops, tanks, guns and planes. Already, Mussolini's Fascists had invaded Abyssinia: the civil war in Spain was a battle between the financially cushioned extreme right and the impoverished left. The Loyalists were the Communist and Socialist factions augmented by trade unionists and other radical sympathizers from several countries who together formed the International Brigades, the 15th of which comprised over 600 Britons, Americans, Italians and Dutch, whose departure was applauded by intellectuals like Spender, Isherwood, Samuel Butler, Pablo Casals, Benjamin Britten, Picasso and others who mostly watched on the sidelines.

Miners in revolt had already stormed Spanish police barracks, result-ing in hundreds of deaths. The war was to be a ghastly rehearsal for World War II, a Spain waking from a nightmare within an oppressive sleep. The League of Nations, which many said might have helped, was in total disarray. Madrid and Valencia had been mercilessly bombed, and dozens of villages, like Guernica, virtually wiped out by the Franco forces.

Mrs. Parker was to find war-torn Spain, its olive groves crimson with blood, a long, long way from Fifth Avenue, New York and Hollywood. Her words rang out sharp and clear:

"It was," she wrote, "darling of me to have shared my cigarettes with the men on their way back to the trenches. Little Lady Bountiful. The prize sow."

But if her self-deprecation was limitless, her concern for the peasants of Spain seemed genuine. Certainly, her published words were graphic enough:

. . . the streets are crowded, and the shops are open, and the people go about their daily living. It isn't tense and it isn't hysterical. What they have is not morale, which is something created and bolstered and directed. It is the sure, steady spirit of those who know what the fight is about and who know that they must win.

In spite of all the evacuation, there were still nearly a million people here. Some of them—you may be like that yourself—won't leave their homes and their possessions, all the things they have gathered together through the years. They are not at all dramatic about it. It is simply that anything else than the life they have made for themselves is inconceivable to them. Yesterday I saw a woman who lives in the poorest quarter of Madrid. It had been bombed twice by the Fascists; her house is one of the few left standing. She has seven children. It has often been suggested to her that she and the children leave Madrid for a safer place. She dismisses such ideas easily and firmly. Every six weeks, she says, her husband has forty-eight hours leave from the front. Naturally he wants to come home and see her and the children. She, and each one of the seven, are calm and strong and smiling. It is a typical Madrid family . . .

It helped that Ernest Hemingway was there, too, in the battle zones and writing: "Just as the earth can never die, neither will those who have ever been free return to slavery. The peasants who work the earth where our dead lie know what these dead died for. . . . " Mrs. Parker was in agreement when, moving on into the battle zone, she recorded for *New Masses*:

While I was in Valencia the Fascists raided it four times. If you are going to be in an air raid at all, it is better for you if it happens at night. Then it is unreal, it is almost beautiful, it is like a ballet with the scurrying figures and the great white shafts of the searchlights. But when a raid comes in the daytime, then you see the faces of the people, and it isn't unreal any longer. You see the terrible resignation on the faces of the old women, and you see little children wild with terror.

"I do not think," she wrote in a later dispatch, "there will be any Lost Generation after this war . . . they are fighting for more than their lives. They are fighting for the chance to live them."

Mrs. Parker met briefly with Hemingway in Madrid. She met too with Joris Ivins and Errol Flynn, whom Hemingway accused of reaching the Spanish border and then turning back to return to Hollywood. There had been many sadnesses for her there, including the death in battle of one of Ring Lardner's sons, a boy who had felt a burning passion to "do something" to help.

Mrs. Parker went back to Paris and spent a week there with Alan, Lillian Hellman and Hammett, before returning to New York with her husband. There she wrote "Soldiers of the Republic," a simple first-person account in short-story form, which was essentially an essay on the plight of the common people. Set in Spain, it could have been anywhere where people were suffering oppression of mind, body and spirit. A soldier spoke, she recorded, with concern for his wife and three children, and their ragged clothes. "She has no thread," he kept telling us. "My wife has no thread to mend with. No thread."

Mrs. Parker sent the piece to Harold Ross at *The New Yorker*. Glad to have Dorothy Parker back again, he published it. Aleck Woollcott was the first to respond, telephoning his congratulations and insisting on paying the costs to have it published in pamphlet form with wide distribution throughout the country. The article was to give her credibility as a serious writer; "Dorothy Parker quits her role as humorist," wrote Leon Schloss of the Los Angeles *Times*. But Mrs. Parker had her own explanation when speaking before a distinguished audience of social and political leaders at the home of New Deal economist Leon Henderson, in Washington, D.C.:

"A humorist in this world is whistling by the loneliest graveyard," she said. "There is nothing funny in the world any more. If you had seen what I saw in Spain, you'd be serious too. And you'd be trying to help those poor people."

When she finished speaking she was crying. So, too, was the Spanish ambassador, de los Rios.

But the metamorphosis of Dorothy Parker into a serious, dedicated, champion of the underdog was not fully accepted by most of the public. Many wanted her to continue to be funny, to be "Tonstant weader all fwowed up." The impassioned humanist was not, surely, *quite* her role. As John Keats wrote:

" . . . a sophisticate . . . is one who dwells in a tower made of Dupont substitute for ivory and holds a glass of flat champagne in one hand and an album of dirty postcards in the other . . . "

In those terms, Mrs. Parker had totally rejected her past; seemingly she no longer wanted part of that world. The horrendous reality of the war had all but overwhelmed her. Indeed, she took herself to task in *New Masses*, telling her readers that the days when poets of light verse wrote about disliking parsley or ladies' clothes were over. "It is no longer," she said, "the time for personal matters—thank God! Now the poet speaks not just for himself but for all of us—and so his voice is heard and so his song goes on."

To the world of harsh reality it was a sad, embittered song. Idealists, Alan told her, were born losers and the Loyalists of Spain were no exceptions to the rule. That, of course, was the attitude of a cynic but Alan preferred to call it the attitude of a realist.

The Loyalists were being overrun and massacred by the thousands. Where now could she turn?

She turned to God. Her turn towards Catholicism was not, perhaps, as extroverted, if that is the right word, as that of her old friend Heywood Broun, who somewhat publicly was brought to the faith by the celebrated converter Monsignor Fulton J. Sheen. Mrs. Parker's turn was of a quiet, deeply thoughtful nature, which might conceivably provide the inner peace she had always desperately lacked. Her friends were predictably suspicious. Scott Fitzgerald, for one, was cryptically cynical. He wrote to Gerald Murphy:

"The heroes are the great corruptionists or the supremely indifferent —by whom I mean the spoiled writers. Hecht, Nunnally Johnson, Dottie, Dash Hammett, etc. That Dottie has embraced the church and reads her office faithfully every day does not affect her indifference. So is one type of commy Malraux didn't list among his categories in *Man's Hope* —but nothing would disappoint her so vehemently as success."

Even in Mrs. Parker's terms, it was inevitable that the road to holiness must perforce pass through the secular world, the world of hate and enmity, the world of war, greed, of evil.

By her actions, it is clear that she believed that man cannot reconcile himself to his God without attempting to achieve what little good he can in everyday action. This was, as she had learned at school, an eternal verity; it was the same truth the Greeks had grappled with, the same truth that Goethe and later the Victorian intellectuals had struggled with in the discomforting knowledge that subjective pressures were invariably stronger than objective ones. She had also learned that with mere mortals it was possible to achieve spiritual serenity in one's private world and yet be forced—often unwillingly, sometimes realizing that precious years of life were being wasted—into the harsh world outside, as Kierkegaard had discovered on his way to truth. Malraux, too, had been forced to face that same truth in just that way, as had Einstein. The rejection of the romantic idea of the artist had been the clear result. Such an idea could not survive in the years of ferocity, the years of hatred, the years of now. The pathetic grandeur of human existence, of human innocence —were these tenable, believable, in a world of degradation, human misery and insupportable evil? The answer, she knew, had to be no.

Mrs. Parker talked about her moral dilemma to a few, but not to Alan. Acutely perceptive of her needs and of what was good for her, he tried to talk down her religious fervor. She had drastically cut down on her drinking and would walk, in conflict with her conscience, alone in the fields of Doylestown for hours on end, trying to reach her God.

It soon became apparent to her friends that Mrs. Parker's flirtation with the Deity was not to last long. She was still Dorothy Parker; her public image was well established for all to know, her inner pain largely concealed. Only at meetings where she talked about her experiences in Spain would she raise her visor a little:

I cannot talk about it in these days. All I know is that there I saw the finest people I ever saw, that there I knew the only possible thing for mankind is solidarity. As I write, their defense in Catalonia against the invasion of the Fascists has failed. But do you think people like that can fail for long, do you think that they, banded together in their simple demand for decency, can long go down? They threw off that monarchy, after those centuries; can men of ten years' tyranny defeat them now? I beg your pardon. I get excited.

The answer to her question was answered soon.

Madrid fell to the Falangists on March 28, 1939. When the news reached Mrs. Parker in Bucks County, she once again rejected her God.

· 4 O ·

A Uniform for Alan

DESPITE Alan Campbell's plea that his wife relax her radical stance, Mrs. Parker swept his arguments aside and continued to preach against Nazism and discrimination against blacks in America.

It was ruining her reputation, Alan protested, which seemed borne out by the fact that during 1939 neither had been offered a single writing assignment in Hollywood. Thus, early in 1940 Mrs. Parker sold the lease of her canyon house to Laurence Olivier and Vivien Leigh. According to movie director George Cukor, who had spent Christmas that year with the Oliviers, the house was "a melancholy place." Mrs. Parker had herself said, "There descends on the house in the late afternoon what I would call a suicide light," a description that was perhaps predictable coming from a somber personality, who at this time had much to be melancholy about.

There was already a strong movement on the part of many Hollywood producers to avoid "leftie" writers. Hollywood's romance with communism was cooling; the Anti-Nazi League had lately and discreetly changed its name to the Hollywood League for Democratic Action, concentrating its activities not on "concerted action against Hitler" but on "neutrality," denouncing everything that seemed to be leading America into war. Alan believed that his wife was being watched by the Federal Bureau of Investigation, and he was afraid. Moreover, he knew that there had to be others who were watching the watchers.

All the signs of the coming world struggle were obvious to thinking men and women. In 1931, Japan had invaded Manchuria, crushing Chinese resistance. A year later, the same country had set up the puppet state of Manchukuo. Italy, having succumbed to fascism, had enlarged her boundaries in Libya and in 1935–36 had conquered Ethiopia. In Germany, Adolf Hitler had organized his National Socialist Party and had seized the reins of government, reoccupied the Rhineland and undertaken large-scale rearmament.

As the true nature of totalitarianism became painfully clear, and as Germany, Italy and Japan continued their aggressions, attacking one small nation after another, American and British apprehension turned to burning indignation.

In 1938, after Hitler had incorporated Austria into the German Reich, his demands for the Sudetenland of Czechoslovakia made war seem possible at any moment. The American people, disillusioned by the failure of the crusade for democracy of World War I, announced that under no circumstances could any belligerent look to them for aid or comfort. Neutrality legislation, enacted piecemeal from 1935 to 1937, prohibited trade with or credit to any belligerent. The objective was to prevent the involvement of the United States in a non-American war.

Mrs. Parker continued to write, lecture and address meetings until the final blow. On August 23, 1939, Soviet Russia signed a non-aggression pact with Nazi Germany. Mrs. Parker's world fell apart. The Communists had linked arms with the Nazis. What now was to become of the American Dream?

Warm, kind, ordinary men, women and children had been relentlessly butchered abroad and here was the Russian Bear embracing the Jew-baiting, inhuman Fascist forces for which all those brave people had fought and died on the red earth of Spain, and elsewhere. Like most of her fellow radicals, she was certain that another world war was imminent. It came, just over a week after the signing of the Russo-German pact.

Before a month had passed, the German Luftwaffe and Hitler's ground panzer units swept across Poland, while from the east the Russian army and air force did their work. Britain and France responded by declaring war on Germany. Neville Chamberlain's wispy "piece of paper" had been snatched up by the winds of war and had disappeared in the dust of battle. Then Denmark, Norway and Holland fell victim to the Nazis while Russia halted in Poland to gather up her spoils.

The immediate reaction of the Americans was to stay out of the European conflict, but they soon understood that what threatened world security also threatened American security. Congress prepared to enact the first peacetime conscription bill in American history.

For Dorothy Parker, reason, cogent argument, and intellectual logic had all been proven false. There was now no moral precept left in the United States for which to fight except, perhaps, discrimination against blacks. She resigned all her affiliations with the anti-Nazi movements, the "pink" leagues and associations. She was totally disillusioned. It was only a matter of time before America allied herself with Britain, its Commonwealth, France, and the Low Countries to become a part of a second world conflict during her lifetime.

She turned once again to her writing, gathering up her fiction for a new volume. She would be including "Soldiers of the Republic" and

"Clothe the Naked." She wrote a new short story, "The Custard Heart," about an aging woman's affairs with young men. With twenty-four short stories and essays thus assembled, she published her fifth volume, dedicated to Lillian Hellman, with the characteristically funereal title *Here Lies*; clearly Mrs. Parker could not leave death alone.

"Clothe the Naked," a story about a blind black youth adopted by a washerwoman, had been written in the heat of her radicalism and illustrated the virtues of communism over capitalism. In reviewing the book for *The Spectator*, under the title "The Parker Probe," William Plomer dug deep into Mrs. Parker's psyche:

> The urbanity of these stories is that of a worldly, witty person with a place in a complex and highly developed society, their ruthlessness that of an expert critical intelligence, about which there is something clinical, something of the probing adroitness of a dentist: the fine-pointed instrument unerringly discovers the carious cavity behind the smile . . . Mrs. Parker may appear amused, but it is plain that she is really horrified. Her bantering revelations are inspired by a respect for decency, and her pity and sympathy are ready when needed.

That these had been ready when needed had been all too evident in the immediate past; the exposure of both had helped neither her nor her career. Certainly her work in Hollywood had not been helped either. Dorothy Parker, the idealist, had learned the truth of Wilde's maxim, that "the wicked prosper in a wicked world." For that matter, she had had plenty of evidence in Spain of another Wilde truism, that "the sick do not ask if the hand that smoothes their pillow is pure, nor the dying care if the lips that touch their brow have known the kiss of sin." They were unhappy paradoxes, trenchantly fitting the world in which she lived.

Although she and Alan were still having marital problems, he still adored her but she continued to snipe at him in public and private. One of her friends, perturbed by her behavior towards Alan, protested to her, "Dottie, what are you complaining about? You're married to a charming, handsome man who adores you. What more do you want?"

"Presents," said Mrs. Parker.

Her attitude towards Alan at this time was not sufficiently abrasive to make him her mortal enemy: on the contrary, for his part, he loved to quote her quips, her witticisms, and adored telling friends about the night they had gotten tattooed with matching symbols, a star on the inside of their upper arms. Alan said that it had seemed all right at the time, but his wife later complained that it had condemned her to long sleeves for the rest of her life. "Well," said Alan, "there we were in a bar or something in Greenwich Village, and a rather delicate sort of fellow recognized Dottie and asked her, for some reason, if she liked fairy stories."

"My dear," she had replied, "let us not talk shop."

Alan was usually there when, as often happened, girls would stop her in the street and say: "I've always loved your lines—'Men never make passes at girls who wear glasses.' " Alan would playfully wag his finger and sharply correct them: "*Seldom*, not never," he would adjure. "Men *seldom* make passes . . . "

If she still approved of the adulation created by her celebrity status, Mrs. Parker did not show it, but she would sometimes drop names in nostalgic remembrance of her friends. She had often said that she felt sorry for those like Fitzgerald who lacked humor, although she thought him the best writer among her friends, with the exception of Hemingway. Of Scott, she said:

"He was attractive and sweet and he wanted to be nice—Ernest never wanted to be nice, he just wanted to be worshiped. He was a bore then —and he remained so—but the damndest thing about Scott, he just didn't know what was funny. He could be funny in his books, but not about life."

Reminiscing about Scott Fitzgerald would invariably turn Mrs. Parker's attention to a memory of Zelda, for whom she had never cared:

"She was living in the day of the shock techniques. That wears off very quickly, don't you think?" she would ask as an aside. "Sitting at a dinner where nothing in particular was being said, Zelda would turn to a neighbor"—here Mrs. Parker would assume an outlandish Southern accent—"and would say: 'Ah do think Al Jolson's a greater man than Jesus Christ, don't yew?' "

Such stories were assiduously collected and filed away in Alan's memory bank. Although he sometimes could not stand her moods, depressive silences and derisory references to him in front of others, he remained the constant fan of his wife, the literary celebrity and wit, and he believed that it would not be long before Hollywood would see the light and recall them both again.

He was right. In 1939 they had attended the Baltimore opening of Lillian Hellman's play *The Little Foxes*. During production of the subsequent film version with Bette Davis, Hellman was urgently called to New York and Dorothy Parker had helped out by writing some additional scenes for the movie. Apart from that and a couple of magazine pieces, "Song of the Shirt" and "Are We Women or Are We Mice?" there had not been much work. But in 1941 offers came in again.

Hollywood beckoned once again and together they scripted *Weekend for Three*, from a story by Budd Schulberg, for producer Tay Garnett. The film was to win few accolades. Thomas M. Pryor, in *The New York Times*, reported that: "The fine acerbic hand of Miss Parker is only fleetingly detectable in a couple of situations." However, there was soon another assignment: Mrs. Parker was asked to adapt her own short story "Horsie" as part of a screen trilogy of original stories, titled *Queen for a Day*; May Robson, celebrated for her "little old lady" screen characterizations, would star.

In 1942, Alfred Hitchcock signed her with Peter Viertel and his own assistant, a blonde Englishwoman named Joan Harrison, to script the original screenplay for *Saboteur*, Hitchcock's contribution to the European propagandist war effort. It was all about spies and lies which, as Mrs. Parker said, amounted to the same thing.

On the bright Sunday morning of December 7, 1941, America's antiwar faction was shattered by the Japanese attack on Pearl Harbor. The following day Franklin D. Roosevelt addressed Congress and the American people:

Yesterday, December 7, 1941—a date which will live in infamy—the United States of America was suddenly and deliberately attacked by the Empire of Japan. It will be recorded that the distance of Hawaii from Japan makes it obvious that the attack was deliberately planned many days or even weeks ago. During the intervening time the Japanese government has deliberately sought to deceive the United States by false statements and expressions of hope for continued peace. The attack yesterday on the Hawaiian Islands has caused severe damage to American naval and military forces. I regret to tell you that very many American lives have been lost . . . No matter how long it may take us to overcome this premeditated invasion, the American people in their righteous might will win through to absolute victory . . . I ask that Congress declare that since the unprovoked and dastardly attack by Japan . . . a state of war has existed between the United States and the Japanese Empire . . .

Under a series of further conscription acts, the armed forces of the United States were up to a total of 15,100,000 men and women. By the end of 1943 it was to increase that number by twice as many in uniform or in essential occupations.

Soon after the United States was drawn fully into the war, it was decided that the essential military effort of the Allies was to be concentrated in Europe, the Pacific theater being secondary. However, during 1942, some of the first important American successes had emerged from actions in the Pacific, which were primarily accomplishments of the

Navy and its carrier-borne aircraft; these involved heavy Japanese losses in the Coral Sea, which in turn had forced the Japanese navy to forgo striking at Australia, a source of considerable allied armament and man power. There had also been severe damage done to a Japanese flotilla of ships off Midway Island, and in August a joint army–navy action which had resulted in an American landing on Guadalcanal, and yet a further victory for the United States in the Battle of the Bismarck Sea.

Intensified production of American armaments had helped the British when their forces broke the German drive aimed at Egypt which, in turn, had pushed Rommel back into Tripoli, thus ending the immediate threat to Suez.

Alan Campbell knew that the time had come for him to make a decision. A graduate of the Virginia Military Institute, he felt he had much to offer his country. His wife concurred, and together they left Fox House Farm for the Philadelphia Enlistment Center. Alan was forty, too old to be reached by any draft then in force. But would the armed forces take him in? His former military training swung the balance in his favor. He did not then apply for a commission, and was accepted into the lowly rank of private.

Mrs. Parker and her husband had sorted out their dog problems, too. Writing to Ruth Gordon from Bomoseen on August 21, 1942, Aleck Woollcott reported: "Poopee Parker, a French poodle *ingenue* owned by the Alan Campbells, was shipped here just before Mr. Campbell left for camp. She was deflowered by Cocaud two minutes after her arrival and, with the tranquility born of inexperience, is awaiting nine blessed events."

Mrs. Parker seemed proud of Alan. She voiced that pride in a letter to Woollcott in New York: "All the while we were there, that line kept lengthening and men were still coming in when we left. That goes on every day, all day. Jesus, Aleck, I guess we're all right." She filled in the details:

The greater part of the room is for the men who are going to camp that day. They all have their bags and the only time I busted was at the sight of a tall, thin young Negro—"lanky" I believe is the word always employed—carrying a six-inch square of muslin in which were his personal effects. It looked so exactly like a bean-bag . . . And then I realized I was rotten to be tear-sprinkled. He wasn't sad. He felt fine. I was ashamed of myself. And yet, dear Aleck, I defy you to have looked at that bean-bag and kept an arid eye. That, of course, has nothing to do with war. Except, also of course, that a man who had no more than that was going to fight for it. . . .

She went to the Doylestown railroad station to see Alan off to the Army Air Force Training Center in Miami Beach. There her fame caught up with her, which she had to tell Woollcott about:

While we were standing there, there came up to me a fat, ill-favored, dark little woman who said to me, "Parn me (*sic*), but aren't you Dorthee Parker? Well, I've no doubt you've heard of me. I'm Mrs. Sig Greenbaum, Edith Greenbaum, you'd probably know me better as: I'm the head of our local chapter of the Better Living Club, and we'd like to have you come talk to us; of course, I'm still a little angry at you for writing that thing about men not making advances at girls who wear glasses, because I've worn glasses for years, and Sig, that's my husband, but I still call him my sweetheart, he says it doesn't matter a bit, well, he wears glasses himself, and I want you to talk to our club, of course, we can't pay you any money, but it will do you a lot of good, we've had all sorts of wonderful people, Ethel Grimsby Loe that writes all the greeting cards, and the editor of the *Doylestown Intelligencer*, and Mrs. Mercer, that told us all about Italy when she used to live there after the last war, and the photographs she showed us of her cypresses and all, and it would really be a wonderful thing for you to meet us, and now when can I put you down to come talk to us?"

For all her previous impassioned pleas on behalf of the poor, the oppressed and the ignorant, Mrs. Parker's sharp sense of satire took priority. She continued with her five single-spaced pages to Woollcott, each full of typographical errors:

I said I was terribly sorry, but if she didn't mind, I was busy at the moment. So she looked around at the rows of men—she hadn't seen them before, apparently; all they did was take up half the station—and she giggled heartily and said, "Oh, what are those—? More poor suckers caught in the draft?"

And an almighty wrath came on me, and I said, "Those are American patriots who have volunteered to fight for your liberty, you Sheeny bitch!" And I walked away, already horrified—as I am now—at what I had said. Not, dear, the gist, which I will stick to and should, but the use of the word "Sheeny" which I give you my word I have not heard for forty years and I have never used before. The horror lies with the ease with which it came to me—and worst horror lies in the knowledge that if she had been black, I would have said, "You nigger bitch!" Dear God. The things I have fought against all my life. And that's what I did.

Well, so anyway, then they came down to the train, and then I left before the train pulled out, because flesh and blood is or are flesh and blood . . .

On September 12, 1942, Woollcott wrote to Charles Brackett in Hollywood: "I think I have never read any letter with greater interest than the one Dorothy Parker wrote me after she had seen Private Alan Campbell off to the war."

· 41 ·

A Month with Maugham

ON HER RETURN from the Enlistment Center, Mrs. Parker telephoned her brother and sister, both of whom she had neglected to inform that she was back East; but she had little to do with them, anyway. When she told her sister that Alan had enlisted, her sister replied: "Oh, isn't that terrible. Well, it's been terrible here, too, all summer. And I never saw such a summer. Why, they didn't even have dances Saturday night at the Club. . . . "

Mrs. Parker tried her brother, but got her sister-in-law instead. According to Mrs. Parker, her response was equally bland. "Oh, really?" she said. "Well, of course, he's had a college education." At that, her sister-in-law switched the talk to her own son, Bertram, who was thirty-five. It was, it seemed, a college education that was holding Bertram back. "He'd just love to be an aviator, but of course he hasn't got a college education." Mrs. Parker skipped over Bertram's advanced age for the aviation corps and explained that the college-educated Alan had enlisted as a mere private. This met with "Oh, really? Oh, listen Dot, we're going to take a new apartment, the first of October. It's got two rooms that the sun simply *pours* in, and you know how I love sun!"

"I don't, Aleck," was Mrs. Parker's comment to Woollcott as she reported what had happened. "Honestly, if you were suddenly to point a finger at me and say, 'What is your sister-in-law's opinion of sun?' I should be dumbfounded." She added, "Jesus Christ! People whose country is at war. People who live in a world on fire, in a time when there have never before been such dangers, such threats, such murders . . . Well!"

Dorothy Parker did not have much in common with what remained of her family. Clearly, the estrangement was valid.

While with Eddie Parker, back in the grim days of World War I, Dorothy had joined him whenever she could. Now she followed a similar pattern. She caught up with Alan at Miami Beach and elsewhere. She reluctantly accepted an invitation to talk to a class at Smith College. After a short leave in New York, Alan and his unit were posted overseas.

Mrs. Parker was alone again. But this time she decided to act and not descend into depression.

Just shy of fifty, she applied to join the Women's Army Corps, hoping she might be posted abroad, perhaps joining Alan in Europe. Her application was turned down flat, no reason given. She could not understand why she had been rejected. She should, perhaps, have known that governments have long memories and that Washington, D.C., had files on people who had tried to buck the system. In the past she had allied herself to the "pink patriots" and the Women's Army Corps naturally had proximity to sensitive military material. One cancelled out the other.

Smarting from this rejection, she declared she would try again to do warwork, this time in her own bailiwick, so to speak. She applied for accreditation as an overseas war correspondent, which, if successful, meant that under wartime rules she would be granted a fresh, emergency passport. Her application induced a further examination of the files. There it all was—"premature anti-Fascist" and "possible subversive." She was accordingly and inevitably refused accreditation. Clearly, there was nothing she could do about it: Should she not have listened to Alan's warnings? Had the watchers caught up with her?

She moved restlessly between the farm, New York and Hollywood, writing magazine pieces, using war themes in her stories. *The New Yorker* republished her "Song of the Shirt," about a serviceman's foreshortened leave with his wife, which had originally been published by the magazine in 1941. The Modern Library again brought out her collected stories—a reprint of *Here Lies*—for which her old friend Franklin Pierce Adams wrote the preface.

Aleck Woollcott included some of Mrs. Parker's work in two anthologies, *Innocent Merriment* and *As You Were*, which he edited for servicemen. Mrs. Parker's last political piece appeared on the bookstalls: an introduction to a limited edition of Lillian Hellman's play *Watch on the Rhine*, which was published by the Joint Anti-Fascist Refugee Committee to raise funds for the cause. In this she wrote:

The woman who wrote this play and the men who made the drawings give this, their book, to those who earliest fought Fascism. Most of those warriors died: on the stiff plains of Spain, behind the jagged wire of French prison camps, in small echoing rooms of German towns. Few of their names are told, and their numbers are not measured. They wear no clean and carven stones in death. But for them there is an eternal light that will burn with a flame far higher than any beside a tomb . . .

Between her work and her wanderings, she stayed occasionally at Lillian Hellman's home on Martha's Vineyard. It wasn't far from New York and she enjoyed the company of Hellman, a lady not given to suffering fools, who in turn enjoyed Mrs. Parker. This was doubtless because, as Miss Hellman wrote in later years:

I never gave her all the good words she got from so many others, and I always cut off her praise of my work, never sure that she meant it, never really caring. We were polite, we were reticent, but very little fakery was given or required, although certainly we both lied now and then about each other's work and we both knew it. I once wrote a short story, my first since I was very young, and gave it to her to read. She had warm words for it, but the fact that she picked up a phrase—I no longer remember what phrase—and kept praising its originality and delicacy, worried me. A few months later she asked me what I had done with the story. I said I had decided it was a lady-writer story, not about anything. She protested, she quoted the phrase again, she said how much impressed she had been, and she tripped over a group of poodle puppies that we had brought along on our walk. As she stooped down to console them, I said, "God is not just. He punishes puppies for the lies of pretty ladies to their friends."

Lillian Hellman, a wise lady, gave Mrs. Parker no quarter and perhaps for this reason the friendship was sustained by its inherent honesty for many years.

It was a similar sort of friendship to that which Dorothy Parker shared with Beatrice Stewart, now known as Beatrice Ames since divorcing Donald Ogden Stewart. Stewart celebrated the divorce by marrying the fiercely radical Ella Winter.

Beatrice had always been fun. In her meetings and talks with Dorothy Parker she would relive the languorous weekends in the Stewarts' Adirondacks ranchhouse; the parties at Fox House Farm; and those incredible, somewhat indecorous, soirees in Hollywood.

Beatrice now lived alone in a New York apartment, receiving occasional visits from her children. Like Hellman, she had formed a warm attachment with Mrs. Parker going back many years and was the recipient of detailed accounts from Alan's letters, which were becoming markedly fewer and fewer. Shortly before leaving the United States he had received his commission as a Lieutenant in the Army Air Force Expeditionary Force, which was now headquartered in London.

Visiting Dorothy one day at her temporary apartment on Madison Avenue, Beatrice was told by an excited Mrs. Parker, "I have been invited to stay with Somerset Maugham!" Maugham was perhaps the most prominent Englishman of letters of his time, and clearly, it was a prospect that appealed to her.

Woollcott had told Dorothy that Maugham always traveled with a set of her books bound in leather. It seemed that Maugham, whom Dorothy Parker had last met and dined with in Hollywood, was spending a long holiday in South Carolina on the estate of Nelson Doubleday, his American publisher. Out of the blue, Maugham had telephoned and asked in clipped, stammering words if she would join his house party on the plush Doubleday estate.

Mrs. Parker went to South Carolina anticipating a stimulating time. Instead, she encountered a house party of homosexuals, headed by Maugham's vicious boyfriend, Gerald Haxton. Haxton organized and supervised every meal, outing, pastime, event with a polished, evil assurance, illustrating his total domination of Maugham. "God," she was later to comment to Beatrice Ames, "that was no place for a woman—or a man, unless he was prepared to show his petticoat!"

As far as Maugham was concerned, Mrs. Parker's presence had been no less disastrous. Afterwards he declared: "That old lady is a c-c-crashing b-bore . . . " except that there were those who remembered that the word he used was not "crashing."

By Maugham's standards, she was a bore. Not even a wit such as Mrs. Parker could compete with the continuous spate of bitchiness over those tiresome weeks. Bridge, Maugham's primary amusement, had monotonously held sway, bridge having never been Mrs. Parker's favorite game.

She returned to New York and wrote articles for *Collier's, Harper's Bazaar, Scribner's, Vogue, Reader's Digest,* among others. She missed Alan terribly, who was growing more and more lackadaisical in his responses to her constant letters. From the photographs, he looked younger and more dashing than ever in his uniform. It had always been to his advantage that he had looked younger than his age. In officer's sleek tailoring, he hardly looked a day over thirty.

Visiting him in Miami Beach, Dorothy had bought expensive clothes and underwear to please him, and had enjoyed the role of a serviceman's wife. To many of her friends this period had been characterized by her meek acceptance of the passive role of being, simply, Mrs. Alan Campbell, wife of a soldier-airman. To many, the time seemed to produce a fresh, reinvigorated Dorothy Parker. In truth, it had produced no such thing, but simply a return to the past, when she had been the wife of another serviceman, Edwin Pond Parker II, in another now largely forgotten war.

In the intervening years she had won success—fame, even —but she had also grown somewhat dumpy, and had developed lines in her face and a peeping jowl. But she knew that with imagination, the heart can keep one young and full of hope, and she had again fallen in love with Alan.

Beatrice Ames kept begging Mrs. Parker to write verse again. She took this advice, producing "War Song," in which the jealousy she felt about Alan was pitted with irony:

> Soldier, in a curious land
> All across a swaying sea,
> Take her smile and lift her hand—
> Have no guilt of me.
>
> Soldier, when were soldiers true?
> If she's kind and sweet and gay,
> Use the wish I send to you—
> Lie not lone till day!
>
> Only, for the nights that were,
> Soldier, and the dawns that came,
> When in sleep you turn to her
> Call her by my name.

Mrs. Parker dedicated the poem "To Lieutenant Alan Campbell" and sent it to him.

He did not reply.

· 4 2 ·

"Dead, Dead, Dead"

DESPITE her defensive wish of his infidelity, Mrs. Parker's revived love for Alan became obsessive, all the more when he did eventually write her amid the pressures of his busy life in London. Such letters recounted excited stories of his encounters with members of the London social set, never among her favorites. Earlier she had written: "Whenever I meet one of those Britishers, I feel as if I have a papoose on my back," a statement strengthened by her visit to Maugham in South Carolina. She had long believed that Britain and America were hopelessly divided by a common language. *Homo britannicus* was not her pet species; patrician vowels were seldom music to her ears.

Alan was now enjoying "bomb-stricken London," having the time of his life meeting up with the Oliviers, the Lunts, George Kaufman, Sybil Colefax, Juliet Duff, Tom Driberg, "Binkie" Beaumont, John Perry, Chips Channon, Peter Glenville and the rest of the smart theatrical and social set. And Dorothy Parker felt jealous and lonely.

She was resentful of her life in New York as Alan lived it up in London, even finding time to socialize in the elegant Claridge's Hotel while attempting to write a play with George Kaufman, *The Lipstick Wars*. Kaufman wrote to Moss Hart: "I've an uneasy feeling that the show I'm on with Alan is rather dated." He was right.

Mrs. Parker wrote angry letters to her husband, letters that were soon to stop completely. But before that happened, she used her status "Married to Lieutenant Alan Campbell, who is with the Army Air Force in England" in an editorial preamble to an article published in *Vogue*, which had now wholly absorbed *Vanity Fair*. The piece was called "Who Is That Man?" and it claimed to echo the feelings of the American girls who were left behind. She released the tear ducts with:

When my husband first went overseas, I wanted to do only what I was told to do. I shied away from decisions; I wanted to be instructed. Perhaps you remember—it has died down now—there was a spate of cheery messages by women for women, as to how to behave when your husband is off to the war. The disrupted are the gullible," she wrote, "and so I followed all the words that were put out . . . The lady writers gushed comfort to the lorn, made it, indeed, seem a positive picnic that your man was out of the house and into the front lines, and you could go to bed with cream on your face. But I found few practical suggestions—practical, that is, for me.

"I live," she continued,

in two rooms on a corner of Madison Avenue, and I skipped those pages that explained what a comfort it is to the heart to crush between the fingers the first leaf of basil from one's herb garden; or maybe it had nothing to do with my living on Madison Avenue. While I had no argument whatever to advance, I merely skimmed the paragraphs which pointed out that, though you see it alone, a sunset is still a sunset. I attended while I was told that war-time is the ideal time for The Girl He Left Behind Him to go in for reading. But I could already read very nicely indeed; so there I was.

Mrs. Parker found that the lady writers provided her with two pieces of advice on which she could act positively. The first was to put on her prettiest bed jacket at night. With only two such jackets, she did as she was bade and awaited results. None, according to her, came.

The second piece of advice, from a writer named Sybil, was to give Sunday brunches. Accordingly she invited some of her friends. "They were," she said, "a somewhat hardy lot." "Brunch," they said. "My God!" and shifted the talk to plans for dinner next Tuesday.

Mrs. Parker went on:

Clearest in my memory was the young man whose glance went like a dotted line in a comic strip, direct to a photograph of my husband, taken some three years before, in civilian dress. The young man snatched up the photograph, held it at first close, then at the length of his arms, "Oh, my dear," he cried, "what a *dream* of a necktie. *Where* did he get it?"

Dorothy Parker was obviously mixing with the wrong kind of people for a Lady Left Behind.

But she knew how her readers felt, especially those who, like herself, were among those whose men had gone to war.

"I do not say, and certainly I do not mean," she adjured,

that life is soft, sweet going for you, while you stay here and your husband is at least a sea away. Worry walks with you by day, and you lie with anxiety by night. Loneliness gnaws your heart like a great, grey rat. You do not grow used to this half-a-life you are left with; you do not want to grow used to it. Every dawn trails after it another unwanted day. Time takes on two measures—the slow, stumbling days, one after one after one, and the fierce rush of months and years whirling past, out of your life, out of your life with him. Well—you know about all that. And it is not, to put it mildly, what you want.

As she said, "There are other matters. You say goodnight to your friends, and know that tomorrow you will meet them again, sound and safe as you will be. It is not like that where your husband is. There are the comrades, closer in friendship to him than you can ever be, whom he has seen comic or wild or thoughtful; and then broken or dead. There are some who have gone out with a wave of the hand and a gay obscenity, and have never come back. We do not," Mrs. Parker enjoined her readers, "know such things, probably will never know them, prefer, and wisely, to close our minds against them."

Mrs. Parker was still in an emotional frame of mind as she went on to tell the harrowing story of a letter she had received which told of a twenty-two-year-old boy she had met, who had called her Ma'am. The boy had been shot down in Germany, and the letter was asking what should be done with the boy's personal effects. "There the handwriting in the letter broke," Mrs. Parker recorded, "as a voice breaks. What," she asked, "do you do with a dead man's laundry?"

"For who," she now inquired in pursuit of her title, "is the man who will come back to you? . . . What have you to offer this man, except half of the bed? That," she claimed,

was perhaps the most important thing, and maybe it will solve much, but not everything. The lovely companionship you had together—he will want that, he will even need that, but he has had companions who have been with him through death and hell . . . Life, after all, is something to be shared; and of this great part, this greatest part of his life, you have no portion. That is where you start, and from there you go on to make a friend of that stranger from across a world.

The truth, she advised, is "that women's work begins when war ends, begins on the day their men come home to them. And I wish to God," she concluded, "for you and me and all of us, that it were today!"

This was Dorothy Parker, the romantic idealist, exhorting her readers to believe that all would come right if you made a real friend of that stranger from across a world.

The year 1945 had arrived to presage more hopeful developments in the world conflict. That year, victory in Europe was proclaimed at 5:19 A.M. on May 8. President Harry Truman had ordered the dropping of the bomb on Hiroshima, creating a "bell-shaped flame brighter than anything seen on earth," followed quickly by a further atom bomb on Nagasaki where, too, hundreds of thousands of victims were fried alive.

Mrs. Parker continued to raise money for war charities, appealing to the Women's Division of the New York War Fund to give funds to the USO and the United Nations. She also identified herself with the Emergency Conference to Save The Jews of Europe at a conference at New York's Commodore Hotel and appealed for children's books as a member of the National Council of American-Soviet Friendship.

The previous year Viking had published *The Viking Portable Dorothy Parker*, which quickly went into several printings. For this, the publishers had enlisted the help of Somerset Maugham to write the introduction, paying him $250. He had praised Mrs. Parker's "faultless ear," her "beautifully polished poetry" and said her work was of "enduring significance." In *The New York Times*, her old friend John O'Hara reviewed the book warmly, but Donald J. Adams, in the same paper, claimed that "an aura of artificiality" enveloped the work.

In 1945 she undertook the task of choosing the contents for Viking's *The Portable F. Scott Fitzgerald*, but, lacking the will, she convinced John O'Hara at the last minute to do it.

She had lived with the hope that Alan would soon return, but was disappointed to learn he had been ordered to remain in London awhile. The news seemed to be a curious echo of the past. On hearing it, her disappointment turned to anger. Her friends recalled that she conjured up visions of Alan being at the center of London's victory celebrations and its attendant high life, while Alan told her nothing to disprove these images. She developed a bitter hatred for him bordering on malevolence. To their friends in New York and Hollywood she declared she was finished with her "pansy husband," that "he's over there playing hostess to a court of queens." "Alan," as far as she was concerned, "was dead, dead, dead."

Vincent Sheean called on her and told her how sorry he was at the news of their breakup. What did she suppose Alan would do without her? he asked.

"Don't worry about Alan," she said. "Alan will always land up on somebody's feet."

· 4 3 ·

Another Man, Another Play

MRS. PARKER, drinking heavily, was consumed by bitterness and resentment. She wrote to Alan telling him of her intention to file for divorce but did not act immediately on her threat.

To her friends, she blamed the collapse of her marriage on a homosexual affair supposedly conducted by Alan in London. Thereafter, for nearly two years, she did virtually nothing with her life until, in 1947, Alan filed for divorce in Las Vegas, claiming that separation had made them strangers. The action was halted while the two sets of lawyers haggled. On May 21, Alan finally agreed to allow her to divorce him. It was all over in a short hearing: no longer did the lilt of love suffuse her life.

Mrs. Parker returned to Fox House Farm, called in the real estate people and put the place up for sale. The agents were quick to find a buyer at $40,000, a loss in excess of $80,000.

On November 21, she received a call from playwright Philip Barry in Hollywood, who told her that Robert Benchley had died suddenly of a cerebral hemorrhage. There was to be no funeral ceremony as such, just a wake of sorts at Romanoff's, to be presided over by her, he hoped. She was invited to stay at Barry's cottage, at the Garden of Allah, an offer she accepted.

Leland Hayward was still acting as her film agent. He called her with news that producer Walter Wanger wanted her to collaborate with Frank Cavett on the screenplay for *Smash Up—The Story of a Woman*, for Universal-International. It was an original story for the screen earlier drafted by her and Cavett, which bore certain similarities to her own situation. The film starred Susan Hayward, who gave a good performance; nevertheless the critics found the script "unconvincing and arbitrary, a kind of soap opera."

She was honored, however, when James Thurber asked her to write the preface to a new edition of his book of drawings, *Men, Women and Dogs*. Her old friend Death made its appearance in this preface, handled by Dorothy's familiar mordant humor:

"I had long ago made my design for what was to become of me when the Reaper had swung his scythe through my neck," she began.

I was to be cremated after death—at least, I always trusted it would be after death. I even left instructions to this effect in my will, a document that might otherwise be writ in a large, school-girl backhand on the head of a pin. Now, with the publication of this book, I must change those words, and with them my plans for the long, long rest. Now I want to be left as approximately is, so that I may be buried in a prominent place on a traveled thoroughfare through a wildly popular cemetery. Above me I want a big white stone—you will see why it must be big—on which I want carven in clear letters: "Uncover before this dust, for when it was a woman, it was doubly honored. Twice in life, it was given to her below to introduce the work of James Thurber. Reader, who around here, including you, can tie that record? I like to think of my shining tombstone. It gives me, as you might say, something to live for . . .

Thurber's gesture was not the only tribute she received at this time. In 1944, Lillian Hellman had dedicated *The Searching Wind* to her, a play about Fascist Italy in 1922 and Nazi Germany in 1923, full of the "spiritual appeasements of war."

Despite the bad press she had received for her work on Wanger's *Smash Up*, Mrs. Parker was still in demand as a scriptwriter. She worked on one or two other scripts that, like so many Hollywood projects, did not get off the ground. Then Hayward called and said he had made a deal for her to script a screen version of Oscar Wilde's *Lady Windermere's Fan*, to be retitled *The Fan*, along with Walter Reisch and a young writer named Ross Evans. It had originally been envisaged as a vehicle for Greer Garson and Helen Hayes but both ladies had lost interest in the idea. The man who had persuaded Twentieth Century–Fox to put up the considerable funds was a fierce-looking actor turned director-producer named Otto Preminger. Preminger had cast Jeanne Crain as an unlikely Lady Windermere, Madeleine Carroll as Mrs. Erlynne, George Sanders as Lord Darlington and Richard Greene as Lord Windermere. But even this array of names did not prevent the film from becoming a gigantic flop. Many said that Wilde's immaculately tailored situations and dialogue, which, of course, had been designed expressly for the theater, were totally lacking in understanding, perception and imagination under Preminger's heavy-handed directorial treatment.

It was rumored that Ross Evans had dreamed up the whole movie package, but that wasn't true; it had been Preminger's idea, an almost insolent conception of seeking to "adapt" Wilde's mountainous skills for transference to a medium it clearly was never designed to fit.

With Alan out of her life, Mrs. Parker looked around at her male friends and took stock of the situation. Evans, who claimed to be "a young novelist and screenwriter," was well-built and witty, and seemed to fulfill most of her requirements. Her friends said he was "the Dottie Parker type," tall, broad-shouldered and extremely handsome. Married before, he had written two unsuccessful novels, had had three off-Broadway plays produced and had written for the movie studios. Joe Bryan, who met him at this time, has since described Evans as "a pleasant, shambling hobbledehoy with huge, lump-toed Army boots that instantly inspired his children to call him 'Li'l Abner', in tribute to Al Capp's lamented naïf, Abner Yokum."

To those in the know, Evans was regarded as an opportunist. Beatrice Ames, a shrewd judge of character, had noted that he rarely missed an opportunity to ingratiate himself into their circle of friends. To Mrs. Parker, however, he had worldly panache and a body to fit. Clearly, she was all set for further punishment. As she had earlier said of herself: "I don't like my state of mind. I am bitter, quarrelsome and unkind. I hate my legs and hate my hands . . . my soul is crushed, my spirit sour . . . I don't like me any more. I quarrel, grumble, grouse . . . I am due to fall in love again . . ."

She took Ross Evans off to New York to look up old friends and to introduce her new man. Vincent Sheean remembered the time:

We were then living in an apartment in Marion Davies' house at Fifty-fifth and Madison when Ross and Dorothy called. They sat on our great, over-sized red-and-green tartaned sofa. We drank—it was one of our main occupations. About two or three in the morning, they began to make love.

I tried to avert my eyes and took a great interest in the New York skyline at night. Later, as she and Mr. Evans were leaving the apartment, Dorothy Parker apologized. "You know," she said, "this hasn't happened for about six months. Hope you don't mind." She paused and added, "We must have looked awfully picturesque."

Back in Hollywood, she went without Evans to a party at Donald Ogden Stewart's mansion, confiding to a roomful of people there, "You know, everybody thinks Ross is banging me every night." This was followed by a long pause, to which she added, "I only wish to God he were."

There was, however, another side to the romance. Evans was clinging to her while she doled out money to pay travel, restaurant and household bills. Other bills were paid only when creditors pressed hard. It was Mrs. Parker displaying her customary contempt for money, writing checks without any reference to bank statements or household accounts. She wrote a substantial number of checks at that time, many in reference to Ross Evans, who broadcast the fact that not only was he Mrs. Parker's new collaborator, he had also taken Alan Campbell's place in her life.

It was a collaboration that was eventually to prove both unrewarding and highly unprofitable for Mrs. Parker.

She and Evans started to write *The Coast of Illyria*, a piece of "faction" loosely based on Charles Lamb's bizarre relationship with Mary, his insane sister. It opened at the Margo Jones Theater in Dallas, Texas, in April 1949. The portrayal of the tortured lives of the Lambs took its title, sardonically, from Shakespeare's *Twelfth Night*, which was underscored when the Lambs were seen to be transcribing for children: "There were a brother and sister . . . who were shipwrecked off the coast of Illyria . . . " Partly historical, it was a dramatization of loneliness, terror and despair, three ingredients with which Mrs. Parker was familiar.

Time reported that the play was well liked in Dallas, the best of the season, and predicted a Broadway run. When Broadway showed no interest, Leland Hayward tried to set up a London production. When that failed, the play was listed to open at the prestigious Edinburgh Festival in Scotland. Mrs. Parker fussed with the play and decided the title should be changed to *Strange Calamity*.

When the Edinburgh Society expressed their strong interest, she changed the title once again to *The Incomparable Sister*. A few days later she decided it should revert to its original title, and on March 29, 1949, she altered it yet again to *Mary Is from Home*, a title which the Society roundly rejected. Aided by Evans, she cut the play drastically, revising it so heavily that Flora Robson, who was to be cast as Mary Lamb, gave up and declined to play the role. At this, the artistic director of the Festival gave up, too, announcing that production was suspended and that Peter Ustinov's *The Man in the Raincoat* would be staged instead.

Mrs. Parker and Ross Evans were not deterred, but remained firmly optimistic. In an interview with *Time*, Evans said, "We've tasted blood. We don't want to do anything ever again except write for the theater."

There were many in Hollywood who knew Evans and didn't like him. Stanley Sayer, a respected studio accountant and well-known film budgetary expert, was fiercely outspoken about him: "Evans," he said, "is a pimp and a down-market gigolo who would latch on to any broad for a free meal and a romp in the hay—especially broads who have passed the point of no return."

Was Mrs. Parker one of those? She was now fifty-four, with a markedly depleted bank balance, brought on by her association with Evans. But she was eager to have him by her side as lover and collaborator. Beatrice Ames congratulated her on acquiring such a healthy specimen of manhood, muscular and sun-tanned as he was. "Yes," Mrs. Parker agreed, "he certainly has the hue of availability."

She asked Leland Hayward to find them more assignments, but their failures had not helped their reputations. It was the fashion in Hollywood of the time to say that "you are only as good as your last picture," and if that were true, Mrs. Parker could no longer be called "good."

Hurt and angry, she told Ross Evans that they needed a holiday, and she proposed Mexico. Two or three weeks in another place and then there would be more work, she believed.

They were in Mexico for less than three days when they began to get into violent arguments. She later told Leueen McGrath, George Kaufman's new wife, that "the man turned out to be a shit and a monster." What she did not tell Mrs. Kaufman was that on hearing from her bank that she was heavily overdrawn, she asked Evans to contribute some funds for the trip. At this, he assailed her with a barrage of insults and informed her that had it not been for his creativity, ideas and contacts, she would be out of Hollywood on her backside, pecking for a living, alone and friendless.

The following day he left her to go out drinking and in a hotel bar met with an attractive blonde, who managed a dress shop. Dispensing with preliminaries, he booked a room in the hotel and took the girl straight to bed.

He returned to tell Mrs. Parker he had no desire to continue a relationship "with an old broad who is all washed up," whereupon they started slinging at each other. When things quieted down, Evans ordered Dorothy Parker and her dogs into her car, pushed an airplane ticket into her hands which had been paid for with her money, and drove her, mute with anger, to the airport. There he told her he was keeping two of her dogs. Minutes before the plane was due to leave for New York, he dismissed her with: "Now, piss off. I don't want you in my life again."

Now another man had left her, this time taking virtually all she had left to give. Who could she turn to now?

She moved aimlessly among various of her friends. Joe Bryan remembers: "I'm not sure what Alan did immediately after the divorce. I remember going to see him in New York when he shared an apartment with Tom Heggen (who wrote *Mister Roberts*), but that was only for a short while; Heggen died in the spring of 1949. Dottie came to stay with us that summer—rather, with my wife; I was working in Washington and was home only on weekends. Our household consisted of us and our three children, Mamie, the cook, and four dogs. Mamie had been a dresser for the Dolly Sisters. She was small and black and a quiet drunkard. When the fit was on her, she simply kept to her room, even though it might be an evening when we were having guests to dinner or, more likely, the next morning. Dottie called her 'a tower of Jell-o.'

"On one of Mamie's 'mornings,' it fell to me to get breakfast. I asked Dottie what she'd like. 'Just something light and easy to fix,' she said. 'How about a dear little whiskey sour. Make it a double, while you're up.' 'While you're up,' was one of her pet additives. She'd tear a strip off some poor wretch, then add reflectively, 'And his wife's a shit, too, while you're up.' "

(It is interesting to record that Mrs. Parker's "while you're up," became a sort of catch phrase throughout America. Grant's, the Scottish whiskey distillers and exporters, mounted an expensive advertising campaign for their "Stand Fast" whiskey based on the expression—"While you're up, get me a Stand Fast.")

Joe Bryan continued: "Another of her pets was 'for my sins,' as in 'I had to go to this *dreadful* party, and there, for my sins, I saw. . . . ' *All* parties were becoming *'dreadful.'* I think she continued to go to them only because they gave her something to do, and because they offered her fresh targets. She took her dog to one of them, where it promptly vomited on the rug. Dottie explained to the hostess: 'It's the company.' "

Joe Bryan went on:

"My friend Stockton Rush and his son John, aged six, stayed with us one weekend while Dottie was there. Saturday night was a rough one. Sunday morning, when Stockton tottered down to breakfast, he asked me shakily: 'Be all right if I cut my throat?' Dottie came in just then. She told him, 'Move over on the blade and make room for me.'

"I saw her again, just after Dame Edith Sitwell gave a reading in New York and, recognizing Dottie in the audience, bowed to her. The gaunt Dame had her own way of dealing with Mrs. Parker, saying, 'Your grett Ameddican pwettess, Miss Doddothy Wadden.' 'Wadden, for Christ's sake,' Mrs. Parker snarled. 'Why, that goddam Limey!'

Joe Bryan, in the mid-1980s, is reservedly generous to his late friend. "Granted," he says, "that she was wonderful company, life with her was life on thin ice. You never knew when she would turn on you and denounce you as a Fascist, a neo-Malthusian, or something equally ridiculous. Almost any epithet would serve. It didn't need even a smidgen of justification. The barb of her wit made it stick where it hit, and the victim was tagged forever after . . . like the Hollywood producer of whom Dottie said, 'He hasn't got sense enough to bore assholes in wooden hobbyhorses.'

"A sentimental occasion like a wedding always brought something absurd from her—or like Christmas, as witness the telegram she sent my wife and me from Hollywood: IN ORDER TO WISH YOU A MERRY CHRISTMAS I AM INTERRUPTING WORK ON MY SCREEN EPIC, LASSIE GET DOWN. And, when someone mentioned Meg Mundy, then starring on the New York stage in *The Respectable Prostitute*, Dottie affected never to have heard of her: 'Meg Mundy? What's that, a Welsh holiday?' And, too, there was her quip on a certain English actor, a notorious homosexual—'He simply buggers description.' "

· 4 4 ·

A Time of Evil

THE LATE FORTIES and early fifties were to become a time of evil for Lillian Hellman and Mrs. Parker and many of their friends who had worked in Hollywood. Senator Joseph McCarthy and the House Sub-Committee on Un-American Activities (HUAC) was now making another raid on the movie industry. HUAC had originally been set up in 1938 as a political ploy to benefit a group of extreme right-wing Republican politicians. In 1947, it had conducted a witch-hunt following the naming of Mrs. Parker and Lillian Hellman, among others, as alleged Communists. As a result, the "Hollywood Ten"—Alvah Bessie, Herbert Biberman, Lester Cole, Edward Dmytryk, Ring Lardner, Jr., John Howard Lawson, Albert Maltz, Samuel Onitz, Adrian Scott and Dalton Trumbo—had been sent to prison, with varying sentences, for refusing to testify before HUAC. Each had invoked the Fifth Amendment, and each had refused to name names.

Artists like Sterling Hayden, Adolphe Menjou, Elia Kazan, Larry Parks, Robert Taylor, Gary Cooper, Clifford Odets and others had played Judas. E. B. White had written in *The New Yorker:* "Ten men have been convicted, not of wrong doing, but of wrong thinking; that is news in this country and if I have not misread my history, it is bad news . . . "

In the words of presiding Chairman J. Parnell Thomas, the purpose of the continued investigations was "to reveal subversive, Communist and Un-American influence in motion pictures," which led naturally to the presumption that influences such as that already existed in American films; HUAC had earlier tried to prove such allegations against those who were now in prison. And that was not all. Thomas let it be known that when this was completed, the HUAC intended to extend its investigations into the areas of books, plays, radio, magazines, labor and education.

For the present, however, it was Hollywood that McCarthy and Thomas were after. It was a move specifically designed to attract international publicity to the Committee through the interrogation of 205 celebrated artists, actors, composers, musicians, producers, directors and writers. Thus, Thomas and his lieutenants, who included Chief Investigator Robert E. Stripling and Congressman Richard Nixon, could project themselves as the saviors of American institutions and family life, protecting it from the "pink 'uns" who had "infiltrated Hollywood movies, injecting those movies with the Red message."

In September 1951, screenwriter Martin Berkeley revealed to HUAC the name of Dorothy Parker as a Communist, confirming the "leaked" allegation.

Mrs. Parker, it was claimed, had been involved in supplying material of the Anti-Fascist Refugee Committee to overseas libraries and information centers. The subpoena to appear before the committee arrived late in 1952. A U.S. deputy marshal delivered the bright pink document to her at her Hollywood home, which summoned her to "appear before the Un-American Activities Committee . . . in their chambers in the city of Washington . . . and there testify touching matters of inquiry committed to the said Committee, and not to depart without leave of said Committee. Herein fail not . . . " The signature on the pink form was "J. Parnell Thomas, Chairman."

It was, to quote writer Gordon Kahn, "a command to perform— perform before a legislative ringmaster at a grand three-ring investigation of Hollywood."

Mrs. Parker remained calm, almost disinterested. Thomas, guided in the wings by McCarthy—both men working with many of the studio bosses, notably Cecil B. DeMille and his hatchet man Albert S. Rogell— had earlier leaked to the international press the names of the "saboteurs." Mrs. Parker, so named, had been inundated with requests for interviews and statements. She had given several of both, but did not apologize for her past affiliations, nor did she display the slightest regret regarding her opinions or about expressing them. Unlike others, she consistently refused to name names or condemn any of her friends of the left. She rose above the scene with studied hauteur, crushing disinterest, pouring dismissive scorn on Thomas, McCarthy, and their fellow inquisitors, referring to them as "rats gnawing at empty holes."

With the integrity displayed by many of the subpoenaed she told reporters that she would invoke the Fifth Amendment, which permitted her, under the rights of the Constitution, to decline to give evidence or make comment which might incriminate herself or her friends. She was not prepared to insult her own intelligence by even acknowledging HUAC's statutory right of inquiry. As far as she was concerned, the committee did not exist; and if it did exist, it was a disgrace to the precepts of freedom and democracy on which the American Constitution was based. This was precisely the line Lillian Hellman took.

Out one evening for a drink, Mrs. Parker was accosted by a man who voiced his agreement with the "protectionist campaign of the Hollywood bosses against the Reds." She rose from her seat, regarded the man with icy anger and said, "With the crown of thorns I wear, why should I be bothered with a prick like you?" and walked out.

HUAC had the legal right under the law of the land to compel listed "offenders" to appear before it to defend or admit the accusation on pain of imprisonment. If a prima facie case was made against them, they must name their left-wing activist friends or risk imprisonment.

HUAC was particularly interested in Dorothy Parker's case, especially since she had shown such contempt for them. Lillian Hellman offered to go to the hearing with Mrs. Parker. The reply she received was full of genuine surprise.

"Why, Lilly?" she asked.

Miss Hellman was later to say: "I don't think it occurred to her that the ruling classes were anything but people with more money than you had. She acted before the Committee as she acted so often with their more literate, upper-class cousins at dinner, as if to say, 'Yes, dear, it's true that I'm here to observe you, but I don't like you and will, of course, say and write exactly that.' "

Throughout the long days of the hearing, Mrs. Parker displayed quiet disdain. To her the whole business was an indecent farce. She parried all questions with the same infuriating aloofness that seemed to some to reduce her inquisitors to a state of near-ataxia.

"Are you now or have you ever been a member of the Communist party?" was the repeated question of Thomas and his aides.

"I was and am many things, to myself and to my friends. But I am not a traitor and I will not be involved in this obscene inquisition," was Mrs. Parker's reply. And that, as far as she was concerned, was the end to it.

They cross-examined Edward G. Robinson and others about their knowledge of Mrs. Parker's political affiliations:

MR. OWENS: Are you, Mr. Robinson, acquainted with Dorothy Parker?

MR. ROBINSON: Yes, I am.

MR. OWENS: What is the nature of your acquaintance with her?

MR. ROBINSON: Just as a friend and in the arts, and socially on occasions.

MR. OWENS: Do you have any knowledge of her alleged Communist affiliations?

MR. ROBINSON: No.

MR. OWENS: Do you know Donald Ogden Stewart? . . .

And so on.

The committee had dug deep into the FBI archives and had come up with a long list of Mrs. Parker's political affiliations. The list was read; some of the affiliations are cited here:

a co-signatory with Helen Keller of an appeal letter, The United American Spanish Aid Committee; congress sponsor, The American Continental Congress for World Peace, along with Stewart and Dashiell Hammett, Clifford Odets and some fifty others; sponsor, The Scientific and Cultural Conference for World Peace, held in March 1949 in New York City, along with Leonard Bernstein, Marlon Brando, Jules Dassin, Norman Mailer, Lillian Hellman, Dashiell Hammett, Arnold d'Usseau, Lee J. Cobb, Betsy Blair, Aaron Copland, and some eighty others; instigator and leader of The Voice of Freedom Committee; member, The Western Writers Congress; member, National Committee of the American League for Peace and Democracy; member, the board of People's Songs, Incorporated (formed to stimulate and develop an understanding and appreciation of worthy American music, songs, cultural and civic traditions), along with Pete Seeger, Leonard Bernstein, Burl Ives, Lena Horne, Oscar Hammerstein II, Larry Adler, Paul Robeson; speaker, meetings of The Progressive Citizens of America; member, Win the Peace Conference; member, Friends of the Abraham Lincoln Brigade; member, American Committee for the Protection of Foreign Born; member, The American Council for a Democratic Greece, along with Donald Ogden Stewart and Thomas Mann; member, the American Labor Party, along with Sam Wanamaker, Arnold d'Usseau, Lillian Hellman and Paul Robeson; member, The Artist's Front to Win the War, along with Hellman, Jose Ferrer, Dalton Trumbo, Jules Dassin; member, Contemporary Writers Organization, along with Arthur Miller, Louis Untermeyer, John Howard Lawson and Arnold d'Usseau; member, The Civil Rights Congress, along with Artie Shaw and Albert Einstein; member, International Workers Order, along with Paul Robeson, Ella Winter; member, Joint Anti-Fascist Refugee Committee, along with Thomas Mann, Jose Ferrer; member, American Friends of Spanish Democracy, along with Ring Lardner, Jr., and Donald Ogden Stewart; patron, Southern Conference for Human Welfare, along with Leonard Bernstein, Paul Robeson; member, Stage for Action, along with Arthur Miller, Sam Wanamaker; member, Voice of Freedom Committee, along with Hellman, Edward Chodorov, Jose Ferrer, Paul Robeson . . .

The committee found that Mrs. Parker was one of the twenty-seven named who had been affiliated with thirty-one to forty Communist-front organizations, determined as such by the Attorney-General.

Despite the "evidence," Mrs. Parker consistently invoked the protection of the Fifth Amendment which proclaimed:

No person shall be held to answer for a capital or other infamous crime unless on the presentment or indictment of a Grand Jury, except in cases arising in the land or naval forces or in the militia, when in actual service, in time of war or public danger; nor shall any person be subject for the same offense to be twice put in jeopardy of life or limb; nor shall be compelled in any criminal case to be a witness against himself, nor be deprived of life, liberty or property, without due process of law; nor shall private property be taken in public use without just compensation.

Thomas and his lawyers had met their match. They quietly dropped their case against Mrs. Parker, as they had done with Lillian Hellman. The government correctly assessed that there would be public outcry against the imprisonment of the women. They could, and had, put several men away with comparative ease but to do the same with the two celebrated literary ladies was to risk the opening of a much more formidable can of worms for McCarthy and his fellow inquisitors.

Eventually the committee was condemned.

McCarthy went back to his whiskey bottle and, soon, to his premature death; Nixon to his law practice; Miss Hellman and Mrs. Parker to their private griefs.

America still had much to learn of the principles of democracy, but it *was* learning—the hard way.

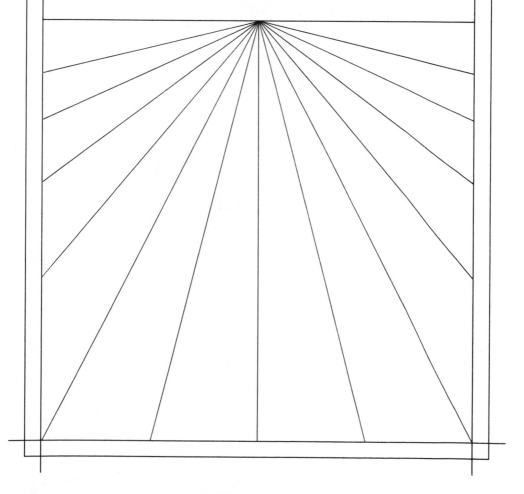

BOOK·FOUR

The
End

· 4 5 ·

Dinner with Miss Nesbitt

OFF MADISON AVENUE in the East Sixties, within walking distance of Central Park, the Volney Hotel was now Mrs. Parker's New York hideout. Earlier in the century, it had been used almost exclusively by tourists. Now, somewhat faded in decor and composed of small suites and single rooms, it housed mainly widows, although a few married couples and divorcées also lived there.

For Mrs. Parker, who could no longer afford to stay at her favorite hotel, the Plaza, it was a convenient place to put down one's grip, just far enough away from her familiar patch which stretched from Times Square to Columbus Circle. It was sufficient that she was back in New York.

While Mrs. Parker had been enduring the pressures of HUAC, Alan had kept in touch with her. Despite their separation, he was still deeply concerned for her welfare. Now, in 1956, at a time of great strain and unhappiness, Alan was ringing from Hollywood. "Alan," she said, "are you as lonely for me as I am for you?" "I still love you," he replied. "Stay there. I am coming to get you."

Alan arrived at the hotel full of his customary optimism. There was no point in their remaining in New York, he said. Hollywood was where the opportunities were. He was now living in a small house in Norma Place, West Hollywood, an area where the houses had originally been those of railroad workers.

In the early days of Hollywood, actress Norma Talmadge had built a studio on the site of Norma Place, which now bore her name. Alan had bought his lease in the days when Nina Foch, John Dall and Carleton Carpenter had lived there, and the place had gone on to accommodate a succession of moderately well-known people who had been, and still largely were, connected with the industry. The frame building that had been Miss Talmadge's dressing-suite still dominated the little street, exactly one block long. The largest house had been broken up and converted into apartments and small houses.

Screenwriter Wyatt Cooper, who was soon to work alongside Mrs. Parker at Twentieth Century–Fox, was to remember Mrs. Parker's arrival at Norma Place:

Dottie's arrival in the area caused a momentary sensation, of course, and she became an instant landmark. She was pointed out politely as she took her dogs for a walk. Norma Place was a close community. Everybody knew everybody else. There was much dropping in on each other, few secrets were possible. And, it seemed, nothing that went on there was beneath Mrs. Parker's notice.

The bank, the post office, the laundromat and the supermarket were clustered around the corner and down the hill, and if you had an errand in any of those places you were likely to encounter Troy Donahue or the like, and find out who was working today on what film, who had gone to the beach and who was having drinks with whom. There was also a bar called the Four Star, where one might glimpse Patsy Kelly shooting a mean game of pool, or a former wife of the English actor Louis Hayward passing the time with a couple of pals and a few assorted dogs. I remember Dottie's delight when Tuesday Weld's mother moved in . . . She would ask the neighbors: "Have you met Tuesday Weld's mother, Wednesday, yet?"

If life had been empty for her of late, she now had her reunion with Alan and her introduction to Norma Place. In Wyatt Cooper she found a friend who shared her interests and sense of humor.

Estelle Winwood, an elderly character actress whom Mrs. Parker had known back in the Algonquin days and who was destined to live for over a century, had an apartment on the block. Cooper recalled she had a front room near the sidewalk which one could pass at almost any time to view the occupant, "somewhat on display, like a mannequin in a shop window, perpetually pouring tea and always carefully groomed and wearing a hat . . . Later, when I mentioned that Miss Winwood was acting in *Camelot*, Dottie commented, 'Playing a battlement, no doubt.' "

"Now and then we had a little extra excitement," continued Cooper,

like when a character lady's canary got out and all the fellows joined, unsuccessfully, in trying to recapture it, while the tearful owner jogged along, calling out to the fugitive bird, and Dottie tried to keep up, offering comfort as best she could.

Or maybe somebody got drunk and fell off a porch and broke a toe—that kind of thing happened from time to time. Rumors were forever spreading—that Judy Garland was visiting one of the residents, or that Dorothy Dandridge had looked at a house that was for sale, or that a certain couple was breaking up; we all took a lively interest in such things.

Once everybody was invited for the unveiling of a portrait of one of the most popular Norma Placers. His living room was small and the portrait was big. In it, our host was life-sized and stark naked, seated, facing front, with carefully drawn genitals that seemed to tumble out at you. Dottie was most genteel and admiring, murmuring things like, "It's so real, you almost feel he could speak to you, don't you?"

But the biggest sensation at that time was what came to be known as Bathsheba Glyn's rape (not her real name, of course). Wyatt Cooper fills in the details:

Miss Glyn, an authoress with a number of plays and scenarios to her credit, had a habit of lying nude in her bedroom watching television, and her window shade did not seem to reach all the way to the bottom of the window. Now, to be fair, it should be pointed out that this window was not readily visible from the street; you were not likely to see it unless you happened to be hanging around in her neighbor's driveway, but we did a lot of hanging around in each other's driveways in those days, and if you had any particular excuse for being in that particular driveway, Miss Glyn's charms were there to be seen and so near that if you couldn't actually reach out and touch them they were certainly within spitting distance. Not half bad charms, either, all things considered.

As a sort of running gag, Alan and I were always inviting each other to stroll down and take a look before turning in and once or twice Dottie, who never entirely believed that Miss Glyn was there, unadorned for all to see, was about to go and see for herself but she would lose courage before she got there. Imagine, then, her fascination when news spread that poor Bathsheba had been raped at five o'clock in the morning. Dottie expressed horror like everybody else, but only when company was present. She relished every last detail and details were not sparing. Since Bathsheba had called in a few neighbors, as well as the police, as soon as her surprise guest had departed, it didn't take long for word to get around. Apparently, she had fallen asleep watching *The Late Show*, leaving the light on. It seems safe to assume that some casual passer-by was overcome by the sight and lost control of himself, but, according to Bathsheba, the intruder told her (in a post-coital conversation over drinks) that he had seen her in the supermarket, become obsessed by a passion for her, and, knowing that he could never possess her in any other way ("I don't know why people jump to such conclusions," said Dottie), had taken this tack. He was eighteen years old, or so he told her, and he was blond—this Bathsheba could tell by the texture of his skin, as she was not allowed to see his face, which was covered by a shirt.

We spent some time trying to figure out how he maneuvered his drink with that shirt over his head, but reluctantly concluded that in desperate situations such things can be managed. She had promised to co-operate on condition that he would afterwards discuss his reasons for such outrageous behavior, an arrangement to which he agreed with alacrity. I am omitting some of the more explicit details, but would feel remiss if I did not report Dottie's reaction to the disclosure that a certain jar of Vaseline had figured in the act, since the lad found some difficulty effecting entry . . . because he was so large or she was so small— "in either case a fantasy," said Dottie. She refused to believe any of it, even after police found footprints and the kitchen knife with which he had threatened his victim. Dottie further claimed to have heard a rumor that Bathsheba was to be arrested for contributing to the delinquency of a minor by giving him the alcoholic beverage. It was with reluctance that we departed on those days, even for a short time, so fearful were we of missing new developments. Little writing got done in any case, as we were in constant touch by telephone, working out new theories and speculations . . .

On Alan and Mrs. Parker's return to Hollywood, they had struck lucky with the film people. Both had been engaged by Twentieth Century–Fox to write a screenplay titled *The Good Soup*, rumored to be a vehicle for Marilyn Monroe, the hottest property in the city. The movie did not get off the ground, but the work at Fox with Alan, and the exuberant company of Wyatt Cooper, who was now also on the payroll there, provided plenty of diversionary fun, as Cooper was to recall:

When Alan, Dottie and I were working at the studios, they had a secretary who had absolutely no humor. This fascinated Dottie and she and Alan used to promise each other sleds for Christmas if they could get her to smile. Dottie swore that everything about the girl was artificial, and I believe it was true. Breasts, eyelashes, hair, finger nails, teeth, all seemed false. Dottie used to surprise her in the rest room, hoping to catch her with some of the beauty aids removed. She kept wondering whether there was anything at all there. Everyday at lunch they would report to me the secretary's personal phone calls, which were the major events of their day. Once, when the secretary had two tickets to a movie premiere, she spent the morning calling various fellows, trying without success to find a date. She was, needless to say, unaware that the pair were eavesdropping and, when Dottie guilelessly inquired who was taking her to the movie, she replied airily, "Oh, I'd rather just go with a nice girl than with some man I don't like." It was our favorite saying for a while and we used to say it to each other rather a lot, and then roll about with laughter.

We took long lunch hours, driving off the lot and going down towards Santa Monica to find a place to eat. Getting away always took a long time because Dottie would go to the rest room, which was filled with secretaries talking, and get into a booth to listen. Each day she would stay longer, and Alan would get impatient, as we were waiting in the car, but when she appeared she had many goodies to report, and she remembered every word; if she didn't, no matter, for she had made up something better.

Mrs. Parker and Alan soon decided to remarry, and telephoned their friends, inviting them to help celebrate the occasion.

Time had proved the strength of their relationship, and had, too, revealed the weaknesses of each other's personalities, but they had survived, to become husband and wife again.

The irony of the situation did not escape Mrs. Parker. Looking around the room during the reception, she said, "People who haven't talked to each other in years are on speaking terms again today, including the bride and groom." Life was full once more. She delighted her friends with the story of how, in bed the night before their remarriage, she had pulled the covers high up to her neck and said teasingly to Alan, "No peeking now. Mustn't see the bride before the wedding!"

With their relationship repaired, the couple started work on a play and almost as quickly abandoned it. But to their friends, and to Wyatt Cooper in particular, their feelings about each other became a blend of pride and exasperation.

"Alan was constantly starting home improvement projects, adding a bathroom or making the garage into a guest cottage to be rented out, and they were rarely completed," recalled Cooper. "Dottie would announce with the air of a true martyr, 'I don't know *where* Alan is; he just pulled two boards up out of the floor and went off to the post office!' " "Or," remembers Cooper, "if he took a chair to be covered in a pretty fabric—he had a strong nest-building instinct—Dottie would share his enthusiasm for the result, taking loving pride in his taste but, shortly afterward, when the dogs had done their inevitable destruction to it, she was almost gleeful in pointing out the damage." "Sometimes," Cooper recalled, it seemed "they were determined to behave symbolically: when Dottie arrived with her poodle Cliche, Alan who up to then had seemed content without a dog of his own, went out and bought a bad-tempered Sealyham puppy, and the two animals were never at peace. From their first meeting, they engaged in a running contest to see which could wreak the greater havoc."

"At the same time," went on Cooper,

Alan and Dottie could be fiercely protective of each other. When she suffered through quite a bit of repair work on her teeth, Alan was visibly distressed by her pain. Once, when we were driving along in my car and Alan was describing some untalented screenwriter, saying, "He would write a line like: 'You're mashing hell out of my finger,' " Dottie was busily reacting, saying: "Imagine writing a line like that!" and I, ever eager to learn, was trying to figure out what was wrong with the line if the character's fingers were actually being mashed, not connecting it with the fact that I was also, at that moment, pressing a button, the function of which was to raise a window on Alan's side of the car. I had no way of knowing that he'd stuck his fingers down into the space where the window was rising, and it took some time and quite a lot of yelling on Alan's part to make the connection for me. Dottie laughed heartily at his predicament, reversing her former position by saying, "It seemed like a perfectly good line to me," until she saw that there was actually blood on his fingernail and then she was all concern for him and mad at my idiocy.

Although they were both drinking a good deal, which often led to tantrums and bad temper, "whatever their anger at each other," recalled Cooper, "they presented a united front when guests were present, each elaborately ignoring any misadventures on the part of the other."

There was a particular dinner party attended by Cooper. Among other guests was the serene English actress Cathleen Nesbitt, who as Rupert Brooke's first great love had inspired the poet to write some of his finest lyric poetry. When Miss Nesbitt arrived, Cooper instantly "recognized the glassy unfocused look in Alan's eyes as a signal that we were headed for trouble. Drinks stretched on and on, with Alan making unsteady trips to the kitchen from time to time to check the progress of a roast. Dottie was fine—his bad behavior brought out her best—she was entertaining and amusing, as was Miss Nesbitt . . . " The actress spoke charmingly of her affection for Dottie's poem "One Perfect Rose":

> A single flow'r he sent me, since we met.
> All tenderly his messenger he chose;
> Deep-hearted, pure, with scented dew still wet—
> One perfect rose.
>
> I knew the language of the floweret;
> "My fragile leaves," it said, "his heart enclose."
> Love long has taken for his amulet
> One perfect rose.
>
> Why is it no one ever sent me yet
> One perfect limousine, do you suppose?
> Ah, no, it's always just my luck to get
> One perfect rose.

Cathleen Nesbitt "told us about seeing Noel Coward's new musical in London, describing it in quite gracious terms, while Alan interrupted unpleasantly and frequently, snarling, 'Let's face it, what you're trying to say is, it stunk!' "

"That," recalled Cooper,

was not what Cathleen Nesbitt was trying to say, but she never lost her aplomb, nor did Dottie, as stomachs began to rumble and dinner failed to appear. Alan's trips to the kitchen took longer and longer and he angrily refused any offers of help.

It was well after ten o'clock before food was forthcoming, and we were so busy not noticing his lurching walk which was, by now, that of a sailor on deck in the worst sort of storm, that it was not until I had a fork loaded with salad and on the way to my mouth that I noticed the presence in it of long strips of gaily-colored aluminum wrap. God knows what Alan had thought he was doing as he shredded it so carefully, but there it was disappearing down Miss Nesbitt's elegant throat, while Dottie complimented her husband on the excellence of his cooking.

For her part, Mrs. Parker rose above the complications of mundane social and domestic scenes. She was still "filled with sympathy for all society's victims," extended to anyone accused of a crime; so long, remembered Cooper, "as they were found guilty she was convinced of their innocence. It had been clear to her at the time he was in jail that Dr. Sam Sheppard had been railroaded. On the other hand, Lizzie Borden, having been acquitted, would be forever guilty in Dottie's eyes, and she took it personally when a book appeared which asserted the girl's innocence." "I can sympathize with almost any wrongdoing," she told Cooper. "People are horrified by child molesting, but it seems perfectly understandable to me. The only criminal activity with which I don't completely identify," she said, "is arson."

She had long since decided on cremation for her own end, fire always seeming to have a strange, mystical effect on her. Many thought that her proclaimed dislike of arson in reality displayed a Freudian attraction to it, as during one of Hollywood's periodic fires when thousands of acres and hundreds of houses were destroyed. Cooper dropped in on Alan and Dorothy, and found her

listening to an account of the fire on the radio. I took Alan aside and asked if he thought she would like to see it. He said that she was dying to, but would have to be persuaded. I broached the subject, mentioning off-handedly that the holocaust was visible from a nearby hilltop, and that I had been thinking of driving up for a quick look. "Oh, I couldn't bear it! What a terrible sight it must be!" she was saying as she pulled on a sweater and headed for the door. We got to the hilltop and couldn't see anything. We went further, and still couldn't. Should we keep going? Might as well. We traveled, finally, some ten or fifteen miles, with Dottie protesting all the way, until suddenly there it was, the entire horizon aflame. Miles of fire. Dottie's face was hidden in her hands, but she was peeking out between her fingers. "It's like Dante's *Inferno*, isn't it? The end of the world," she was saying in genuine distress. "Think how frightened all the little animals are: the little squirrels, the little rabbits, all the little birds," then, without a change of voice, "Do you think we could get any closer?"

Dorothy and Alan could not be happy together or apart. In many respects, they were a highly engaging couple, he sociable and witty with perhaps, a discernible chip on his shoulder; she, accomplished, wise and celebrated. They had spent many years of their lives together yet, apart from their newspaper and show business acquaintances, they had few real friends, excepting Dorothy's friendships with Beatrice Ames and Lillian Hellman.

Many people were afraid of Dorothy Parker. One of her Norma Place neighbors had described to her a minor automobile accident in which the woman had received a small scratch on her face. The woman told Mrs. Parker, "I did hope there wouldn't be a scar," to which Mrs. Parker muttered, "As opposed to all those women who *like* looking as if they went to school in Heidelburg." Clearly, Mrs. Parker's attitude towards people did not engender a harmony of spirit. One actor she was introduced to had an unbecoming nose and deeply receding chin and believed that in Mrs. Parker he had met a kindred spirit. The man thus poured out to her all his considerable hopes of fame and fortune in Hollywood. "Oh, really," she told him, "they've been *searching* for a new Cary Grant."

To many, her remarriage to Alan was a glaring mistake, which she gave rise to by saying, "I've been given a second chance—and who in life gets a second chance?" or, after being asked where she was staying, before they had remarried, by replying coquettishly, "At Alan's. Isn't that disgraceful?" Keats reported that at the reception following their remarriage, Alan told some of the guests that Mrs. Parker was receiving an average of $10,000 a year in royalties. "I never believed Alan, and no one else believed him," said one later. "But what a darling thing of him to say. He was saying 'I am not marrying her to try to make her work because she needs money, because she doesn't need money.' He was marrying her because he wanted to help take care of her. Alan was so wonderful for her, and she would crucify him, but she relied on him and he was lovely to her."

The cynics who had prophesied doom for their remarriage were mostly those who were afraid of the icy contempt expressed in the expected quip which so often cut the recipient to the quick. Few, it seems, even those who believed they were close to her, felt really at ease with her. Cooper admitted he didn't; even Alan at times appeared to feel uncomfortable. For his part, Cooper was frank:

"Probably everybody has somebody with whom he is never completely himself. The reasons for this may be varied—awe of a hero, respect for a talent, or just plain fear." It seemed to be a combination of all three for him: "In all the years I knew her," he was to say much later, "and however often I saw her, I was never totally at ease with her . . . I could not escape seeing myself as I imagined I looked to her; an Ichabod Crane, all awkwardness and absurdity, the nervous laugh always at the ready, just in case . . . I never stopped feeling, somehow, like an adolescent covered in runny pimples."

She was still more than capable of delivering the ultimate line. Someone, it is believed to have been Cooper, remarked in idle conversation that Christine Jorgensen, who had undergone a celebrated sex change, was going to visit her mother in the United States. "And what sex, may I ask, is the mother?" inquired Mrs. Parker.

For all her moods and quirks, Alan still adored her. As most people around them knew, she was incurably jealous of him, no doubt helped by the fact that he was much younger. She continually accused him of infidelities that, according to him, simply did not exist. "He had," said Cooper, "a happy capacity for friendship, many of them with cultivated and interesting women. Of one, who was perhaps a little more formal and unbending than most, Dottie said in anger, 'I know you aren't laying her, Alan. If you were, you'd have splinters in your prow.' "

Could her irascibility have been caused by her insecurity in Hollywood following the McCarthy hearings? Screenwriting had always been an unsatisfactory occupation, achieving little for her and Alan except a few screen credits and enough money to sustain their high life-style. They had been given screen credit for some of their work, but a good many of their writing assignments had not been translated into film and when they had, some soon became buried without a trace. *Crime Takes a Holiday, Five Little Peppers and How They Grew, Weekend for Three* and *Gentle Gangster* could be counted among those that dried up.

Little work was coming in, and it did not help that Hollywood was the one place where inferior minds made superior people feel inferior. Perhaps she should have heeded the words of Donald Ogden Stewart, who had earlier evolved a set of rules for a writer's survival in Hollywood. The first was the simple edict, "Find out who the star of your film is going to be. It's disconcerting to have written something for Joan Crawford only to find it is Lana Turner whom the producers have settled on." Secondly, "Never, never tackle a screenplay at the beginning of its development. Let the producer and his other writers mess it up and then, when they're faced with an actual shooting date, you do the final job." Finally, he added, "whatever happens, you must learn not to let them break your heart."

· 4 6 ·

Social Security and
Another Parting

THE RENEWED TENSIONS between Mrs. Parker and Alan were not helped by their increased drinking and lack of screenwriting assignments. She could not seem to apply herself to magazine writing, which resulted in a considerable drop in their joint income. They discussed the problem with Wyatt Cooper, who said he

. . . [I] persuaded them to file for unemployment compensation which I was already drawing. It is a perfectly honorable procedure and a rewarding one. You got quite a lot, considering that it was tax-free; it seems to me that it was about $75 a week, and for the two of them it amounted to a worthwhile sum by the end of the month. All you had to do was to go in once a week and sign a card saying that you were available for work. It was a pleasant and even a rather chic thing to do; you not only caught sight of such stars as Marlon Brando from time to time, but you also ran into old chums you hadn't encountered for ages, whom you were happy to see, as long as you didn't have to spend a lot of time with them. The parking lot always had a Rolls or two along with an abundance of sporty Cadillacs and we once decided that you saw just as many celebrities there as you would lunching at Romanoff's; furthermore, as Dottie was quick to comment, "It's a much nicer set."

The first time you go, however, there is a certain amount of bother. Papers must be filled out, and you are sent from desk to desk and asked such questions as "Have you been looking for employment?" "Are you enrolled in any school?" and "What other skills have you that might be of use in other fields?" They never bat an eye at the large sums you have been paid for your studio services; they've heard it all before.

On the way down to the unemployment office, Cooper coached Alan and his wife carefully,

. . . necessary because both were behaving as if they were about to perjure themselves into prison.

We kept assuring each other heartily that, after all, we paid enormous taxes and were entitled to our rights like anybody else. Alan and I collaborated in filling out their preliminary forms as it was an undertaking for which neither of us had any talent, and for which Dottie was hopeless.

276

They could not, however, accompany her to the actual interviews.

We stood watching as she was shuttled from clerk to clerk, looking like a lamb on its way to slaughter. "Ah, she'll be all right now," Alan said as she approached one desk, "That one has glasses on." Sure enough, the lady with the glasses started to read Dottie's record, looked up, asked a question, grinned broadly, took off her spectacles, shook hands, and called several other girls over to touch the author of the familiar line. We were too far away to hear what was being said, but we could see several pairs of lips moving as they recited the poem to her, and Dottie's expression on this occasion was one of deep gratitude. Everyone was most cooperative after that and it was even arranged that the Campbells' reporting time would coincide with mine so that we could make a weekly jaunt of it.

Despite the facade of equanimity assumed for the benefit of their friends, it was not a good time for Mrs. Parker and Alan. There was now no work coming in and their drinking habits were becoming worse. It was, as Mrs. Parker was later to recall, "a time of demons."

Their deep and bitter quarrels reached another climax. She again accused him of having homosexual affairs. She told him she wanted to go back to New York to live alone. He, for his part, had suffered enough tensions through unemployment without having to withstand his wife's constant accusations. Each agreed to go his own way. Alan stayed on for a time at Norma Place; Mrs. Parker returned to New York and the Volney Hotel.

While there, she attended a cocktail party where she met again with her old friend Arnold d'Usseau, the left-wing intellectual who had served on war committees with her in Hollywood. He was the author of five plays, including *Tomorrow the World* and *Deep Are the Roots*, and a thoughtful man with a good sense of humor. What was he writing? she wanted to know.

"I'm resting," he joked, "but I'm soon to start work on a play with Dorothy Parker . . . "

She smiled. "That's strange," she said. "Only the other day I was discussing an idea for a play I'm planning to write with Arnold d'Usseau . . . "

They met and talked again. It was indeed true that she had an idea for a play. Her life at the Volney had inspired her to think about portraying a group of middle-aged and elderly women living out the rest of their lonely lives in a small shabby New York hotel. Together she and d'Usseau set the action within a hotel they called the Marlowe, in the East Sixties. The result turned out to be a penetrating study of death in life.

Mrs. Parker and d'Usseau decided to call it *Ladies of the Corridor*, a title they took from T. S. Eliot's *Sweeney Erect*. Clearly, Mrs. Parker, aided by d'Usseau, knew her drama. Professor Kinney makes just this point in dealing with the character of Mildred Tynan:

Mildred . . . seems at first a typed dipsomaniac. Drink, she tells the maid Irma, "makes you a different person. You're not yourself for a little while, and that's velvet . . . A couple of drinks and I've got some nerve. Otherwise I'm frightened all the time." Mildred has, though, a desperate kind of wit—"I'm giving up solitaire. I can't win even when I cheat. . . . Maybe I could give music lessons to backward children? . . . I finally got so I could play *The Minute Waltz* in a minute and a half," displaying how frightened the character remains, even after drinking. For her, drinking is a consequence not of fear in the present but of searing memories from the past with her husband: "Once I got started—God, how he hurried me along. So when we went to the country club, Mrs. John Tynan would fall down on the dance floor and her husband would carry her out. And everybody would say, 'Oh, that poor man, and look how sweet he is to her! Poor, dear man. Holy John Tynan, the Blessed Martyr of Santa Barbara! Yes, and the call girls, two and three at a time, and the whip in the closet . . . ' "

That sounded remarkably like Mrs. Parker.

Arnold d'Usseau and doubtless Mrs. Parker herself knew that the chief character of Lulu Ames bore an uncanny resemblance to Hazel Morse, the Big Blonde of Mrs. Parker's earlier short story.

LULU: Is there a man, Connie?
CONNIE: No, oh, no. After Ben died there was a long stretch when I sat and looked at the wall. Then, a long time after that, there was a man—a lovely man. I was young again.
LULU: [*Gently*] What happened, Connie?
CONNIE: He found somebody who was young for the first time. So then there was a succession of transients. If that shocks you, Lulu, it shouldn't. The one-night stands don't do any good. I found that out. There's got to be fondness and there's got to be hope. Lulu, please— this new life must be all you want it to be. Only don't let yourself get lonely. Loneliness makes ladies our age do the goddamndest things. . . .

After Boston and Philadelphia tryouts, the play opened October 21, 1953, at the Longacre Theater, New York, staged by Harold Clurman and starring Edna Best, British actress, former wife of movie star Herbert Marshall; Betty Field; and Walter Matthau. George Jean Nathan named it the best play of the year.

"It was," Dorothy Parker was to say, "the only thing I have ever done in which I had great pride." It was, however, a pride that was not to last long. After the opening, Clurman demanded that she and d'Usseau change the play's ending, a decision so demonstrably wrong that it brought about a premature end to the play's run after only forty-five performances. As Lillian Hellman had said: "Failure in the theater is more public, more brilliant, more unreal than in any other field." As usual, Miss Hellman was right.

Mrs. Parker's time of demons had not ended.

In February 1955, the New York State Joint Legislative Committee discovered misuse of the Joint Anti-Fascist Refugee Committee funds and called on Mrs. Parker, who had been national chairman and had signed most of the checks, to testify. She denied knowledge of the committee's financial affairs and records, but she freely admitted signing checks which, she said, had been used "to help people who were helpless." She was again asked if she were a Communist. In reply, she again pleaded the Fifth Amendment.

How could one reconcile Mrs. Parker's impressive list of humanitarian actions with her constant approval of the more fortunate of mortals, the rich and famous? Did Lillian Hellman touch on the truth when she wrote:

She liked the rich because she liked the way they looked, their clothes, the things in their houses, and she disliked them with an open and baiting contempt; she believed in socialism but seldom, except in the sticky sentimental minutes, could stand the sight of a working radical; she drank far too much, spent far too much time with ladies who did and made fun of them and herself every inch of the way; she faked interest and sympathy for those who bored her and for whom she had no feeling, and yet I never heard her hit mean except where it was, in some sense, justified; she herself was frightened of being hit, being made fun of, being inconvenienced.

There were those who, like Miss Hellman, had recognized that in her attitude to the legislative committee, although not displaying any outward sign of terror, Mrs. Parker had been wearing a mask, obscuring her deep fears.

It was shortly after Mrs. Parker's appearance before the committee that Wyatt Cooper met again with Alan Campbell in New York. He had not spent a great deal of time with either Alan or Dorothy Parker in a while. He later recalled this meeting with Alan:

The experience was disturbing to me . . . remembering it now is oddly discomforting . . . I had seen Alan here and there and though he was one of the most charming, witty and sociable gentlemen alive, he also had a surprising defensiveness that made me wary of him. I was surprised then, when in the elevator after a gathering at George Kaufman's, he suddenly asked, like a man desperate not to be alone, "I have to go see Dottie. Will you go with me?" As my previous encounters had not been pleasant ones—this was an unhappy period of her life—I must have hesitated, though it is doubtful if I hesitated long, my curiosity being what it was.

"My memory," said Cooper,

is of a stark, bare, colorless and impersonal room, with a large bone on the floor, dog toys on the gravy-colored sofa, a dog, of course, and an agonized Alan facing a stricken-looking Dottie, who was, as incredible as it seems now, actually fat. My impression was of a sad, bewildered young girl, angrily trapped inside an inappropriate and almost grotesque body. Of the desolate conversation, I remember only that she apologized repeatedly: for the disorder of the room, for her own appearance, for the behavior of the dog, and for the absence of anything to drink. There was a sense of unreality about it: the darkened room, the sad and lost lady, the man ill-at-ease and poised for flight, and the stranger to them both, with no reason whatever for being present. It was painful to witness the estrangement of two people who were forever to be deeply involved with each other. Loneliness and guilt were almost like physical presences in the space between them, and they spoke in short, stilted and polite sentences with terrible silences in between, and yet there was a tenderness in the exchange, a grief for old hurts, and a shared reluctance to turn loose.

If there was loneliness and guilt there was also some hope. Dorothy Parker was writing again. Despite its short run, *Ladies of the Corridor* and Nathan's approval of it had inspired her. The following year, 1955, *The New Yorker* took two of her stories, "I Live on Your Visits" and "Lolita," both fictional spinoffs of her play written with d'Usseau.

And now came the good news that Hollywood wanted the return of the Parker-Campbell writing team to script a remake of *A Star Is Born*, this time starring Gloria Swanson and William Holden. The project was stillborn.

If Dorothy Parker and Alan couldn't live together, they assuredly could not live apart. Mrs. Parker moved back in with Alan at Norma Place, near Hollywood. They had some bright spells in their lives once again. "They were," as Cooper said, "very much alike; much more alike than most people realized. Not only their humor—Alan wrote the funniest letters I've ever read—but their likes, their dislikes, their prejudices, their fears, and their critical judgments were almost interchangeable. They had the kind of unspoken communication of those who know all there is to know about each other."

It was not long before they were again living on alcohol and unemployment checks. Lillian Hellman persuaded the producers of her operetta adaptation of Voltaire's *Candide,* which was in rehearsal and for which Hellman had written the book, to hire Mrs. Parker to write lyrics with Richard Wilbur and John Latouche to Leonard Bernstein's music. She wrote two songs: One, for Candide to sing in the Eldorado scene, was promptly dropped; the other, "Gavotte," was sung in the play by the character Sofronia. *Candide,* later described as a "spectacular disaster," ran for only seventy-three performances. It was a disaster for both Lillian Hellman and Dorothy Parker, who later voiced distinct disapproval of Bernstein's attitude towards her.

Dorothy Parker was interviewed by Marion Capron at this time:

"I don't want to be classed as a humorist," she said firmly. "It makes me feel guilty. I've never read a good, tough, quotable female humorist, and I never was one myself; I couldn't do it. A 'smart-cracker' they called me, and that makes me sick and unhappy. There's a helluva distance between wisecracking and wit . . . There aren't any humorists any more," she added, "except for Perelman. There's no need for them. Perelman must be lonely."

But why was there no need for the humorist? persisted Capron.

"It's a question of supply and demand. If we needed them we'd have them. The new crop of would-be humorists doesn't count. They're like would-be satirists. They write about topical topics. Not like Thurber and Mr. Benchley," she said. She still respectfully referred to him as *Mr.* Benchley.

"Those two," she emphasized, "were damn well read and, though I hate the word, they were *cultured.* What sets them apart is that they both had a point of view to express. That is important to all good writing. It's the difference between Paddy Chayefsky, who just puts down lines, and Clifford Odets, who in his early plays not only sees but has a point of view. The writer," she stressed, "must be aware of life around him."

"And what," Capron asked her, "of the current crop of writers?" Did Mrs. Parker read them?

"I will say of the writers of today that some of them, thank God, have the sense to adapt to the times. Mailer's *The Naked and the Dead* is a great book. And I thought William Styron's *Lie Down in Darkness* an extraordinary thing. The start of it took your heart and flung it over there. He writes like a god. But for most of my reading I go back to the old ones—for comfort. As you get older you go much further back."

The advent of yet another flop, *Candide,* did not help the morale of either Dorothy Parker or Alan Campbell, who both continued their heavy drinking. Back on the coast at Norma Place, with intermittent trips to New York with his wife, Alan continued to do the cooking and the cleaning, aided by a part-time maid.

Mrs. Parker had long nursed an idea for a play about life in a convent. She started it in 1957, then threw the manuscript away. She then wrote another short story, "The Banquet of Crow," a morsel bitingly analogous to her life with Alan, and sent it off to her old friend Arnold Gingrich, editor of *Esquire*, who had been associated with one or two of the committees she had served on during the war. Gingrich promptly bought it, suggesting that she also contribute regular book reviews to the magazine. He was prepared to pay her $750 for each piece she wrote. Gingrich, who had done so much to rescue Scott Fitzgerald from alcoholism, regarded the gesture as nothing more than a tribute to Dorothy Parker, the literary legend whom he greatly admired. Perhaps, though, it was not all that altruistic; Gingrich was an inventive journalist and editor, and he knew there were millions of Americans who could still quote the quips, epigrams and verses of Dorothy Parker. His offer, then, apart from helping her, would be good for circulation.

From the West Coast, Mrs. Parker put through a call to Gingrich in New York to thank him, saying she would be flying to New York in a few days and would be at the Volney. Gingrich promised to send over an editor to firm up the arrangement, who would bring with him a parcel of review copies for her to choose from.

Mrs. Parker arrived at the Volney, and within hours received Harold Hayes, a young editor from *Esquire*. Let him take up the story:

"I expected a wisecracking hot-shot, a very old one," he said, "but when I met a woman who was more insecure than I was—as a young editor—I was charmed."

Harold Hayes's opinion of Dorothy Parker as a dignified, warm and genuinely concerned woman never changed thereafter. He was, however, shortly to find that she was not the most dependable of book reviewers, nor the easiest writer for an editor to handle. "Editing her," he told John Keats, "was a terrifying experience." What was particularly terrifying was that when *Esquire* issues for press closed her copy would still be missing.

This was confirmed by Alan. Back in California with his wife he used to call on Wyatt Cooper and announce grumpily:

"I'm supposed to get out of the way so that Dottie can do her *Esquire* piece. It's already five days late and she's not going to do it. I put a hair on the typewriter and, when I get back, it'll still be there. Wait and see, she's going to claim she's finished it and sent it in."

That was about the measure of it. As Keats reported: "She began her column well enough and on time in the December 1957 issue, but there was no Parker column in January, February, March or April, 1958." She was, indeed, to miss a good many other issues. What was the reason? "She seemed," reported Hayes, "sincerely to detest writing. She truly hated to write. She'd just lie about how far along she was with a piece. She fled from the problem of doing anything."

Gingrich himself put it another, more graphic way: "It is a high-forceps delivery every time we manage to get a piece out of her."

· 47 ·

Return to Yesterday

THE WILL TO WORK might have left Dorothy Parker, but the clarity and irony of her wit were still very evident in the pieces she did bring herself to tackle for Gingrich.

She reviewed a collection of the "Best Fiction of 1957" in December of that year, as a salute to the year's end, revealing her sadness at the trend of late fifties' literature:

> The cases of euphoria among book reviewers have reached alarming figures; perhaps my opportunity to see this, once-a-year, what they are daily faced with makes a little more understandable to me the fact that any reasonably grammatical novel brings on such attacks of cheer-leading, hat-tossing, and dancing in the streets, as make the critiques of Alexander Woollcott seem those of a man of ice and iron. Miserable-child stories are surprisingly absent. English authors, though their books may not quite succeed, write better than almost anybody, and Irish authors, better than anybody.

She did not like the trend of new novelists having their photographs on the back dustcovers of their books, "You never saw so many lumberjack shirts in your life," she deplored. Nor did she approve of explicit sex in novels:

> Poor dear sex is crammed into spaces where there is scarcely room for it by itself, and its joy must be left outside. The nowadays ruling that no word is unprintable has, I think, done nothing whatever for beautiful letters. The boys have gone hog-wild with liberty, yet the short flat terms used over and over, both in dialogue and narrative, add neither vigor nor clarity; the effect is not of shock but of something far more dangerous—tedium.

This was vintage Dorothy Parker.

And erratic though her contributions to *Esquire* were, she could still assess, often with devastating irony or understatement, pillars of the American literary establishment like Ellery Queen, John Steinbeck, Truman Capote, John Updike, Katherine Anne Porter, Shirley Jackson, and old friends like Edna Ferber, Edmund Wilson and James Thurber and even some of the "New Wave" writers like Jack Kerouac.

While lyrical in her praise of Mr. Wilson's *The American Earthquake*, she applauded, too, the format, print, paper and cloth binding of Mr.

Kerouac's *The Subterraneans,* but showed her claws when dealing with his generation:

Doubtless my absence of excitement over Mr. Kerouac's characters is due to a gaping lack in me for, and I regret the fact, I do not dig bop. I cannot come afire when I hear it, and I am even less ecstatic in reading about it. I am honestly sorry about this, for who could not do with a spot of ecstasy now and then? I envy the generation its pleasure in music. And that is all I envy it.

Did she find echoes of any ecstasy in her reading of Edna Ferber's *Ice Palace?*

Miss Ferber, who so thoroughly travels her country, came most recently upon Alaska. She was deeply impressed with the dramatic beauty of the place, and so, through her eyes, are you, and she is finely indignant over the stupidity of not admitting the territory to statehood . . . Otherwise the book, which is going to be a movie, has the plot and characters of a book which is going to be a movie . . .

Dorothy Parker had never been enamored of Miss Ferber or her writings and, for her part, Miss Ferber felt the same about her. But Mrs. Parker did want the reader to know a little about Miss Ferber's central plot:

"Well, it seems this young couple was out walking in the wilds, and suddenly there were unmistakable signs that Baby was about to make three . . . "

Years before, Edna Ferber had been introduced to a pretty lady, Tell Schlesinger, whose writing was said to be imitative of Mrs. Parker's. The meeting had apparently engendered cool feelings between the two. Preparing to return to New York, Miss Ferber was surprised to be greeted at the station by a group of Hollywood authors and scenarists who included Tell Schlesinger. They had come unexpectedly to see Miss Ferber off to Manhattan.

The story went that Ferber wandered across to a bookshop and arrogantly demanded of the salesman, "Where's my latest book?" Miss Schlesinger, who also boasted a recently published volume, also inquired, somewhat less aggressively, "And where's *my* book?" At this, Ferber leaned across, reached for a copy of Dorothy Parker's *Enough Rope* and, turning to Miss Schlesinger, said pertly, "Why, here it is!"

Weeks before its American publication, Mrs. Parker bravely called Vladimir Nabokov's *Lolita* "a fine book . . . a great book . . . " and poked derisive fun at John Gordon, editor of the London *Sunday Express,* for having described it "without doubt . . . the filthiest book I have ever read." But, then, Mr. Gordon hailed from Scotland where his Presbyterian upbringing and the stringencies of the Kirk did not admit the existence of fornication with teenagers.

If, apart from her occasional *Esquire* pieces, Mrs. Parker had all but given up writing, there were those who remembered her halcyon days and wished to pay tribute to Dorothy Parker, the lady of letters. On April 30, 1958, the National Institute and American Academy of Arts and Letters awarded her a citation and the Marjorie Peabody Waite Award for her outstanding fiction and poetry, later inducting her as a member of the academy.

In November 1958, she joined Robert Gorham Davis to conduct a symposium at the Writer's Club of Columbia University's School of General Studies. She was also invited to appear on David Susskind's television show, "Open End," when she applied a scythe to the new fiction sent to her by *Esquire*. It was, she said, "appalling!" But this certainly didn't apply to John Updike. Seizing on that writer's *The Poorhouse Fair*, she proved that she could still laugh at herself: "Perhaps this is a purely personal matter, but I am always drawn to reading a book about a poorhouse—after all, it is only normal curiosity to find out what it will be like in my future residence."

When reviewing James Thurber's nostalgic *The Years with Ross*, a vivid recollection of his time with Harold Ross on *The New Yorker*, Mrs. Parker was on familiar ground. The book recalled for her many amusing memories. She remembered one of her own encounters with Ross:

"Once I used the word 'stigmata' in a piece. The proof came to me from Ross with no questions: only the exclamation 'No such word' in the margin. When friendship was restored, Ross conceded that maybe 'stigmata' had something to do with defective vision." She concluded her review with: "After all, only God or James Thurber could have invented Ross."

To her credit, when she did fulfill her writing obligations to *Esquire*, she usually entertained her readers, retaining her capacity to assess in a single paragraph a complete review of a book, as she did with Shirley Jackson's *We Have Always Lived in the Castle*:

"There is still sunshine for us. The miracle is wrought by Shirley Jackson. God bless her, as ever unparalleled, more than ever in her latest book . . . as leader in the field of beautifully-written, quiet, cumulative shudders. This novel brings back all my faith in terror and death. I can say no higher of it and her."

To Gingrich's credit, even though Mrs. Parker often failed to keep her commitment, he still sent her a check. Thus, there was still enough coming in to keep "body and soul apart." With her twice-yearly royalty checks, reprint fees, occasional foreign payments, sporadic college lecture fees, and the $750 a month from *Esquire*, she could still afford to live a good life, often spending a considerable amount on liquor. In addition, as a promotional gimmick for *Esquire*, Gingrich, along with a New York television station, produced *The World of Dorothy Parker*, a record which brought in more money.

She had already recalled the weariness of her years when she had written: "Hey, what's the good of fooling? People ought to be one of two things—young or old," correcting herself with, "No, people ought to be one of two things—young or dead." But for all her dark attitudes, she constantly showed compassion to her old friends. When she visited Oscar Levant during one of his bouts of psychological illness, he described his hospital day and said that "Dinner is at a quarter-to-five." "That," said Mrs. Parker, "makes for nice long evenings." Levant asked her if she took sleeping pills. "In a big bowl with sugar and cream," she assured him.

There was, perhaps, a small hope that her life would finally level out, which might have been fulfilled had it not been for her heavy drinking and liberal doses of Veronal.

Life at Norma Place proceeded uneasily with its pattern of little food and too much booze; there was little that could alter the degenerative pattern.

Alan despaired of pleasing his wife. He said that no matter what he did, she felt victimized. Mrs. Parker's affinity to distress became especially related to money matters. When royalty checks came in, they were hastily put away in the backs of drawers, there to remain unopened while she went about worrying how they could pay the bills. As Cooper recalls, "God help anybody who tried to come to Mrs. Parker's aid." He cited Alexander Woollcott's description of Mrs. Patrick Campbell in her declining days as "a sinking battleship firing on her rescuers," which certainly could have been applied to Mrs. Parker without fear of exaggeration.

"There was," Cooper said,

something quite fierce and splendid about her. She resisted friendship with all her might. God forbid she should let anybody get the idea she was popular. The phone would ring and she would exclaim, "Ah, here's fresh help!" and answer the instrument in an apprehensive voice. Upon hearing the name of the caller, she would curtly say: "Not in," replace the receiver and then turn to me and say: "I don't want to speak to Mr. X now, or ever, do you?" Later, she would complain that she never hears from the same Mr. X anymore.

"I don't suppose anybody ever thought of her as old," Cooper mused. "She wasn't . . . her fragility had nothing to do with age; the deep lines across her cheeks," so evident now, "came not from the piling up of the years, but from staring wide-eyed at the human comedy. The mind remained quick and severe and young, with the anger and daring and hope of youth."

· 4 8 ·

"Get Me a New Husband"

ALAN CAMPBELL, now fifty-eight, went to bed at Norma Place in the early hours of June 14, 1963. He had been drinking a good deal and had swallowed several sleeping tablets. His wife joined him in bed half an hour later.

In the morning, Mrs. Parker awoke, touched her husband's shoulder and called his name. He did not respond; his body was cold to her touch.

Mrs. Parker called the police and one or two of their close friends, including Peter Feibleman, who was with her when the coroner took Alan's body to the mortuary. Mrs. Jones, a neighbor, who had been fond of Alan and pretended to like his wife for his sake, was there too. Mrs. Jones loved to fuss and meddle in the affairs of others, but she clearly meant it when she said to Mrs. Parker, "Dottie, tell me, dear. What can I do to help you?"

Mrs. Parker turned to her with a sterile look and said: "Get me a new husband."

There was an awful silence, broken only by Mrs. Jones's horrified words: "Dottie, I think that is the most callous and disgusting remark I ever heard in my life." Mrs. Parker looked straight at the woman, sighed and in a soft voice, said: "So sorry. Then run down to the corner and get me a ham and cheese on rye and tell them to hold the mayo."

Wyatt Cooper was away in Tuscaloosa, Alabama, where Governor George Wallace and the National Guard were barring two black students from entering the University. Cooper had gone there on a personal visit to stay with the president of the university, a relative of his, and had kept in touch with Dorothy and Alan by letter. There he received word of Alan's passing:

Shaken and emotional, I called Dottie, not really expecting her to be in any condition to come to the phone. She did, however, and there ensued a most disconcerting conversation. While I was still making blubbery and incoherent noises of sympathy, she cut me off by saying, as calmly as if continuing a conversation interrupted only five minutes earlier, "The whole world thanks you for what you are doing." I could not think what she was referring to unless it was the act of calling her. "I could hardly not . . . " I began, but she interrupted me with:

". . . And let's face it, dear, it's not for yourself you're doing it; it's for all mankind. . . . "

By now, Cooper was, as he said, "hopelessly at sea." Mrs. Parker continued: "I think," she said, "we can say Alan died with your letters clutched in his hand." It was at that point that Cooper

. . . had a vague idea of what she was trying to do. She was removing herself from her grief by talking of something else, something untrue, and she was outrageously giving me credit for accomplishing the integration of the university. . . . I asked her who was with her, and she replied that no one was, although I could hear voices and had recognized that of their close friend Bill Templeton, when he had answered the phone. I ran through a list of their friends and she said flatly that she had heard from none of them which was, of course, not true. She was in a state of suspended emotion, moving automatically, and she seemed to want to talk. She gave me an account of her discovery of Alan's body, speaking as one might to a newspaper reporter, getting the facts straight. She said that he'd asked to be awakened at a certain time, and that when she touched him rigor mortis had already set in. This last she said with some coldness, as if that condition were somehow his fault. A final affront.

She was to repeat the words describing Alan's death again and again to friends over future years, commenting "I didn't know what 'in shock' meant, but I was in it."

Although Alan's death had clearly been caused by an excessive intake of alcohol, combined with too many sleeping pills, the coroner blandly certified his passing as being from natural causes.

Alan's mother, Hortense, arrived at Norma Place from Virginia. With no regard to Mrs. Parker, she assumed responsibility of the funeral arrangements which, in the event, was just as well because her daughter-in-law pointedly could not have been less interested.

Feibleman was there when Hortense told Mrs. Parker that Alan had always wanted to be buried in his hometown of Richmond; Hortense wanted a short service at the Episcopal church there. But Mrs. Parker, as if in a sudden, bizarre attempt to invade the permanent sleep of her Jewish father and with a firmness that took Hortense aback, decreed that Alan Campbell, of Scottish descent and Christian by birth, should be buried in Richmond's small and crowded Hebrew cemetery. After an argument, she eventually compromised by agreeing to an Episcopalian priest, a former rector of Virginia Military Academy who had known Alan, plus a rabbi.

As Cooper had earlier observed, "Of course, the idea of Dottie having a mother-in-law of any sort was unsettling at best." Mrs. Parker, in one of her many complaints about Hortense, had said: "The way she gushed over me when we got married, calling me 'my little daughter,' when I wasn't her little anything." This had not gone down well with Hortense; neither had Hortense's allegation that Dorothy had "snatched that boy out of his cradle" gone down well with Mrs. Parker.

Now Mrs. Parker was even more disdainful of Hortense. "This," she said of her mother-in-law, "will be her coming-out party!"

Mrs. Dorothy Parker, for whom age had put aside the conceits of youth, was now seventy and alone again. Alan, her husband and friend through the good times and the bad, had gone to his Maker. Joe Bryan, who had known Alan Campbell in Richmond when they were boys, had returned to that city at the time of Campbell's death. Years later he remembered the sad period:

Alan's family asked me to be a pallbearer, with several other of his boyhood friends. I assumed that Dottie would come to the funeral, so I telephoned Hollywood and left an invitation for her to stay with us. No answer. The next I heard, she was in New York, in a suite at the Volney Hotel. At first I used to ring her when I came to town and ask if I might stop in for a drink, but she was always "just going out"; and if I called well in advance, it was always, "If *only* you'd phoned five minutes earlier."

I was reassured to learn before long that she was avoiding almost everybody, so I stopped bothering her.

The California heat was stifling that summer, and not long after Alan's death, Mrs. Parker was sitting in the living room at Norma Place with Wyatt Cooper. The heat was particularly intense that day, and the windows, which went all the way to the floor, could not be opened for fear the dogs would run loose. As Cooper remembered, "That afternoon, there arrived on the scene a very altruistic lady, a former movie star, as gracious as she was charitable, who had gone to the trouble earlier of measuring the windows and then having screens cut to fit.

"With the cheerfully bustling air of the well-intended, she lugged the screens in while Dottie went on effusively about her inability to repay 'such kindness, such sweetness, such compassion, such benefi- cence . . . ' " While Mrs. Parker continued with her exhortation, the visiting lady asked Cooper to find a hammer and nails, whereupon Mrs. Parker stopped her recitation of praise, turned to Cooper and, freezing him with a gaze of exaggerated sympathy, observed: "If there's anything I can't stand, it's a bossy woman."

During this time friends made sure Mrs. Parker had food; without such concern she probably wouldn't have eaten. Alan had once told

Cooper that rather than cook anything, she would go into the kitchen and eat raw bacon. The kind and compassionate, alas, found the going hard. "None of the good Samaritans lasted long," recalled Cooper. "There was quite a turnover of new faces. They all started out with much enthusiasm but, after a while, retired looking somewhat subdued."

Mrs. Parker decided to sell the house in preparation for her final move back to New York. One neighbor who happened to be rather effete brought a couple to look over the place. Cooper recalled this day: "While the prospective homeowners gingerly picked their way among the little piles of doggie waste, which seemed to have a way of accumulating since Alan's death, the neighbor perched tentatively on a chair facing Dottie. 'It's so kind of you to do this,' Dorothy was saying, 'but then, that's just the way you are, warmhearted, tender, compassionate, obliging . . .'

"The fellow," Cooper went on, "gushed quite a bit, quite pleased with himself, out of all proportion really, as he did expect to make a commission on the deal. He then excused himself to see how his clients were doing in their examination of the property. He was barely out of his chair," said Cooper, "and certainly not out of earshot, before Dottie said, 'There he goes, tossing his little Shirley Temple curls.' "

"I doubt," said Cooper later, "that this is a distinction that would hold up in court, but I really don't think it was the person who had rallied around to help for whom she meant the back of her hand. Not the person, but the self-congratulating pleasure that the do-gooder takes in his deed—that's what aroused her ire. Being grateful for an extended period produces a hell of a strain and, as virtue was obviously rewarding itself, Mrs. Parker couldn't resist a little annihilation."

It was the same sort of annihilation that she used on her mother-in-law, about whom she now said: "Can you believe it that after all those years of going to the Episcopal Church, she buried Alan in the Hebrew cemetery. I see you *can* believe it. I'd hoped you couldn't."

Now, with Alan gone and little work on the horizon, Mrs. Parker was restless again. Her experience with d'Usseau in writing *Ladies of the Corridor* had been a happy one; she now started to collaborate with him again, but their sessions tailed off and their idea came to nothing. Another old friend, Frederick B. Shroyer, suggested that she succeed Christopher Isherwood as the Distinguished Visiting Professor of English at California State College in Los Angeles, teaching courses in twentieth-century American literature and major British writers. How was Mrs. Parker on major British writers?

She had years earlier told Marion Capron:

I read Thackeray's *Vanity Fair* about a dozen times a year. I was a woman of eleven when I first read it—the thrill of that line, "George Osborne lay dead with a bullet through his head." Sometimes I read, as an elegant friend of mine calls them, "who-did-its." I love Sherlock Holmes. My life is so untidy and he's so neat. But as for living novelists, I suppose E. M. Forster is the best, not knowing what that is, but at least he's a semi-finalist, wouldn't you think? Somerset Maugham once said to me, "We have a novelist over here, E. M. Forster, though I don't suppose he's familiar to you." Did he think I carried a papoose on my back? Why, I'd go on my hands and knees to get to Forster. He once wrote something I've always remembered: "It has never happened to me that I've had to choose between betraying a friend and betraying my country, but if it ever does so happen I hope I have the guts to betray my country." Now doesn't that make the Fifth Amendment look like a bum?

She finally agreed to teach at California State College. Continually getting lost in the maze of corridors, she told the Los Angeles *Times* that she found 18,000 students and 150 parking lots not to her liking. She also told Wyatt Cooper that she hated the students, some of whom had interviewed her for the student press. She felt they were too quick to settle for too little, that their range of vision was too short. She also claimed the students hated her, and when she heard that Christopher Isherwood had remarked how mad about her they were, she laughed and said, "You know how much sense Christopher makes!" These feelings, however, did not extend to the blacks. She believed in their future and expressed her regard for Martin Luther King.

Her classes in 1963 were largely informal and of a personally reminiscent nature. Whatever she herself may have felt about her influence at the college, Professor Charles Beckwith, chairman of the English department, recalled that "the students adored her."

Mrs. Parker was slowly picking up the pieces of her life. She sold the house and furniture at Norma Place and moved for the last time to New York, for her "a hell of a place."

She was met at the airport by Beatrice Ames, and it was a warm reunion. "This is my city, this is my town, why did I ever leave it?" she asked Mrs. Ames. "You are back. That is all that matters," her friend said. "New York has been waiting for your return." She was interviewed by a reporter from Associated Press. To him she said: "There was nothing more fun than a man. Alan Campbell and I had twenty-nine great years together." She had gotten her numbers wrong: for more than twelve of those twenty-nine years they had been apart, through the exigencies of war or choice.

Once again she settled at the Volney, close to her familiar environs of Park Avenue and Times Square. "A silver cord," she had written, "ties me right to my city." But had things changed?

In a newspaper she read that Frank Case was suffering from a terminal illness. He was asked what had become of the Round Table, to which he replied, "Whatever became of the city reservoir at Fifth Avenue and Forty-Second Street? It gave place to the public library. These things do not last forever."

What Case did not say was that Woollcott, before his death, had enlisted the aid of Beatrice Ames to reestablish a sort of latter-day Vicious Circle, to be called The Elbow Room in the Berkshire Hotel, Manhattan. One rainy morning Woollcott had taken Leonard Lyons, Lucius Beebe, Elsa Maxwell and Gerald Murphy along to see the place, which had been decorated in varying shades of blue by Norman Bel Geddes. On seeing it, Murphy said: "All you have to do is to let the rain in and it'll make a great swimming pool." The idea had not been pursued.

But if there was little call for a revival of such an idea, Mrs. Parker retained her appeal as a literary figure. There was still magic attached to her name, as was confirmed when Richard Avedon asked her to sit for his camera. She duly sat and told her friends afterwards that she was displeased with the result, which most agreed was not Avedon's fault.

Caedmon Records, who in 1956 had suggested that she record some of her work on tape, approached her again. She taped excerpts from her work with Shirley Booth, and in the fall of 1964 read some of her works for Spoken Arts and Verve Records. She was also interviewed on WBAI by Richard Lamparski and by the BBC over a line from London.

Now and then she produced book reviews for *Esquire*. In November 1964, she published her last work for magazines, captions for John Koch's paintings of New York City for *Esquire*. In her captions, she wrote: "As only New Yorkers know, if you can get through the twilight, you'll live through the night." For her, writing was becoming increasingly difficult, and she was lonely and drinking heavily, sometimes drunk for days.

Back in the twenties, her dear friend Robert Benchley had said that "Love always ends with tears or a wry shrug." Her love for Alan, within full view of the public, had ended with just such a wry shrug. And despite the fact that her reputation seemed to grow with the passing of the years, she believed that her verse and short stories, indeed most of her creative work, was inconsequential and meaningless.

· 4 9 ·

"Promise Me I'll Never
Grow Old..."

N OW, whenever the subject of old friends came up in conversation, Mrs. Parker would say: "If I had any decency, I should be dead. Everybody I ever cared about is."

That was true largely. But Donald Ogden Stewart was still alive, and had settled with his wife, Ella, in Ramsay MacDonald's house in Hampstead, England, with the wish that there together they might end their days, which they did within two days of each other in August 1980. Heywood Broun had died in 1939, and Alice Duer Miller had suffered a fatal heart attack in 1942. Dashiell Hammett died in January 1961. And Alan and her dear and lovely friend, Robert Benchley, were now gone. Woollcott had told many people that Benchley and Mrs. Parker had been lovers, forever citing the story of when he and a young college boy had seen Benchley and Mrs. Parker at a Times Square theater opening. The boy had asked Woollcott, "Would that be Mrs. Benchley?" Woollcott replied, "Yes, that would be Mrs. Benchley, were it not for the fact that there already is a Mrs. Benchley."

On being told the story at "21" Benchley and Mrs. Parker had laughed loud and long. "Why don't we get married right now?" she had suggested. Lillian Hellman was to say in the mid-sixties: "Robert Benchley had loved her, I was told by many people, and certainly I was later to see the devotion he had for her and she for him." But it didn't matter now.

Ring Lardner, too, had died, in 1933, and Ernest Hemingway, who had found it too difficult to live with being a Nobel prize winner; "Papa," a moody, selfish, abusive and sometimes vicious figure, had blown his brains out in 1961.

On January 23, 1943, Aleck Woollcott was due to go on the air for a roundtable discussion concerning the tenth year of Hitlerism in Germany. Guests were to include Henry D. Gideonse, president of Brooklyn College, Marcia Davenport, the novelist, Rex Stout, the mystery writer and chairman of the Writer's War Board, and Dr. George N. Shuster, president of Hunter College. While sitting at a desk, he suddenly leaned forward, and, panting for breath, desperately commanded a receptionist to get his nitroglycerin tablets. He died on the way to Roosevelt Hospital. Afterwards, a radio technician on the show was interviewed about Woollcott, the radio star. "It was Aleck's show," he said, "and by God, nobody's name was announced on that show unless it was made plain that Aleck Woollcott was the star—the big star—that it was *his* show. The bastard. God rest his soul."

Franklin Adams had died too, as had Frank Crowninshield, George Kaufman, Harold Ross, Robert Sherwood and many others of the Algonquin days. So many of her friends, if they had indeed been that, were now memories only, including the maddening, talented, humorless Scott Fitzgerald, who died on Christmas Eve 1940 of a coronary occlusion. The Bishop of Baltimore would not allow him to be buried in consecrated ground, because the Catholic Church deemed his books "immoral"; they had also refused him last rites. But at the funeral his friend Mrs. Parker, the friend of his wild years, had been there to repeat over his dead body the words Fitzgerald had written for Gatsby's interment: "The poor son of a bitch."

As she remembered, D. H. Lawrence had written: "The dead don't die. They look on and help," or words to that effect. But Mrs. Parker perceived, because she wanted to perceive, no help at all; certainly none from the dead, and little enough now from the living.

She sat at home in the Volney with her two black poodles, Misty and C'est Tout; packs of cigarettes to suppress any appetite and a couple of bottles of whiskey which, as Yeats said, "blunted the edges of many things."

She took stock of her future.

Her eyesight was bothering her. One friend, fearful of the gloom that surrounded her, suggested she move down to the Plaza, her familiar watering place on Central Park. But there was no question of holing up there to suffocate her sorrow in a welter of assumed affluence that clearly she couldn't afford. The Plaza cost money, real money, like the Hôtel du Cap on the Côte d'Azur, like the Beverly Hills Hotel, shunned by her in her Hollywood days as "the place where the elephants go to die." No, she was as happy—if that was the right word—as she could hope to be in the Volney where something over forty dogs of many breeds and varieties could find uncomfortable if erratic companionship with Misty and C'est Tout. She had had the mechanistic slaveries of Sodom-near-the-sea out there on the West Coast; the place didn't matter any more. She was back in the city where her triumphs had emerged, held sway, where in past days she had caught her own breath in a lust for life.

She tried to meet her *Esquire* commitment, and told Beatrice Ames she was resolved to read lots of books, acquaint herself fully with the current literary scene. She also said she wanted to write more short stories: "I want to be taken seriously as a short story writer, and by God I hope to make it," she would say. One friend suggested she return to academe, but she wasn't interested. She thought students of the day very narrow, citing the example of Steinbeck's *Grapes of Wrath*, which her students in Los Angeles had found "too dirty." When, not long after, Steinbeck had won the Nobel Prize for Literature, "the students had behaved as if they had given it to him," she recalled.

She was now, in her own way, a fable for those same students and most of their elders, and there were still those in New York's charmed literary circles who acknowledged that fact.

She received a call from Atheneum Publishers, asking whether she would be interested in a senior editorial post. She hesitated. Then, no doubt thinking of the regular income that would supplement her fees from *Esquire*, she said, "Well, I might . . . "

"Fine," the caller said. "Do drop by and we'll talk about it."

She accepted a post as a senior editor at Atheneum. Mr. Thomas Ober, long a New York and New Jersey literary agent who is now retired in Pennsylvania, today produces letters from Dorothy Parker of Atheneum in response to his 1965 suggestion that the publisher might like to offer an option against a first novel by his then client, movie actor Gilbert Roland. Mrs. Parker appeared to slip easily and confidently into the role of publishing editor. She wrote to Ober on January 26 of that year:

Dear Mr. Ober,

Thank you for your letter of January 20 acknowledging our interest in Gilbert Roland's manuscript.

I'm afraid it is against our practice to offer an option against first look at a first novel, even by so illustrious a name. In view of this I hope you will still feel Atheneum belongs on top of your list of possible publishers for *Blood on the Horns*.

Sincerely yours,
Dorothy Parker

A few weeks later, on March 1, she followed up with:

Dear Mr. Ober,

I look forward to seeing Mr. Roland's novel as soon as it is ready. Thank you for sending along the three stories that will be part of a collection. Unfortunately, Atheneum is trying to go rather slowly on short stories now, and would in any case prefer to publish a first novel before a story collection by the same author. I've read these short pieces, and thought they had a nice feeling to them. I'd prefer to wait for the novel before making any decision, if that's all right with you.

Sincerely,
Dorothy Parker

She wrote many such letters and read a number of manuscripts herself, as many as her impaired eyesight would allow. But she did not stay long in publishing. The administrative routine was not for her, and she wanted to get back to her own work.

But writing was becoming more and more difficult, not for lack of inspiration, but because it was difficult for her to see, often made worse by her inability to find her glasses.

With the death of Hammett and the trauma of HUAC, Lillian Hellman had gone through hard times. Speaking of Mrs. Parker at this time, she said:

> We saw each other, of course, but after the first few times I knew I could not go back to the past. The generation differences between us seemed shorter as I grew older, but I was irritable now with people who drank too much and Dottie's drinking made her dull and repetitive, and she made me sad. I had money again but no longer enough to give it without thought before it was needed which is the way it used to be between us; but mainly, plainly, I did not want the burdens that Dottie, maybe by never asking for anything, always put upon her friends. I was tired of trouble and wanted to be around people who walked faster than I and might pull me along with them.
>
> And so . . . I was not the good friend I had been. True, I was there in emergencies, but I was out the door immediately they were over. I found that Dottie's middle age, old age, made rock of much that had been fluid, and eccentricities once charming became too strange for safety or comfort.
>
> Dottie had always, even in the best days, clung to the idea that she was poor. Often she was, because she was generous to others and to herself, but more often it came from an insistence on a world where the artist was the put-upon outsider, the épaté rebel who ate caviar from rare china with a Balzac shrug for when you paid. I had long ago given up trying to figure out her true-poverty-periods from the pretend-poverty-periods, and the last sick years seemed no time to argue.
>
> She had, many years before, given me a Picasso gouache and a Utrillo landscape, saying as she gave them that she was leaving them to me anyway, so why not have them now? It was her charming way of paying off a debt and I remember being impressed with the grace. A few years after the gift, when I thought she was short of money, I sold the Utrillo and sent her a check. (She never told me that she had received the check, we never spoke of it at all.) Now, in 1965, she needed money and so I decided to sell the Picasso. It was a good, small picture, sold immediately for ten thousand dollars, and I took the check to Dottie the day I got it. Two days later, a woman unknown to me phoned to say that Dottie was

in the hospital, sick and without money. I said that couldn't be, she said it was, and would I guarantee the hospital bills. I went to the hospital that day. Dottie and I talked for a long time, and as I rose to go I said: "Dottie, do you need money?"

"She's been calling you," she said, "the damned little meddler. She's called half of New York to make me into a pleading beggar."

"She meant no harm. She thinks you're broke."

"I *am* broke, Lilly. But I don't want people, not even you—"

"You're not broke. I gave you a check two days ago for ten thousand dollars. Where is it?"

She stared at me and then turned her face away. She said, very softly, "I don't know."

And she didn't know, she was telling the truth. She wanted to be without money, she wanted to forget she had it.

Proust had written, "The only certainty of life is change," and Dorothy Parker, the once lovely and proud, had changed with the onset of age. In the wake of Wilde, she had many times said to her friends, "Promise me I'll never grow old." "Dottie," Wyatt Cooper had told her, "you're like time itself—eternal!" and for once she had called out joyfully, her dark eyes sparkling, "Do you really think so?"

She received an offer to write her autobiography and called in Cooper to help. It was to be like the novel about which there had been much talk back in the summer of 1928, while staying with the Murphys at Chalet La Bruyère in Montana-Vermala. Between bouts of heavy drinking, she had told the visiting George Oppenheimer that she was well into the novel, indicating a large stack of manuscript which, she declared, was already finished, under the title of *The Events Leading Up to the Tragedy.* She had been reluctant to let the publisher see it, because the stack of alleged manuscript consisted largely of undestroyed carbons of her old articles, padded further with correspondence.

Now she was determined to tackle the job of writing her life story. Or was she? Cooper remembered the day she received the letter from the publisher:

She exhibits the crumpled letter and her eyes sweep the room in hopeless supplication of those invisible but omnipresent forces that so capriciously shape our destinies; the huge, pleading eyes seem never to stop searching for some sort of sympathetic understanding that they damn well know they aren't going to find.

"I'd never be able to do it," she says, "but I wish to God I could!" The ladylike voice progresses from resignation to a final note of triumph and defiance. "I'd like to write the damn thing, just so I could call it *Mongrel!*"

. . . She seemed to want to get her story down—"It would give me something to live for," she said, sitting for a few dozen hours talking into a tape recorder while I, who saw her not only as a thoroughbred but as best of breed and best of show as well, prodded her with apprehensive questions. She began by saying, "Let's make it gay; if it's not fun, there's no point in telling it," and then plunged into a narrative that was all one color and that color was black . . . If the accuracy of her reporting fluctuated, the mood did not. She could, and did, stand one's hair on end with the chronicle of the adversities of a waif with the unfortunate name of Dorothy, a chronic victim whose misadventures were enough to make a piker out of de Sade's *Justine*.

"I apologize for introducing nobody but dreadful characters," Dottie would interject cheerfully as she waded on in a saga of a childhood filled with such obstacles as ignorant nuns. "Boy, did I think I was smart! Still do." And the hostile children? "They weren't exactly your starched-crinoline set, you know. Dowdiest little bunch you ever saw . . . " There were, too, the wretched stepmother . . . the malicious servants . . . all exaggeration of course, but creative exaggerations that throw a fascinating light on what the truth must have been.

The sessions invariably turned into visits and, as one of the things we had in common was a shameless lust for gossip, the resultant tapes, except for the times when I had the presence of mind, and the discretion, to shut the damned thing off, reveal much more happy and inventive speculation about the secret lives of some of the more beautiful of the "Beautiful People" than about Dottie's days among the golden circle at the Algonquin Round Table, a circle which, in any case, she now maintained, she'd never been part of. ("Mr. Benchley and I weren't there for the simple reason that we couldn't afford it. It cost money, and we weren't just poor, we were penniless.") And then she would say the most outrageous things about Jews, her father, and libel her friends.

Clearly, for Cooper, it was time to leave. But Mrs. Parker had not finished her reminiscences. She told an Associated Press reporter more about the Algonquin days—and nights:

Think of who was writing in those days—Lardner, Fitzgerald, Faulkner and Hemingway. Those were the real giants. The Round Table was just a lot of people telling jokes and telling each other how good they were. Just a bunch of loud-mouths showing off, saving their gags for days, waiting for a chance to spring them. "Did you hear about my remark?" "Did I tell you what I said?" and everybody hanging around, saying, "What'd he say?" It wasn't legendary. I don't mean that—but it wasn't all that good. There was no truth in anything they said. It was the terrible day of the wisecracks, so there didn't have to be any truth, you know. There's nothing memorable about them. About any of them. So many of them died. My Lord, how people die . . .

At first, I was in awe of them because they were being published. But then I came to realize I wasn't hearing anything very stimulating. I remember hearing Woollcott say, "Reading Proust is like lying in somebody else's dirty bath water."

And then he'd go into ecstasy about something called *Valiant Is the Word for Carrie*, and I knew I'd had enough of the Round Table.

"Woollcott," she said reflectively, "was ridiculous. He had a good heart, for whatever that was worth, and it wasn't much. George Kaufman was a mess.

"But," she said, "Mr. Benchley was very funny and wonderful; FPA was a lovely man, disagreeable and rude—but lovely. Harold Ross," she added, "was almost illiterate, wild and rough, never read anything, didn't know anything, but had a great gift as an editor and was awfully nice to the people who worked for him."

And what of the women of the Round Table?

"We were little black ewes that had gone astray; we were a sort of ladies' auxiliary of the legion of the damned. And, boy, we were proud of our show."

Mrs. Parker abandoned her autobiography. *Mongrel* had not been such a good idea anyway; she had always wanted to be a thoroughbred. And there was another problem.

The girl who wore glasses, now an elderly lady, was going blind.

· 5 0 ·

Mrs. John F. Kennedy
Regrets...

THEY CAME to ask if she would prepare a book, *The First Dorothy Parker Quartette*, which they hoped would be the forerunner of further quartettes of her work. Mrs. Parker toyed with the idea but did little about it; she was too busy indulging herself in the noble art of killing time.

Sometime before, Scribner editor Charles Pettee had suggested that she and her friend Frederick B. Shroyer co-edit a collection of short stories, to be called *Short Story: A Thematic Anthology*. Shroyer remembered: "We began by each of us submitting to the other a list of around one hundred short stories we thought were very good. I'm proud to say that many titles appeared on both our lists!"

It was not too heavy a task for Mrs. Parker. The selection predictably included stories by Hemingway, Fitzgerald, Faulkner and Lardner. It helped that the business of writing the preface was undertaken by Shroyer, after discussions with her. "But," as Shroyer himself observed at this time, "her captains and kings had long departed and she said, in effect, that all those she loved were dead and that she, herself, had been dead for a long time."

She recalled in her talks with him the madcap days of the twenties and thirties—"I think the trouble with us was that we stayed too young."

It might have been either Cooper or Shroyer who suggested to her that television presented creative possibilities for her, but she shunned the idea. Back in May 1962, a trilogy of her work, "The Lovely Leave," "A Telephone Call" and "Dusk Before Fireworks," had appeared in dramatized form on WNEW-TV in New York, starring Margaret Leighton and Patrick O'Neal. There had been a short, sharp fracas between Mrs. Parker and the television station. She complained to the press that she had not been paid for the broadcast. She had—but after all, she seldom knew if money had or hadn't been given to her.

Someone remarked that Dorothy Parker had wanted to be a kind of George Eliot of her century but she had never aspired to that. She had, she said, simply wanted to become a writer as good as Ernest Heming-

way, but she knew that she could never become that. Hemingway, en-
meshed in his own time slot, was an original, who had dissipated much
of his life, but few, if any, of his talents. True he had taken life by the
throat, lived dangerously and courted death and destruction; so had she,
but not in the same way. Curiously, in another way his pattern had been
similar to hers.

Hers had long been an almost passive confrontation with both life
and death, occasionally aided by barbiturates and a knife at her wrists.
She had labored well enough. Did she now derive any comfort from her
accomplishments and her fame?

We don't know, but we do know that she had almost precisely summarized her present existence in a poem written many years before,
"Inspector for the Ceiling of a Bedroom":

> Daily dawns another day;
> I must up, to make my way.
> Though I dress and drink and eat,
> Move my fingers and my feet,
> Learn a little, here and there,
> Weep and laugh and sweat and swear,
> Hear a song, or watch a stage,
> Leave some words upon a page,
> Claim a foe, or hail a friend—
> Bed awaits me at the end . . .

Unlike the pulsating thirties of which she now said, "They were progressive days. We thought we were going to make the world better—I
forget why we thought it—but we did," there was little now to fill her
days except drink and sleep.

Death was constantly on her mind. Talking to Wyatt Cooper, she
said: "Do you know what they do when you die in this hotel? They used
to take them down on the big elevator in the back, but it's not running
and they take them down that front elevator, and you know how small it
is. They have to stand you up."

"Her rooms again were bare and impersonal," said Cooper,

though more cheerful than the ones I remembered from years before. Except for
a Christmas card with a picture of my son on it on the bureau in her bedroom,
there were no photographs, no attempts at decoration, and no clues to the
identity of its resident, apart from the inevitable pile of books on the coffee table.
Even these she did not keep. Publishers continued to send books to her . . . they
were pressed on the next visitor.

There were only two visible mementoes of her life. One was an old edition of her poems or stories, only recently sent to her by a stranger who had, through the years, cut pictures of her out of the papers and glued them in. When I said that the photographs were beautiful, she said, "My dear, those are pictures. They could fix those up."

When Cooper said that it was a fascinating thing to have, she said gruffly, "Want it?" He put the clippings book down.

"The other souvenir, the only thing so far as I could see that she had salvaged from the California house," remembered Cooper,

was a set of Napoleon's generals, thirteen porcelain figures, that we had come across in a junky sort of antique store in Santa Monica during one of our lunch hours. They were installed in the Campbell living room and Alan even put a special light over them. Here at the hotel, Dottie had had somebody put a shelf in the middle of a wall, and Napoleon, backed by his stalwart generals, brooded down on her as she went about her daily occupations.

Cooper took his son Carter, "an extremely self-possessed and brilliant child," according to his father, to visit Mrs. Parker. It was the boy's second birthday. The child "strolled in, shook hands, and indicating the porcelain figures with a tilt of his head said, 'You like Napoleon?' " Mrs. Parker thereafter was "convinced that I'd coached him to say it before we entered the room," said the proud father. Carter, according to Cooper, "came into this world with a college education" and preferred, it seemed, *The Life of Napoleon in Pictures* to *Winnie The Pooh*, "a literary judgment with which Mrs. Parker found herself in complete agreement."

"She was fascinated by children," declared Cooper, "and seemed to want to like them, but a certain degree of mistrust was apparent in her manner, as if waiting for the little tykes to betray themselves and confirm her darkest suspicions."

Cooper, of comfortable background himself, had married Gloria Vanderbilt, heiress of the Vanderbilt railway millions, who had been the central figure in the sensational child-custody case of the 1930s. At the age of two, she had inherited $4 million, when her mother's sister, Lady Furness, was having an affair with the Prince of Wales. Gloria Vanderbilt had married at seventeen, a union which lasted only three years. At twenty-one she had married again, this time to Leopold Stokowski, bearing the conductor two sons. This marriage had ended after ten years. An actress now, she had gone on to marry film director Sidney Lumet, but this marriage had failed too. She then married Wyatt Cooper and bore him two sons. The Coopers were very happy and enjoyed sharing their happiness with others, keeping high social company which often included Mrs. John F. Kennedy, widow of the president. Cooper relayed this fact to Mrs. Parker at one point. It seems she was devoted to Mrs. Kennedy and wanted to hear everything about her: "What she wore, how she spoke, what we talked about and could she possibly be as enchanting as Dottie fancied her to be?

"We promised Dottie that if she would come with us—she had recently been in the hospital and almost never these days went out—to a recital at the United Nations by Libby Holman, we would invite Mrs. Kennedy," promised Cooper. "Unfortunately," he went on,

Mrs. Kennedy was unable to join us, though she expressed regret at not being able to meet Mrs. Parker, and delight at hearing that she was alive and around. I, accordingly, conveyed this disappointment to Dottie, who agreed to come anyway. The evening went well; she was enthusiastic and energetic, making a luncheon date with Mr. Mainbocher, chatting as happily as a schoolgirl with Mrs. Eugenia Sheppard, whose column she followed conscientiously and, at the concert, enjoying a reunion with Miss Holman.

After such an excursion, her spirits were high for days, and she delighted in describing it . . . though something in her made it necessary that she balance her diversion with some show of vexation, and her pleasure in this particular evening did not prevent her from complaining that we had got her out under false pretenses by promising her Mrs. Kennedy.

There were to be other social occasions for Mrs. Parker.

"Another evening, when she was to come to our house for dinner," recalled Cooper,

the city was hit by the worst snowstorm of the season. Cars could not move and the sidewalks were piled so deep with snow and ice that only the most hardy could navigate. She insisted that she could make it, however, and when Harvey Breit went to pick her up, she happily invited him up to her room to zip her dress. "After thirty years of marriage," she explained to him, "you miss such things." They set out on foot determinedly, but she had to give up before they'd gone a block. Her disappointment was so keen that my wife suggested we give a party for her and ask people she'd like to see—some she knew, some she'd like to meet, some she'd enjoy looking at, and some she'd enjoy talking to.

The Coopers gathered a galaxy of social notables, including Mr. and Mrs. Gardner Cowles, Mr. and Mrs. William S. Paley, Mr. and Mrs. Bennett Cerf, Mr. and Mrs. Samuel P. Peabody, Mr. and Mrs. Martin Gabel, Mr. and Mrs. John Barry Ryan II, Mr. and Mrs. Louis Auchincloss, Mrs. Arthur Bunker, Ms. Gloria Steinem, Miss Jean Parr, Duke Fulco diVentura, Mr. Herb Sargent, Mr. Richard Adler and Mr. Oliver Smith.

"Dottie followed all developments with joyful anticipation," said Cooper, "but a week before the event she suddenly said, 'You know I can't go there with Mrs. Paley and all those people. What in God's name would I wear?' "

"It is true," said Cooper, "she had few clothes. Alan used to take her to buy her dresses, and I don't imagine she had ventured into a store since.

"But," he recalled, "we were prepared for this. My wife was, of course, fascinated by Dottie, and was somewhat worshipful, an attitude that was mutual. Gloria never heard her breathe an unkind word about anybody. Dottie was always at her most genteel in my wife's presence, with malice towards none and charity for all."

Gloria Vanderbilt Cooper confessed to her husband that she always wanted to see Dorothy Parker in some kind of Chinese robe, delicately embroidered and elegant. When, a few months earlier, Mrs. Cooper started to wear kaftans as maternity dresses, she told her husband she wanted to have one made for Dorothy Parker.

Having no measurements to go by, Mrs. Cooper took a chance and had one made in size three, a beautiful garment of yellow brocade with gold trim encrusted with little imitation pearls. Wyatt Cooper took it over to Mrs. Parker at the Volney.

She sat looking at it and touching it in the manner of an orphan with a Christmas present she can't quite believe is meant for her. She went into the bedroom to try it on, and emerged after a long time to say that she didn't know how to get into it. I put it on the floor and, as one would in dressing a child, I lifted her feet to place them inside the dress, pulled it up and fastened it around her. The stand-up collar, the soft color, and the rich material emphasized the essential femininity of her face. She stood looking at herself in the mirror and she was transformed. It was as if for a long time she had been unaware of her beauty, and suddenly she could see what she had forgotten. The dress was too long by at least six inches. I offered to have someone come in and shorten it. "No," she said immediately, "I want it long. Then I have to lift it, like this" . . . at which she pulled herself tall, and with one hand raised her skirt like an Edwardian lady about to step into her carriage. "I want to have that haughty look," she said.

Cooper declared that, indeed, she already had it. "She minced about the room, head held high, body erect and proud, steps lady-like and sure, while her eyes followed her progress in the mirror."

Gloria Steinem and Herb Sargent brought her to the party, and she entered the room "trembling but looking magnificent," said Cooper, "like the last Dowager Empress of China, a creature frail and exquisite but a power not to be tampered with, a lady of grace and modesty but well aware of her own value. She was not unlike," he said, "a great actress who may have been away for a while, but who knows her audience is still waiting for this appearance, and she's going to make it a triumphant one."

Wyatt Cooper saw Mrs. Paley catch her husband's arm.

"Bill," she said quietly, but with some awe in her voice, "do you know who *that* is?" Mr. Paley, records Cooper, "went over to sit beside Dottie and to talk of previous meetings." He was, of course, the head of CBS and other conglomerates.

Others came over to Mrs. Parker. She was unfailingly gracious and charming and impressive. "The evening," says Cooper, "had a certain amount of glitter; everybody looked just right, and Dottie's eyes took in every detail of the women's clothes, jewelry and hairdos; each item was tucked away in her mind to be produced at will later on."

Cooper also remembered that he had a moment with her at this stage and whispered to her that her slippers and bag were perfect. She put on her sorely-tried-but-ever-patient face and said with mock dignity, pronouncing each syllable with elaborate care, "Mr. Cooper, promise me that you will never, never go to Saks to buy gold slippers and a gold handbag with Sara Murphy and that nurse!" Furthermore, Mrs. Parker demanded of him, "If you *do* go to Saks to buy gold slippers and gold handbag with Sara Murphy and that nurse, you won't go to Schrafft's for tea afterwards."

The formal dinner began. "She was seated on my right, of course," recalls the host, "and as we took our places at table, she spoke glowingly of the beauty of the room with the red tablecloths, the gleaming silver, the glowing candles, the flowers arranged with such artful casualness. My wife," said Cooper with some pride, "does these things with tolerable style—but when someone remarked that the wine glasses were beautiful, adding: "I always think that wine tastes so much better in lovely glasses, don't you?" Dottie, quick as a flash, said, "Oh, yes, paper cups aren't right." Mr. Cooper recorded that at that moment he was seized by a fit of nervous coughing.

Mrs. Parker chatted with Mr. Auchincloss, who was seated next to her on the other side. She admired his work and he admired hers. When it was time to turn back to Cooper, they exchanged a few formal remarks, "and then I realized that, after all the years of talking, of letting our hair down, and shooting straight, man-to-man as it were, we had, under the present elegant circumstances, nothing whatever to say to each other, and we began to laugh . . ."

A week later, Misty, one of Mrs. Parker's poodles, died, which left only C'est Tout.

One day shortly after that, looking staggeringly frail and wan, she was visited by Beatrice Ames, who for the past year or more had often traveled from her house on East Eighteenth Street to prepare food for Mrs. Parker. Dorothy put out her hand and said,

"I want you to tell me the truth. Did Ernest really like me?"

· 5 1 ·

The Leader of the Pack

WITH the consummate maturity so evident in several of her short stories, Dorothy Parker, now a myopic old lady, had come a long, often unhappy way since those dizzy days of the twenties when she had laughed gaily at the inanities of the Algonquin crowd, who under the pressures of their own legend had fought hard to provide an overeager public with frequently forced laughter.

Whether she admitted it now or not, apart from her fiction and some of her verse, she had formerly been carried along in a tide of tabloid tidbits of little positive value. But it had all been part of growing up. Those had been the improvident days of hilarity, heady days to be sure; when what she had said at lunch on Monday could well be written up by Franklin Adams or a press agent and placed in Tuesday's gossip columns. Perhaps more than most of the Algonquinites, Mrs. Parker had become the victim, willing or not, of a success she clearly had not bargained for. She had not sought that success, but when it arrived she had not rejected it.

It had come because she had tried to compete with the men, knowing she was clever and witty, and knowing too that the Round Table did not expect women to be either. And because she was a woman who could and did compete with men, she won for herself a firm seat at the Table; there was no way she could be ignored. If she surprised and delighted others with her witticisms, it is likely that she also surprised and delighted herself, but she was far too astute to let on that she had.

The profound literary influences of the twenties and earlier had come from Europe. Mrs. Parker, along with Hemingway, Fitzgerald and others, and to a lesser degree Lardner, Benchley and a few more, had proven that one could be talented, sophisticated, intellectual even—*and* still be American. It was, in its way, a major revelation. There was no longer a need to look towards Europe for Jamesian refinements. Hazel Morse, the Big Blonde, for example, was a home-grown product. The cultural impact of the crop of American writers spawned in the twenties had been a bombshell of sorts to the nation as a whole and to those of the rest of the world who were listening. Each in his or her individual way had indicated that the American writers were at last becoming important among the world literati.

This development was not a one-way street. Many fine European writers, poets and artists found their way to Hollywood during that period.

By Mrs. Parker's elegant turn of phrase, her invention and her audacity, she had helped establish the American literary challenge. She had confronted the male of the species and metaphorically demanded, "move over." In doing so, she had spelled it out to American women that it really was all right to be audacious, self-assured, bright and witty; she had given them the right to use the wisecrack, riposte, and caustic quip. And to her literary peers she had chosen sardonic literary images with which to assault the conventional mores of the established short story form and conventional journalistic habits.

Many thought she had outdistanced her idol, Miss Millay, the leader of the pack, as well as Alice Duer Miller and others.

If her success had proved to be a phenomenon—and there is much evidence that it had been no less than that—there could be little doubt that she had fit its demands, try as she might in later life to play down the fact. She had done much to convince the world that Manhattan was an American center—if not *the* center—of sophistication, talent and creativity.

She had made her impact on the literary scene mainly in the twenties and thirties with her audacious verse and certain of her fictional pieces. Did her stories measure up to the best of the forties, fifties and sixties? The seriocomic content of Mrs. Parker's later fiction is emphasized by the undulating rhythms of her words and the images those words convey. This is particularly noticeable in "I Live on Your Visits," in which a divorced woman, receiving her son during a brief visit to her hotel room, displays a controlled style and hauteur that is both peremptory and skilled. The son arrives, but is in a hurry; there to witness the arrival is Mme. Marah, his mother's friend, who is given to telling fortunes from hand or eye or both. The boy's mother speaks:

"Well, aren't you going to kiss me?" she said in a charming, wheedling voice, the voice of a little, little girl. "Aren't you? You beautiful big ox, you?"

"Sure," he said. He bent down toward her, but she stepped suddenly away. A sharp change came over her. She drew herself tall, with her shoulders back and her head flung high. Her upper lip lifted over her teeth, and her gaze came cold beneath lowered lids. So does one who has refused the white handkerchief regard the firing squad.

"Of course," she said in a deep, iced voice that gave each word its full due, "if you do not wish to kiss me, let it be recognized that there is no need for you to do so. I had not meant to overstep. I apologize. *Je vous demande pardon.* I had no desire to force you. I have never forced you. There is none to say I have."

"Ah, Mom," he said. He went to her, bent again, and this time kissed her cheek.

There was no change in her, save in the slow, somehow offended lifting of her eyelids. The brows arched as if they drew the lids up with them. "Thank you," she said. "That was gracious of you. I value graciousness. I rank it high. *Mille grazie.*"

"Ah, Mom," he said. . . .

"Perhaps," she said, "you will award yourself the privilege of meeting a friend of mine. She is a true friend. I am proud that I may say it." There was someone else in the room. It was preposterous that he had not seen her, for she was so big. Perhaps his eyes had been dazzled, after the dim-lit hotel corridor; perhaps his attention had been all for his mother. At any rate, there she sat, the true friend, on the sofa covered with embossed cotton fabric of the sickened green that is peculiar to hotel upholsteries. There she sat, at one end of the sofa, and it seemed as if the other end must fly up into the air.

"I can give you but little," his mother said. "Yet life is still kind enough to let me give you something you will always remember. Through me, you will meet a human being."

Yes, oh, yes. The voices, the stances, the eyelids—those were the signs. But when his mother divided the race into people and human beings—that was the certainty.

He followed her the little way across the room, trying not to tread on the train of her velvet tea gown that slid along the floor after her and slapped at the heels of her gilt slippers. Fog seemed to rise from his raincoat and his shoes cheeped. He turned out to avoid the coffee table in front of the sofa, came in again too sharply, and bumped it.

"Mme. Marah," his mother said, "may I present my son?"

"Christ, he's a big bastard, isn't he?" the true friend said.

And later, the imperious asininity of Mme. Marah:

"When's your birthday?" she asked the boy.

"The fifteenth of August," he said.

His mother was no longer the little girl. "The heat," she said. "The cruel August heat. And the stitches. Oh, God, the stitches!"

"So he's a Leo," the true friend said. "Awfully big for a Leo. You want to be pretty careful, young man, from October 22nd to November 13th. Keep away from anything electrical."

"I will," the boy said. "Thank you," he added.

"Let me see your hand," the true friend said.

The boy gave her his hand.

"Mm," she said, scanning the palm. "M-hmm, m-hmm, m-hmm. Oh. Well —*that* can't be helped. Well, you'll have pretty good health, if you just watch that chest of yours. There's a long sickness in your twenties and a bad accident some time around forty-five, but that's about all. There's going to be an unhappy love affair, but you'll get over it. You'll marry and—I can't see if there's two or

three children. Probably two and one born dead, or something like that. I don't
see much money, any time. Well, you watch your chest." She gave him back his
hand.

"Thank you," he said.

The little girl came back to his mother. "Isn't he going to be famous?" she
said.

The true friend shrugged. "It's not in his hand," she said.

Every line of Mrs. Parker's short story breathes the alienation of
affection; her dialogue is curiously remote, yet it is at the same time
incisive, accurate.

That Mrs. Parker could often compel the reader to sit up and take
notice in the first paragraph is graphically obvious in the opening of
"Lolita," the story of a wallflower's girlhood and subsequent marriage to
a handsome newcomer. In the story, the girl's mother is instantly in
focus:

Mrs. Ewing was a short woman who accepted the obligation borne by so
many short women to make up in vivacity what they lack in number of inches
from the ground. She was a creature of little pats and prods, little crinklings of
the eyes and wrinklings of the nose, little runs and ripples of speech and movement, little spirals of laughter. Whenever Mrs. Ewing entered a place, all stillness
left it.

But how to introduce the mousy Lolita to the reader? Watch Mrs.
Parker's sleight-of-hand:

Mrs. Ewing had a daughter: Lolita. It is, of course, the right of parents to
name their offspring what they please, yet it would sometimes be easier if they
could glimpse the future and see what the little one was going to look like later
on. Lolita was of no color at all; she was thin, with insistent knobs at the ends of
her bones, and her hair, so fine that it seemed sparse, grew straight.

The irony of the ugly duckling carrying off the important, good-
looking stranger in the face of the local beauties might seem subliminally
to reflect the self-denigrating Mrs. Parker's own search for a Prince
Charming, except that, unlike her author, Lolita wins all the way down
the line, a pattern hardly etched in Mrs. Parker's own life. This time,
however, there was an escape hatch:

"It's just like I tell Lolita," Mrs. Ewing said. "Just like I always say to
her when I write: 'You go ahead and be happy as long as you can.'
Because—Well, you know. A man like John Marble married to a girl like
Lolita! But she knows that she can always come here. This house is her
home. She can always come back to her mother."

Mrs. Ewing, claimed Mrs. Parker, "was not a woman who easily abandoned hope."

Mrs. Parker's story "The Bolt Behind the Blue" can best be described as an exercise in observation; a wisp of trenchant dialogue that today seems curiously dated. It largely recounts a visit by Mary Nicholl, a lonely, impoverished secretary, to an affluent divorcée friend whom she has occasionally visited over the years. Some would call it a tale of morality, the searing injustice of Mary Nicholl's poverty set in counterpoint to her friend Mrs. Hazelton's richness of life-style. Yet we are meant to perceive that richness dwells in Mary Nicholl's drab life. Mrs. Hazelton may well delight in her ceaseless round of invitations, but the essential loneliness of her life, even though blessed with an inquiring young daughter, is bereft of either love or real interest. The emptiness of her days and nights persuades her, when her friend visits, to put on masks which do not fit.

In many ways, Mrs. Parker resembled the comedian who wants to play *Hamlet*. So many of her stories are wrapped in the gloom of pathos, her ubiquitous escort. Yet, when she writes seriocomedy, it is often brilliantly funny, as in "Horsie." In that story, Miss Wilmarth, the trained nurse charged with looking after the convalescing, wealthy Camilla Cruger, appears to her employers to look like a horse.

Through Mrs. Parker's artistry, we almost hear the poor woman neighing. Even the merciless jokes are funny, as when Mr. Cruger, compelled by good manners to dine with the equine-looking Miss Wilmarth while his wife rests supinely on an apricot satin chaise longue in her bedroom, introspectively rehearses his dinner dialogue with the nurse; the scene has all the triteness of imbecility and all the imbecility of contrived triteness:

"Well, I see where they held up that jeweler's shop right in broad daylight on Fifth Avenue. Yes, I certainly don't know what we're coming to. That's right. Well! I see the cat. Do you see the cat? The cat is on the mat. It certainly is. Well! Pardon me, Miss Wilmarth, but must you look so much like a horse? Do you like to look like a horse, Miss Wilmarth? That's good, Miss Wilmarth. That's fine. You certainly do, Miss Wilmarth. That's right. Well! Will you for God's sake finish your oats, Miss Wilmarth, and let me get out of this?"

The comedy is measured, compelling and frequently funny. But those who study Mrs. Parker's work know that, as with much of her frothy light verse, it takes a good deal of heat to make a perfect soufflé. A soufflé is precisely what her story *Horsie* is. It is heated to perfection.

The same skillful comedy vein emerged in several of Mrs. Parker's early stories, notably *Glory in the Daytime*, in which the bridge-playing, vacuous Mrs. Murdock is invited by a fellow player for tea the next day to meet a famous actress, Lily Wynton. Mrs. Murdock is excited, and tells her husband:

"Honestly," she said. "It was the funniest thing you ever heard in your life. We'd just finished the last rubber—Oh. I forgot to tell you, I won three dollars, isn't that pretty good for me?—and Hallie Noyes said to me, 'Come in to tea tomorrow. Lily Wynton's going to drop up,' she said. Just like that, she said it. Just as if it was anybody."

"Drop up?" he said. "How can you drop *up?*"

"Honestly, I don't know what I said when she asked me," Mrs. Murdock said. "I suppose I said I'd love to—I guess I must have. But I was so simply—Well, you know how I've always felt about Lily Wynton. Why, when I was a little girl, I used to collect her pictures. And I've seen her in, oh, everything she's ever been in, I should think, and I've read every word about her, and interviews and all. Really and truly, when I think of *meeting* her—Oh, I'll simply die. What on earth shall I say to her?"

"You might ask her how she'd like to try dropping down, for a change," Mr. Murdock said.

"All right, Jim," Mrs. Murdock said. "If that's the way you want to be."

The arrival of the actress is finely etched satire, displaying Mrs. Parker's gift for smiling, often with sadness, at the exaggerations and postures of the human animal:

Lily Wynton wore, just as she should have, black satin and sables, and long white gloves were wrinkled luxuriously about her wrists. But there were delicate streaks of grime in the folds of her gloves and down the shining length of her gown were small, irregularly-shaped dull patches; bits of food or drops of drink, or perhaps both, sometime must have slipped their carriers and found brief sanctuary there. Her hat—oh, her hat. It was romance, it was mystery, it was strange, sweet sorrow; it was Lily Wynton's hat, of all the world, and no other could dare it. Black it was, and tilted, and a great, soft plume drooped from it to follow her cheek and curl across her throat. Beneath it, her hair had the various hues of neglected brass. But oh, her hat.

"Darling!" cried Miss Noyes.

"Angel," said Lily Wynton. "My sweet."

That night Mrs. Murdock tells her husband of her exciting day, stating "It was something I'll remember all my life." Her husband says, "What did she do? . . . Hang by her feet?" When all is said and done, and the glorious excitement of the day is over, "Wearily, little Mrs. Murdock went on down the hall to her bedroom." There the story ends, and with these words, Mrs. Parker puts her character in storage. She was later to re-create Mrs. Murdock under another name in her play, *Ladies Of the Corridor.*

Mrs. Parker used her familiar dialogue technique in "New York to Detroit," essentially a phone conversation between a young man in Detroit and a girl in New York who are experiencing a poor connection. It is shambling, emotional reportage of a near-hysterical woman frustrated at her man's prolonged stay on a business trip. It is strikingly redolent of "The Lovely Leave," which is not one of her better efforts. Her pervasive sentimentality sought justification, too, in "Sentiment," in which a woman ruminates in a taxi:

"I wonder why it's wrong to be so sentimental. People are so contemptuous of feeling. 'You wouldn't catch *me* sitting alone and mooning,' they say. 'Moon' is what they say when they mean remember, and they are so proud of not remembering." Mrs. Parker continues by having the woman say:

"I can't go on like this. I can't. I can't. I cannot stand this frantic misery. If I knew it would be over in a day or a year or two months, I could endure it. Even if it grew duller sometimes and wilder sometimes, it could be borne. But it is always the same and there is no end." The story goes on, and more of the woman's thoughts are made known. It is, in essence, the woman's valedictory address to her lost love that we hear. And, as such, it is nothing much.

"Sentiment" was one of Mrs. Parker's relatively early stories, fueled by the sadness of her early love affairs. Of all her stories, only "Big Blonde," "Horsie" and "Mr. Durant" stand with the best of the literature written in her best years; perhaps "Mrs. Hofstadter on Josephine Street" and "The Custard Heart" come close, too. But all were written when she was relatively young.

Now, aging and lonely, Mrs. Parker was writing no more, facing her end with alcohol and the comforting presence of her little dog.

Callers were now a rarity, but Dorothy occasionally ventured out to visit her old friend Beatrice Ames Stewart at her apartment, where they would sit around drinking vodka and reminiscing about the old days. She called on her on the evening of Tuesday, June 6, 1967, and her friend later told Joe Bryan of that evening when "she loaded Dottie into a taxi and paid the driver to make the delivery. Half an hour later her phone rang and she heard a mumble—'My bes' frien'! Mos' loyal frien'! On'y frien'! Goodnigh'!' . . . All the pain of the years was in her incoherent words."

· 5 2 ·

"Goodbye, Dottie..."

THE NEXT DAY, Wednesday, June 7, 1967, almost three months after she had worn her lovely satin gown to the Cooper's party, Mrs. Dorothy Parker died in her rooms at the Volney Hotel. She was quite alone, except for C'est Tout. When the police came they found her slumped on the floor, the dog whimpering in the corner of the room. Shakespeare's "amiable and lovely death," the death which she had pursued so ardently throughout her life, had at long last reached out and embraced her.

They took her, as she had known they would, down in the small front elevator to Frank Campbell's chapel at Madison and Eighty-first Street, where she was put in the dress given to her by Gloria Vanderbilt Cooper.

The New York Times ran her obituary on page one; it spilled over to cover a full page inside. Alden Whitman, chief obituary writer for the *Times*, waxed superficial and sometimes erroneous. He listed her bon mots with dull precision—largely as a series of consecutive one-liners, adding: "On one occasion, assured by a drunk who accosted her that he was really a nice person and a man of talent, Miss Parker replied: 'Look at him, a rhinestone in the rough.' " Mr. Whitman continued: " 'This reputation for homicidal humor,' Miss Parker recalled in after years, 'used to make me feel like a fool. At parties, fresh young gents would come up defiantly and demand I say something funny and nasty. I was prepared to do it with selected groups, but with others I'd slink away.' At one party a man followed her around all evening waiting for a bright remark. He finally apologized, saying: 'You're not at all the way I thought you'd be. I'm sorry.' 'That's all right,' Miss Parker rejoined. 'But do me a favor. When you get home, throw your mother a bone.' "

Mr. Whitman touched on Mrs. Parker's "evocation of heartburn." There was, too, it seems "a bit of Donne and a hint of La Rochefoucauld" in "Words of Comfort to Be Scratched on a Mirror":

> Helen of Troy had a wandering glance;
> Sappho's restriction was only the sky;
> Ninon was ever the chatter of France;
> But oh, what a good girl am I!

One is forced to wonder where precisely those influences appear.

Mr. Whitman admitted that she was a careful, even finicky craftsman as, he pointed out, was confirmed by Ogden Nash: " 'To say that Miss Parker writes well,' Nash once remarked, 'is as fatuous as proclaiming that Cellini was clever with his hands.' " Mr. Whitman went on to add: "She had her own definition of humor, and it demanded lonely, perfectionist writing to make the truly funny seem casual and uncontrived. 'Humor to me, Heaven help me, takes in many things,' she once said. 'There must be courage, there must be no awe. There must be criticism, for humor, to my mind, is encapsulated in criticism. There must be a disciplined eye and a wild mind. There must be a magnificent disregard of your reader, for if he cannot follow you, there is nothing you can do about it.' "

The summing up came from Edmund Wilson, who wrote: "She is not Emily Brontë or Jane Austen, but she has been at some pains to write well, and she has put into what she has written a voice, a state of mind, an era, a few moments of human experience that nobody else has conveyed." Wilson had, indeed, said it all, rather in fewer and better words than Whitman who, getting his Chaucerian gender confused, said that Mrs. Parker was the " 'verray, parfit gentil knight' of the squelch, which she delivered deadpan in a clear, mellow, lamb-like voice." Others considered her to be rather more than that.

The funeral service opened with a violinist playing Bach's *Air on the G String*; she would have had something funny to say about that. Over 150 people—friends and enemies—assembled in the chapel to say farewell and to see her remains pass through the curtains into the crematory. Her brother, sister and brother-in-law were there; also the Coopers, Beatrice Ames and many others. And, of course, Lillian Hellman.

Zero Mostel, the actor and political activist who had helped her through HUAC, rose to say that it was Dorothy Parker's wish that formal ceremonies should be dispensed with. "If she had had her way," he said with just the trace of a smile, "I suspect she would not be here at all."

Lillian Hellman, her face lined with the turmoil of the years, delivered the eulogy: "She was part of nothing and nobody except herself: it was this independence of mind and spirit that was her true distinction. And it stayed with her till the end, young and sparkling."

Hellman, who was to outlive her friend by another seventeen years, went on to tell of nights with Dorothy Parker, when "gulping what we called a watered extract of Scotch," they would "put aside the gentle manner and let fly." "Then," she said, "I would roar with laughter at one of her jokes. It was laughter that always ended in sober recognition that the joke hid a brilliant diagnosis of people, or places, or customs, or life." She reminded the mourners that Mrs. Parker had said, "It's not the tragedies that kill us, it's the messes."

"The remarkable quality of Dorothy Parker's wit," she added, "was that it stayed in no place, and was of no time." With further words, she remembered her friend, who "never spoke of old glories, never repented old defeats, never rested on times long ago." She was, Miss Hellman said, "brave in deprivation, in the chivying she took during the McCarthy days, in the isolation of the last bad, sick years." And she had willed these words for her tombstone: "If you can read this, you've come too close."

Then they pressed the button, and a machine whirred.

One or two remembered "The Satin Dress," a poem she had written long ago which had presaged this very day:

> Satin glows in candlelight—
> Satin's for the proud!
> They will say who watch at night,
> "What a fine shroud . . ."

Mrs. Gloria Vanderbilt Cooper's satin dress was just that, a fine shroud.

She had made a will of sorts, leaving $20,000, the bulk of her estate, to Martin Luther King, Jr., and certain of her copyrights to The National Association for the Advancement of Colored Peoples. They had searched through her effects and found Lillian Hellman's $10,000 check, together with eight other uncashed checks, some seven years old or more.

Mrs. Parker, who had lived her last years virtually penniless, with death always close to the surface, had spent her life searching for Dorothy Parker.

She never found her.

Epilogue

It is hard to define a woman. It is harder still to define a woman like Dorothy Parker.

It was said that wit, the humor of the indifferent, was her armor. It is known that death was her friend, her constant companion. But even this she derided: "I like to think of my shining tombstone. It gives me, as you might say, something to live for."

Lillian Hellman said "she was, more than usual, a tangled fishnet of contradictions," and Miss Hellman, a cold, clinical intellectual, was probably the best judge of character Dorothy Parker ever had.

Some tried to get close to Mrs. Parker, to befriend her, but she always pulled away in time. She remained the enigmatic literary journalist, short story writer, epigrammist, essayist, critic, proclaimed wit, poet of sorts, failed playwright, dissident screenwriter; she loathed her work in Hollywood, but took the money, all the while searching for an elusive inner peace that, when threatened with discovery, was perversely out of hand.

To the few who were close to her, she appeared to adore the empty round of parties, yet gave to others the indelible impression that the parties and the people were empty and valueless.

Mrs. Parker hovered over the American literary scene with reverberating effect from 1913 to the late fifties, wavering between restraint and rebellion. Like Oscar Wilde's niece, Dolly, "she was a visual person, she didn't see in images, she saw in phrases." Her worst enemies described her as a flippant show-off who abused her talents; others assessed her as a latter-day, ragtime Ophelia in a black skirt, sweater and pearls, quietly given to crying into her gin.

They said many vicious things about her, mostly because they had been hurt by her, or were afraid of her.

Was she a wit? Wycherley said: "Wit [to a woman] is more necessary than beauty, and I think no young woman ugly that has it, and no handsome woman agreeable without it." On that assessment, Mrs. Parker would have won the Restoration playwright's approval on both counts.

Miss Hellman recalled, "It was a cold spring, and I had decided to set the snapping turtle traps earlier than usual and I was anxious to have a look at them. I hauled up one of the long, wire cages and there was our first turtle of the year. As I put the cage on the ground to look at him, his penis extended in fear. Dottie said, 'It must be pleasant to have sex appeal for turtles. Shall I leave you alone together?' "

Certainly she was more than just a wit. She was a walking enigma whose mind perceived in colors of sepulchral black or dull grey. Introverted, moody, with a longing for laughter to shroud her omnipresent death wish, she perplexed, charmed, reviled and mystified most of those who met her. And, as Miss Hellman has said, "she loved those who never really loved her." Particularly Ernest Hemingway.

Who, then, *was* she? What, in terms of her life and times, did she accomplish? As Woollcott said, her published work does not loom large. And did the evaluation of her friends and acquaintances come anywhere close to the truth of the lady? That she was professionally a frustrated playwright there can be little doubt. She herself said that although her play *Ladies of the Corridor* was a flop, it was the only worthwhile thing she had ever done. With her verse, short stories and literary journalism, she conquered the literati of her time with the disdain of the disinterested. Was Somerset Maugham right when, at the height of his fame, he wrote: "In her stories Dorothy Parker has a sense of form which, in these days, to my old-fashioned mind, is all too rare. Whether in a sketch or a story she knows exactly where to begin and where to end and when you have done reading it you have no questions to ask . . . her style is easy without being slipshod and cultivated without affectation."

Easy without being slipshod? Cultivated without affectation? She frequently quoted La Rochefoucauld, "the big Frog," as she called him. Much of "The Little Hours" is based on what she learned from him. "The only pleasing thing I can remember his saying is that there is always something a little pleasing to us in the misfortunes of even our dearest friends. That cleans me all up with Monsieur [*sic*] La Rochefoucald. *Maintenant c'est fini, ca!*" Pursuing her theme for pages, settling "the old cynic" for being "circa 1650," which may be one way of describing his time span of 1613–1680, she proceeds annoyingly to misquote him.

In her writings, she also misquoted others, ranging from Shakespeare to Greta Garbo. She once averred that "solitude is the safeguard of mediocrity and the stern companion of genius." She did not attempt to credit, justify or argue the thought. Could she be the author of such wisdom? She was not. Carlyle was. It was enough that it sounded intriguing. There had always to be the skittish skirl, as in this morsel of Parkerian philosophy: "If you would learn what God thinks about money, you have only to look at those to whom He has given it." What she did not reveal to her readers is that Sydney Smith said it first in the early nine-teenth century before he became a cleric.

Her friends had mixed feelings about her. Even Robert Benchley described her as "the everlasting ingenue." Some years after her death, John Keats summed her up as "an elfin woman who had two kinds of magic about her. Her first magical quality was that no one could ever consider her dispassionately, and the other was that no one could pre-cisely define her."

Certainly many tried.

Alexander Woollcott aimed, perhaps, for a bull's-eye with his "a com-bination of Little Nell and Lady Macbeth," which friends considered not a bad shot. Edmund Wilson wrote of her:

It is true that Mrs. Parker's epigrams have the accent of the Hotel Algonquin rather than that of the coffeehouses of the eighteenth century. But I believe that, if we admire, as it is fashionable to do, the light verse of Prior and Gay, we should admire Mrs. Parker also. She writes well: her wit is the wit of her particular time and place, but it is often as clearly economic at the same time as it is flatly brutal as the wit of the age of Pope; and, within its small scope, it is a criticism of life. It has its roots in contemporary reality, and that is what I am pleading for in poetry.

Gertrude Atherton, who encapsulated Mrs. Parker and her Algon-quin colleagues in *Black Oxen*, knew her well. She called her a "fe-lion," while Groucho Marx settled for "She's just a gigolette," add-ing, inconsequentially, "but she has a delightful bum." Beatrice Ames said, "She was a storm after a rainbow and a rainbow after a storm." Nunnally Johnson considered her to be "like a bright line in a bad play."

In the 1980s Conor Cruise O'Brien evaluated her as "an incompetent critic" and "quite a nasty woman." Of her *Collected Works* he said: "Taken as a whole [her] poems and stories together carry an unbearable cumulative charge of self-pity, gallantly borne . . . a cloying quicksand . . . most of it is a bore," adding, "what she does best, and most, is to dig up bad books, laugh at them, and get the reader to laugh, too. Occasion-ally, she has the misfortune to dig up what, because of her critical inad-equacy, she wrongly thinks is a bad book, and gives it the same treatment . . . the lady would have been quite at home in the more fashionable streets of Gath or Askelon," a line almost worthy of Mrs. Parker herself.

Actress Eleanor Boardman said that Dorothy Parker "inhabited a world of her own. She was the ascent of a five-feet Venus, with a brain. I wouldn't put her higher than that!" And what about Hemingway? He claimed that "she had a soft side, like blackberry pie. But the bitch was always there, ready to rise with the heat." It was Frank Crowninshield who likened her to Oliver Hertford's crab: "The crab, more than any of God's creatures, has formulated the perfect philosophy of life. Whenever he is confronted with a great moral crisis in life, he first makes up his mind what is right, and then goes sideways as fast as he can. That was Dottie . . ." Her wealthy friend Sara Murphy thought that "she was fun, like falling through a window and finding yourself alive is fun."

Scott Fitzgerald wrote about her to Harold Ross: "Dottie is the lightning in the storm. She illuminates the tawdry for what it is—and her personal thunderbolt crashes on and on. I like her. But she doesn't like anybody . . . most of all, she hates herself. She is desperately unhappy all of the time and time is the only thing she really has. And she doesn't want it."

But was she *such* an incomplete soul, *such* a highly complex, mordant human being? George S. Kaufman, whom she did not like, thought she was.

If she didn't take to you, she bit you, digested you and spat you out. She was not an easy woman to take, either personally or in print. You looked at her and you knew she was sizing you up for a straight left at the appropriate time. Her fun *persona* was feigned. She couldn't come to terms with any real sort of love: her only loves were her fantasies and animals—and neither could talk back . . . she was as deadly as an asp.

Neysa McMein thought her sense of fun a veneer. While painting her portrait she asked, "Why do you assume the air of being a fun person when you know that isn't you? Why, for the good of your talent and your soul, don't you throw it all up, all this Fifth Avenue cha-cha, and get yourself a cottage and write and write and find yourself?" Mrs. Parker quietly replied: "I can't. I don't know how . . . "

"The wittiest woman of our time," declared William Rose Benét of her. Tallulah Bankhead, predictably, was more astringent: "That lady ain't a book lady," she said, "she's a bed lady, like me." Oscar Hammerstein didn't assess her quite that way: "Dorothy Parker is an undrinkable mix of vanity, pain-in-the-ass decorum, conformity and rebellion. In short, she's a mixed-up gal."

Mrs. Parker grows more intriguing as the assessments continue.

When he left her, Edwin Pond Parker said, "I don't want to talk about her. I don't ever want to talk about her. And I never will." He didn't. His silence was almost as enigmatic as Dorothy Parker herself. Her mother-in-law, Hortense Campbell, was not so reticent and proclaimed: "She is a cow. And cows ought to be left out in fields or in the cow house, with muck . . . "

"She needed protection. She always needed protection," said Donald Ogden Stewart, with characteristic grace and gentleness.

She was a frighteningly vulnerable creature, in the early days as pretty as a picture by Renoir. She was vitally honest about most people and things. That was because she abhorred cant and hypocrisy. Don't let the early living-it-up bit confuse you: she was just taking joy out of life to hide her great unhappiness, her painful disillusion. True, she could be acerbic; mightily so, but she had reason to be. It was the only protection to her acute sensitivity.

Arnold Gingrich recalled: "She was her own fable, her own lore. She enriched American literature and she couldn't believe she'd done any such thing. She believed in no one, least of all herself—that was the saddest thing about her . . . She was a legend," and as Gingrich opined, "legends have their place in life just like fried bread."

Ross Evans claimed at the end of their affair: "God, she was a monumental bore," while Swedish journalist Gunilla Wettergren, who knew her well, wrote: "She is like a wisp of gold thread, twisted around the dun-colored lamps of Manhattan. She glitters for all to see and then is swept gently away by the wind before the onset of the exhaust smoke." Mrs. Parker would have liked that lyrical comment.

And Anita Loos, the author of *Gentlemen Prefer Blondes*, declared, "Dottie Parker is a dream. And like dreams, she seldom comes true." Elizabeth Arden said, "That woman Parker is quite a dame. If she'd written the copy for my ads, I might have made another twenty million."

Edna Ferber, whom Mrs. Parker did not enjoy, thought she was "like the bitter taste in an otherwise enjoyable cup of coffee, you can't ignore it."

Elmer Rice said of his collaborator, "She'll go to heaven, that one." And one might be impressed by the view of her friend Wyatt Cooper, who said she entered a room like an apology. "If," he said, "you didn't know Dorothy Parker, whatever you think she was like, she wasn't. Even if you did know her, whatever you thought she was like, she probably wasn't."

In 1934, Woollcott wrote of his friend: "I think it not unlikely that the best of Mrs. Parker's work will be conned a hundred years from now. If so, I can foresee the plight of some undergraduate in those days being maddened by an assignment to write a thesis on what manner of woman this dead and gone Dorothy Parker really was. Was she a real woman at all? he will naturally want to know. And even if summoned from our tombs, we will not be sure how we should answer that question."

Let actress Ruth Gordon, who survived Mrs. Parker by eighteen years, have the last word:

Aleck Woollcott, Dottie Parker and Neysa McMein and to a slightly lesser degree Alice Duer Miller all had streaming eyes whenever the subject was animals.

Out in California where anything is likely to happen and often does, a man living on the edge of wild land had his grounds softly floodlit and after his dinner party would put a big platter of cold cuts, T-bone steaks and other inducements on the lawn, far from the house. Guests got binoculars and watched the deer and rabbits and a spotted lynx leave freedom and get hungup on steak.

Woollcott and Dottie came to dinner, but that night nothing showed up. "It has only happened twice before," the host apologized. "Please come once more, I can't account for tonight. It won't happen again."

Woollcott and Dottie made a second visit. Again nothing came out of the wilderness. At eleven-thirty they gave up.

"Oh, I don't understand it," moaned the host. "How could it happen?"

Dottie shook her head in amazement.

"I thought we'd at *least* get the after-theater crowd!"

Bibliography

To each of the following authors, editors and publishers, I express my grateful thanks for providing either direct quotations used in the text or background and research information.

Adams, Franklin P., ed. *FPA's Book of Quotations*. New York: Funk & Wagnalls, 1952.
———*The Diary of Our Own Samuel Pepys* (2 Vols) New York: Simon & Schuster, 1935.
Astor, Mary. *My Story*. Garden City, N.Y.: Doubleday, 1959.
Atkinson, Brooks. *Broadway Scrapbook*. New York: Theatre Arts, 1947.
Bacall, Lauren. *By Myself*. London: Cape, 1979.
Benchley, Nathaniel. *Robert Benchley*. Foreword by Robert E. Sherwood. London: Cassell, 1956.
Brackett, Charles. *Entirely Surrounded*. New York: Knopf, 1934.
Brown, John Mason. *The Worlds of Robert E. Sherwood*. New York: Harper & Row, 1965.
———*Dramatis Personae: A Retrospective Show*. New York: Viking, 1963.
Brownlow, Kevin. *The Parade's Gone By*. London: Secker & Warburg, 1968.
Bruccoli, Matthew J. *Some Sort of Epic Grandeur*. London: Hodder & Stoughton, 1983.
Burke, Billie. *With a Feather on My Nose*. Foreword by Ivor Novello. London: Davies, 1950.
Capron, Marion. *Writers at Work*. The Paris Review Interviews. ed. Malcolm Cowley. New York: Viking, 1957.
Carter, Randolph. *Flo Ziegfeld*. London: Elek, 1974.
Case, Frank. *Tales of a Wayward Inn*. Stokes, 1938.
Cerf, Bennett. *Try and Stop Me*. New York: Doubleday, 1954.
Chase, Ilka. *Past Imperfect*. New York: Doubleday, 1942.
Coffee, Leonore. *Storyline*. London: Cassell, 1973.
Connelly, Marc. *Voices Offstage: A Book of Memoirs*. New York: Holt, Rinehart & Winston, 1968.
Crichton, Kyle Samuel. *Total Recoil*. New York: Doubleday, 1960.
Day, Beth. *This Was Hollywood*. New York: Doubleday, 1956.
Dayton, Katharine, with George S. Kaufman. *First Lady*. New York: Random House, 1935.
Dietz, Howard. *Dancing in the Dark*. New York: Quadrangle/New York Times, 1974.
Drennan, Robert E. *The Algonquin Wits*. New York: Citadel, 1968.

————*Wit's End*. London: Frewin, 1973.

Eckardt, Wolf Von, with Sander L. Gilman. *Bertolt Brecht's Berlin*. New York: Abelard, 1976.

Edel, Leon. *Bloomsbury: A House of Lions*. London: Hogarth Press, 1979.

Ellis, Davis Maldwyn. *New York: State and City*, trans. William Byron. Cornell University Press, 1979.

Ferber, Edna. *A Kind of Magic*. New York: Doubleday, 1963.

————*A Peculiar Treasure*. New York: Doubleday, 1938.

Gassner, John. *Dramatic Soundings: Evaluations and Retractions*. New York: Crown, 1968.

Geisinger, Marion. *Plays, Players, and Playwrights: An Illustrated History of the Theater*. New York: Crown, 1971.

Geist, Kenneth L. *Pictures Will Talk: The Life and Films of Joseph L. Mankiewicz*. New York: Charles Scribner's Sons, 1978.

Gold, Arthur, with Robert Fizdale. *Mista*. London: Macmillan, 1980.

Gordon, Ruth. *Myself Among Others*. New York: Atheneum, 1971.

Graham, Sheilah, and Gerold Frank. *Beloved Infidel*. London: Allen, 1958.

Grant, Jane. *Ross, The New Yorker and Me*. New York: Reynal & Morrow, 1968.

Gray, James. *On Second Thought*. Minneapolis: University of Minnesota Press, 1946.

Green, Abel, with Joe Laurie, Jr. *Show Biz*. New York: Holt, 1971.

Guiles, Fred Lawrence. *Hanging On in Paradise*. New York: McGraw-Hill, 1975.

Hall, Donald, ed. *The Oxford Book of Literary Anecdotes*. London: Oxford University Press, 1981.

Hammett, Dashiell. *The Big Knockover and Other Stories*, intro. Lillian Hellman. New York/London: Penguin, 1981.

Harriman, Margaret Case. *The Vicious Circle*. New York: Rinehart, 1951.

Harris, Jed. *Watchman, What of the Night?* New York: Doubleday, 1963.

Hart, Moss. *Act One*. New York: Random House, 1959.

Hayes, Helen, with Anita Loos. *Twice Over Lightly*. New York: Harcourt Brace Jovanovich, 1972.

————*On Reflection*. New York: Evans, 1968.

Hecht, Ben. *Charles*. New York: Harper & Row, 1957.

Hellman, Lillian. *Three. (Pentimento, An Unfinished Woman, and Scoundrel Time)*, intro by Richard Poirier. Boston: Little, Brown, 1979.

Hirschfield, Al. *Show Business Is No Business*. New York: Simon & Schuster, 1951.

Howe, Irving, with Kenneth Libo. *The Immigrant Jews of New York*. London: Routledge & Kegan Paul, 1976.

Hoyt, Edwin P. *A Gentleman of Broadway*. Boston: Little, Brown, 1964.

————*Alexander Woollcott, The Man Who Came to Dinner*. Philadelphia: Chilton, 1968.

Huston, John. *An Open Book*. New York: Knopf, 1980.

Jessel, George, with John Austin. *The World I Lived In*. Chicago: Regnery, 1967.

Kahn, B. J., Jr. *The World of Swope*. New York: Simon & Schuster, 1967.

Kanin, Garson. *Tracy and Hepburn*. London: Angus & Robertson, 1970.

————*Movieola*. London: Cassell, 1979.

Kaufman, Beatrice, with Joseph Hennesy. *The Letters of Alexander Woollcott*. New York: Viking, 1944.

Kaufman, George, with Edna Ferber. *The Royal Family of Broadway*. New York: Doubleday, 1928.

———, and Morrie Ryskind. *Let 'em Eat Cake*. New York: Knopf, 1933.

Kerr, Jean. *Please Don't Eat the Daisies*. New York: Doubleday, 1957.

Knef, Hildegard. *The Gift Horse*. Germany: Verlag Molden, 1971.

Kramer, Dale. *Ross and The New Yorker*. New York: Doubleday, 1951.

Laufe, Abe. *Anatomy of a Hit*. New York: Hawthorn, 1966.

Lawrence, Margaret. *The School of Femininity*. Stokes, 1936.

Layman, Richard. *The Shadow Man: A Documentary Life of Dashiell Hammett*. Junction, 1981.

Lesley, Cole. *The Life of Noel Coward*. London: Cape, 1976.

Loos, Anita. *But Gentlemen Marry Brunettes*. New York: Brentano's, 1926.

Mannin, Ethel. *Young in the Twenties*. London: Hutchinson, 1971.

Marx, Harpo, with Rowland Barber. *Harpo Speaks!* New York: Random House, 1961.

Marx, Samuel, with Jan Clayton. *Bewitched, Bothered, and Bedevilled*. London: Allen, 1977.

Maugham, W. Somerset. *Variations on a Theme*. New York/London: Viking, 1944.

Meredith, Scott. *George S. Kaufman and His Friends*. New York: Doubleday, 1974.

Mitford, Nancy. *Zelda Fitzgerald*. London: Bodley Head, 1970.

Mizener, Arthur. *Scott Fitzgerald and His World*. London: Thames & Hudson, 1972.

Nathan, George Jean. *The Intimate Notebooks*. New York: Knopf, 1932.

Niven, David. *The Moon's a Balloon*. London: Hamilton, 1971.

Nolan, William F. *A Life at the Edge*. New York: Congdon & Weed, 1983.

Nugent, Elliott. *Events Leading Up to the Comedy*. New York: Trident, 1963.

Oliver, Donald, ed. *By George*. New York: St. Martin's, 1979.

Oppenheimer, George. *The Passionate Playgoer*. New York: Viking, 1968.

Parker, Dorothy, preface by Lillian Hellman. *A Month of Sundays*. New York/London: Viking, 1970.

———*After Such Pleasures*. New York/London: Viking, 1933.

———*The Best of Dorothy Parker*. London: Methuen, 1952.

———,with Elmer Rice. *Close Harmony*. London: French, 1939.

———*The Collected Dorothy Parker*. London: Duckworth, 1973.

———*The Collected Stories of Dorothy Parker*. New York: Modern Library, 1942.

———*The Collected Poetry of Dorothy Parker*. New York: Modern Library, 1944.

———*Constant Reader*. New York: Viking, 1970.

———*Death and Taxes*. New York: Viking, 1931.

———*Enough Rope*. Boni & Liveright, 1926.

———*Here Lies*. New York: Viking, 1939.

———,with Arnold D'Usseau. *Ladies of the Corridor*. New York: Viking, 1954.

———*Laments for the Living*. New York: Viking, 1930.

———*Not So Deep as a Well*. New York: Viking, 1936.

———*The Penguin Dorothy Parker*, introduced by Brendan Gill. New York: Penguin, 1977.

———*The Portable Dorothy Parker*. New York: Viking, 1973.

————,with Frederic B. Shroyer. *Short Story: A Thematic Anthology*. New York: Scribner's 1963.

————*Sunset Gun*. Boni & Liveright, 1928.

Parrish, Robert. *Growing Up in Hollywood*. London: Bodley Head, 1976.

Pearson, Hasketh. *The Life of Oscar Wilde*. London: Methuen, 1946.

Perelman, Sidney J. *The Last Laugh*. London: Methuen, 1981.

Richards, Dick, ed. *The Curtain Rises*. London: Frewin, 1966.

Robyns, Gwen. *Light of a Star*. London: Frewin, 1968.

Rogers, Agnes, with Frederick Lewis. *I Remember Distinctly*. Harper and Brothers, 1947.

Rubin, Williams, and Carole Lancner. *The Paintings of Gerald Murphy*, foreword by Archibald Macleish. Catalogue of Museum of Modern Art, 1974.

Schwartz, Charles. *Cole Porter*. London: Allen, 1978.

Seldes, Gilbert. *The Seven Lively Arts*. Harper and Brothers, 1924.

Shadegg, Stephen. *Clare Boothe Luce*. London: Frewin, 1970.

Sheean, Vincent. *Dorothy and Red: A Literary Biography*. New York: Houghton Mifflin, 1963.

Simon, Kate. *Fifth Avenue*. London: Sidgwick & Jackson, 1968.

Sternberg, Josef von. *Fun in a Chinese Laundry*. London: Secker & Warburg, 1968.

Stewart, Donald Ogden. *By a Stroke of Luck!* London: Paddington, 1975.

Teichmann, Howard. *George S. Kaufman*. London: Angus & Robertson, 1973.

————*Smart Aleck*. New York: William Morrow, 1976.

Thomas, Bob. *Selznick*. London: Allen, 1970.

Thomas, Gordon, with Max Morgan-Witts. *The Day the Bubble Burst*. London: Hamish Hamilton, 1979.

Thurber, Helen, and Edward Weeks, eds. *The Selected Letters of James Thurber*. London: Hamish Hamilton, 1982.

Thurber, James. *Men, Women, and Dogs*. London: Allen, 1943.

————*My Years with Ross*. Boston: Little, Brown, 1959.

Toohey, John L. *A History of the Pulitzer Prize Plays*. New York: Citadel, 1967.

Veiller, Bayard. *The Fun I've Had*. New York: Reynal & Hitchcock, 1941

Vot Le, Ander. *F. Scott Fitzgerald*. London: Lane, 1984.

White. E.B., with Katherine S. White. *A Sub-Treasury of American Humor*. New York: Coward-McCann, 1941.

Wilk, Max, ed. *The Wit and Wisdom of Hollywood*. London: Cassell, 1971.

Wilson, Edmund. *The Twenties*. New York: Farrar, Strauss & Giroux, 1977.

Winslow, Susan. *Brother, Can You Spare a Dime?* London: Paddington, 1970.

Woollcott, Alexander. *While Rome Burns*. New York: Grossett and Dunlap, 1934.

Zolotow, Maurice. *Stagestruck*. New York: Harcourt Brace and World, 1965.

Zukor, Adolph. *The Public Is Never Wrong*. London: Cassell, 1954.

Index